Norihiro Yagi won the 32nd Akatsuka Award for his debut work, *UNDEADMAN*, which appeared in *Monthly Shonen Jump* magazine and produced two sequels. His first serialized manga was his comedy *Angel Densetsu* (Angel Legend), which appeared in *Monthly Shonen Jump* from 1992 to 2000. His epic saga, *Claymore*, is running in *Monthly Jump Square* magazine.

In his spare time, Yagi enjoys things like the Japanese comedic duo Downtown, martial arts, games, driving, and hard

CLAYMORE VOL. 19
SHONEN JUMP ADVANCED Manga Edition

STORY AND ART BY
NORIHIRO YAGI

English Adaptation & Translation/John Werry
Touch-up Art & Lettering/Sabrina Heep
Design/Amy Martin
Editor/Megan Bates

Published by VIZ Media, LLC
P.O. Box 77010
San Francisco, CA 94107

10 9 8 7 6 5 4 3 2 1
First printing, November 2011

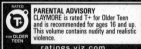

RATED T+
PARENTAL ADVISORY
CLAYMORE is rated T+ for Older Teen
and is recommended for ages 16 and up.
This volume contains nudity and realistic
violence.
FOR OLDER TEEN
ratings.viz.com

THE WORLD'S MOST
CUTTING-EDGE MANGA
SHONEN JUMP
ADVANCED
www.shonenjump.com

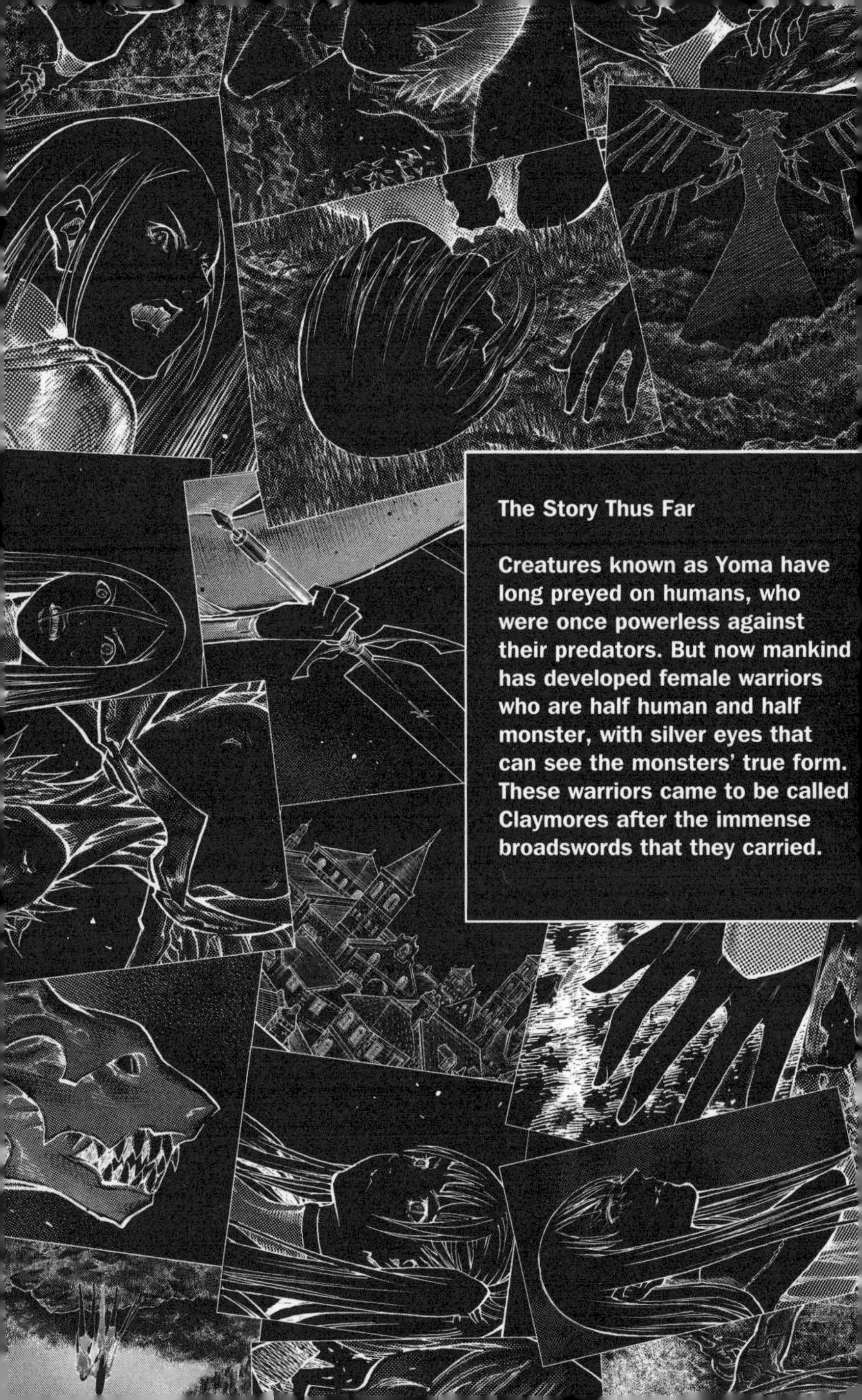

The Story Thus Far

Creatures known as Yoma have long preyed on humans, who were once powerless against their predators. But now mankind has developed female warriors who are half human and half monster, with silver eyes that can see the monsters' true form. These warriors came to be called Claymores after the immense broadswords that they carried.

Claymore

クレイモア

Vol. 19

CONTENTS

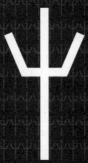

SCENE 102: THE ASHES OF LAUTREC, PART 7

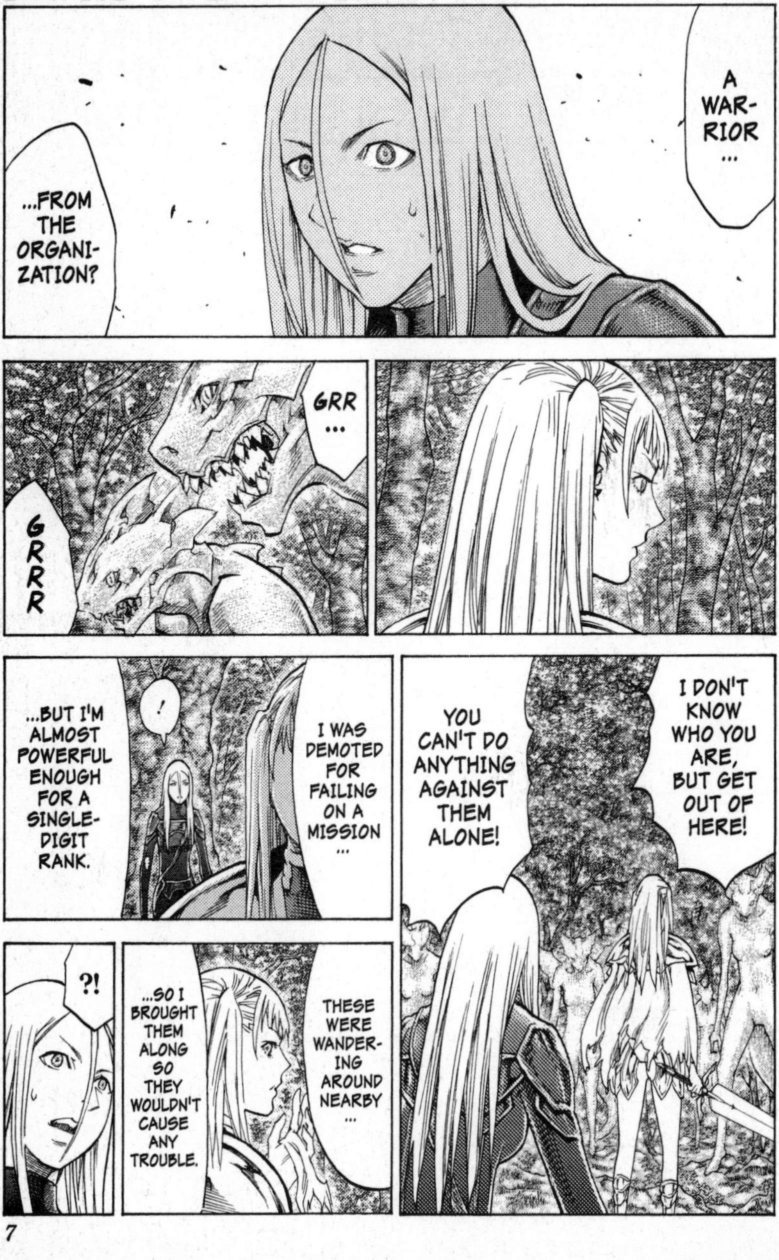
A WAR-RIOR...
...FROM THE ORGANIZATION?
GRR...
GRRR
I DON'T KNOW WHO YOU ARE, BUT GET OUT OF HERE!
YOU CAN'T DO ANYTHING AGAINST THEM ALONE!
I WAS DEMOTED FOR FAILING ON A MISSION...
!
...BUT I'M ALMOST POWERFUL ENOUGH FOR A SINGLE-DIGIT RANK.
THESE WERE WANDER-ING AROUND NEARBY...
...SO I BROUGHT THEM ALONG SO THEY WOULDN'T CAUSE ANY TROUBLE.
?!

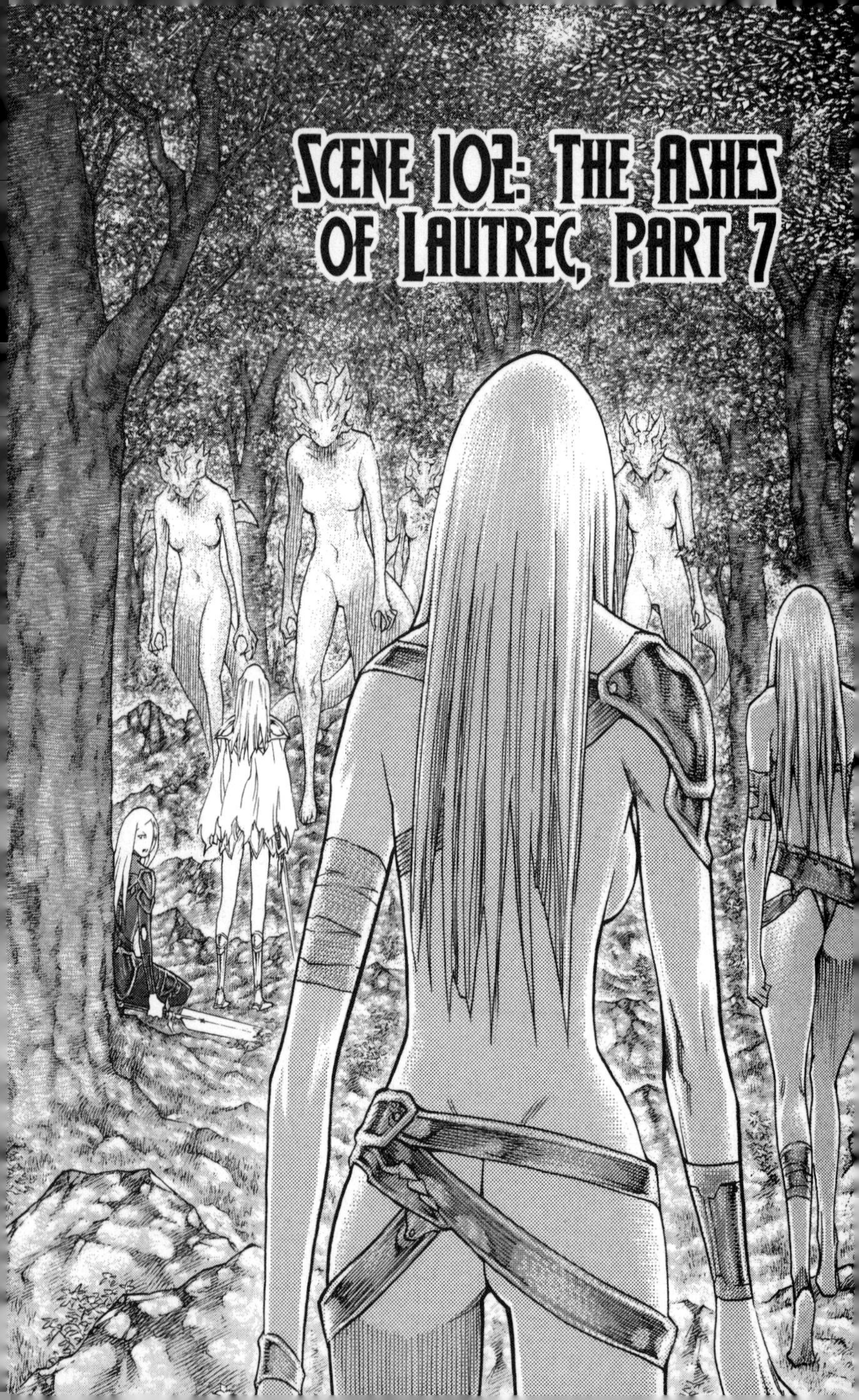
Scene 102: The Ashes of Lautrec, Part 7

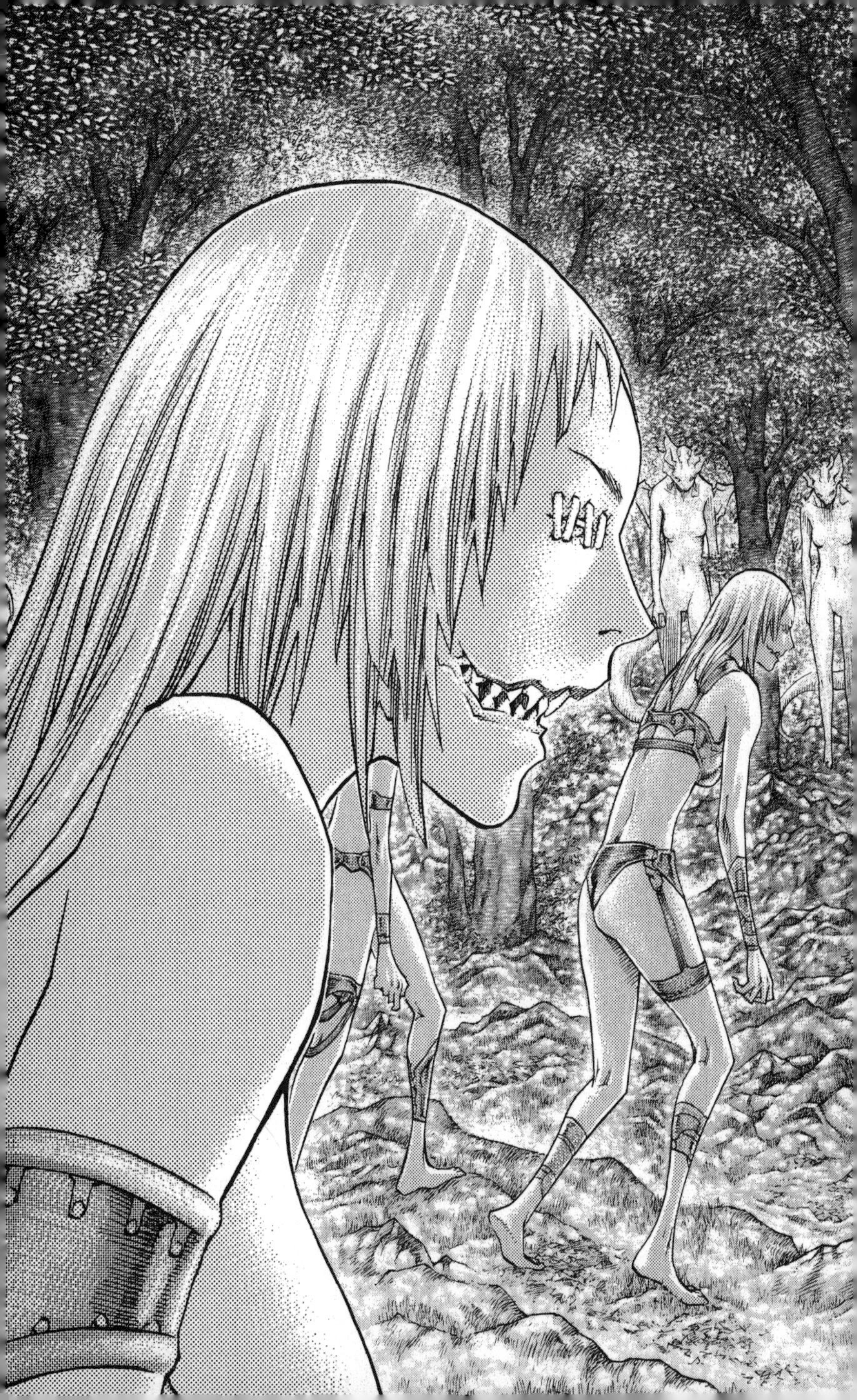

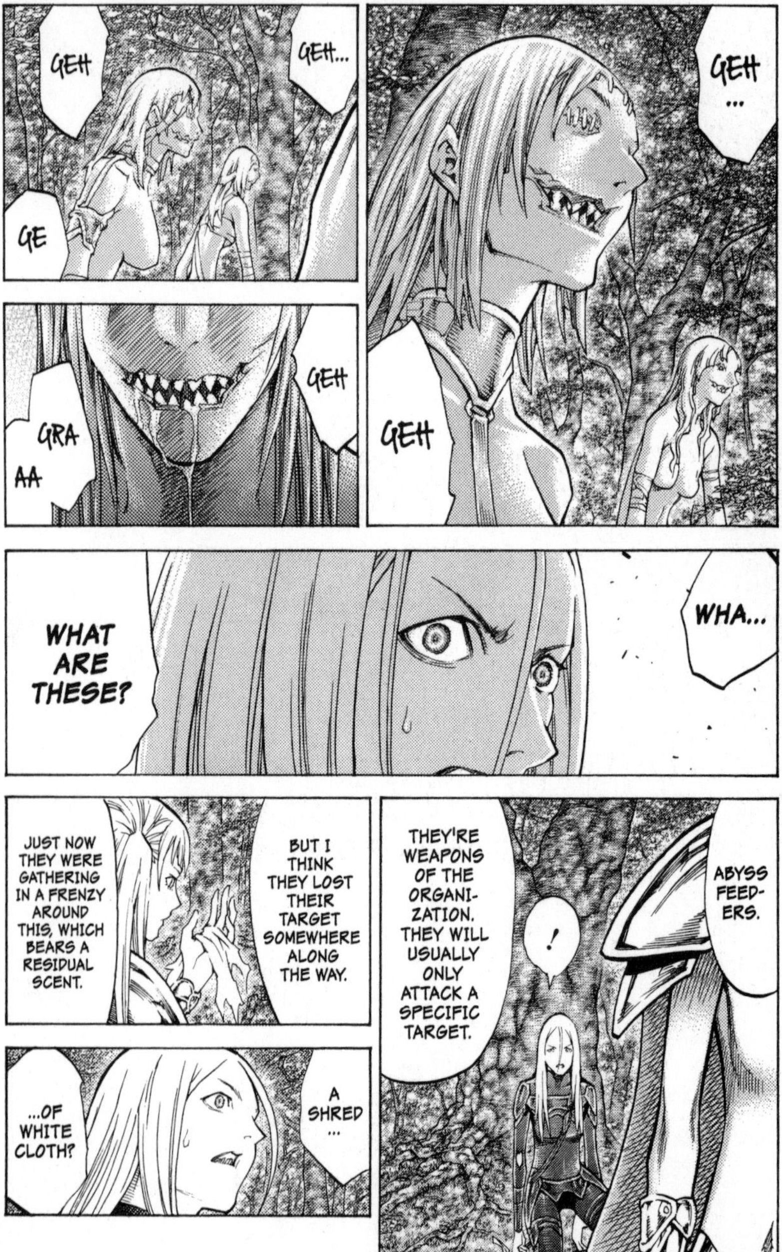
GEH ...
GEH
GEH...
GEH
GE
GEH
GRA AA
WHA...
WHAT ARE THESE?
ABYSS FEEDERS.
!
THEY'RE WEAPONS OF THE ORGANIZATION. THEY WILL USUALLY ONLY ATTACK A SPECIFIC TARGET.
JUST NOW THEY WERE GATHERING IN A FRENZY AROUND THIS, WHICH BEARS A RESIDUAL SCENT.
BUT I THINK THEY LOST THEIR TARGET SOMEWHERE ALONG THE WAY.
A SHRED ...
...OF WHITE CLOTH?

READ THIS WAY

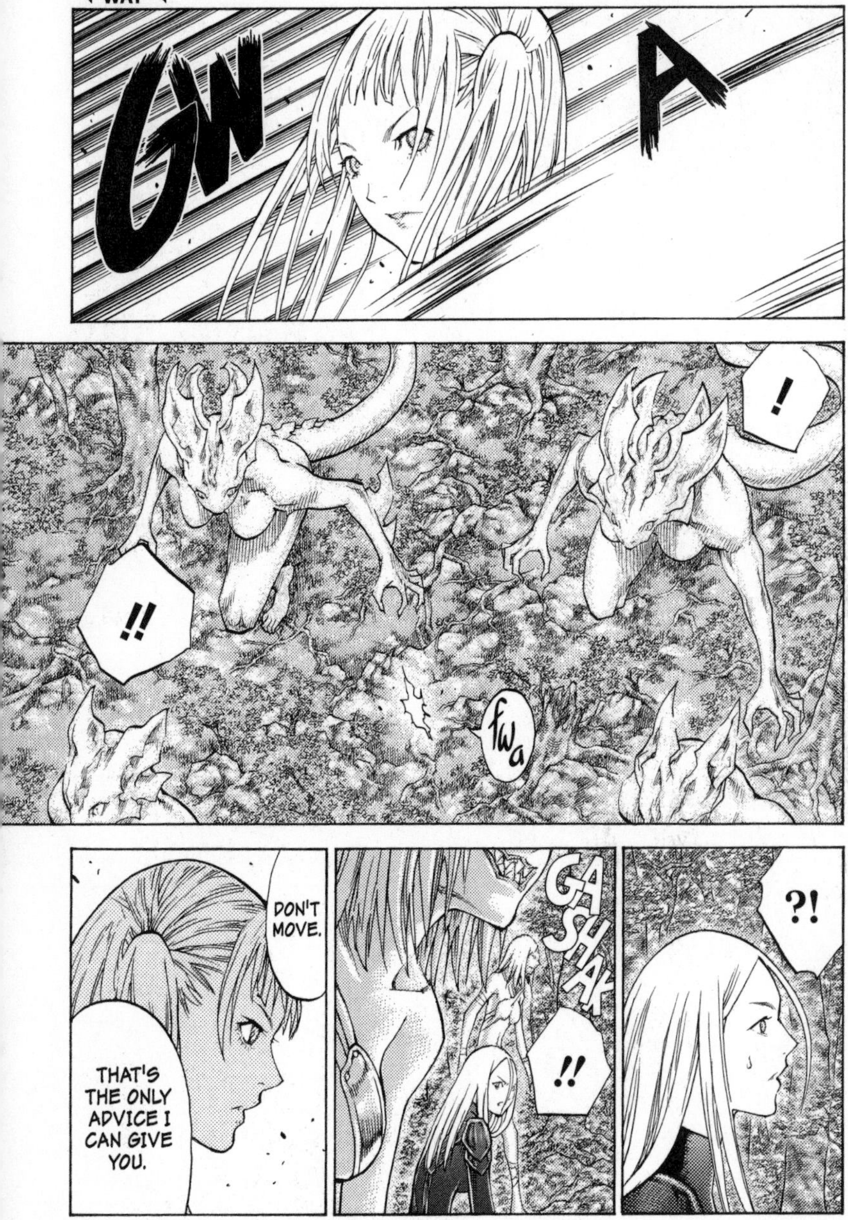

GWA
!
!!
fwa
?!
GASHAK
!!
DON'T MOVE.
THAT'S THE ONLY ADVICE I CAN GIVE YOU.

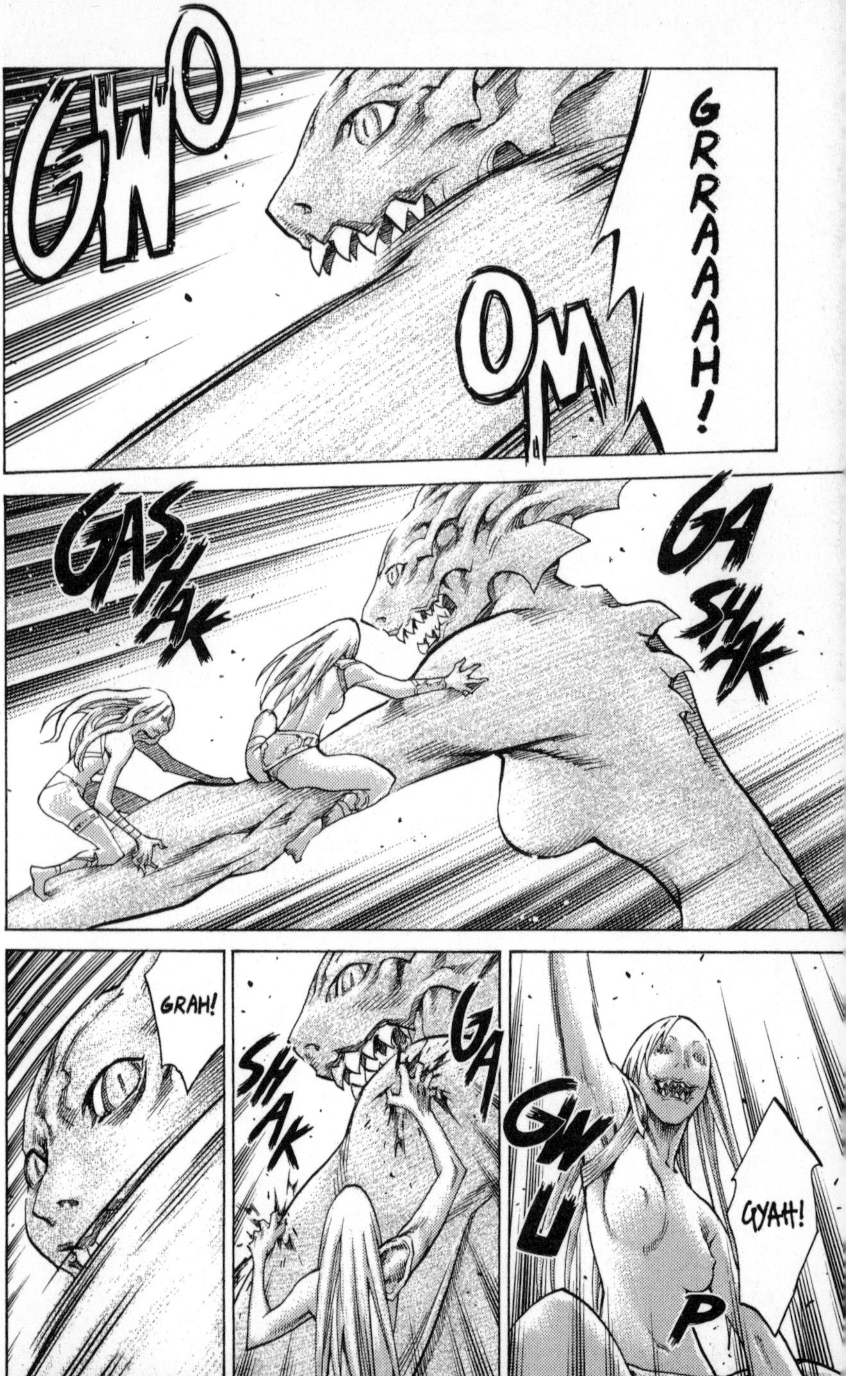
GRRAAAAH!
GWOOM
GASHAK
GASHAK
GYAH!
GWUP
GASHAK
GRAH!

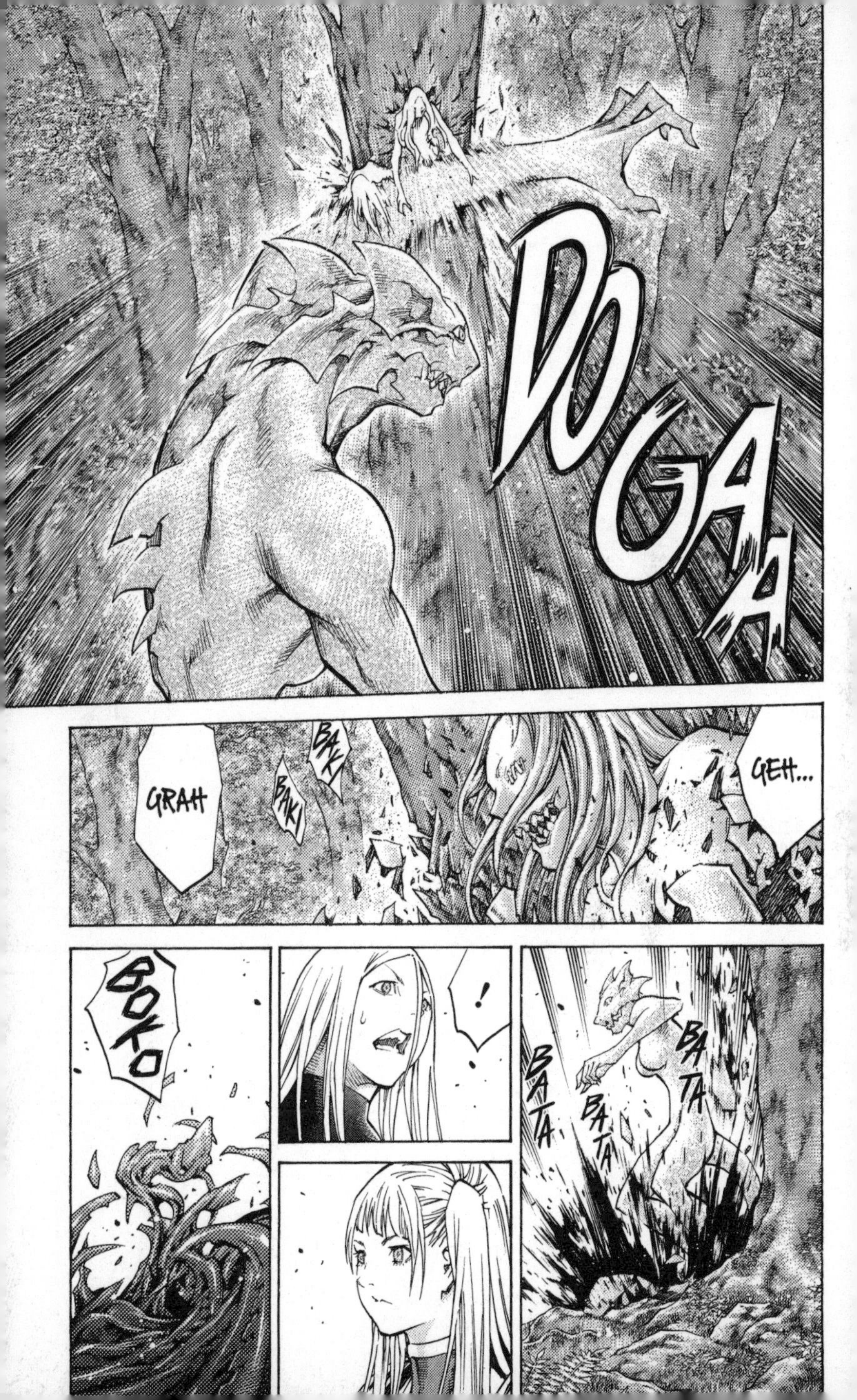
DOGAA
GEH...
BAKI
BAKI
GRAH
BATA
BATA
BATA
!
BOKO

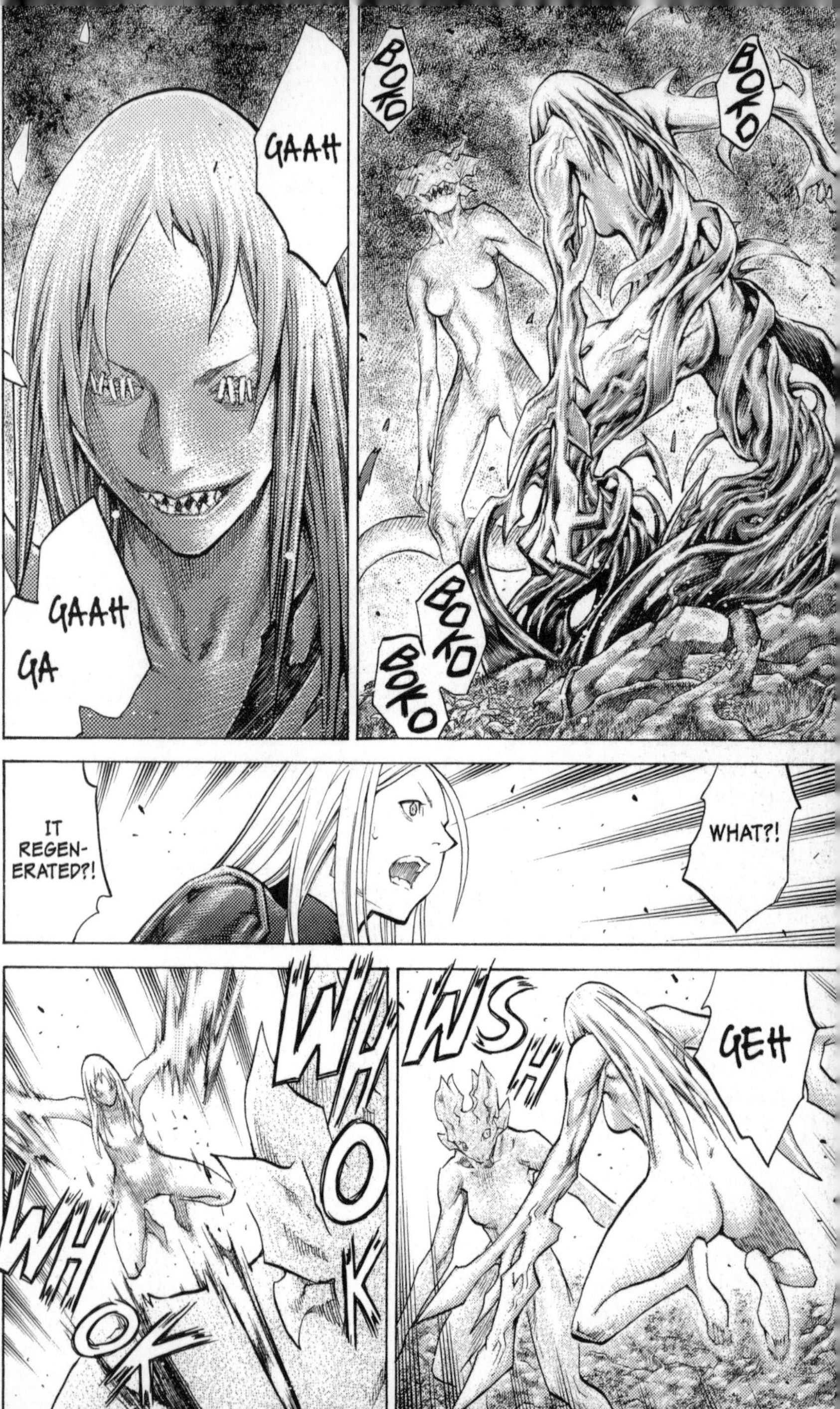
BOKO
BOKO
BOKO
BOKO
GAAH
GAAH
GA
WHAT?!
IT REGEN-ERATED?!
GEH
WWSH
WHOK
WHOK

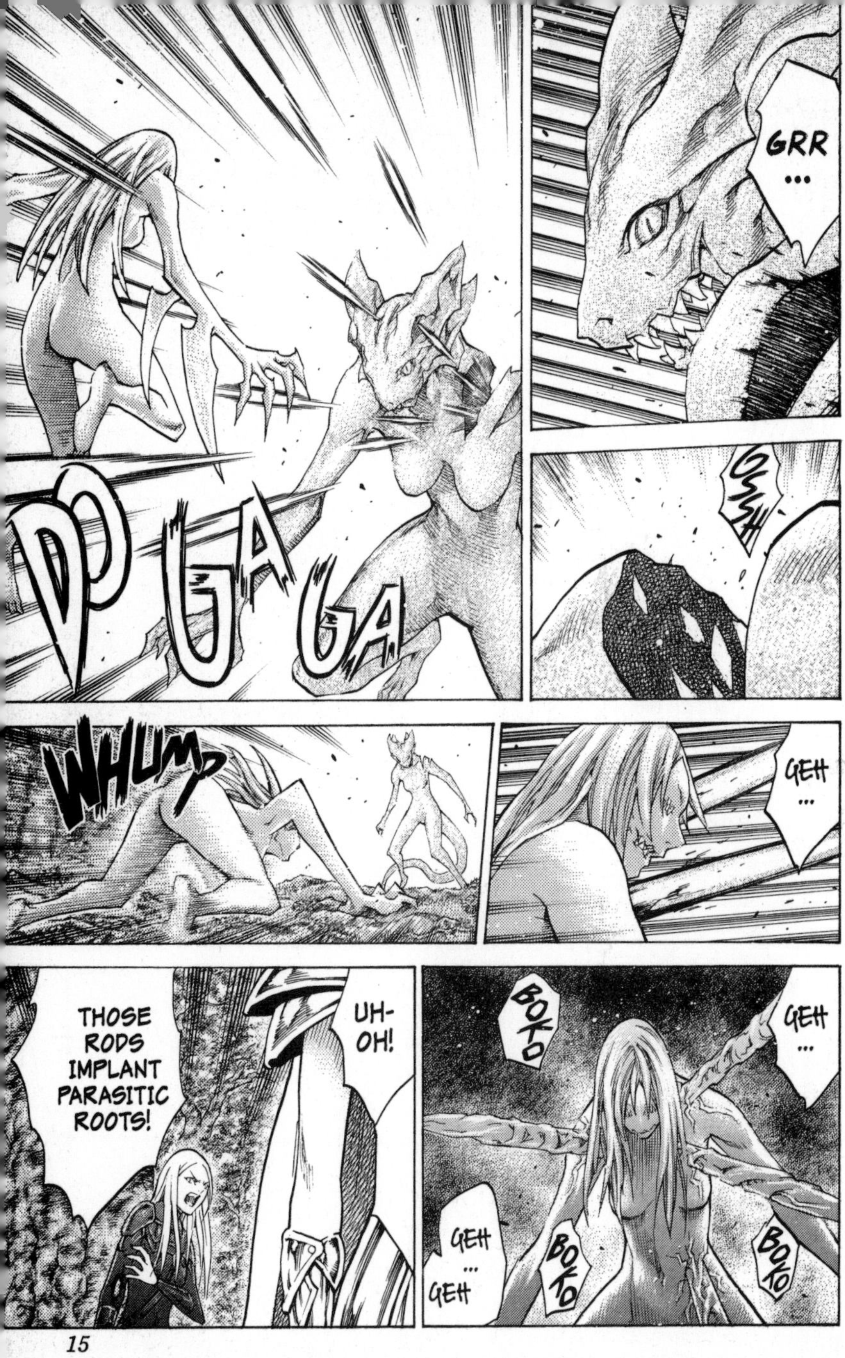
GRR ...
GUSH
DO GA GA
GEH ...
WHUMP
BOKO
GEH ...
GEH ... GEH
BOKO
BOKO
UH-OH!
THOSE RODS IMPLANT PARASITIC ROOTS!

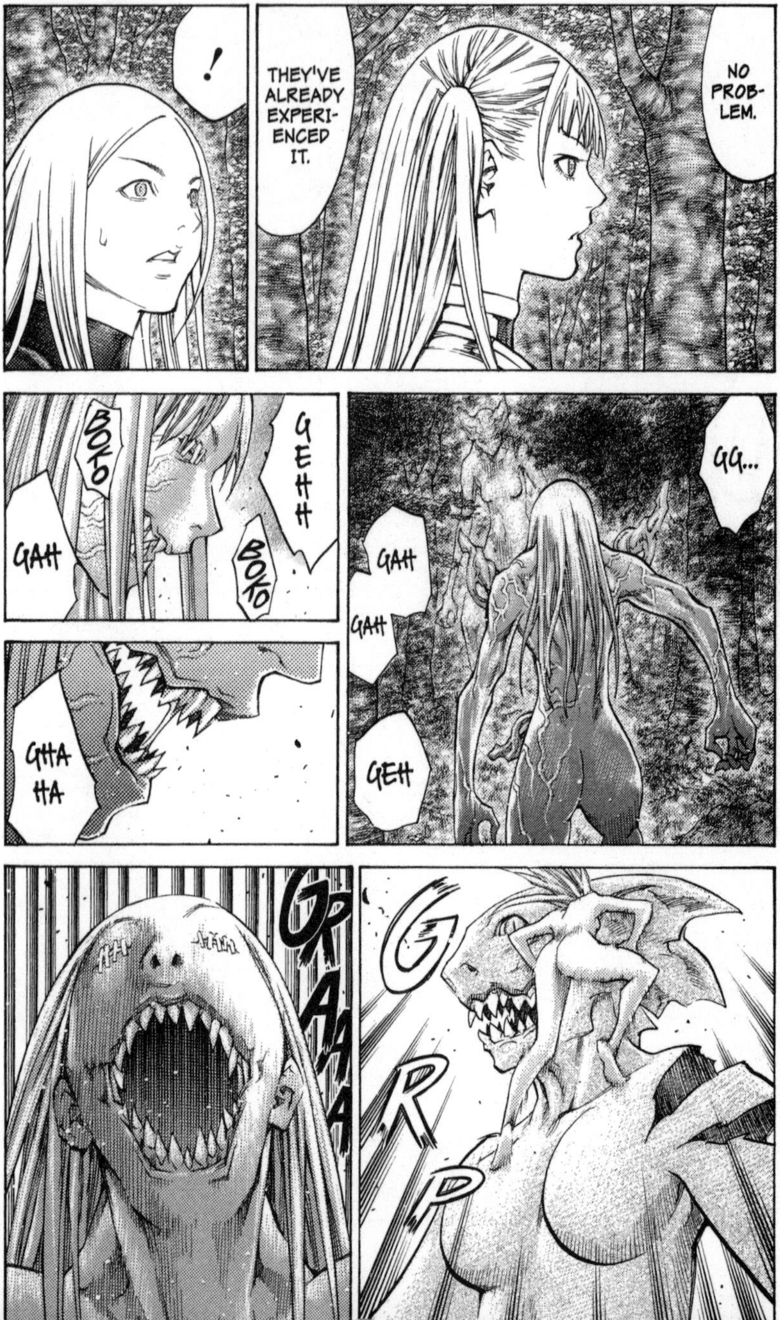
NO PROB-LEM.
THEY'VE ALREADY EXPERI-ENCED IT.
!
GG...
GAH
GAH
GEH
GEHH
BOKO
BOKO
GAH
GHA HA
GRP
GRAAAA

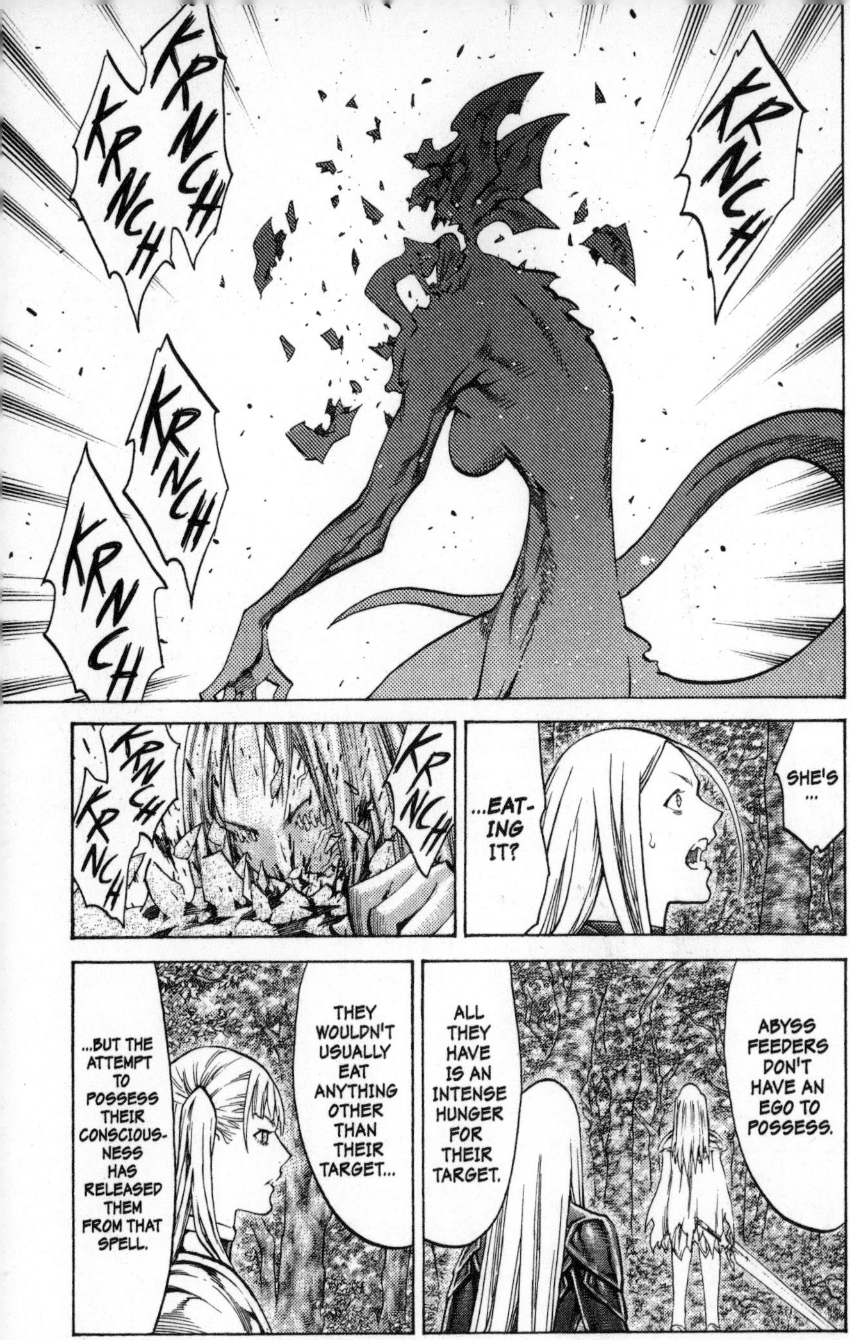

KRNCH
KRNCH
KRNCH
KRNCH
KRNCH
SHE'S...
...EATING IT?
KRNCH
KRNCH
KRNCH
ABYSS FEEDERS DON'T HAVE AN EGO TO POSSESS.
ALL THEY HAVE IS AN INTENSE HUNGER FOR THEIR TARGET.
THEY WOULDN'T USUALLY EAT ANYTHING OTHER THAN THEIR TARGET...
...BUT THE ATTEMPT TO POSSESS THEIR CONSCIOUSNESS HAS RELEASED THEM FROM THAT SPELL.

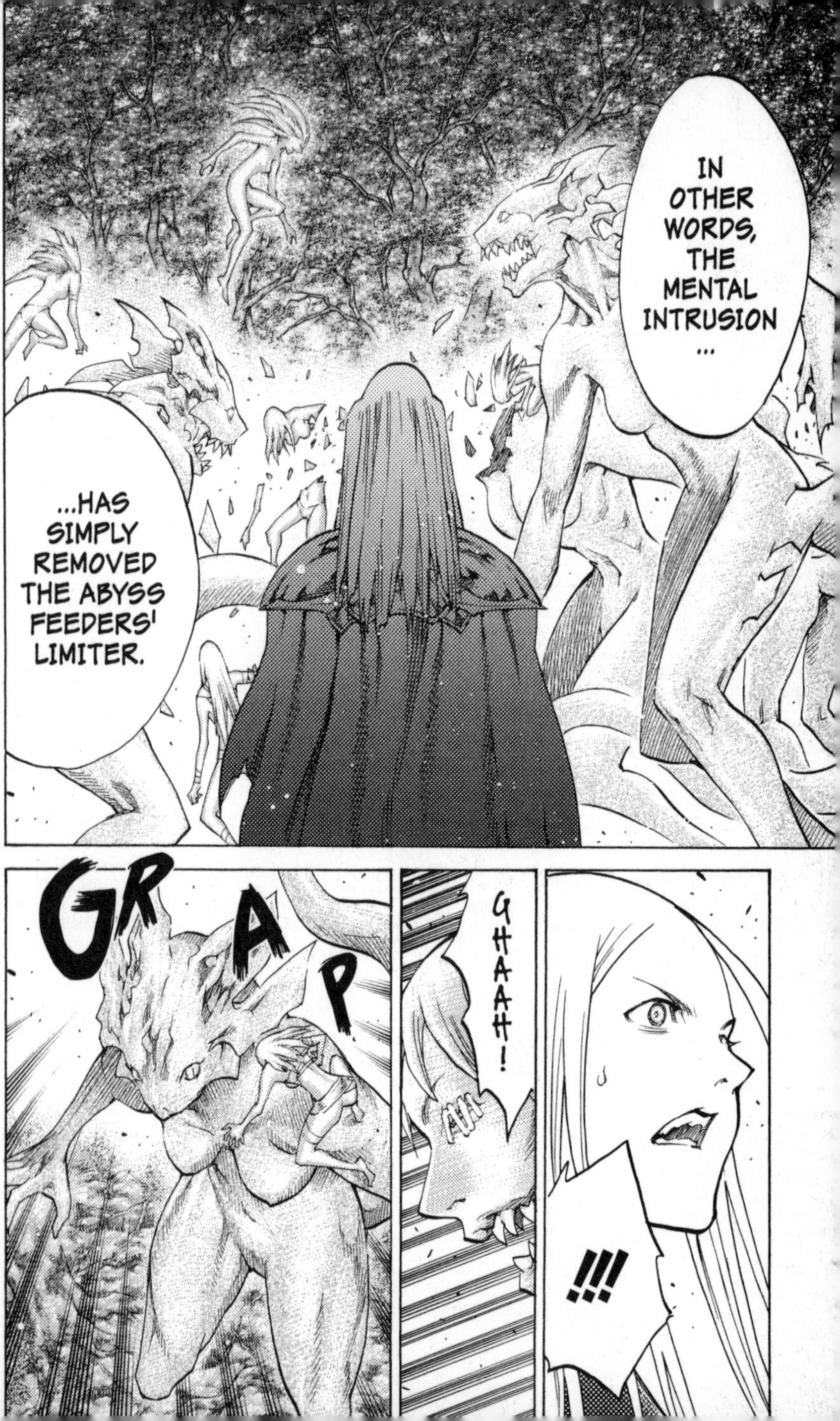
IN OTHER WORDS, THE MENTAL INTRUSION...
...HAS SIMPLY REMOVED THE ABYSS FEEDERS' LIMITER.
!!!
GHAAAH!
GRAP

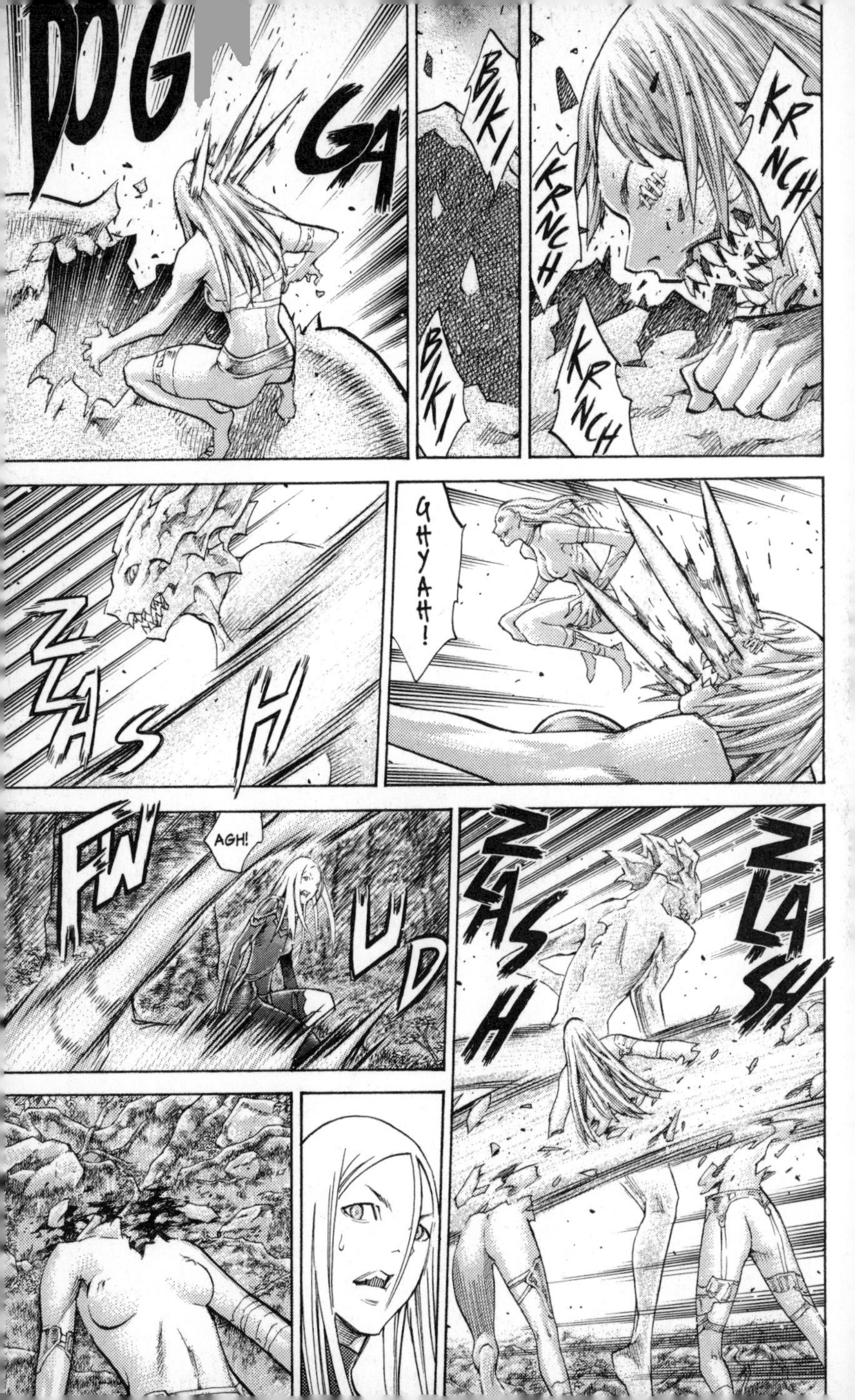
KRNCH
KRNCH
KRNCH
BIKI
BIKI
DOG
GA
GHYAH!
ZLASH
ZLASH
ZLASH
AGH!
FWUD

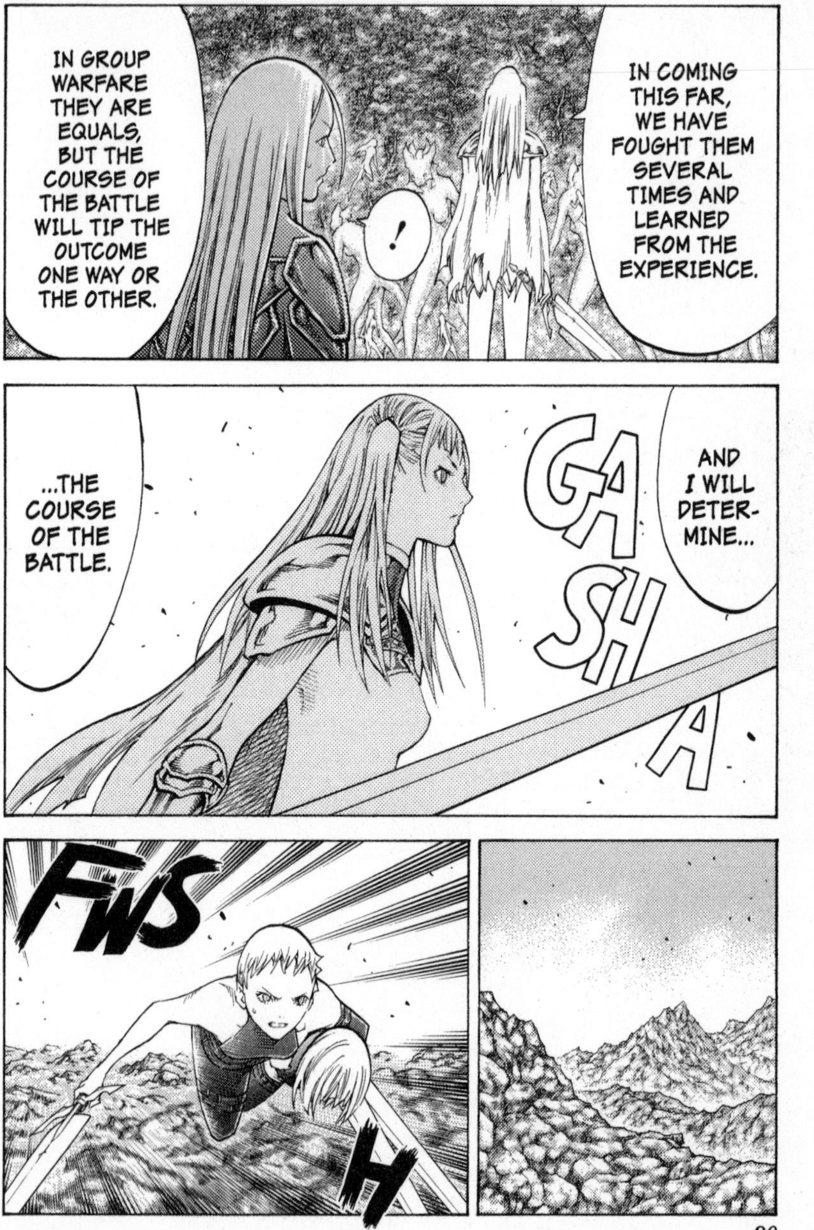
IN COMING THIS FAR, WE HAVE FOUGHT THEM SEVERAL TIMES AND LEARNED FROM THE EXPERIENCE.
!
IN GROUP WARFARE THEY ARE EQUALS, BUT THE COURSE OF THE BATTLE WILL TIP THE OUTCOME ONE WAY OR THE OTHER.
AND I WILL DETERMINE...
GASHA
...THE COURSE OF THE BATTLE.
FWSH

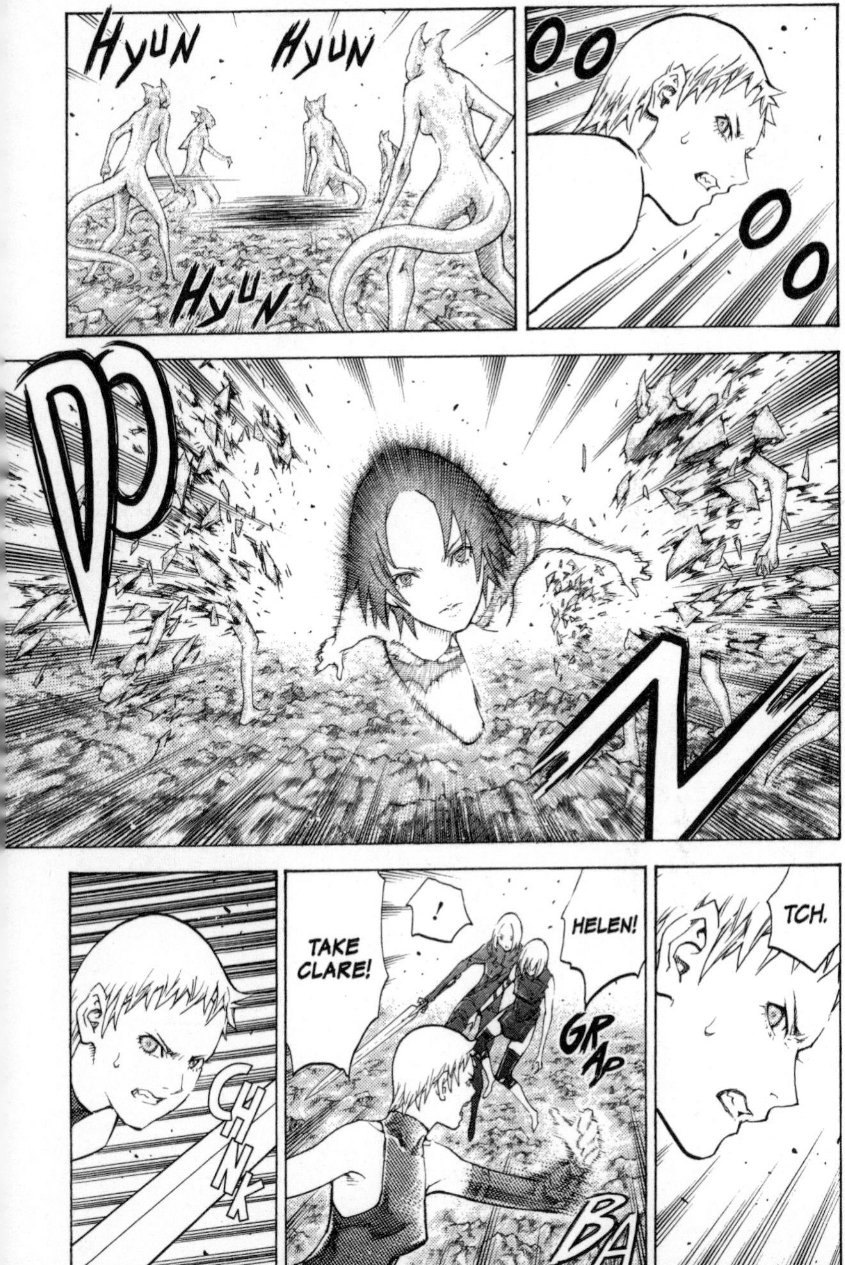

OO
OO
HYUN
HYUN
HYUN
DON
TCH.
HELEN!
!
TAKE CLARE!
GRAP
BA
CHINK

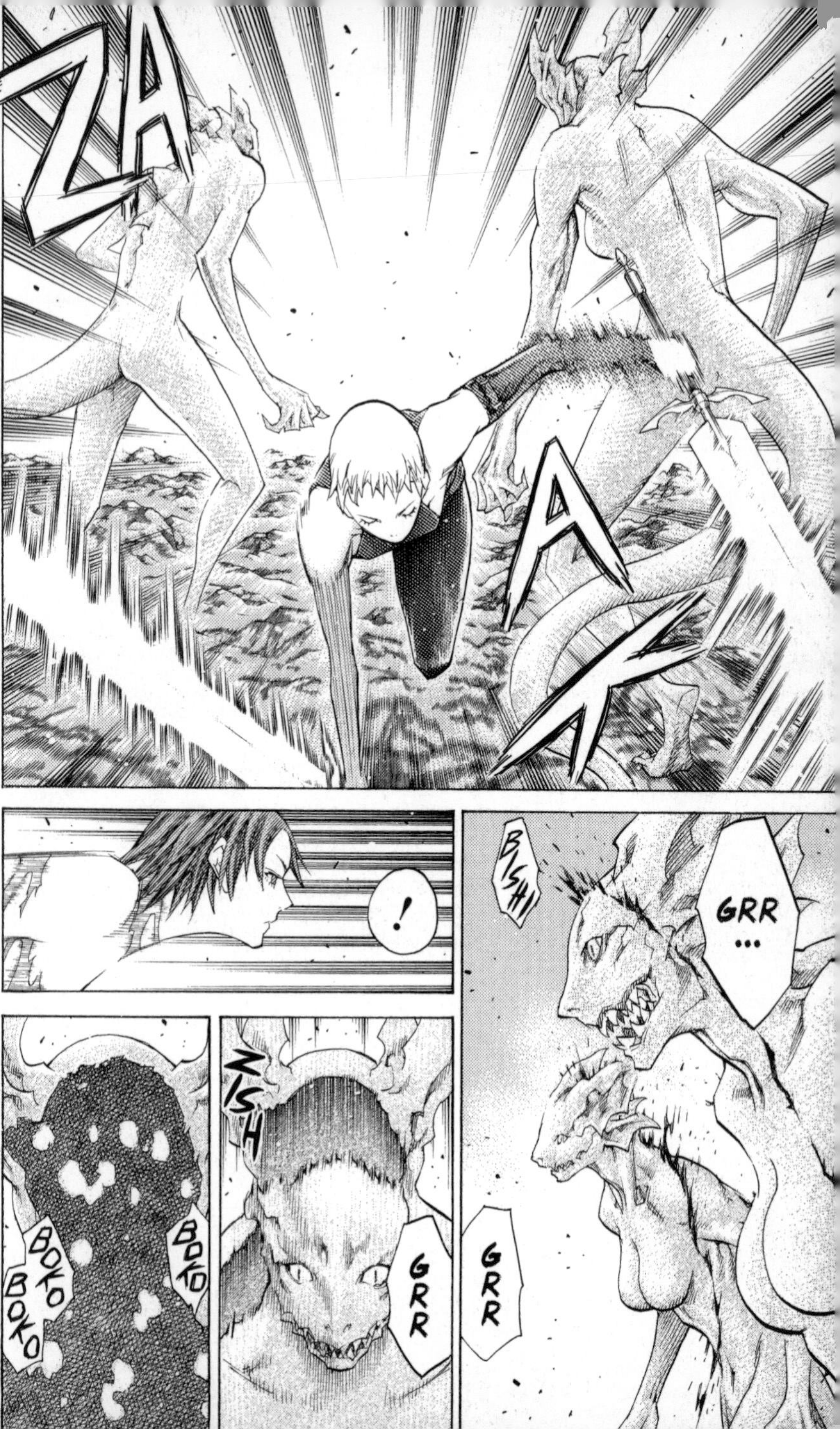
ZA
AK
BISHI
GRR...
GRR
!
ZISH
GRR
BOKO
BOKO BOKO

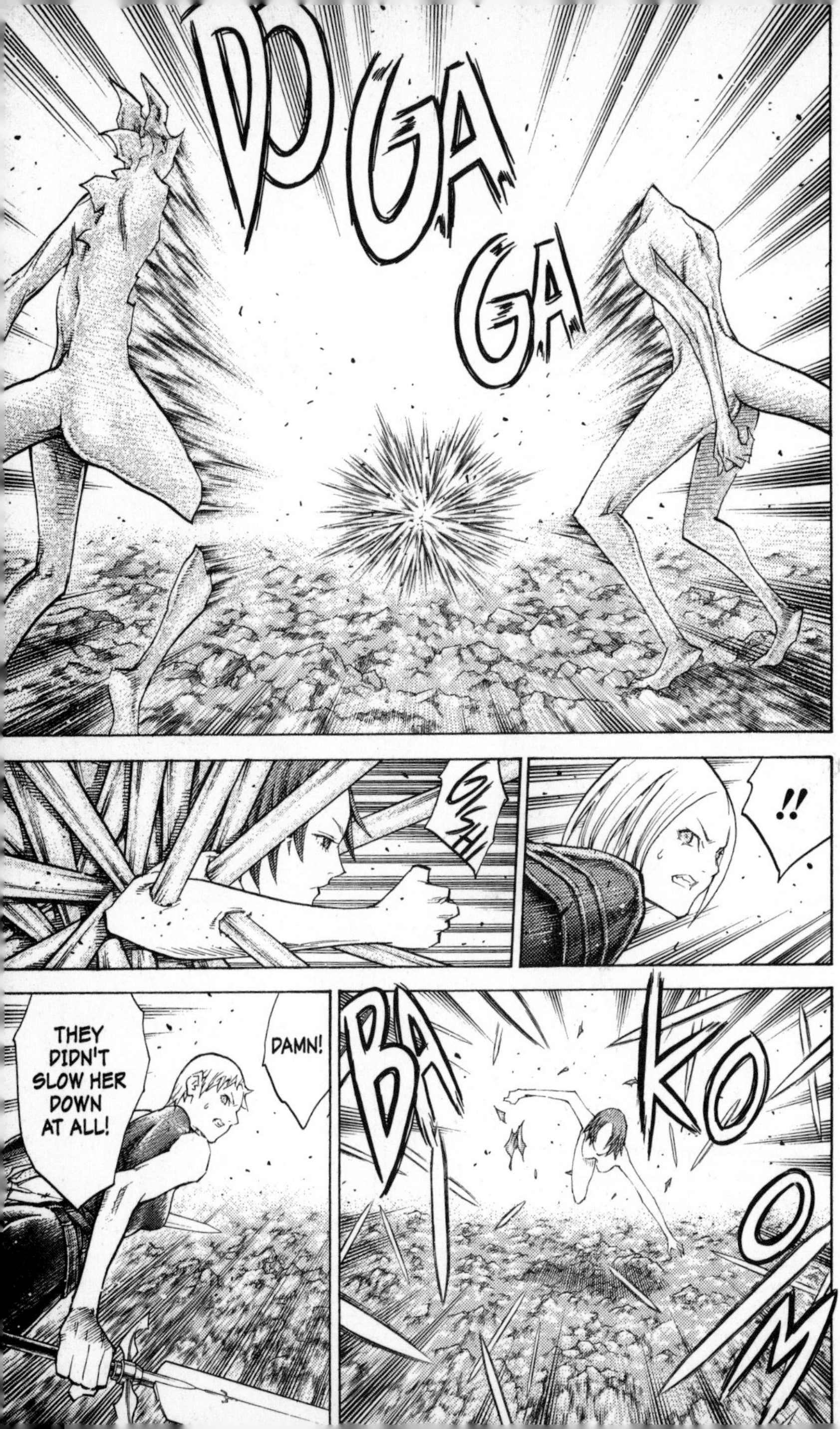
DOGAGA
!!
GISHI
BAKOOM
DAMN!
THEY DIDN'T SLOW HER DOWN AT ALL!

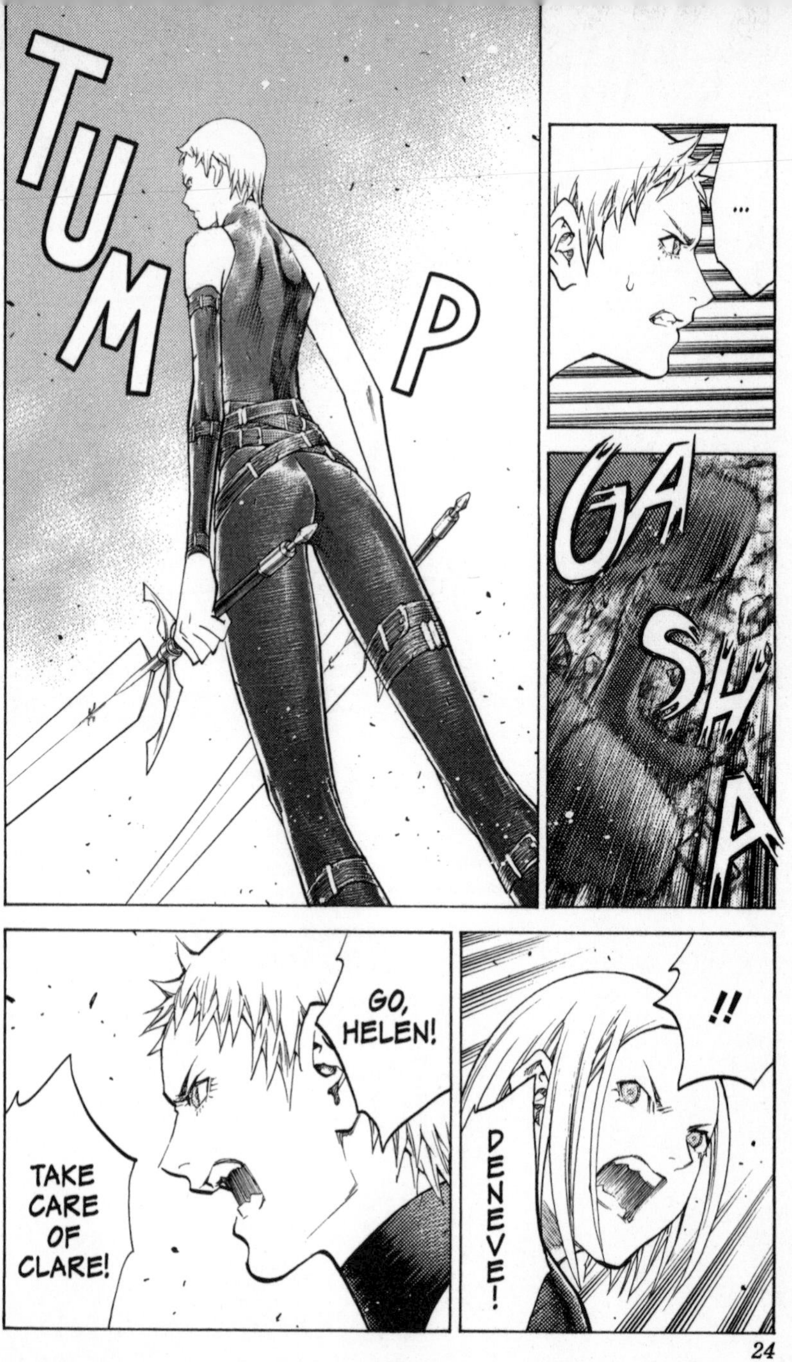
...
GASHA
TUMP
!!
DENEVE!
GO, HELEN!
TAKE CARE OF CLARE!

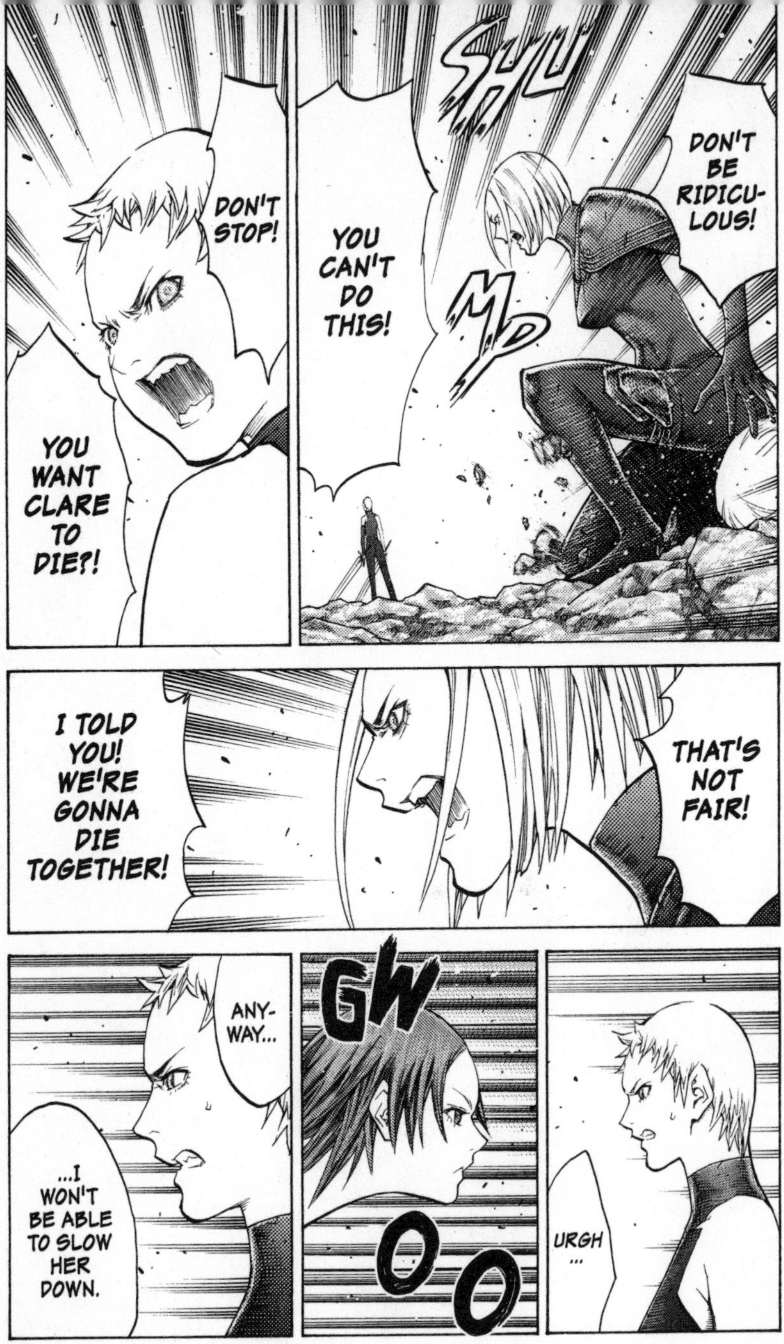
SHU
DON'T BE RIDICULOUS!
YOU CAN'T DO THIS!
MD
DON'T STOP!
YOU WANT CLARE TO DIE?!
THAT'S NOT FAIR!
I TOLD YOU! WE'RE GONNA DIE TOGETHER!
URGH ...
GW
OO
ANY-WAY...
...I WON'T BE ABLE TO SLOW HER DOWN.

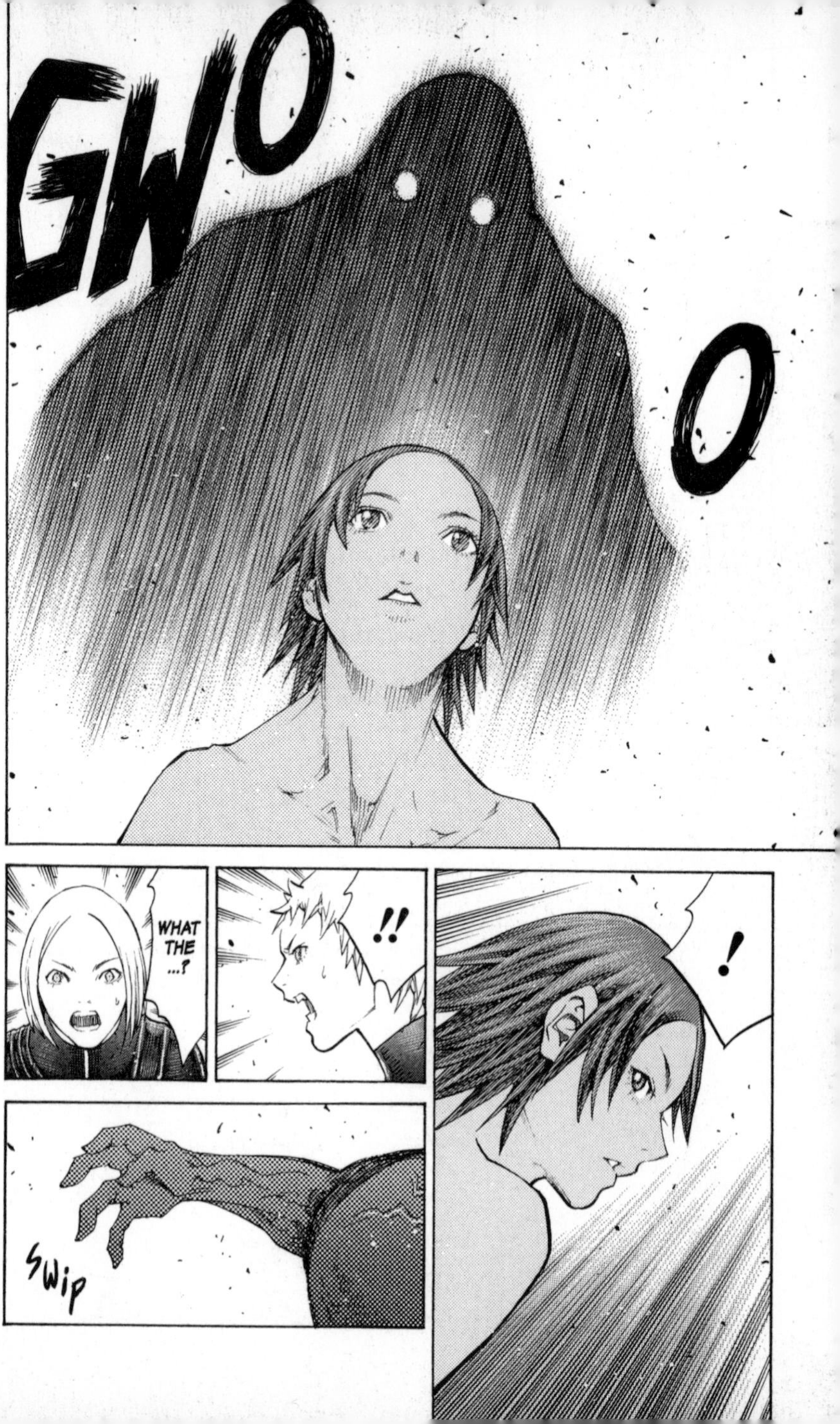
GWOO
!
!!
WHAT THE ...?
SWIP

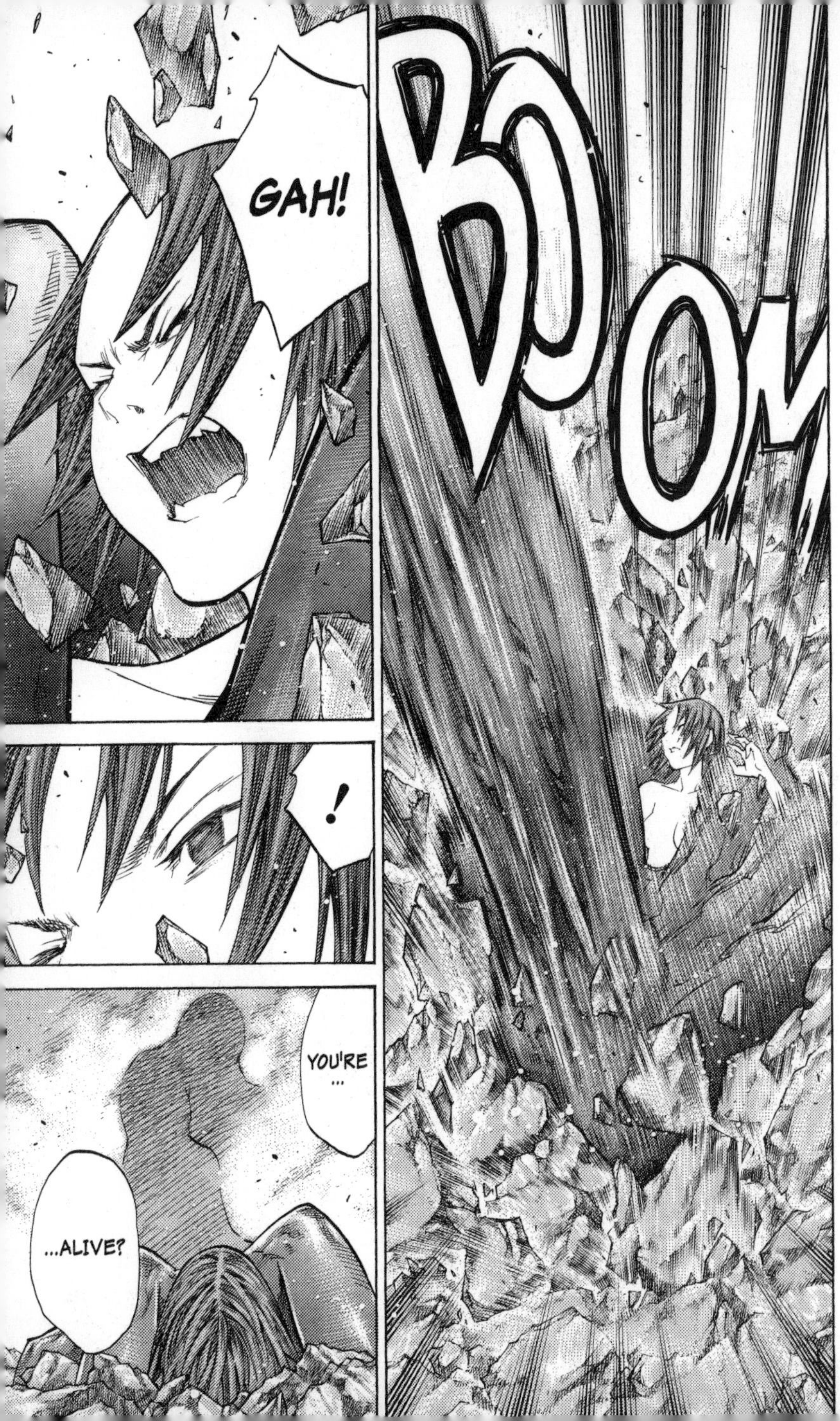
BOOM
GAH!
!
YOU'RE ...
...ALIVE?

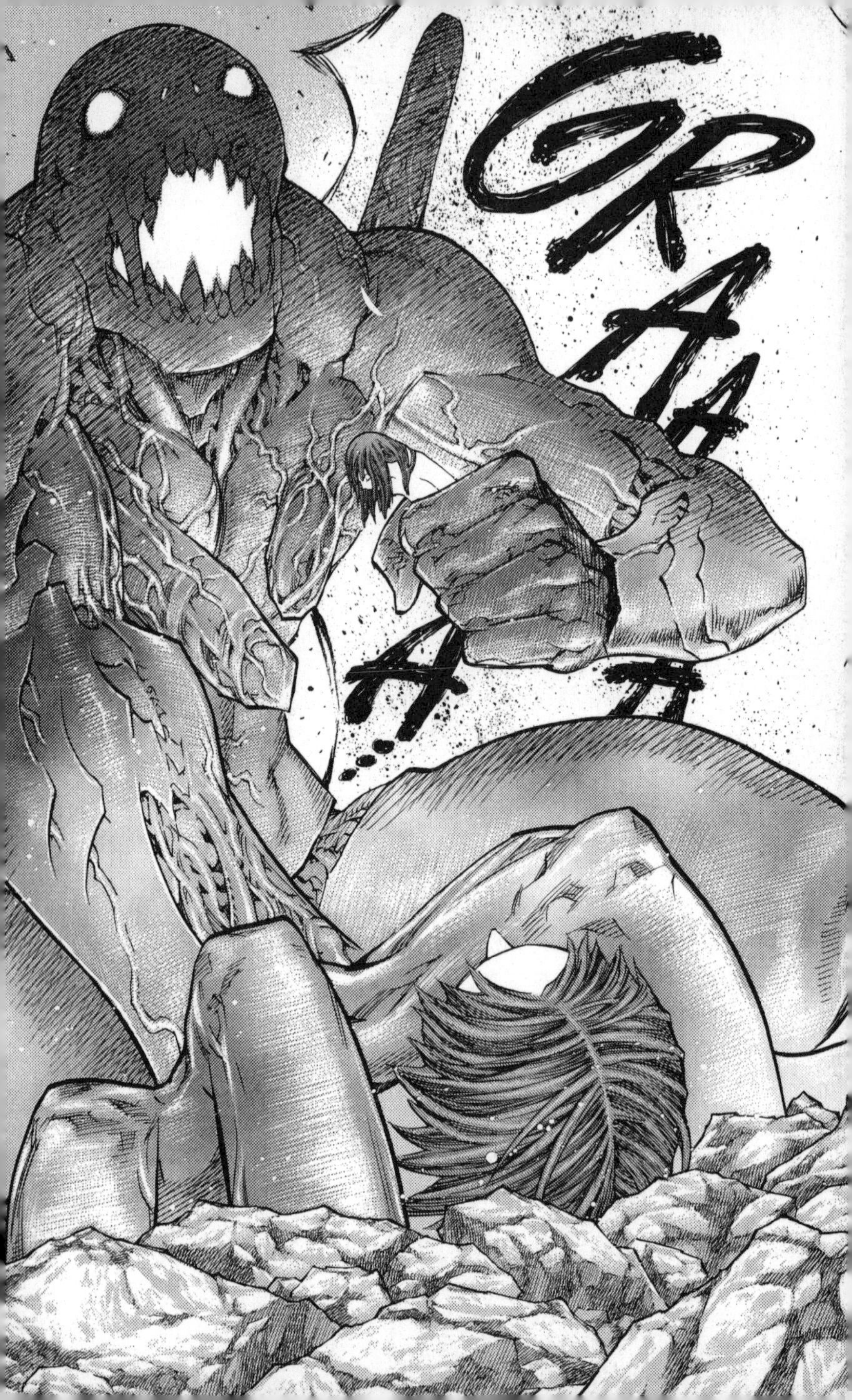
GRAAAAH...

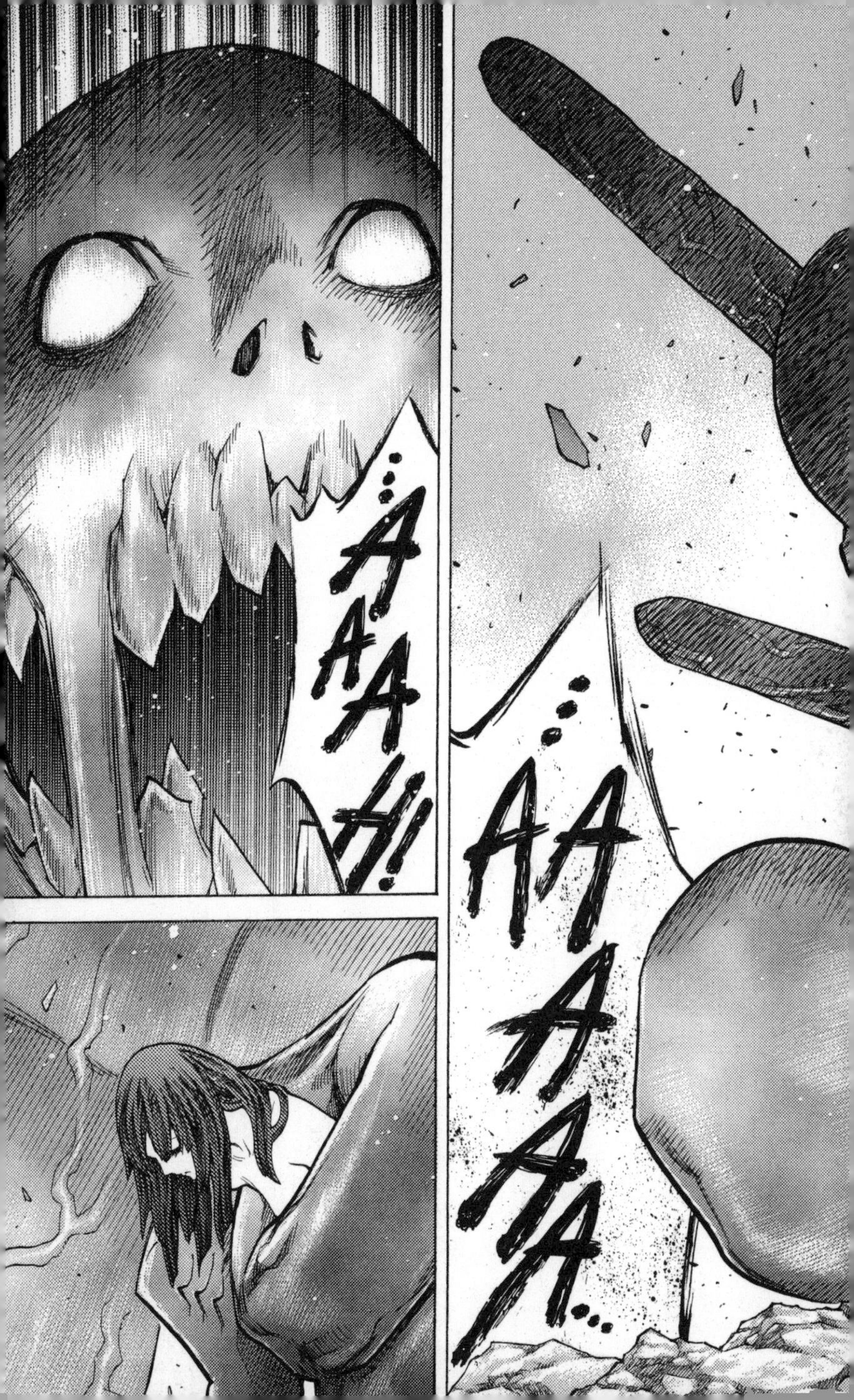
...AAAAAA...
...AAAH!

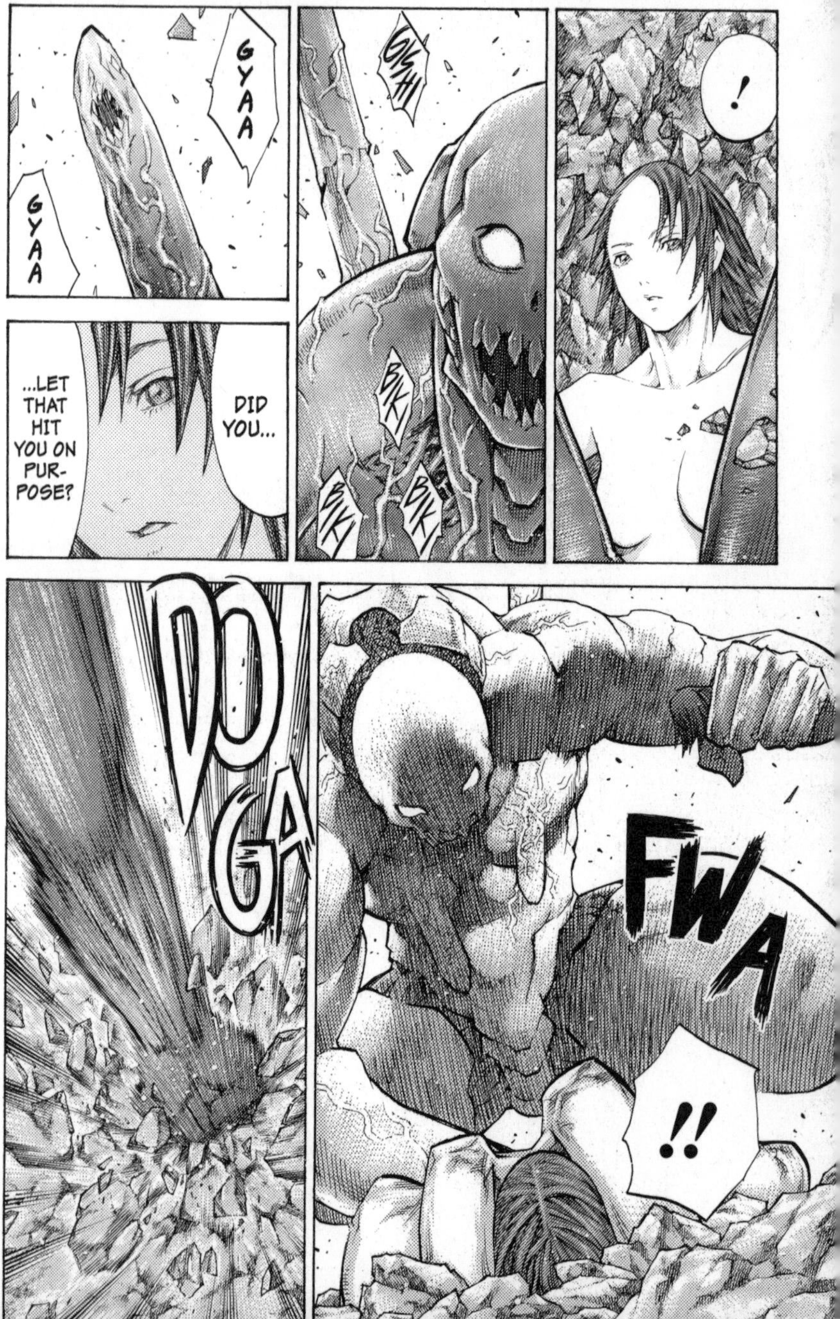
!
GISHI
BIKI
BIKI
BIKI
GYAA
GYAA
DID YOU...
...LET THAT HIT YOU ON PURPOSE?
FWA
!!
DOGA

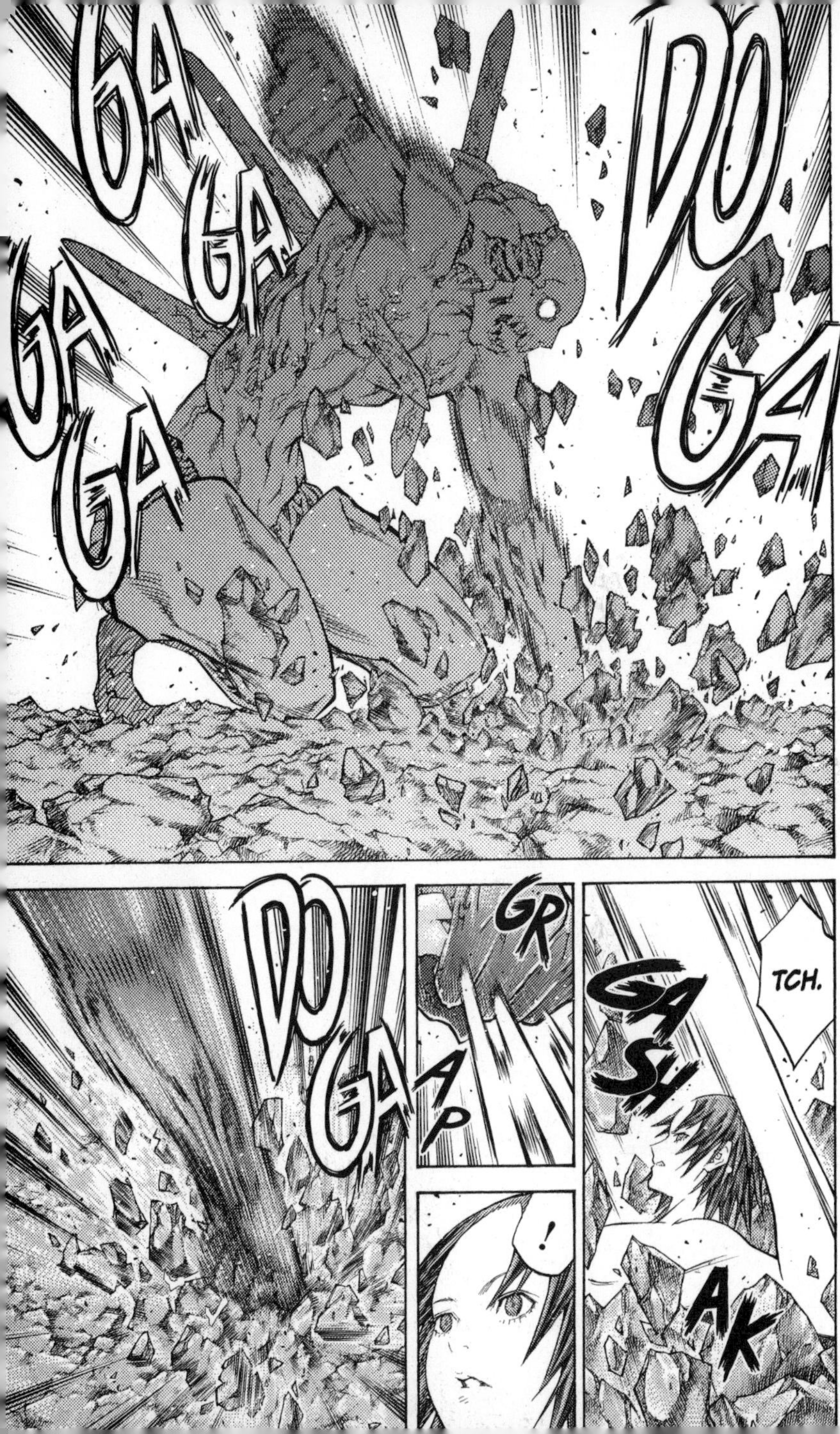
DO GA
GA GA GA GA
TCH.
GASH
AK
GR
GAP
!
DO GA

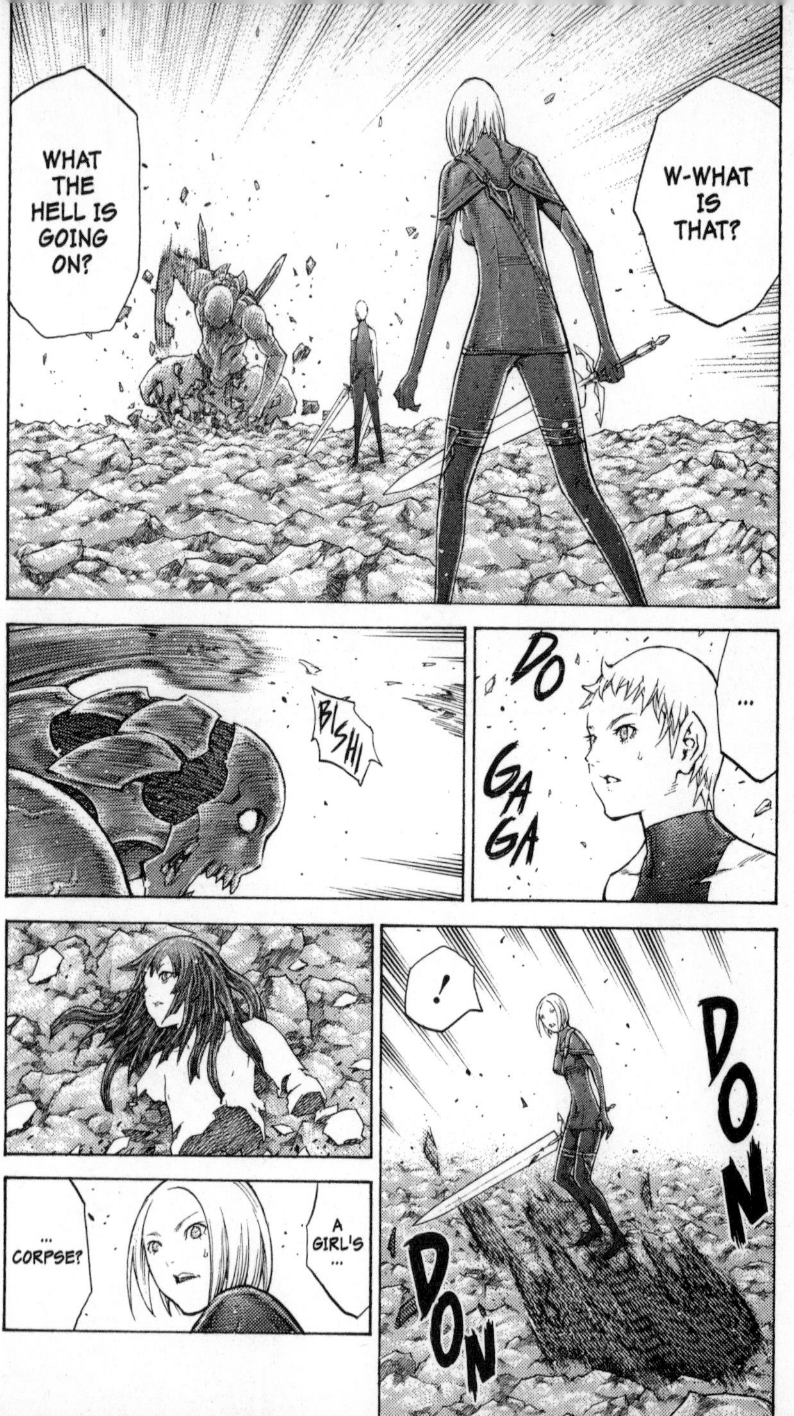
W-WHAT IS THAT?
WHAT THE HELL IS GOING ON?
...
DO
GAGA
GA
BISHI
!
DON
DON
A GIRL'S ...
... CORPSE?

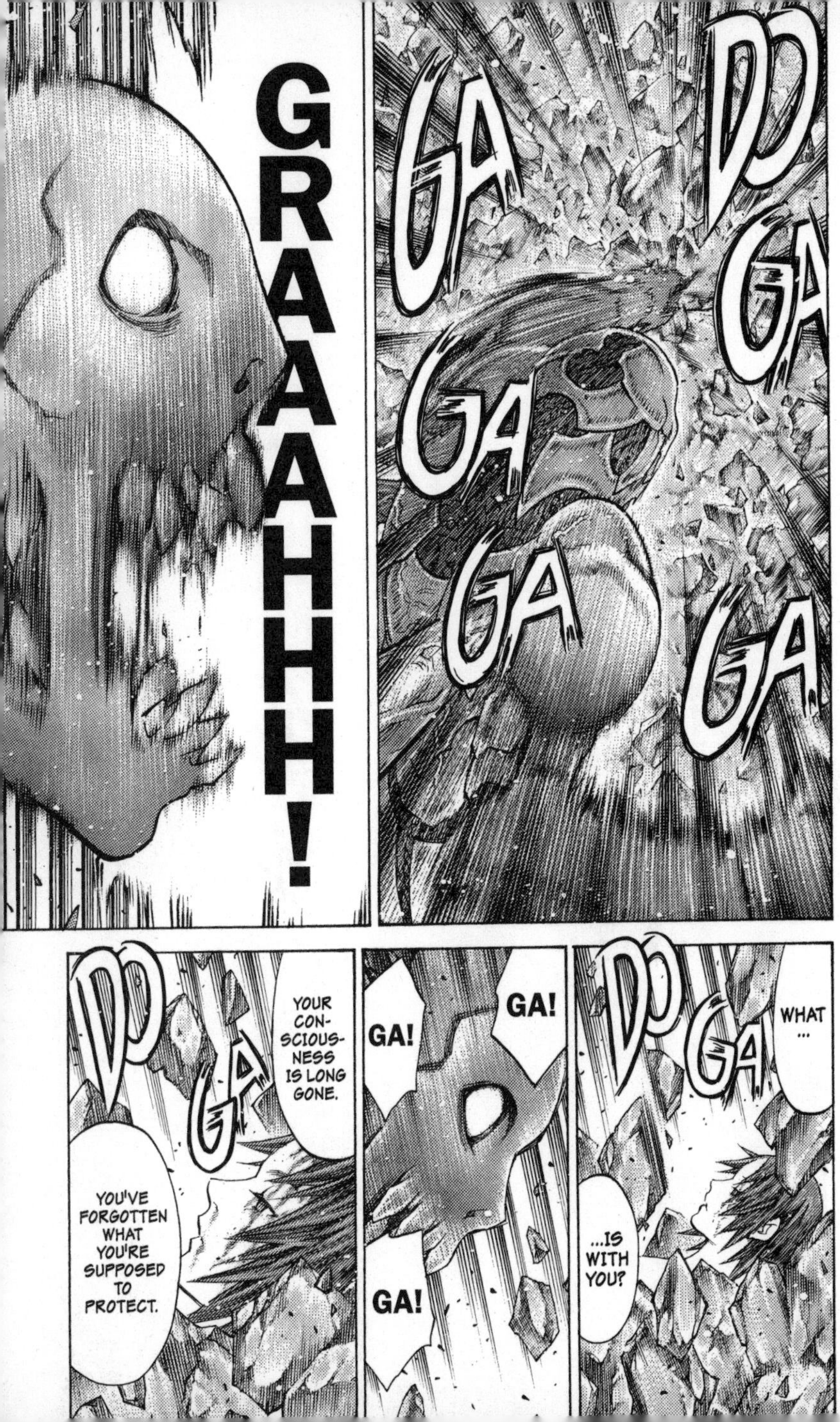

DO
GA
GA
GA
GA
GA
GRAAAHHH!
DO
GA
WHAT...
...IS WITH YOU?
GA!
GA!
GA!
DO
GA
YOUR CON-SCIOUS-NESS IS LONG GONE.
YOU'VE FORGOTTEN WHAT YOU'RE SUPPOSED TO PROTECT.

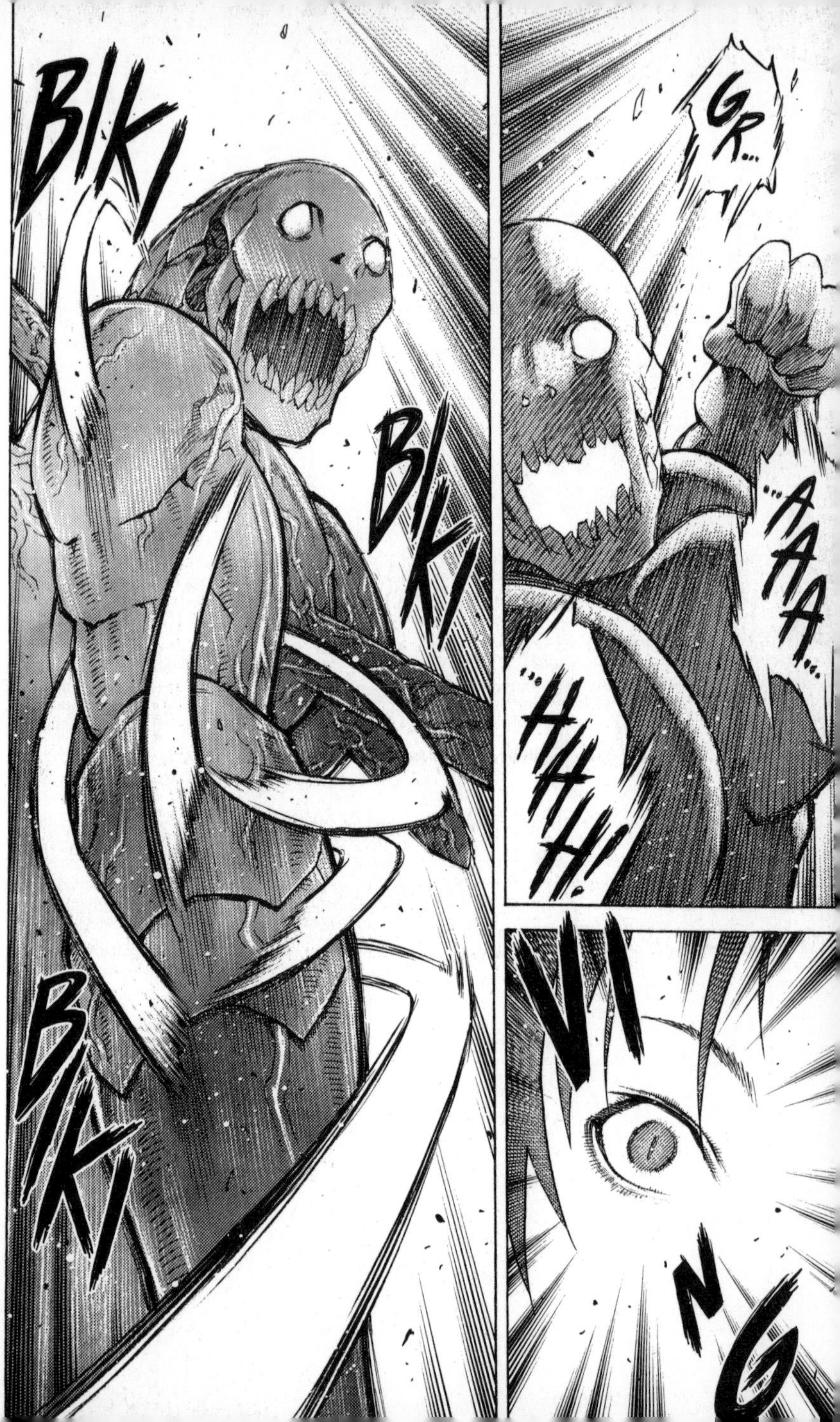
GR...
...AAAA...
...HHHH!
VING
BIKI
BIKI
BIKI

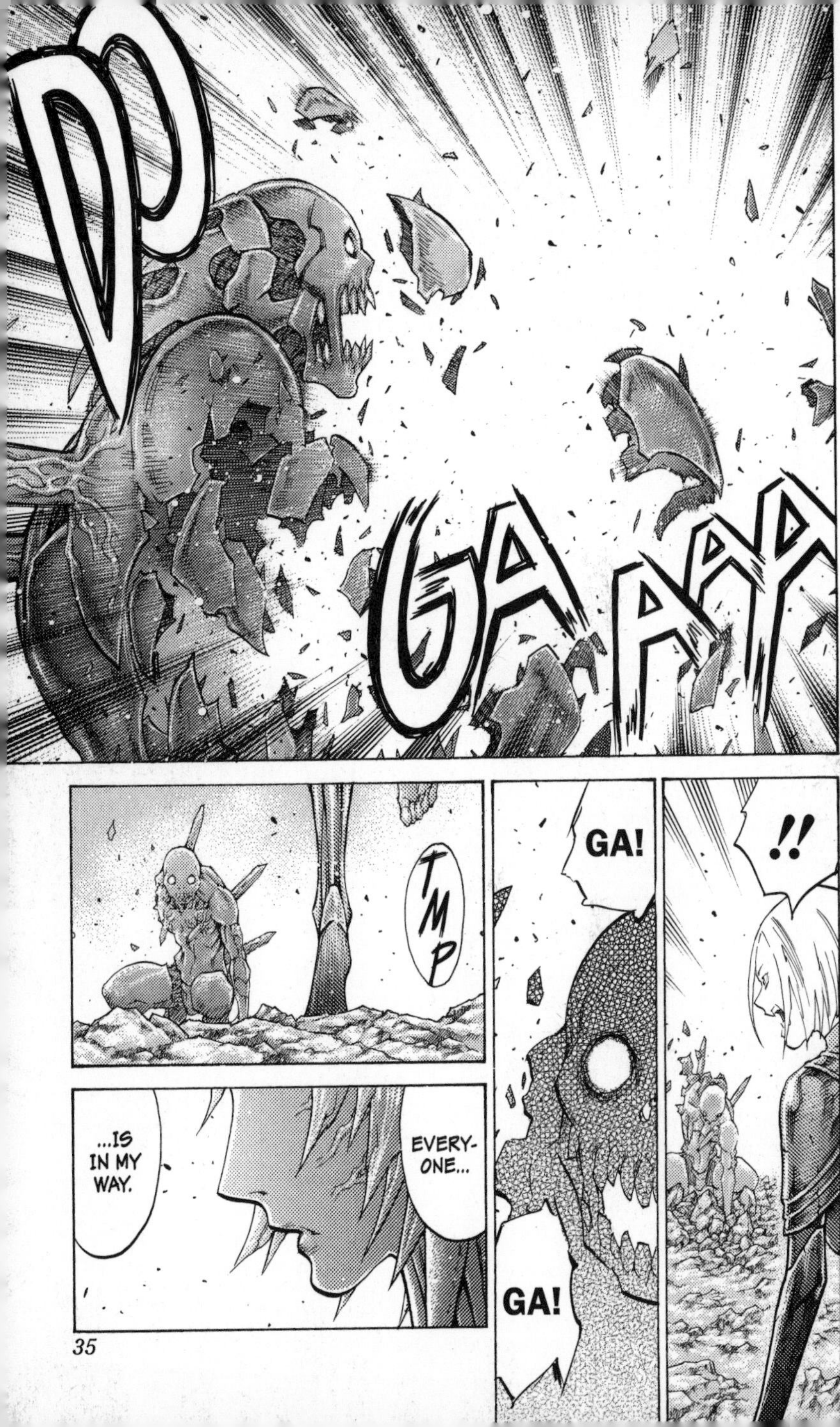
DO
GAAAA
!!
GA!
GA!
TMP
EVERY-ONE...
...IS IN MY WAY.

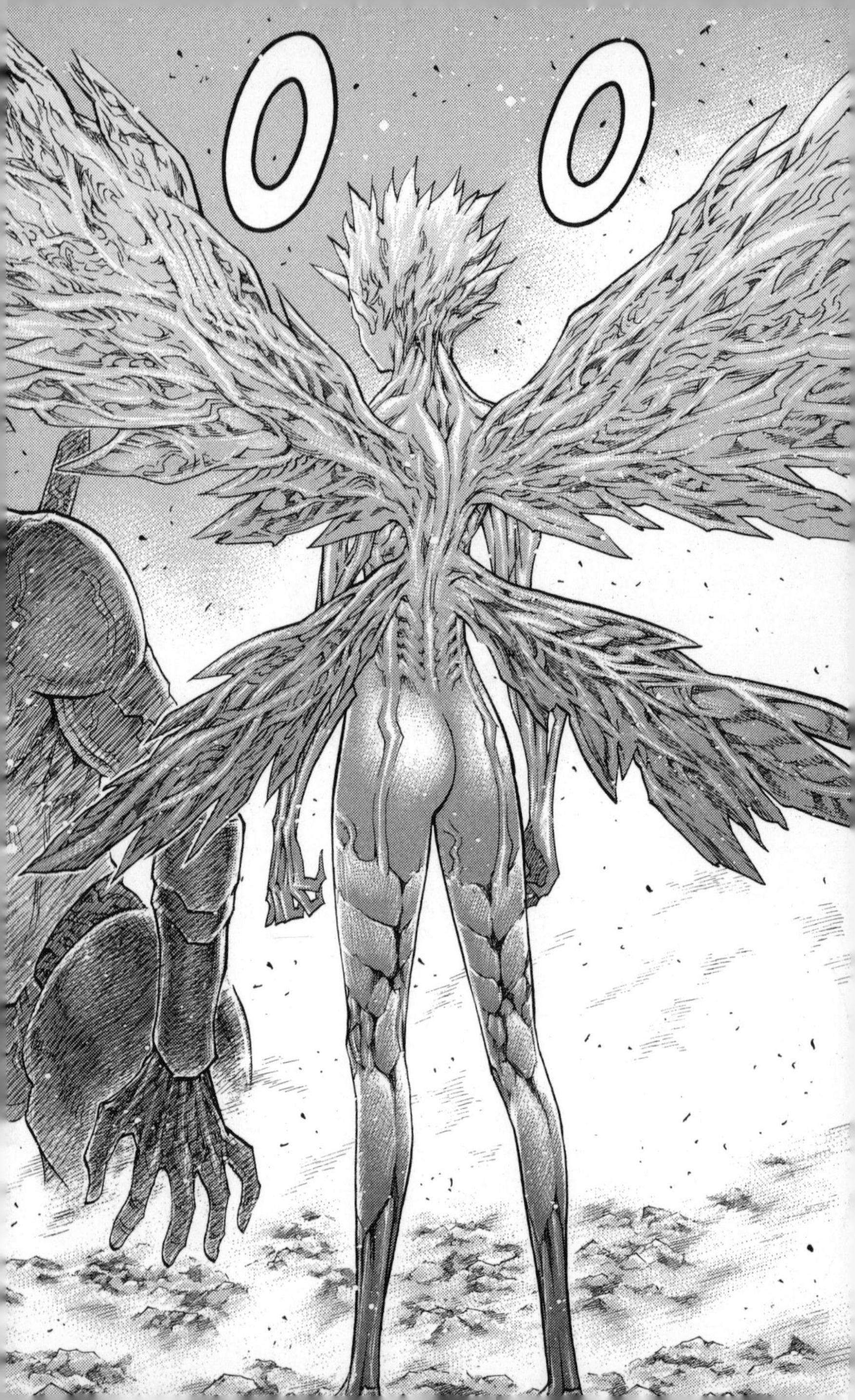

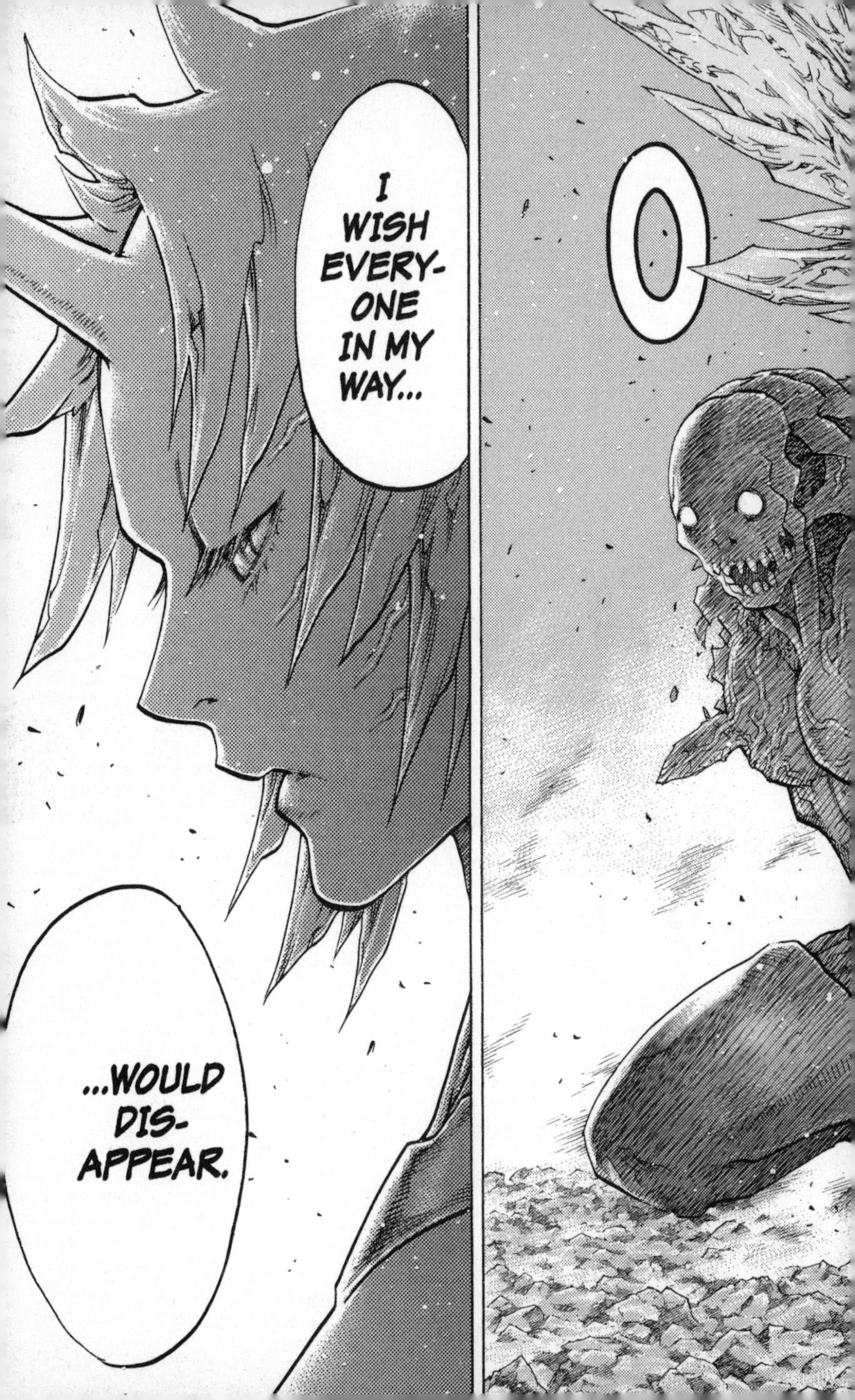
I WISH EVERY-ONE IN MY WAY...
...WOULD DIS-APPEAR.

クレイモア

Claymore

Scene 103: The Ashes of Lautrec, Part 8

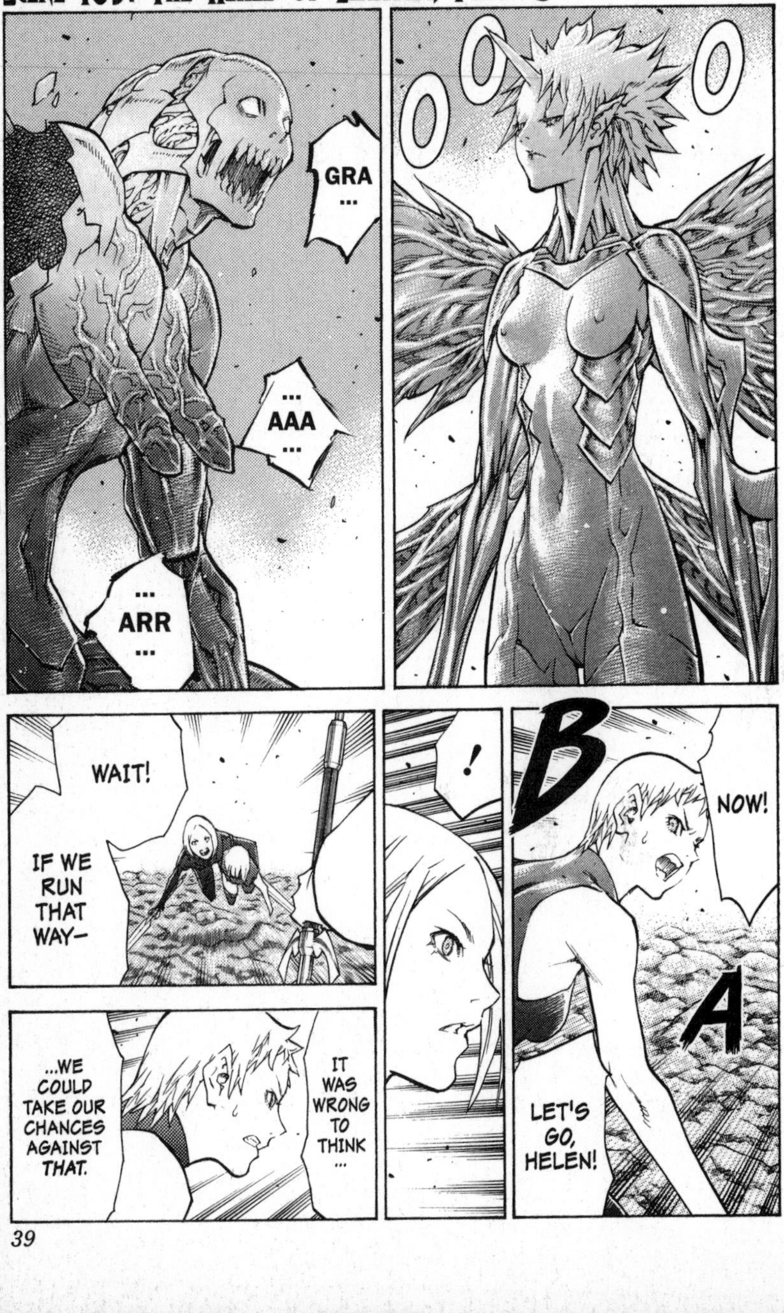
GRA
...
...
AAA
...
...
ARR
...
NOW!
BA
LET'S GO, HELEN!
!
WAIT!
IF WE RUN THAT WAY—
IT WAS WRONG TO THINK ...
...WE COULD TAKE OUR CHANCES AGAINST THAT.

Scene 103: The Ashes of Lautrec, Part 8

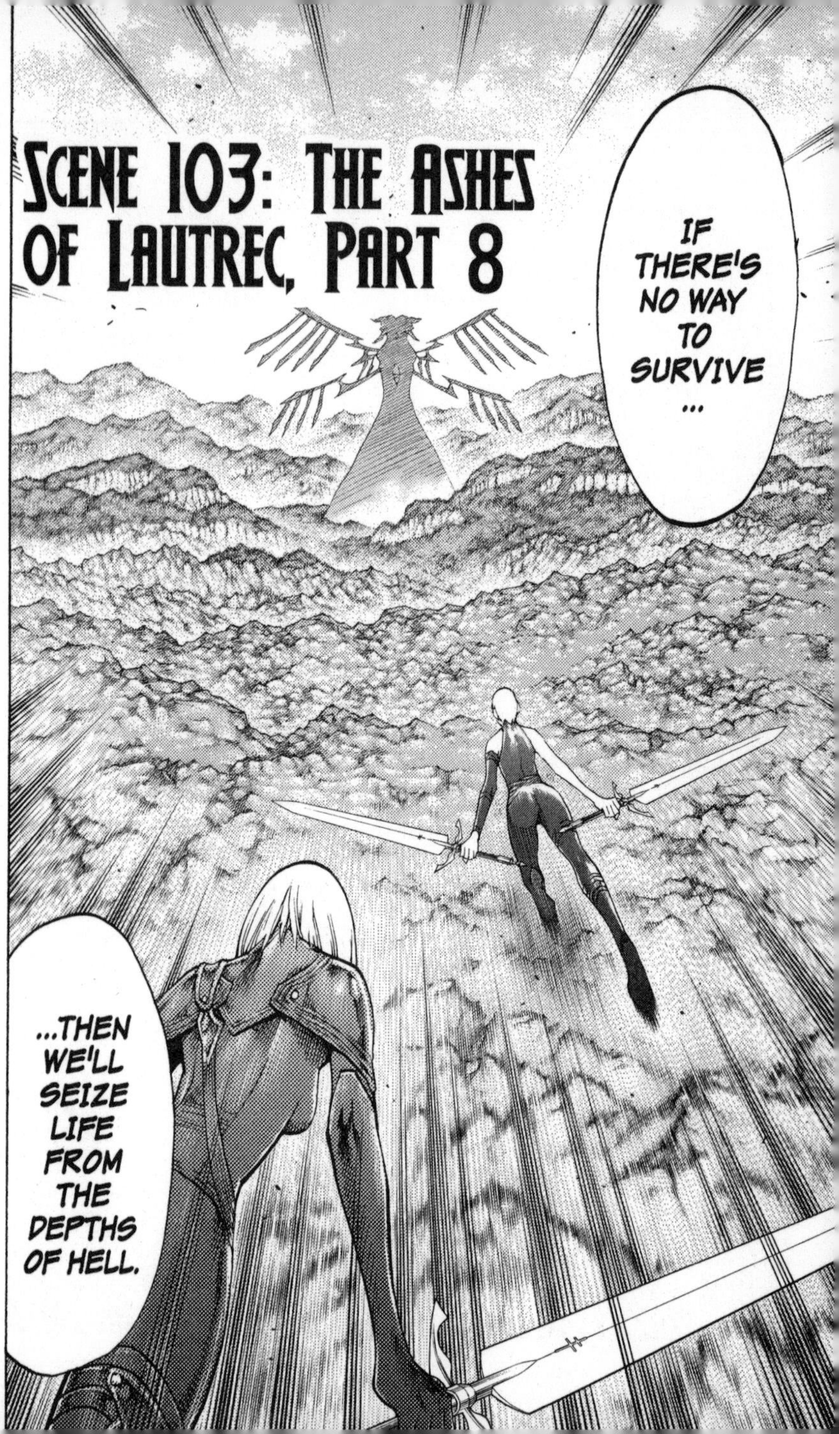

IF THERE'S NO WAY TO SURVIVE ...
...THEN WE'LL SEIZE LIFE FROM THE DEPTHS OF HELL.

READ THIS WAY

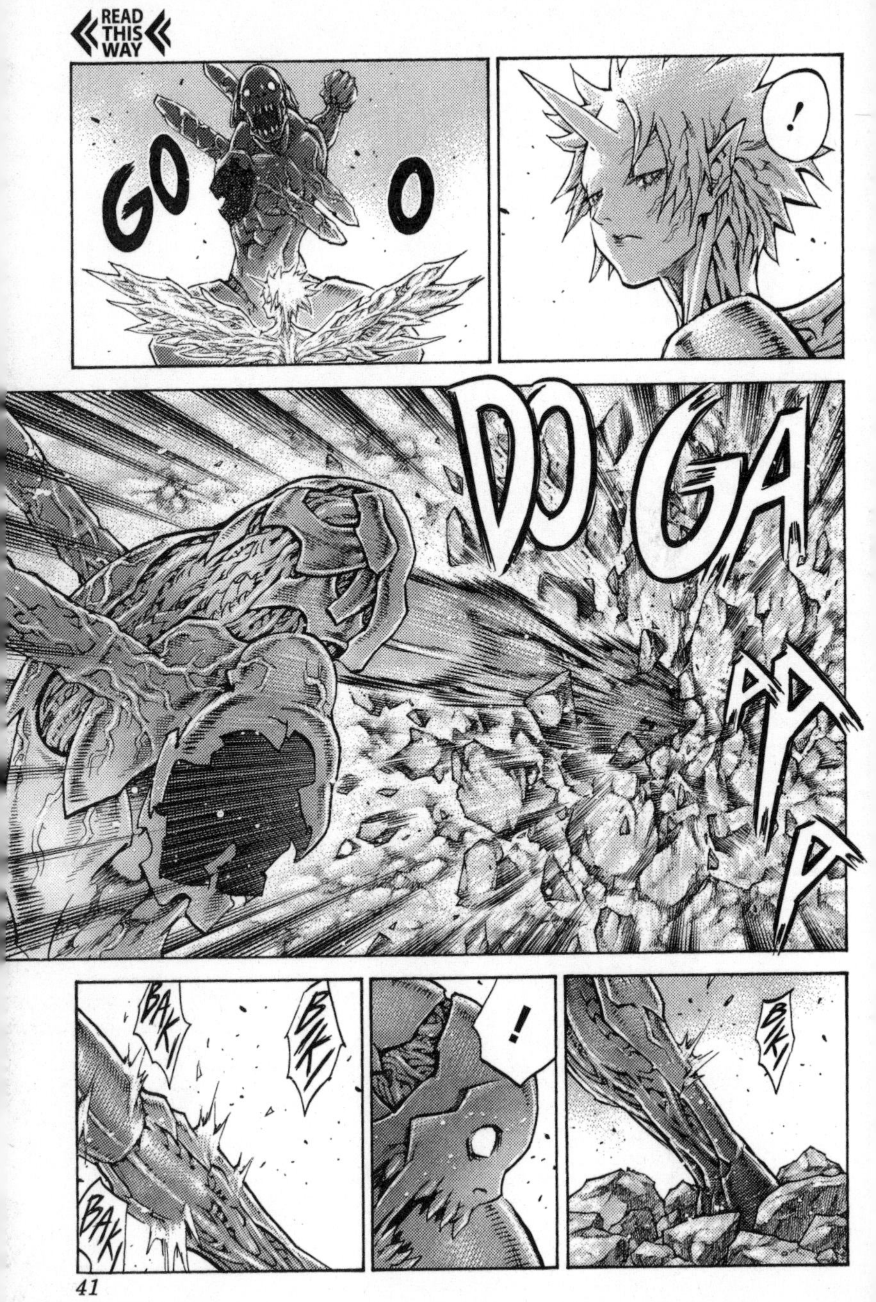
!
GO
O
DO GA
AAA
BIKI
!
BAKI
BIKI
BAKI

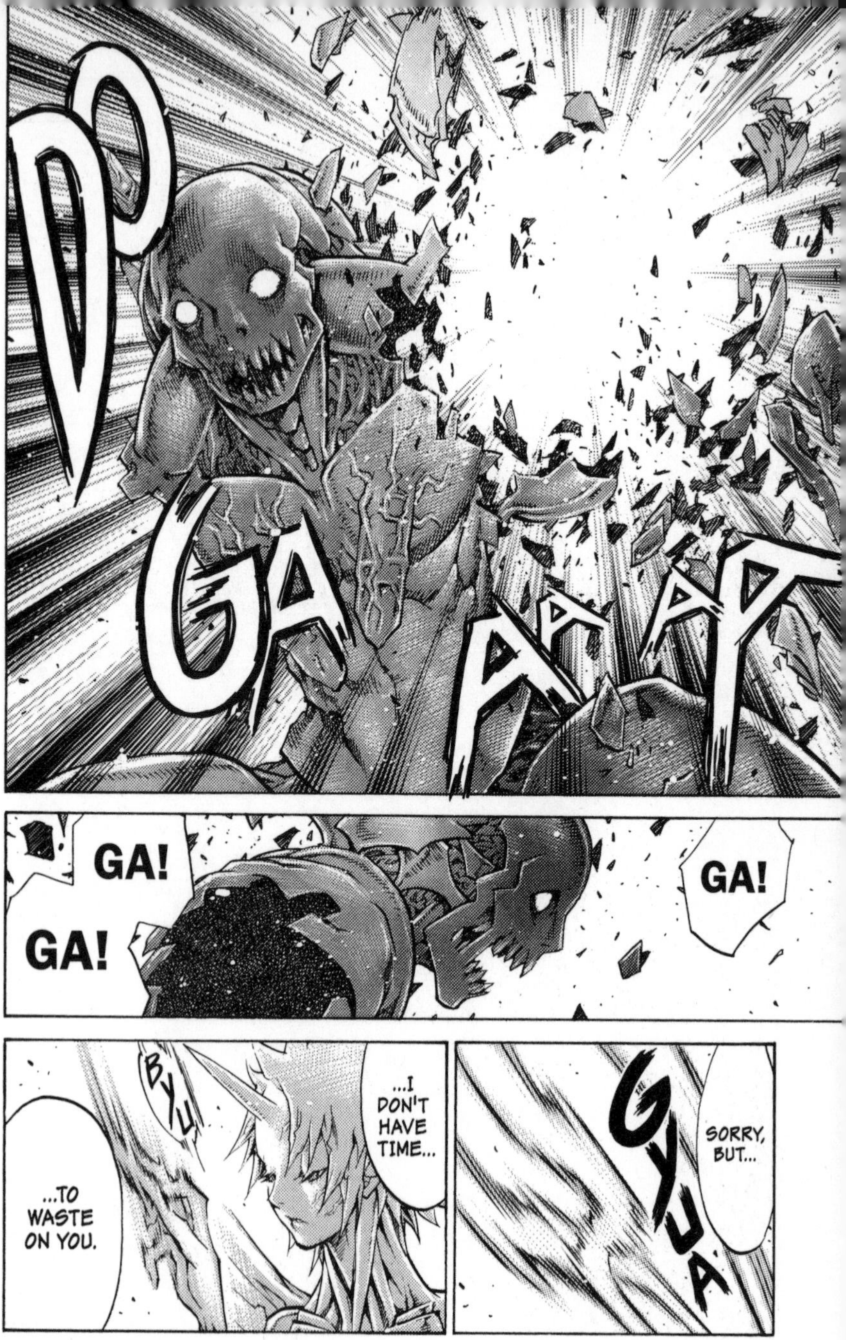
DO
GAAAT
GA!
GA!
GA!
SORRY, BUT...
GYUA
...I DON'T HAVE TIME...
BYU
...TO WASTE ON YOU.

READ THIS WAY

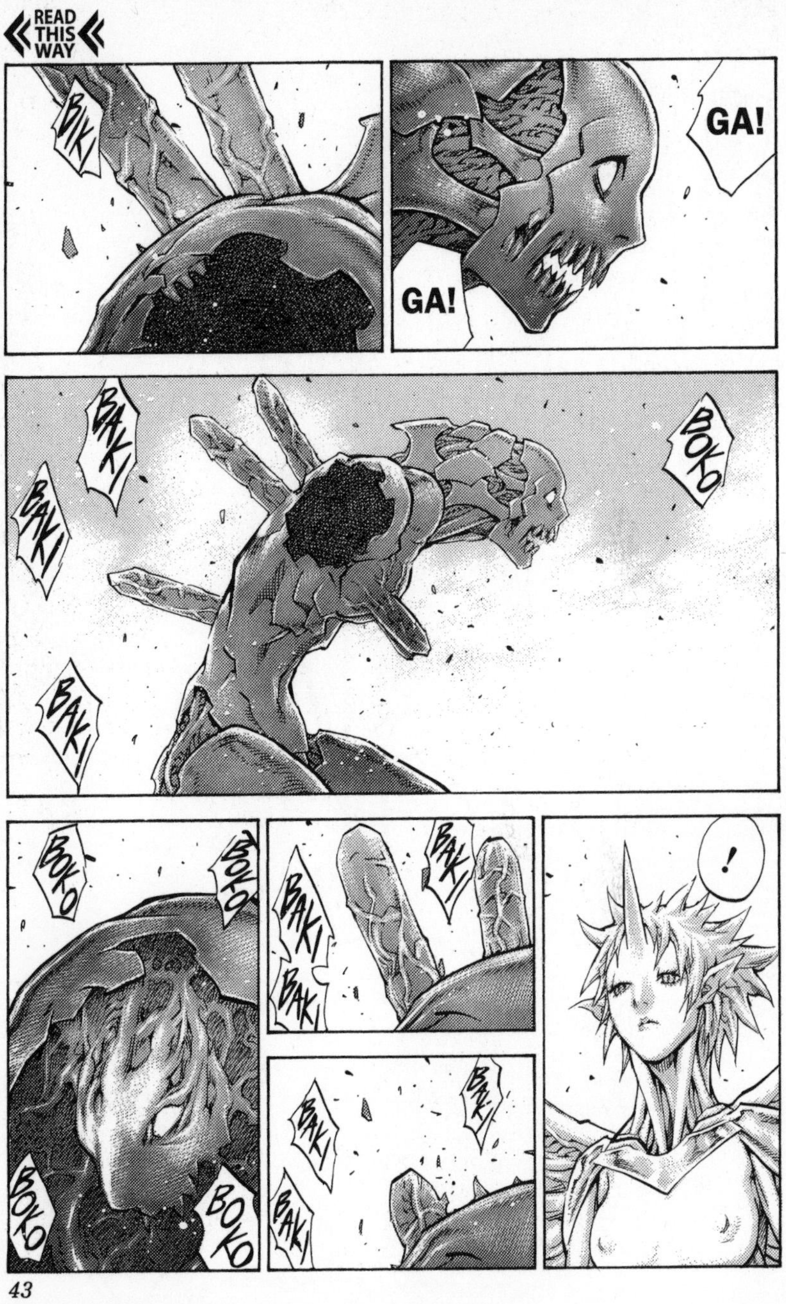

GA!
GA!
BIKI
BOKO
BAKI
BAKI
BAKI
!
BAKI
BAKI
BAKI
BAKI
BAKI
BAKI
BOKO
BOKO
BOKO
BOKO

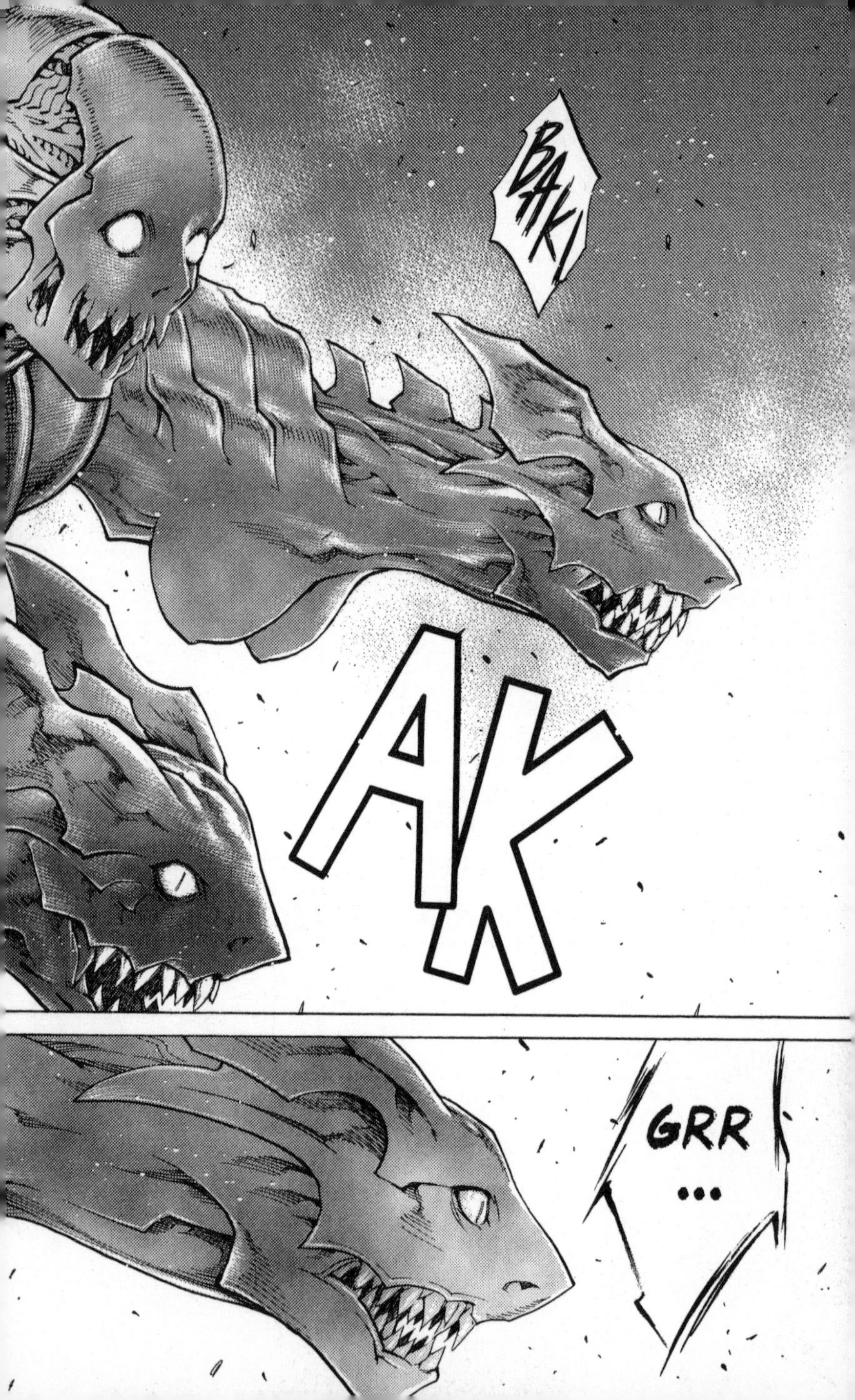
BAKI
AK
GRR
...

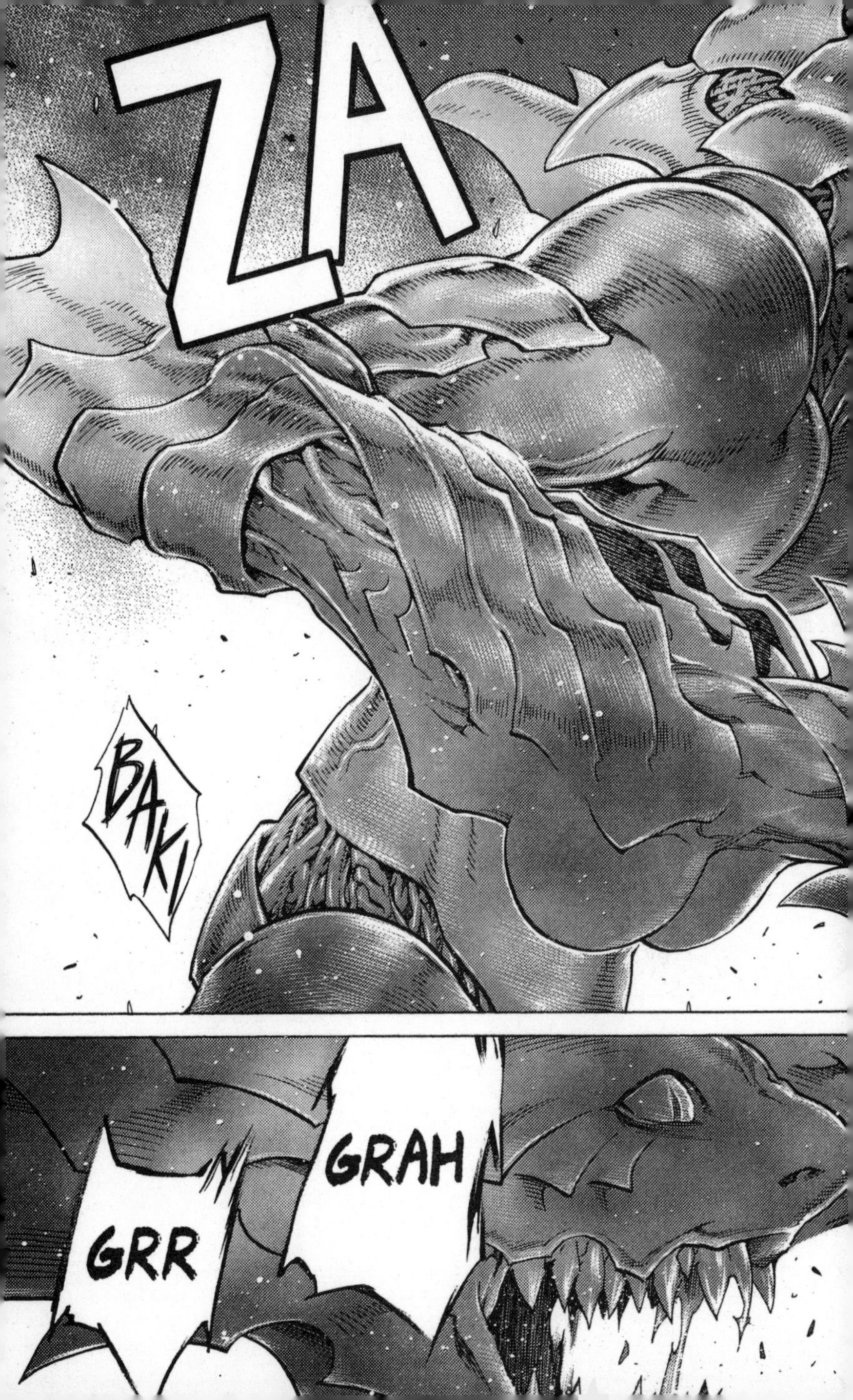
ZA
BAKI
GRAH
GRR

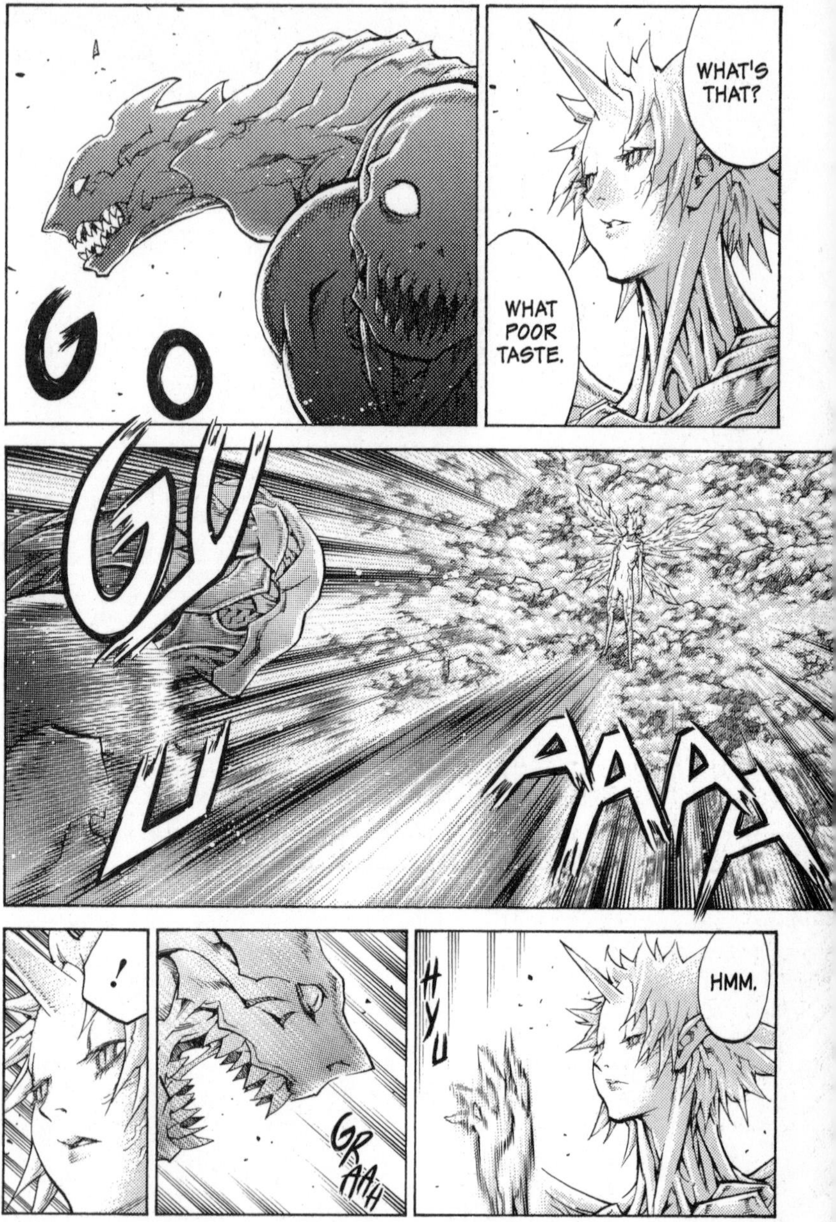
WHAT'S THAT?
WHAT POOR TASTE.
GO
GYU
U
AAAA
HMM.
HYU
GRAAH
!

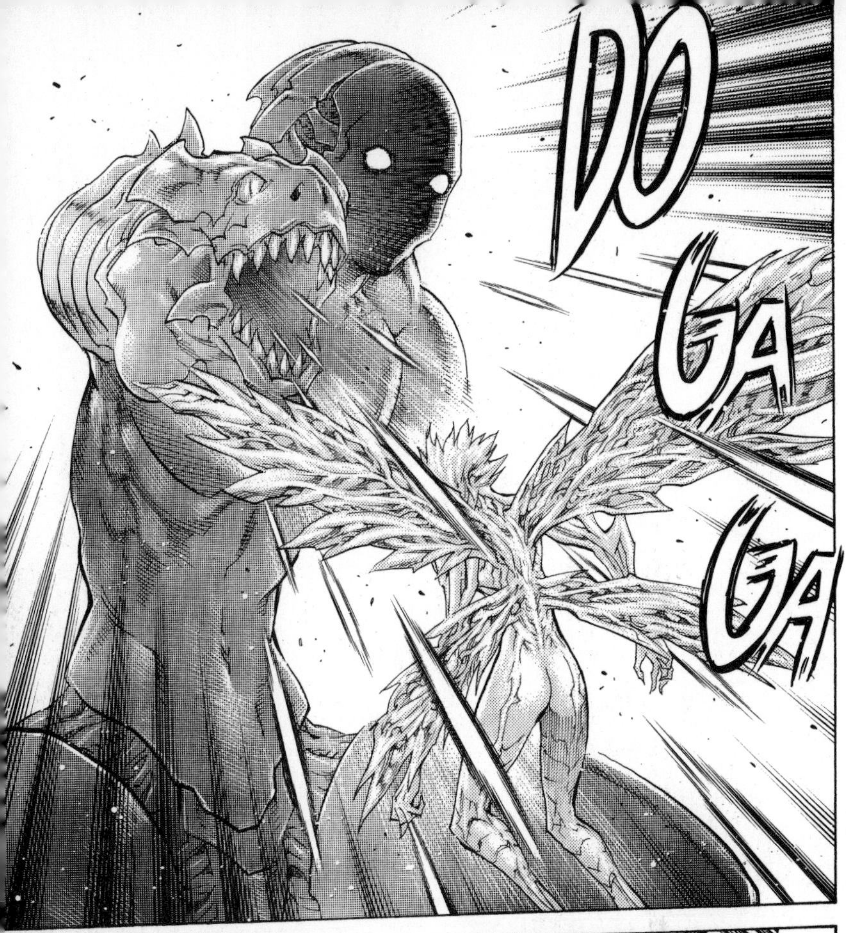
DO
GA
GA
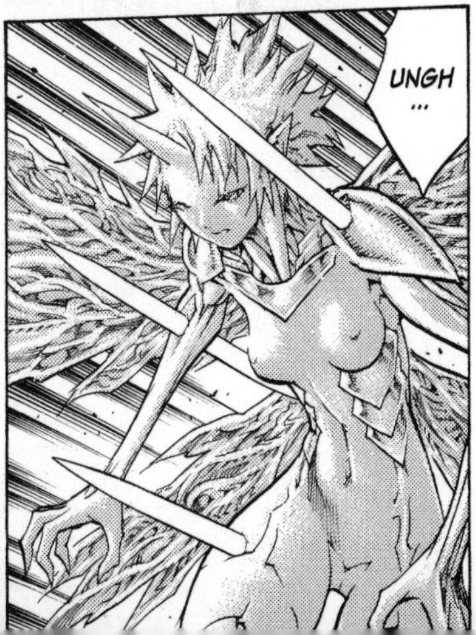
UNGH ...
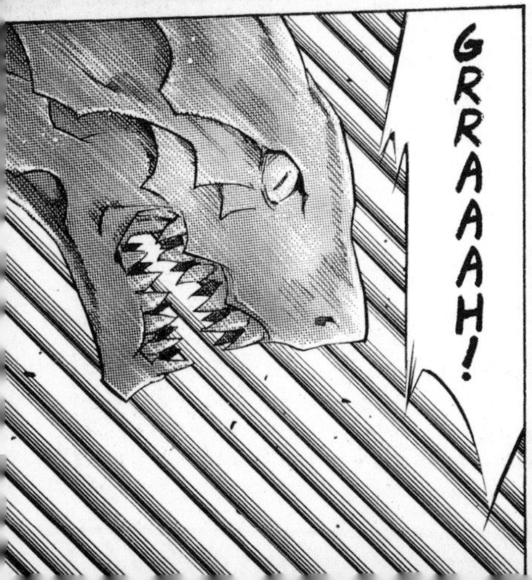
GRRAAAAH!

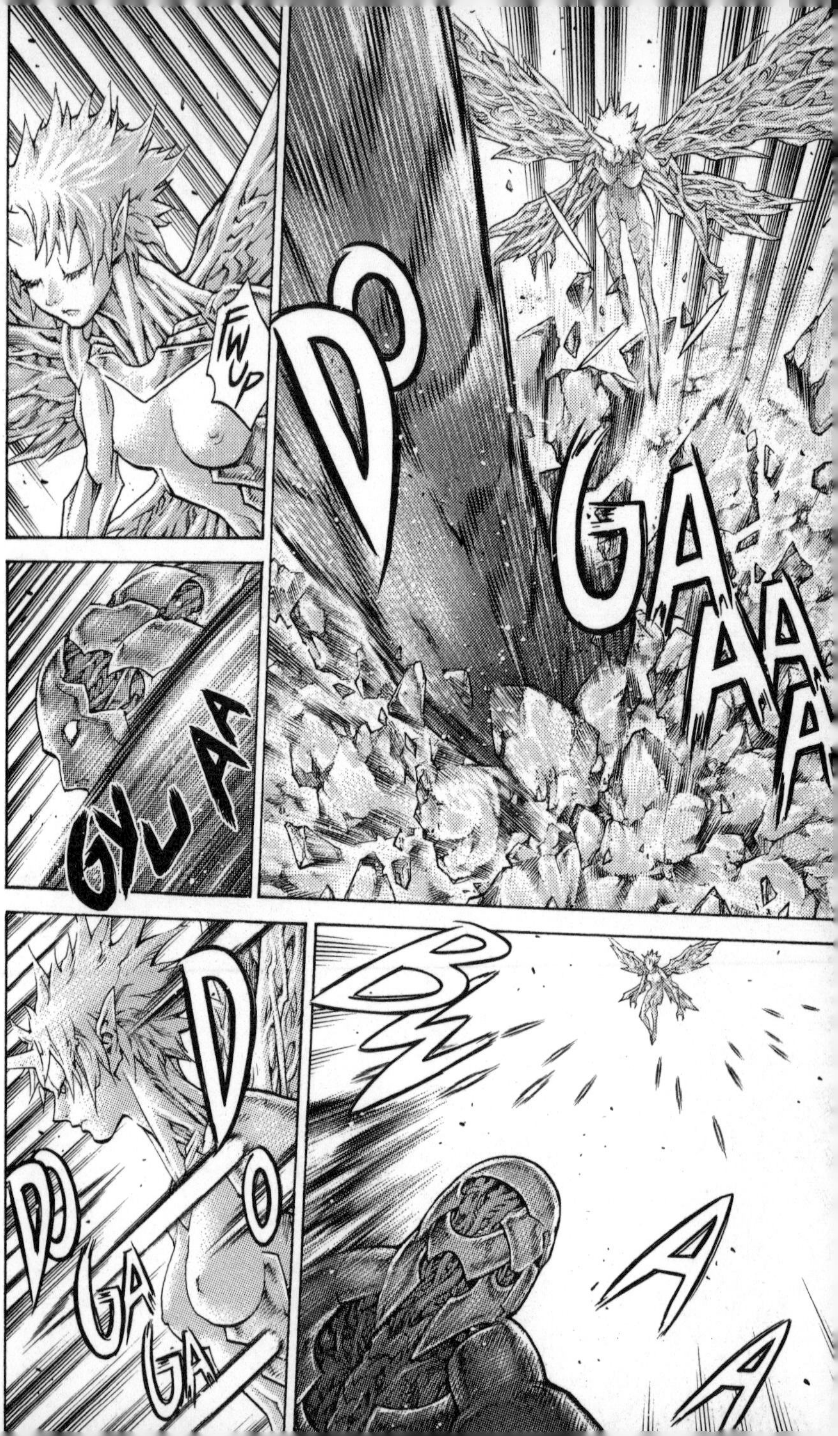
GA-AAAA
DO
FWUP
GYUA
BW
AA
DO
DOGAGA

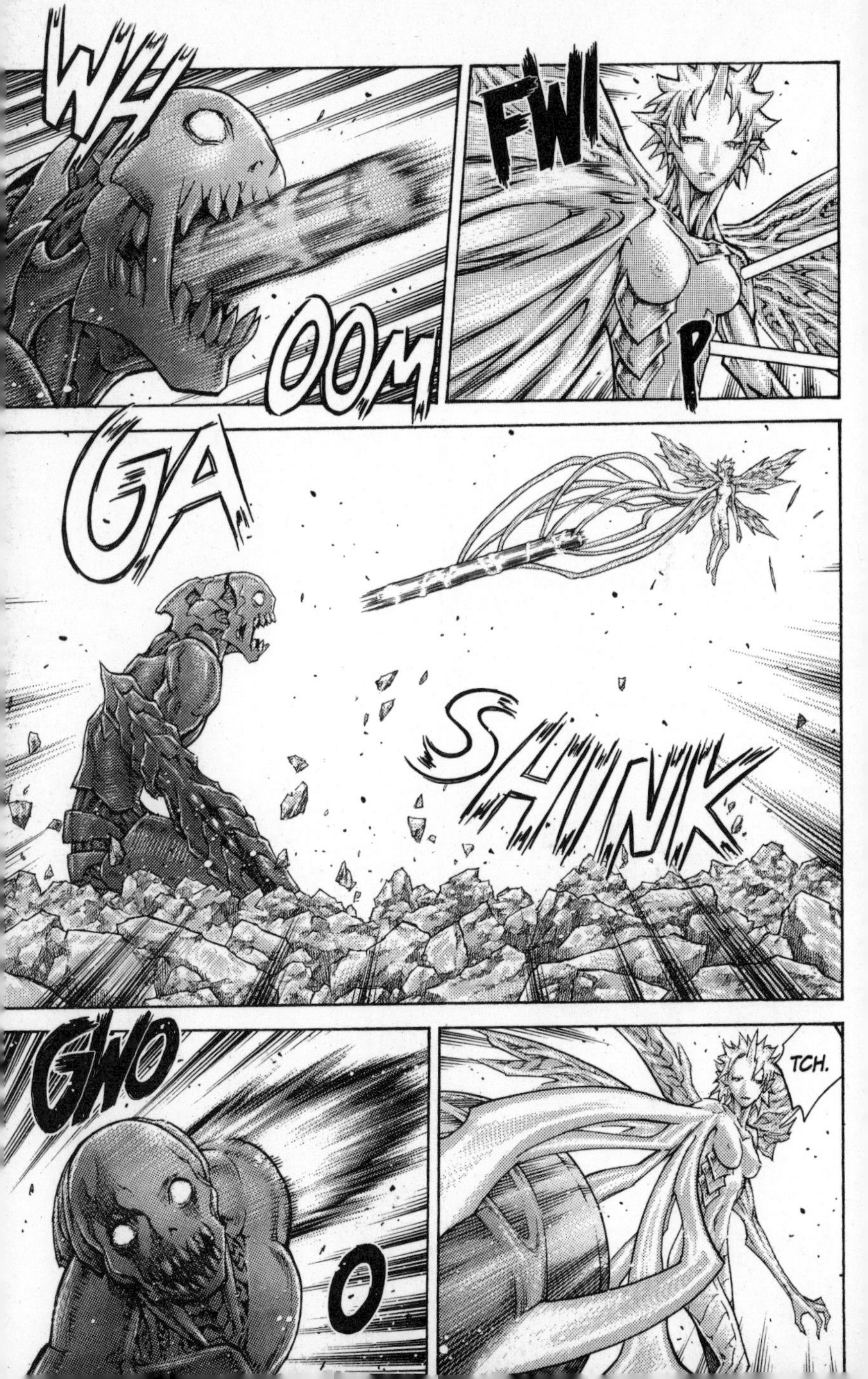
FWI
P
WH
OOM
GA
SHINK
TCH.
GWO
O

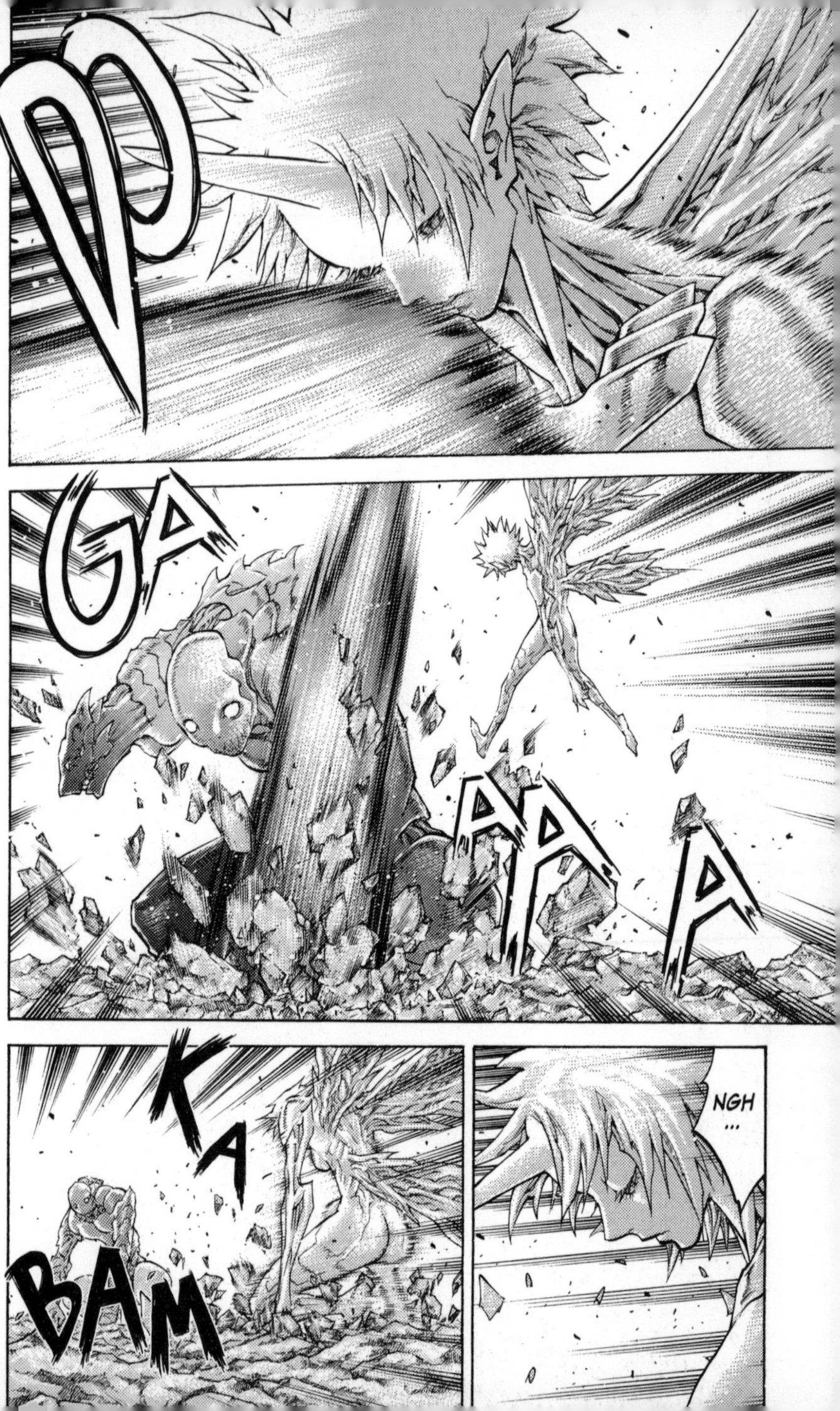
DO
GA
AAA
NGH ...
KA
BAM

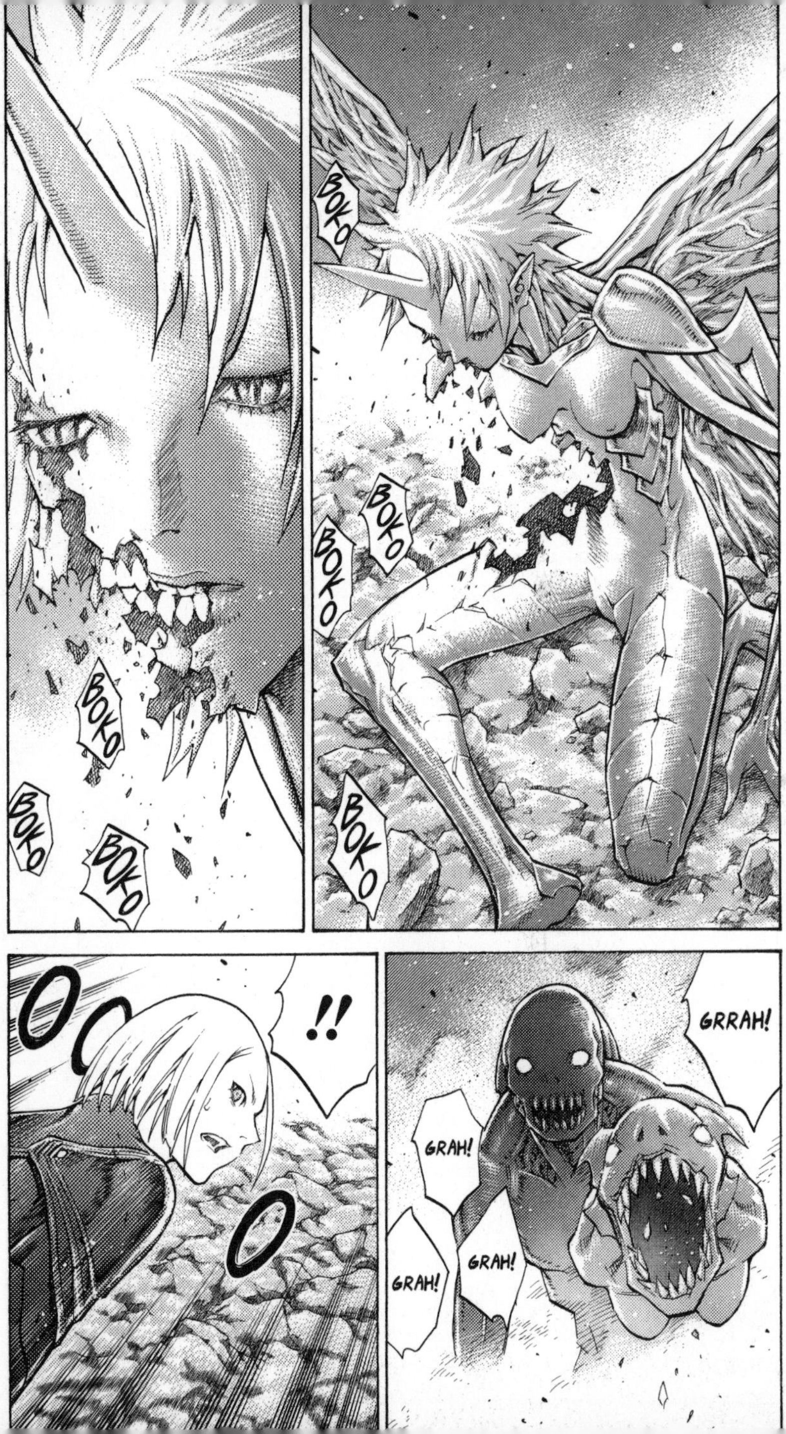
BOKO
BOKO
BOKO
BOKO
BOKO
BOKO
BOKO
GRRAH!
GRAH!
GRAH!
GRAH!
!!
OOO

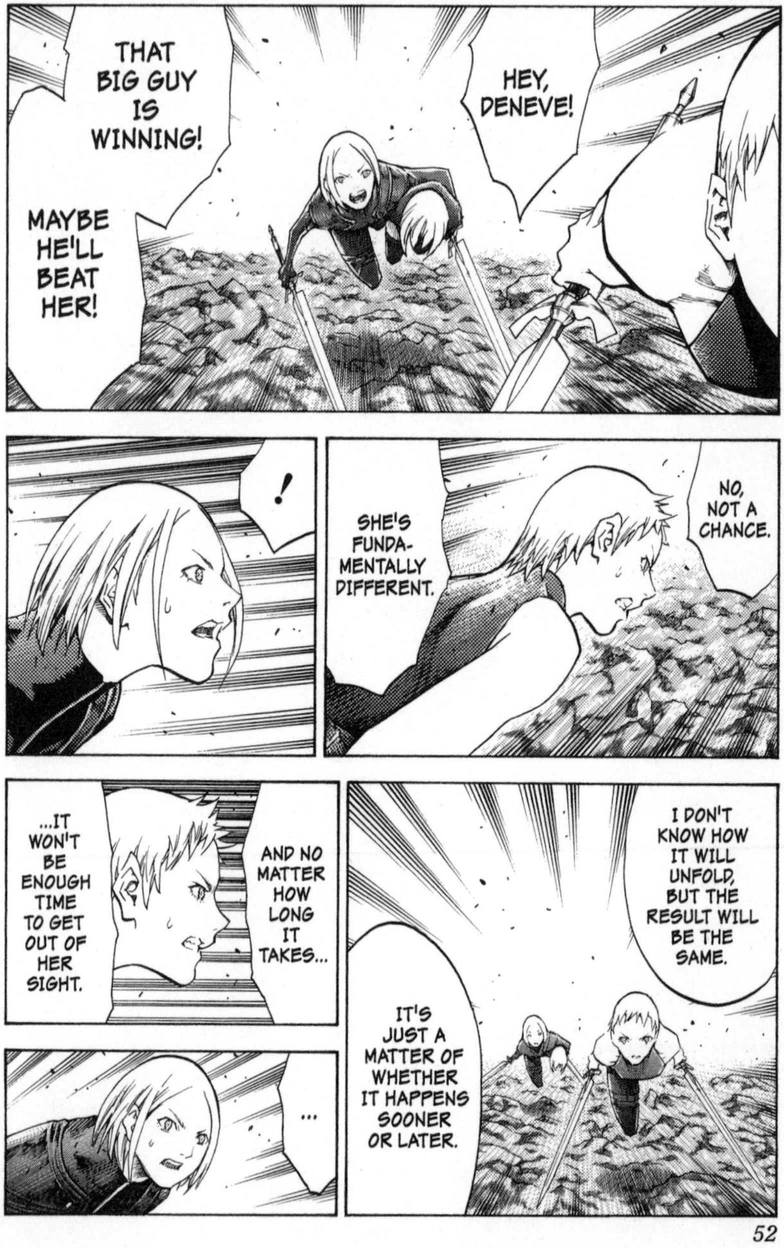
HEY, DENEVE!
THAT BIG GUY IS WINNING!
MAYBE HE'LL BEAT HER!
NO, NOT A CHANCE.
SHE'S FUNDA-MENTALLY DIFFERENT.
!
I DON'T KNOW HOW IT WILL UNFOLD, BUT THE RESULT WILL BE THE SAME.
IT'S JUST A MATTER OF WHETHER IT HAPPENS SOONER OR LATER.
AND NO MATTER HOW LONG IT TAKES...
...IT WON'T BE ENOUGH TIME TO GET OUT OF HER SIGHT.
...

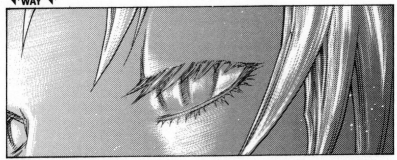

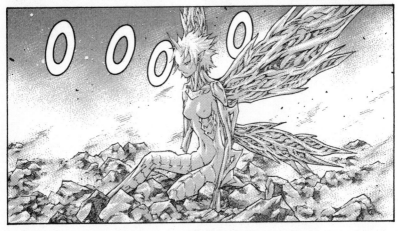

READ THIS WAY

O O O O
BOKO
BOKO
BOKO
BOKO
WHAT'S GOING ON?
I THOUGHT I COULD...
ZAK
!

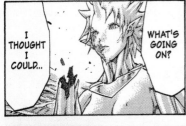

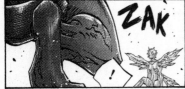

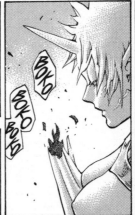

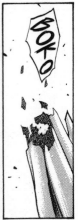

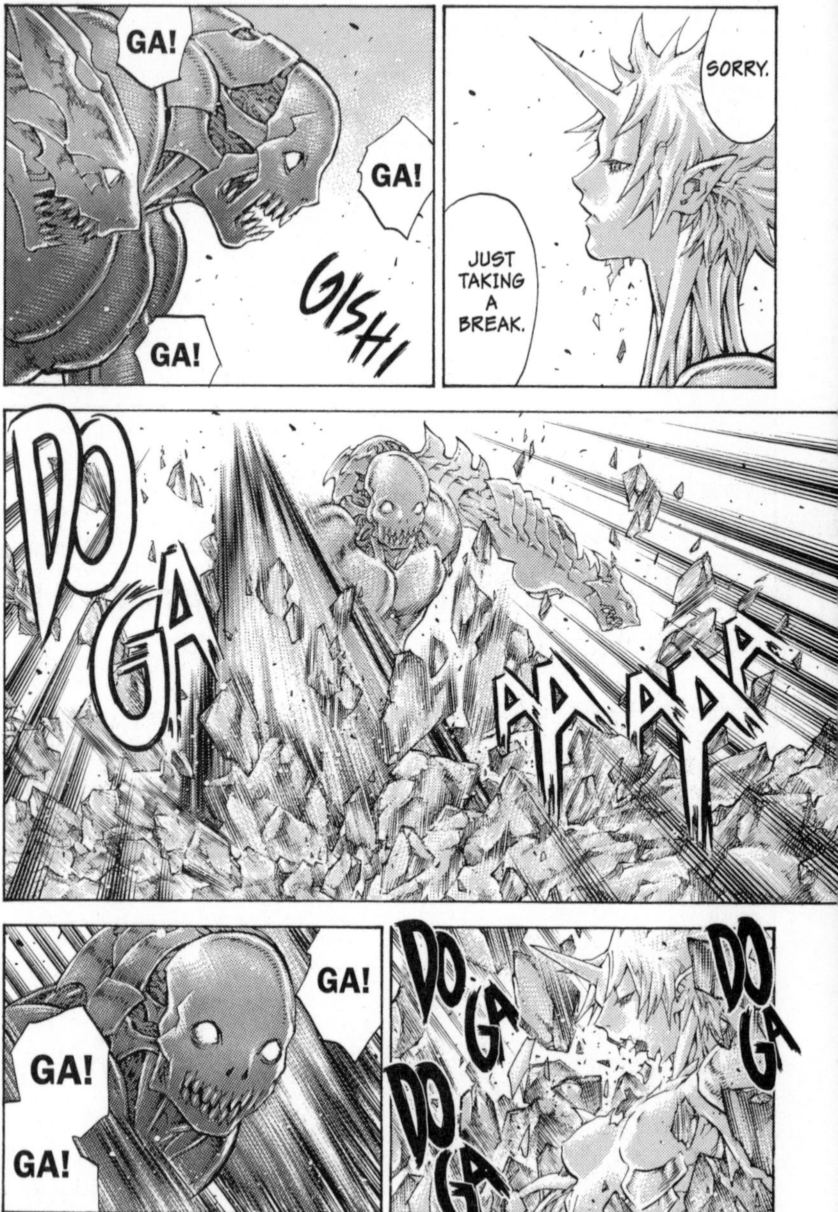
SORRY.
JUST TAKING A BREAK.
GA!
GA!
GISHI
GA!
AAAA
DOGA
DOGA
DOGA
DOGA
GA!
GA!
GA!

READ THIS WAY

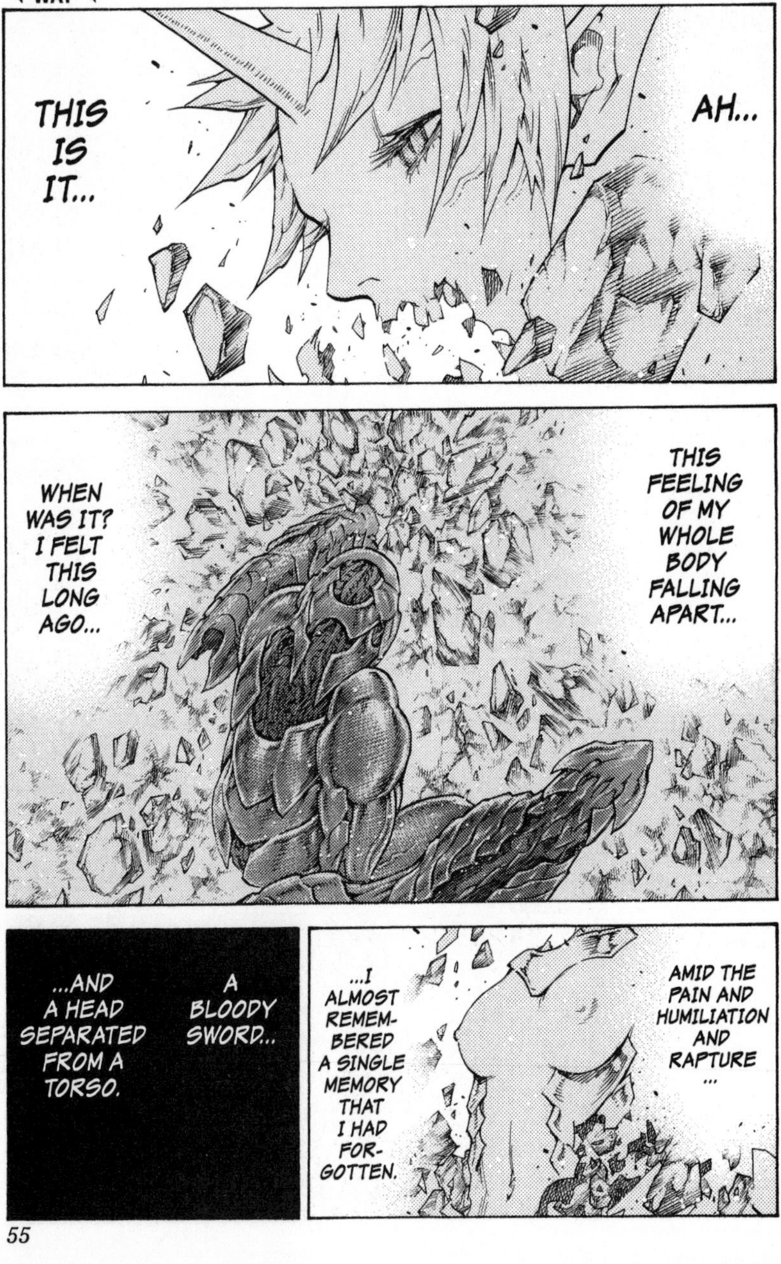
AH...
THIS IS IT...
THIS FEELING OF MY WHOLE BODY FALLING APART...
WHEN WAS IT? I FELT THIS LONG AGO...
AMID THE PAIN AND HUMILIATION AND RAPTURE ...
...I ALMOST REMEMBERED A SINGLE MEMORY THAT I HAD FORGOTTEN.
A BLOODY SWORD...
...AND A HEAD SEPARATED FROM A TORSO.

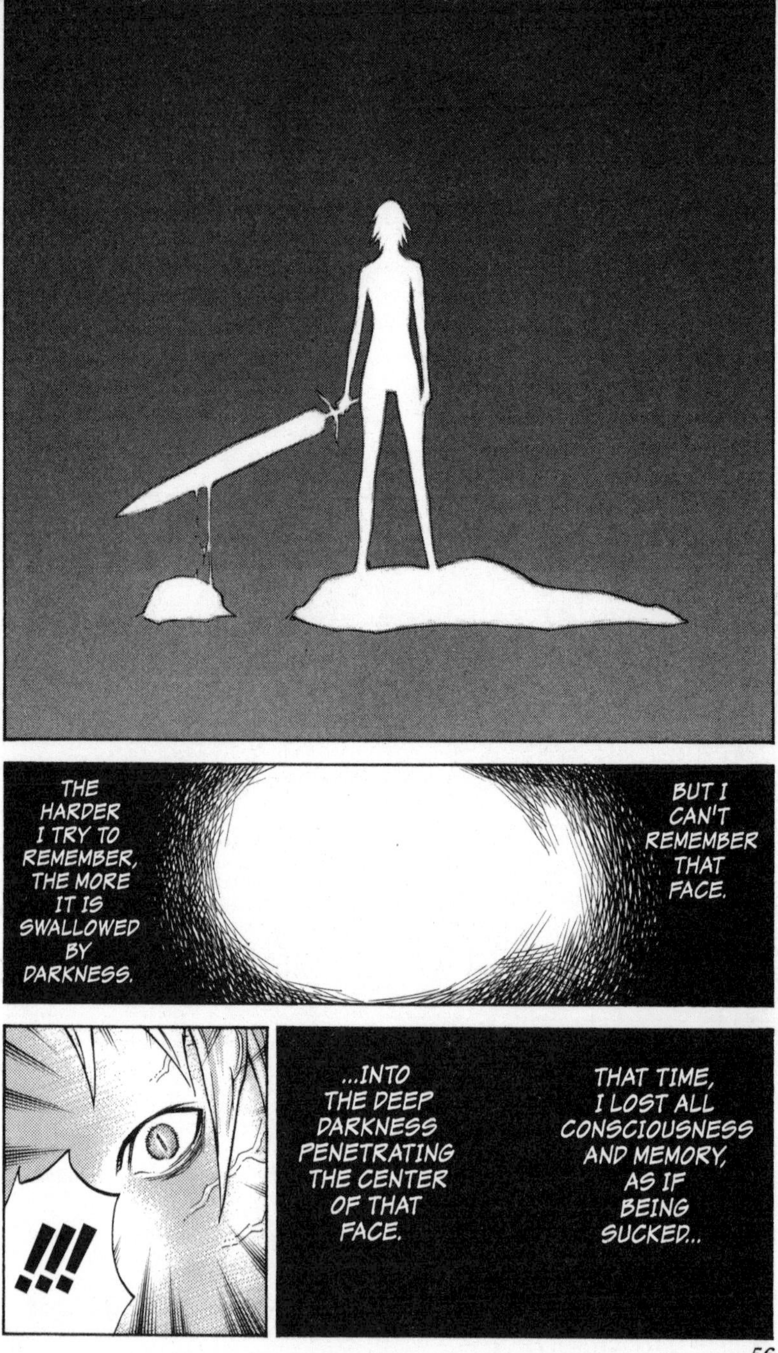
BUT I CAN'T REMEMBER THAT FACE.
THE HARDER I TRY TO REMEMBER, THE MORE IT IS SWALLOWED BY DARKNESS.
THAT TIME, I LOST ALL CONSCIOUSNESS AND MEMORY, AS IF BEING SUCKED...
...INTO THE DEEP DARKNESS PENETRATING THE CENTER OF THAT FACE.
!!!

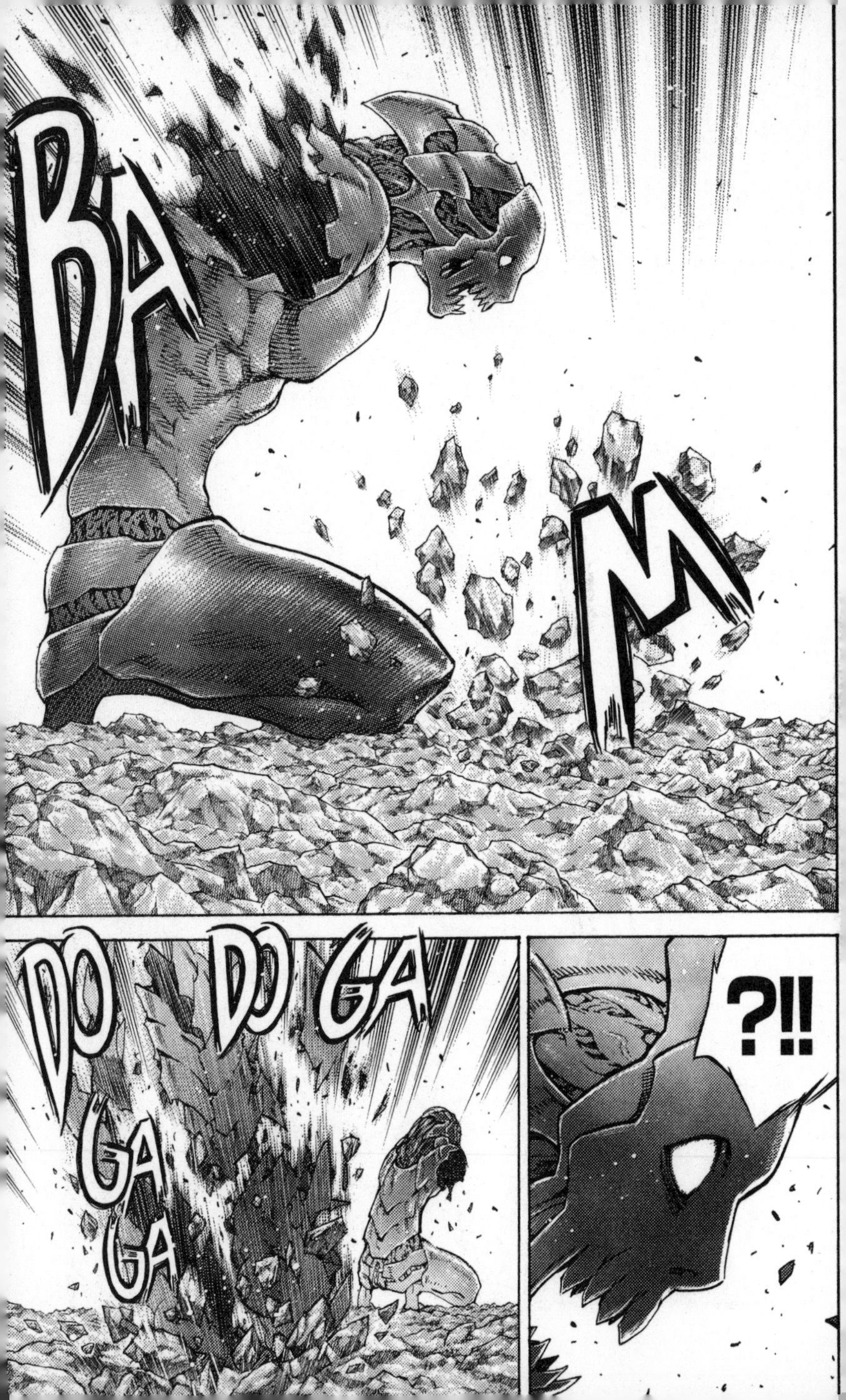
BADAM
?!!
DO DO GA
GA GA

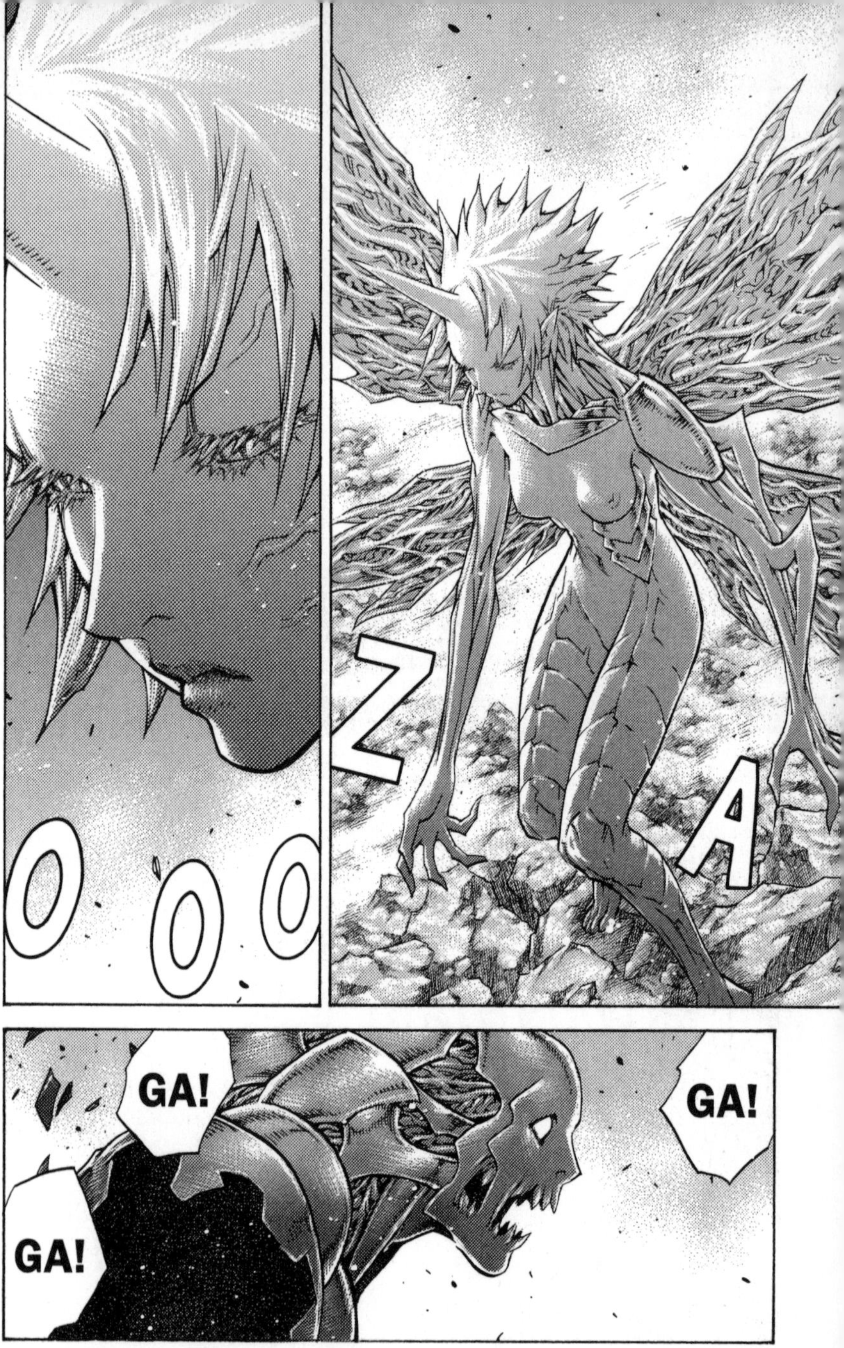

ZA
OOO
GA!
GA!
GA!

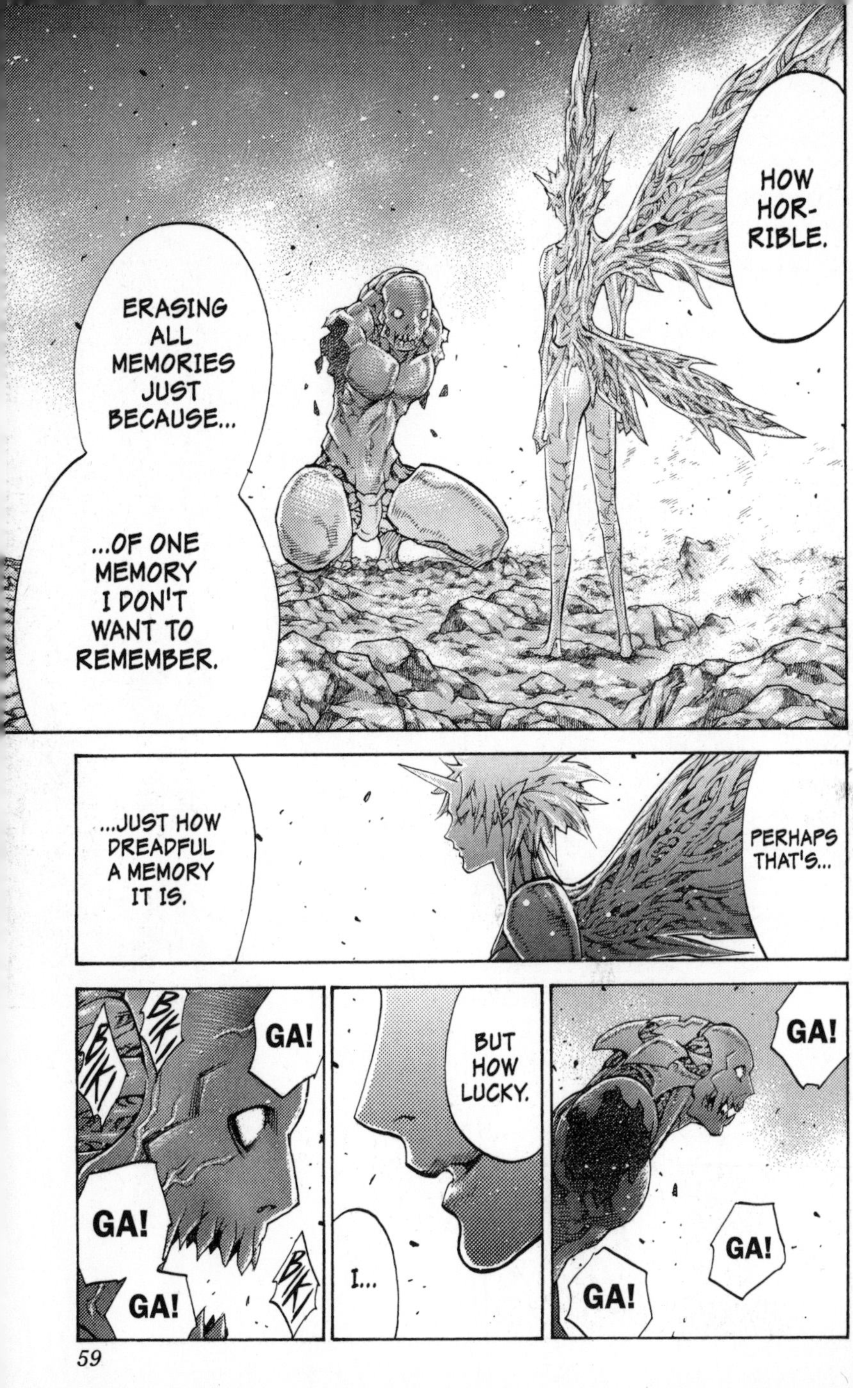
HOW HOR-RIBLE.
ERASING ALL MEMORIES JUST BECAUSE...
...OF ONE MEMORY I DON'T WANT TO REMEMBER.
PERHAPS THAT'S...
...JUST HOW DREADFUL A MEMORY IT IS.
GA!
GA!
GA!
BUT HOW LUCKY.
I...
BIKI
BIKI
GA!
GA!
GA!
BIKI

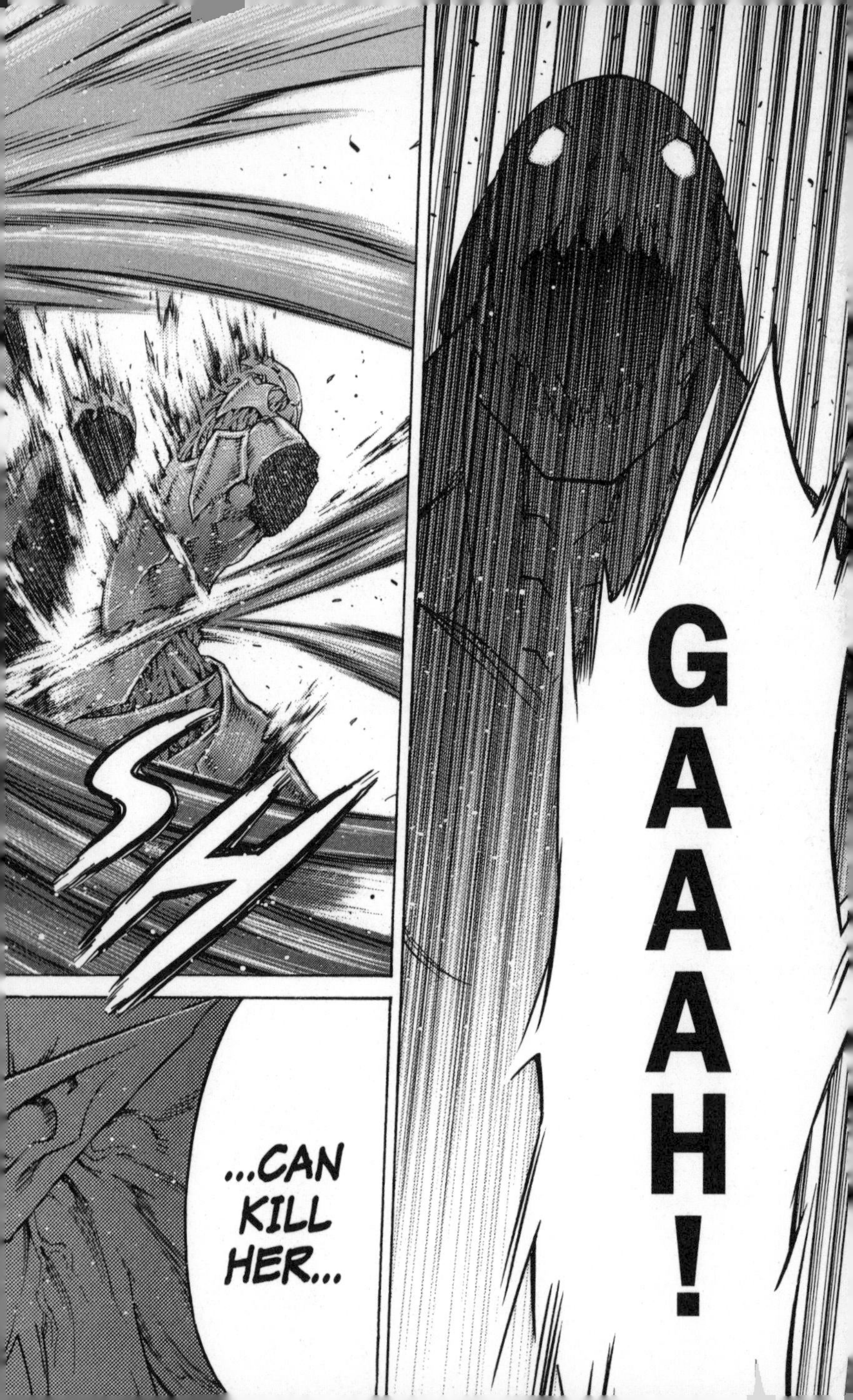
GAAAH!
SH
...CAN KILL HER...

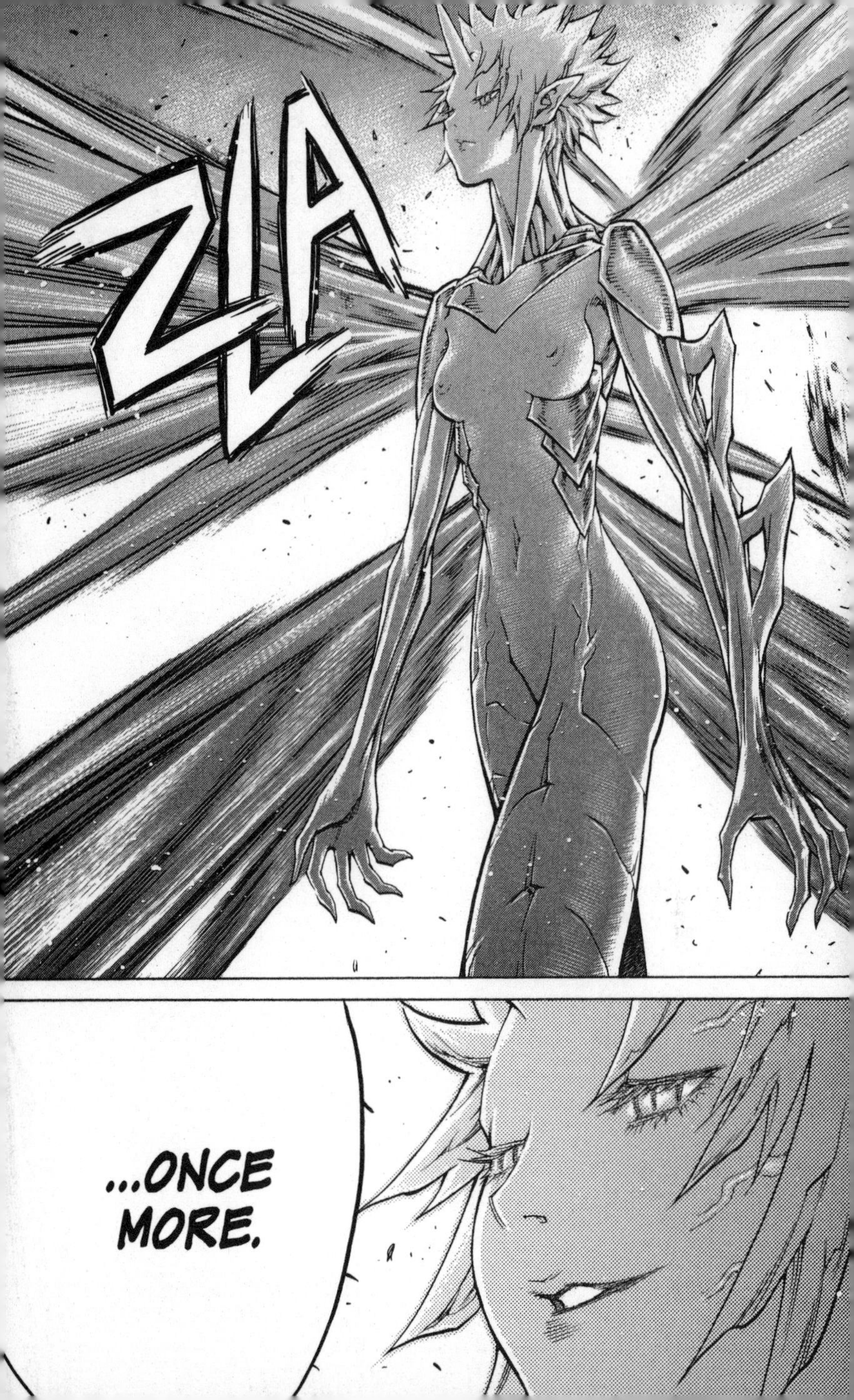
ZIA
...ONCE MORE.

クレイモア
Claymore

Scene 104: The Ashes of Lautrec, Part 9

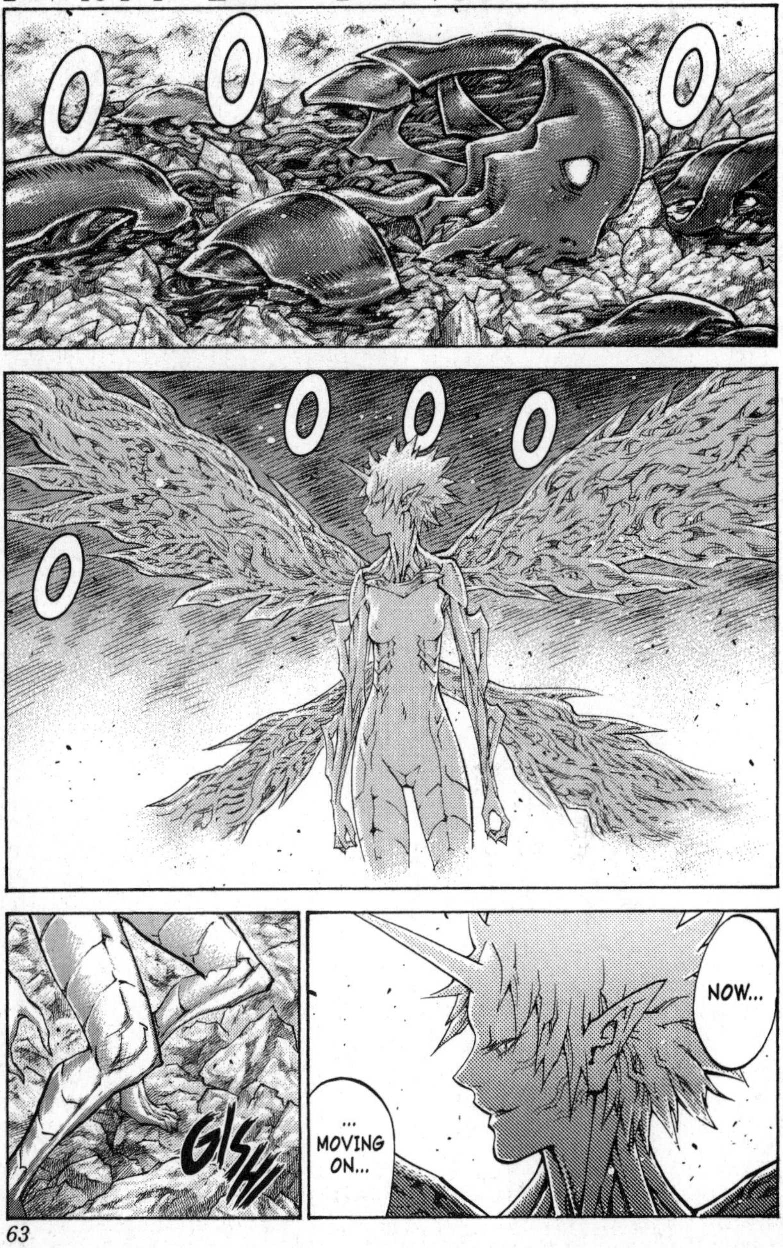
O O O
O O O O
NOW...
...MOVING ON...
GISHI

Scene 104: The Ashes of Lautrec, Part 9

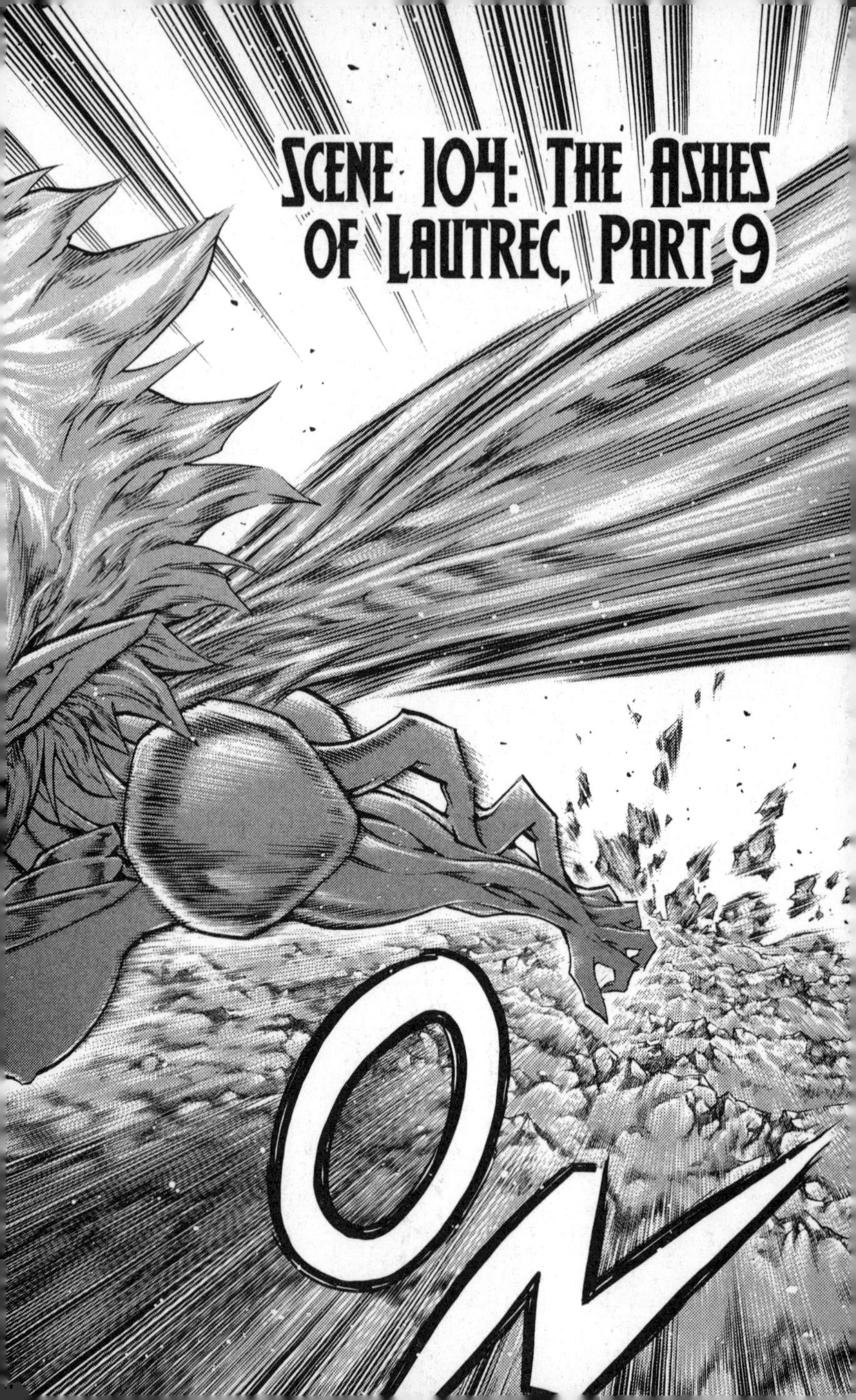
ON

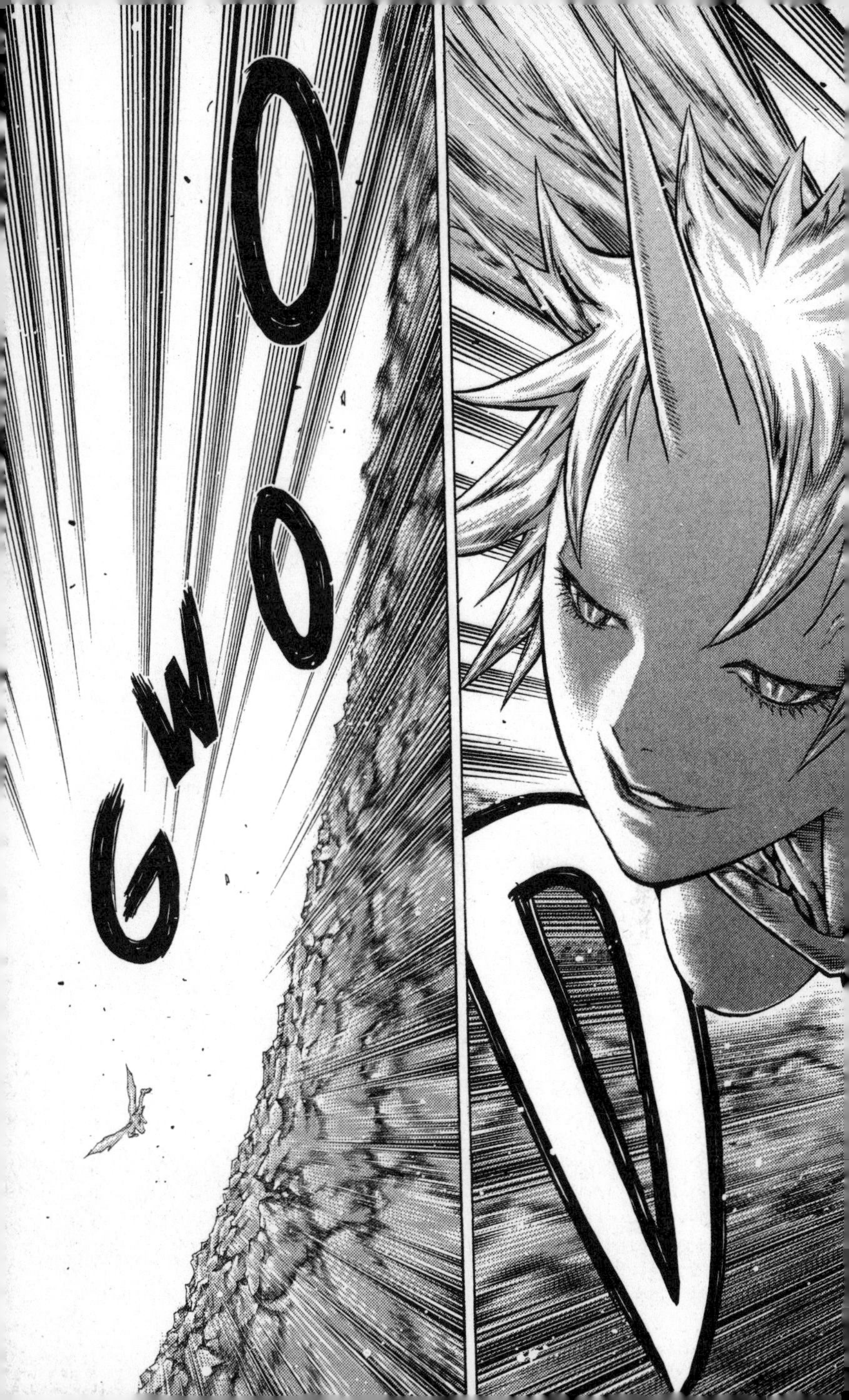
GWOOO

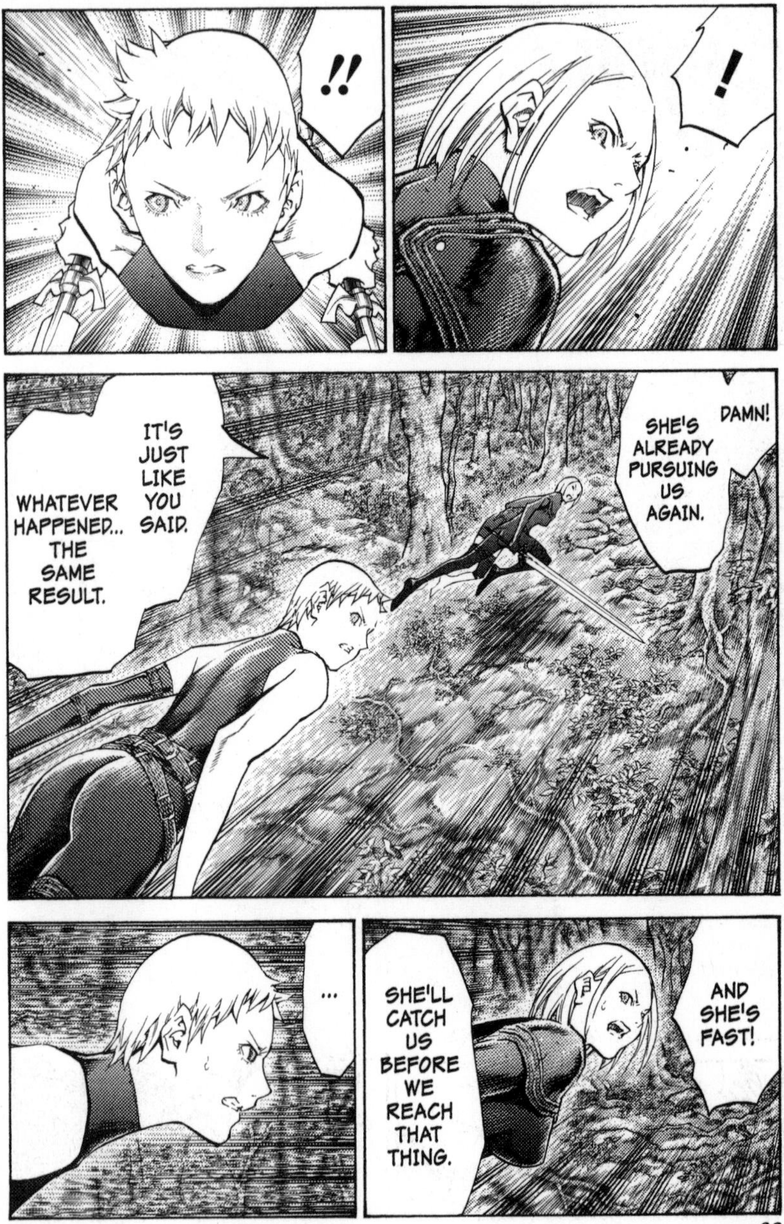
!
!!
DAMN!
SHE'S ALREADY PURSUING US AGAIN.
IT'S JUST LIKE YOU SAID.
WHATEVER HAPPENED... THE SAME RESULT.
AND SHE'S FAST!
SHE'LL CATCH US BEFORE WE REACH THAT THING.
...

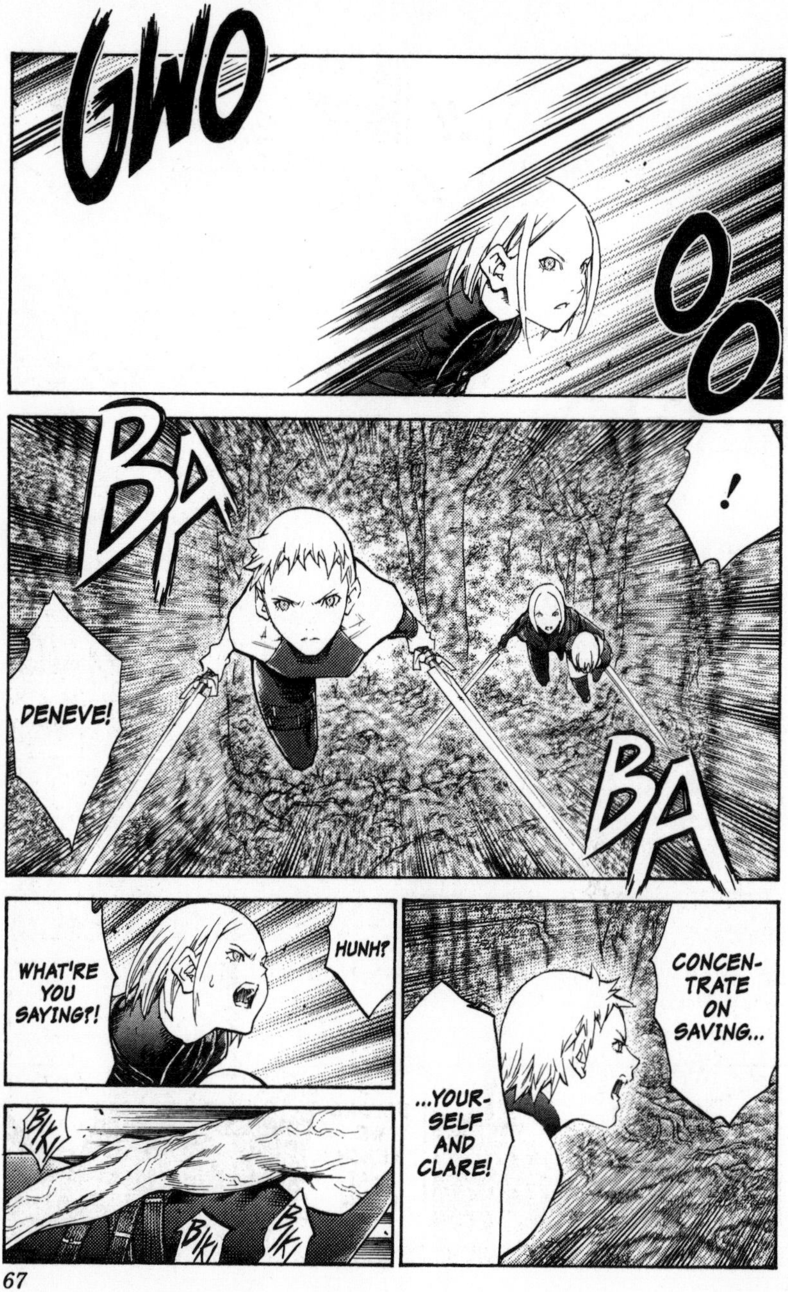
GWO
OO
!
BA
BA
DENEVE!
CONCEN-TRATE ON SAVING...
...YOUR-SELF AND CLARE!
HUNH?
WHAT'RE YOU SAYING?!
BIKI
BIKI
BIKI

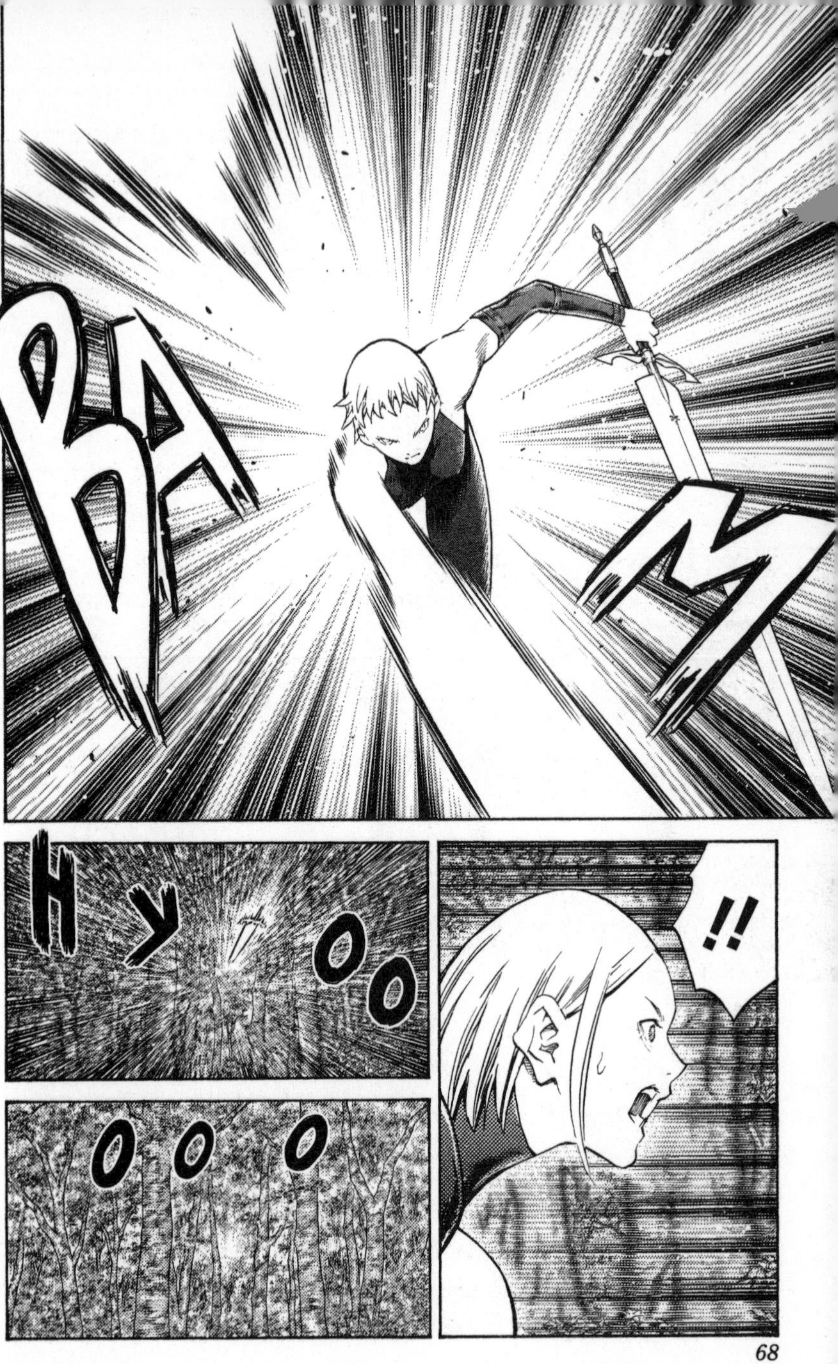
BAM
!!
HYOO
OOO

READ THIS WAY

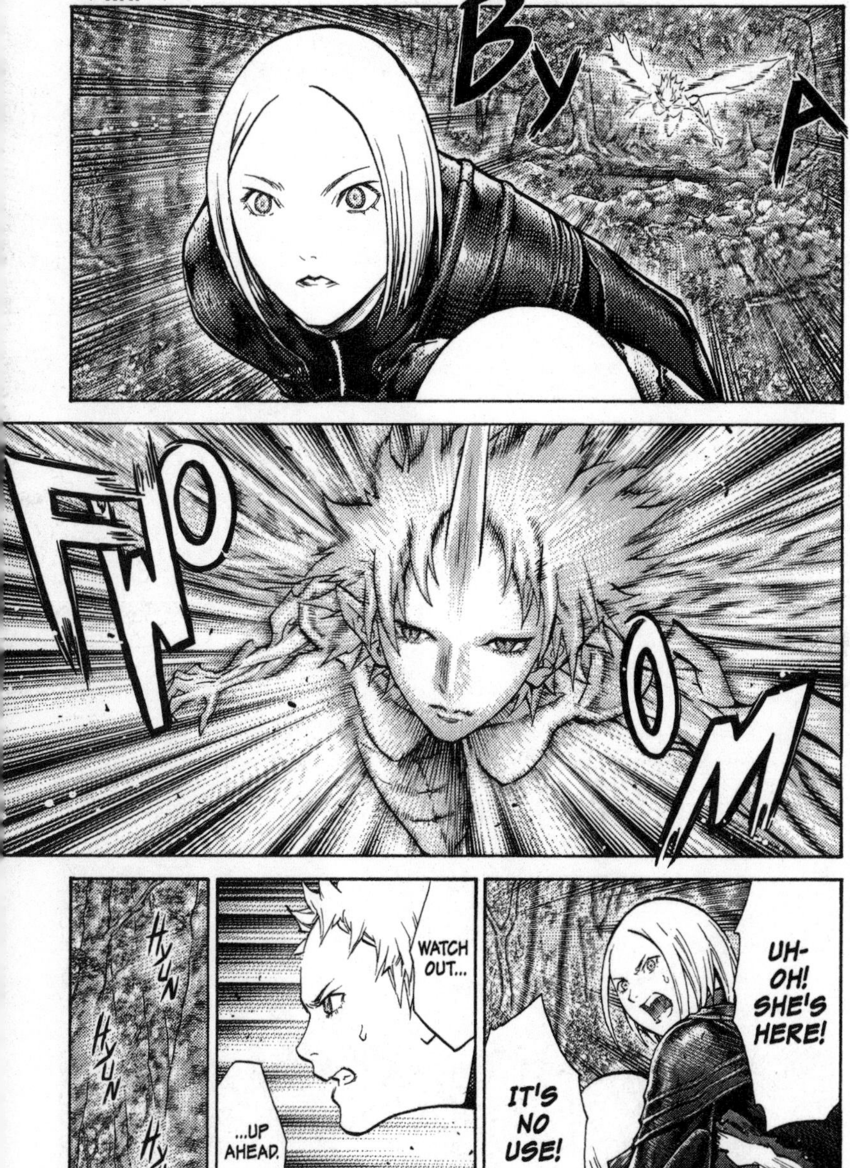
BYA
FWOOM
UH-OH! SHE'S HERE!
IT'S NO USE!
WATCH OUT...
...UP AHEAD.
HYUN
HYUN
HYUN

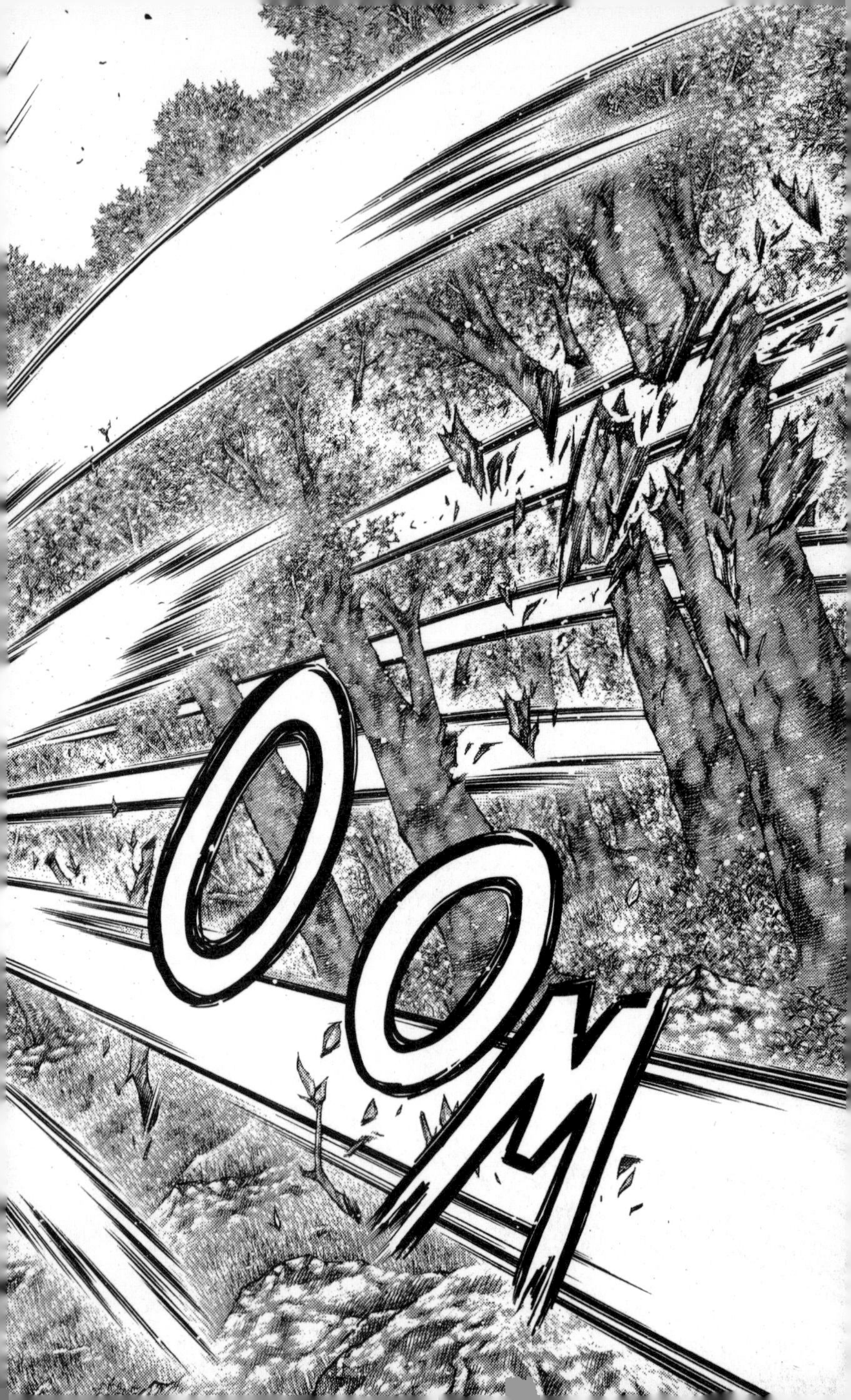
OOM

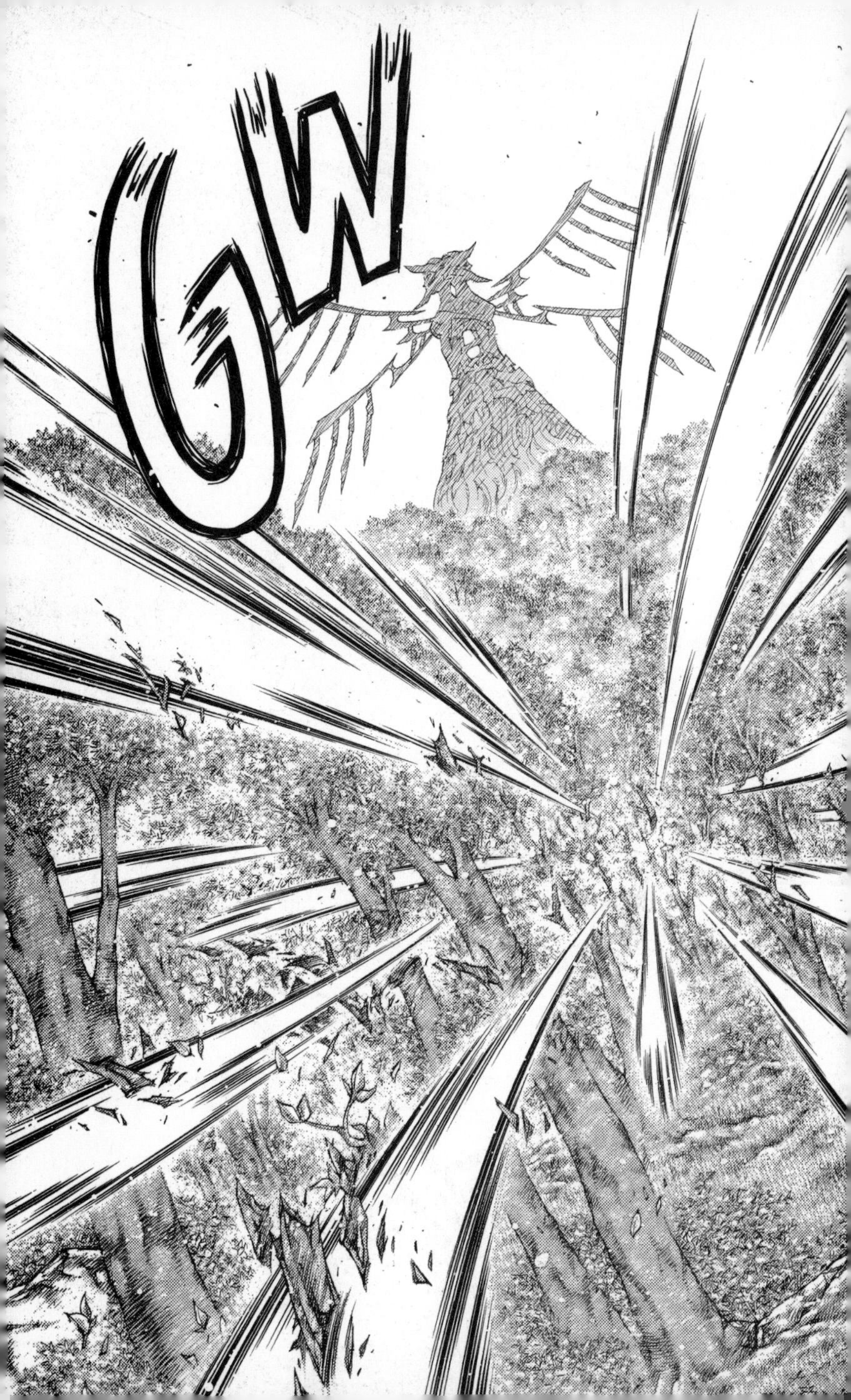
GW

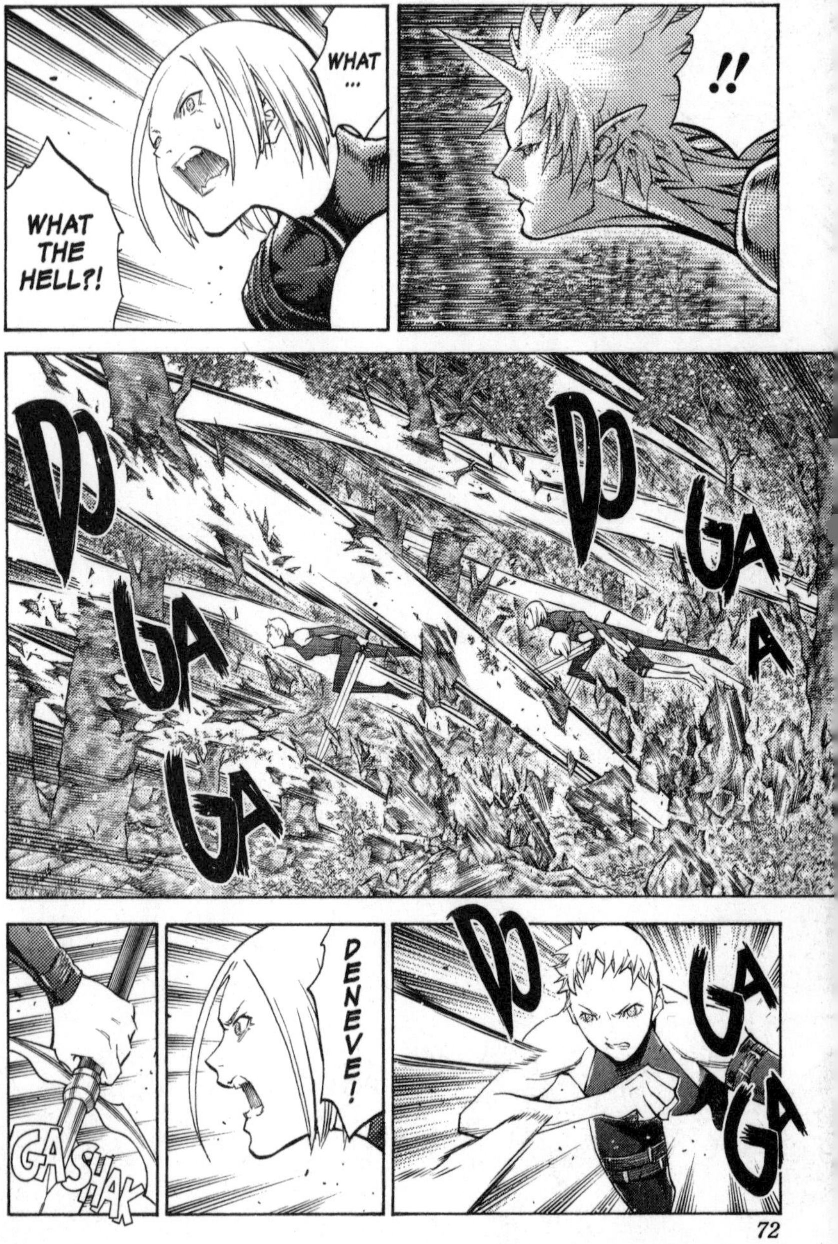
!!
WHAT ...
WHAT THE HELL?!
DO GA GA
DO GA GA
DO GA GA
DENEVE!
GASHAK

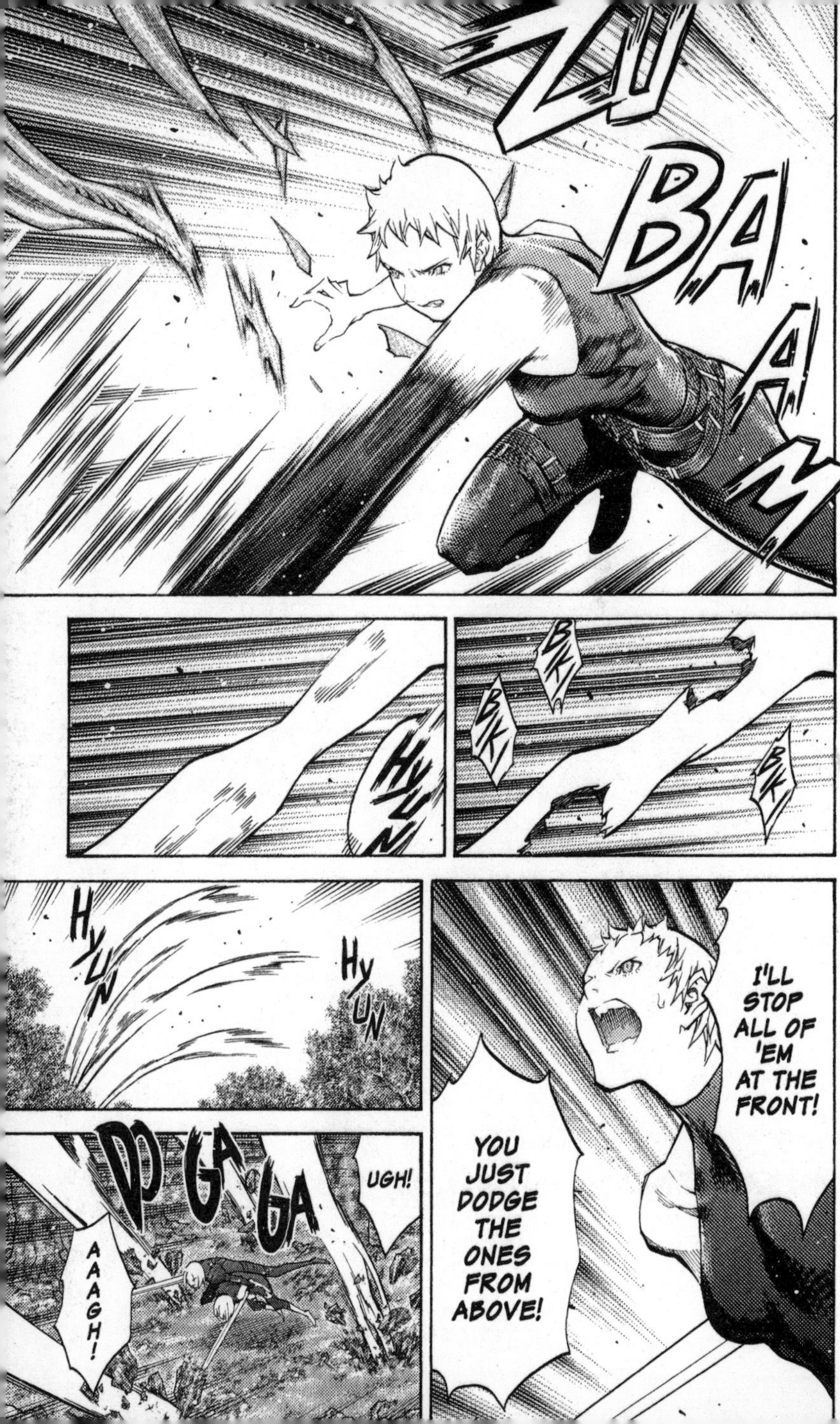
ZUBABAAM
BIK
BIK
BIK
HYUN
I'LL STOP ALL OF 'EM AT THE FRONT!
YOU JUST DODGE THE ONES FROM ABOVE!
HyUN
HyUN
DOGAGA
UGH!
AAAGH!

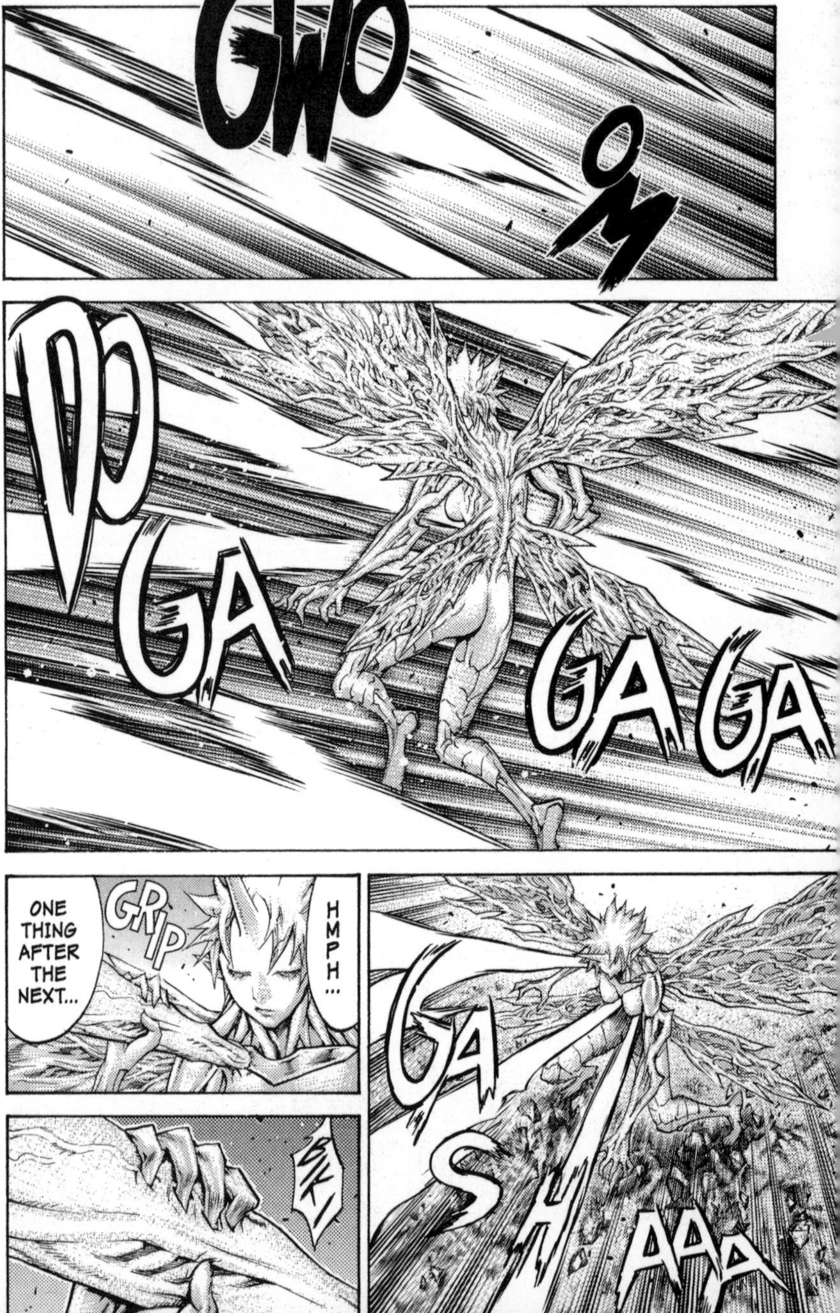
GWO
OM
DO
GA
GAGA
GA
SHAAA
HMPH...
GRIP
ONE THING AFTER THE NEXT...
BKI

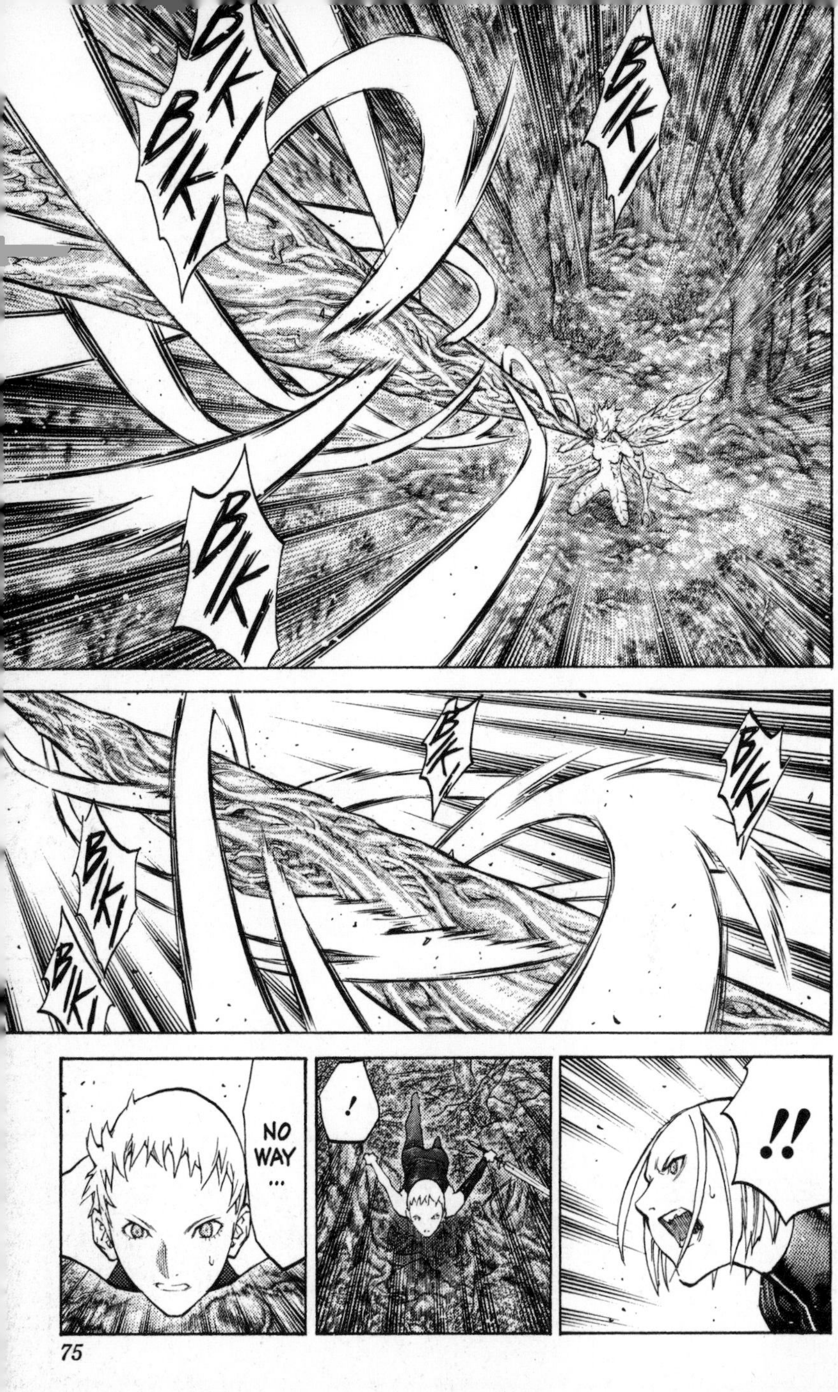
BIKI
BIKI BIKI
BIKI
BIKI
BIK
BIKI
BIKI
!!
!
NO WAY ...

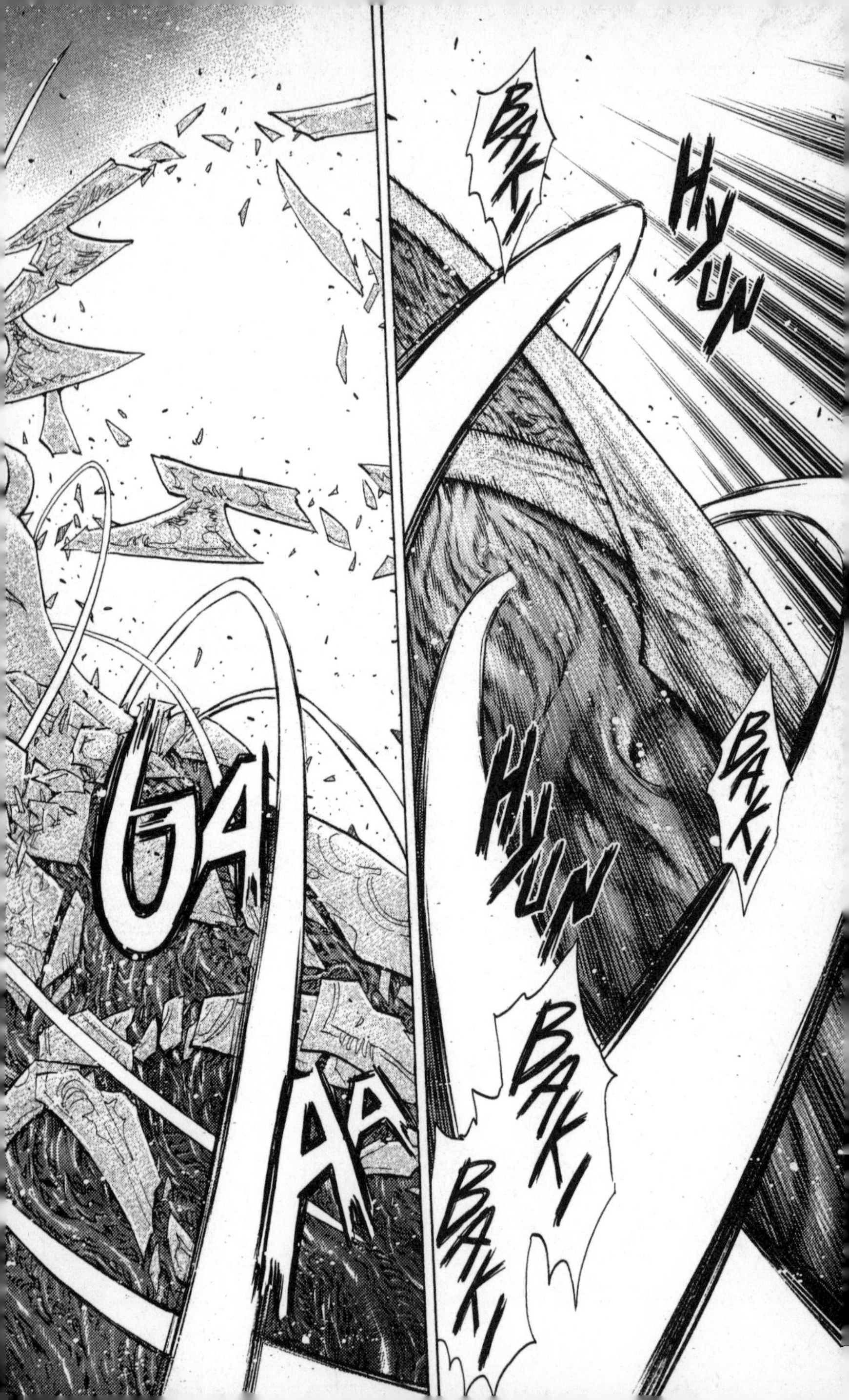
HYUN
BAKI
BAKI
HYUN
BAKI
BAKI
GAAA

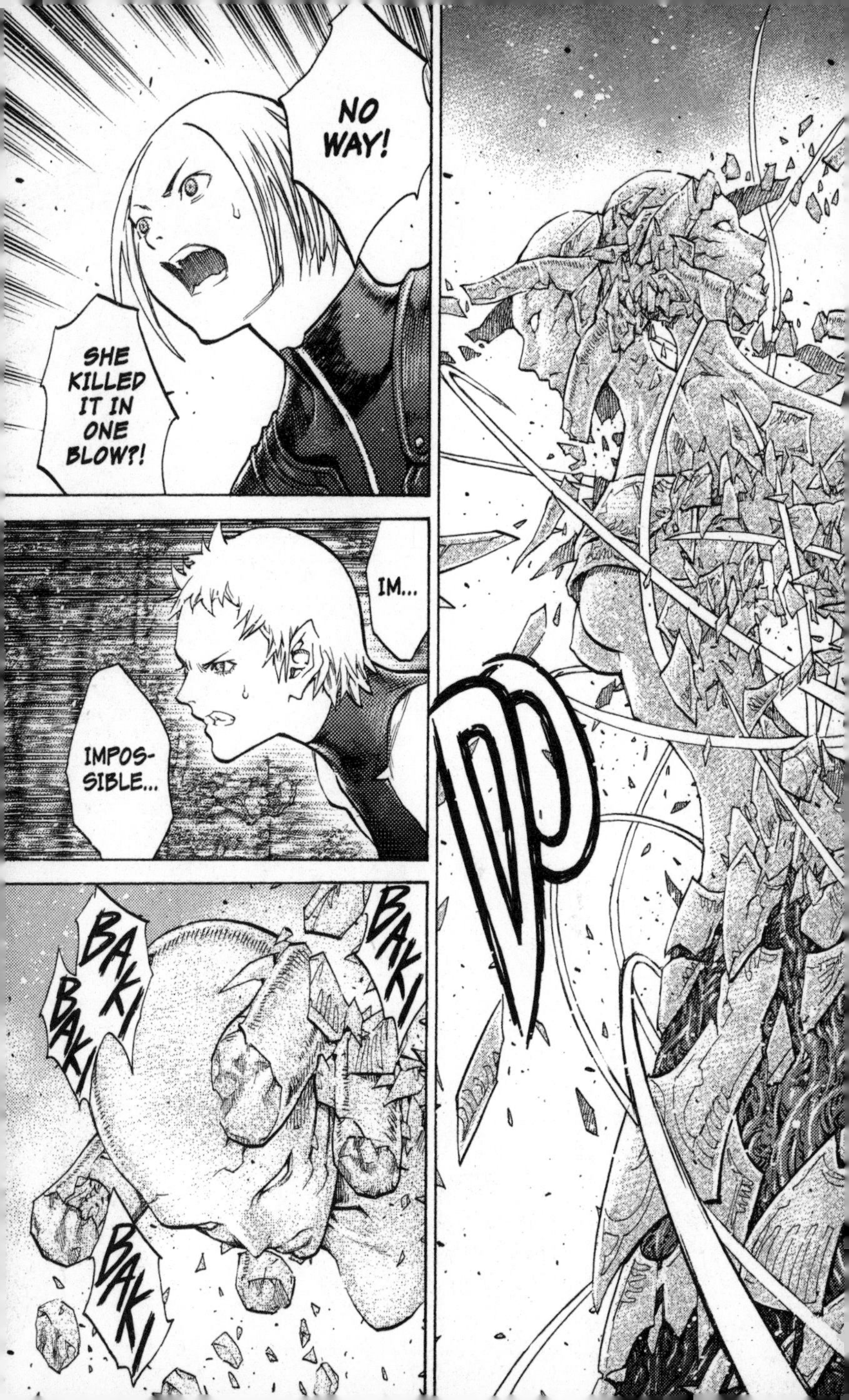
NO WAY!
SHE KILLED IT IN ONE BLOW?!
IM...
IMPOS-SIBLE...
BAKI
BAKI
BAKI
BAKI

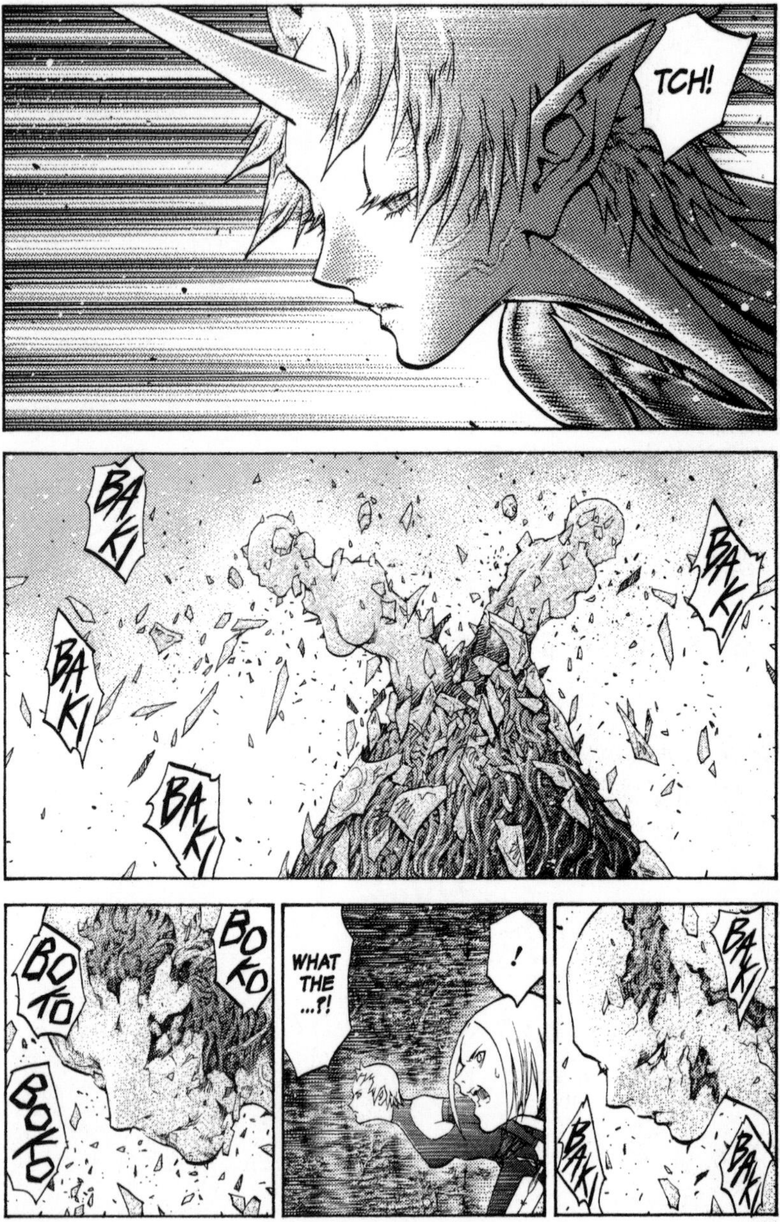
TCH!
BAKI
BAKI
BAKI
BAKI
BAKI
BAKI
BAKI
!
WHAT THE ...?!
BOKO
BOKO
BOKO

READ THIS WAY

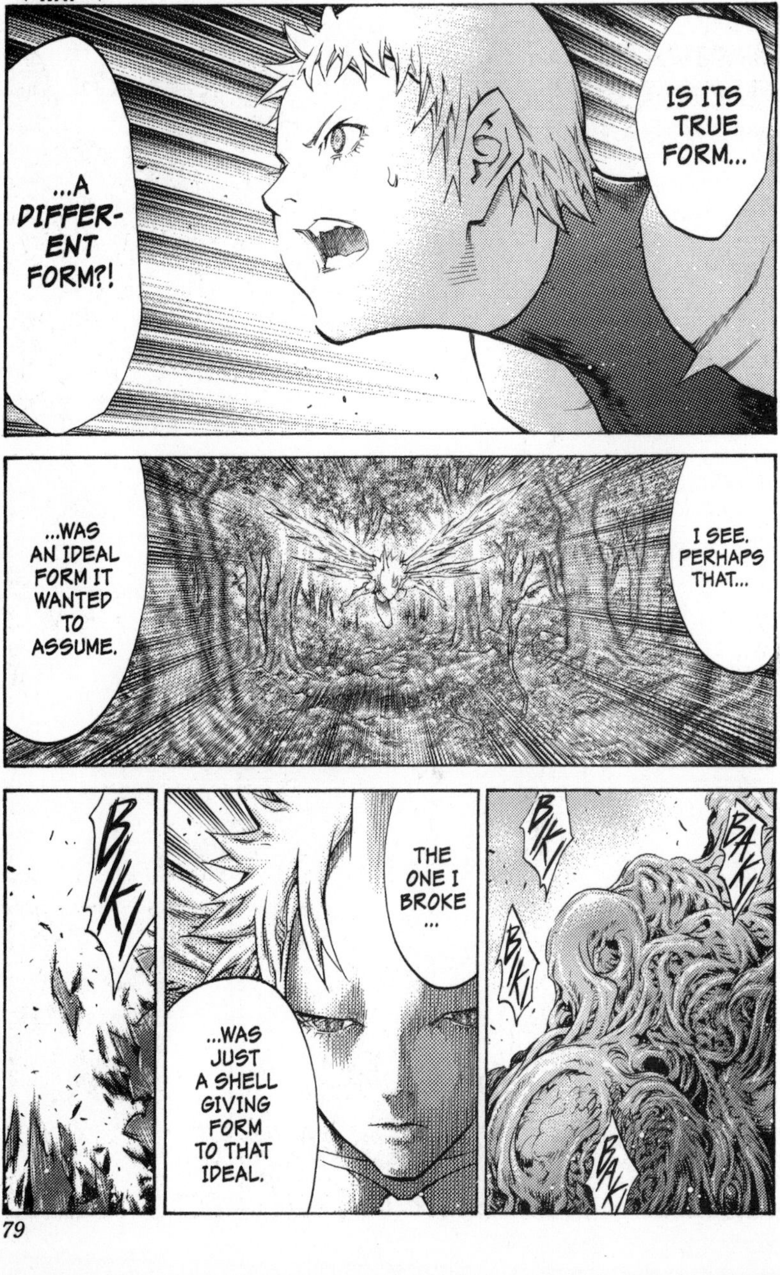

IS ITS TRUE FORM...
...A DIFFERENT FORM?!
I SEE. PERHAPS THAT...
...WAS AN IDEAL FORM IT WANTED TO ASSUME.
BAKI
BIKI
BIKI
BAKI
THE ONE I BROKE...
...WAS JUST A SHELL GIVING FORM TO THAT IDEAL.
BIKI

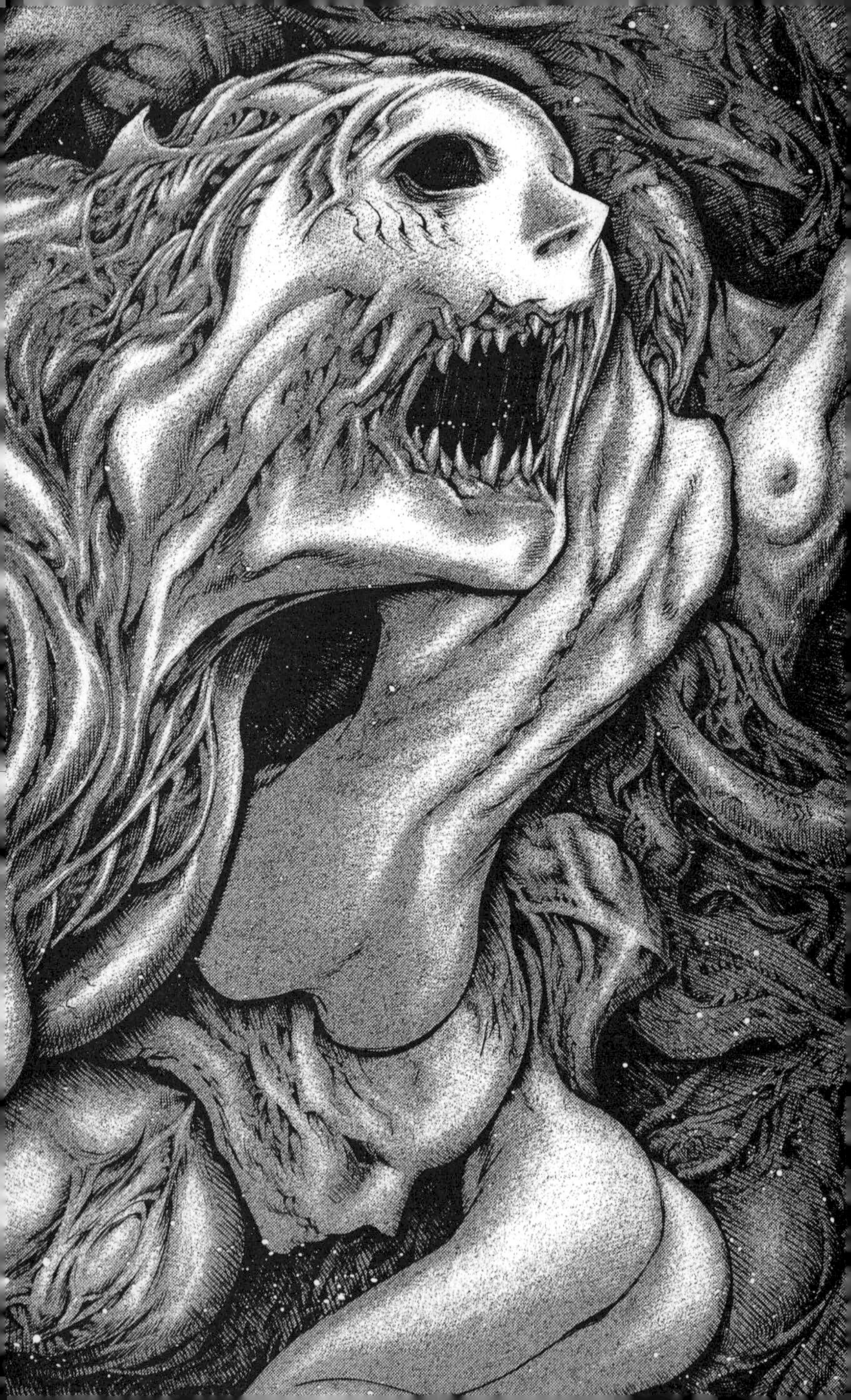

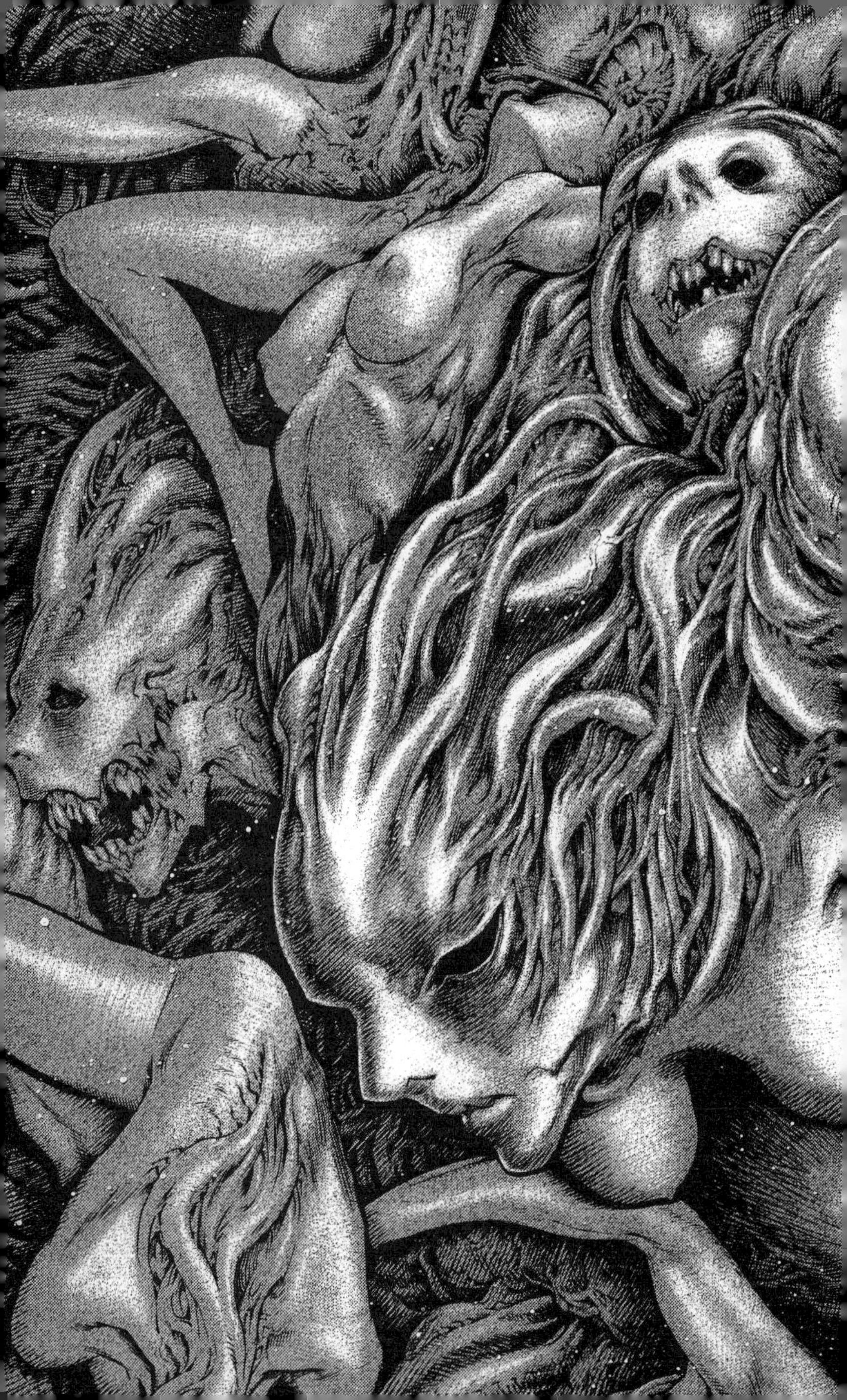

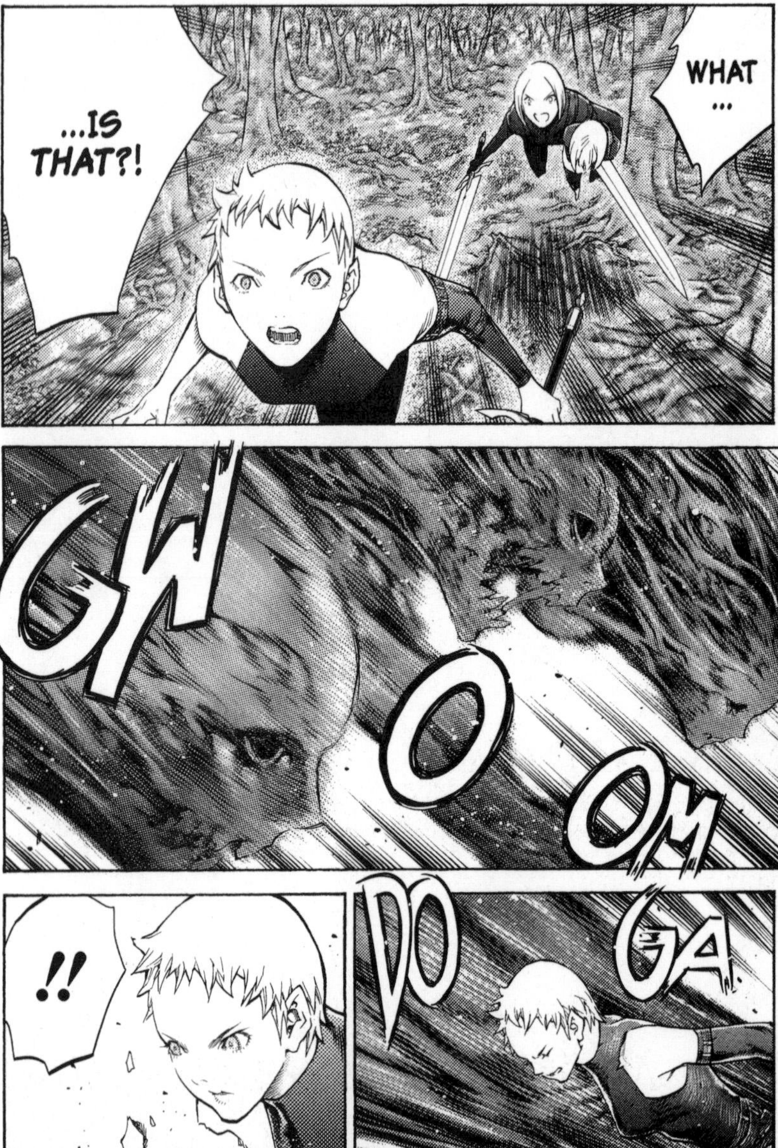
WHAT...
...IS THAT?!
GWOOOM
DO GA
!!

READ THIS WAY

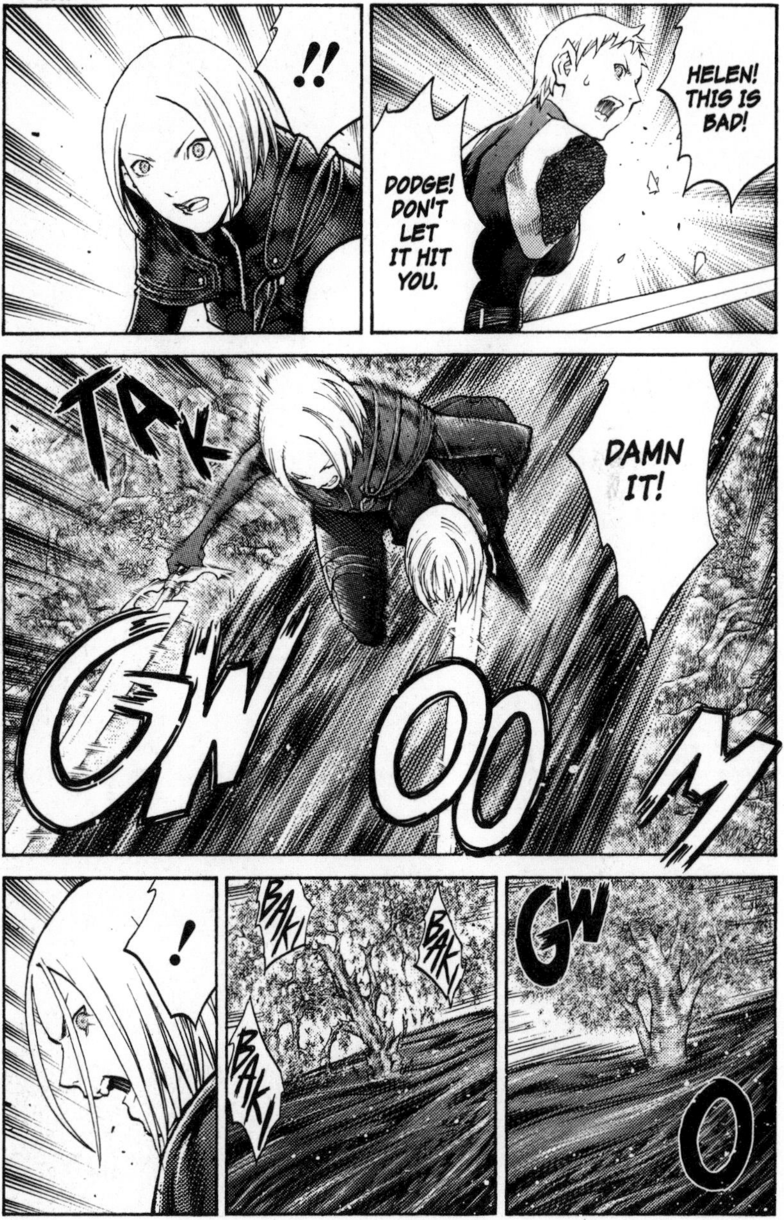
HELEN! THIS IS BAD!
DODGE! DON'T LET IT HIT YOU.
!!
DAMN IT!
TAK
GWOOOM
GW
O
BAK
BAK
BAK
!

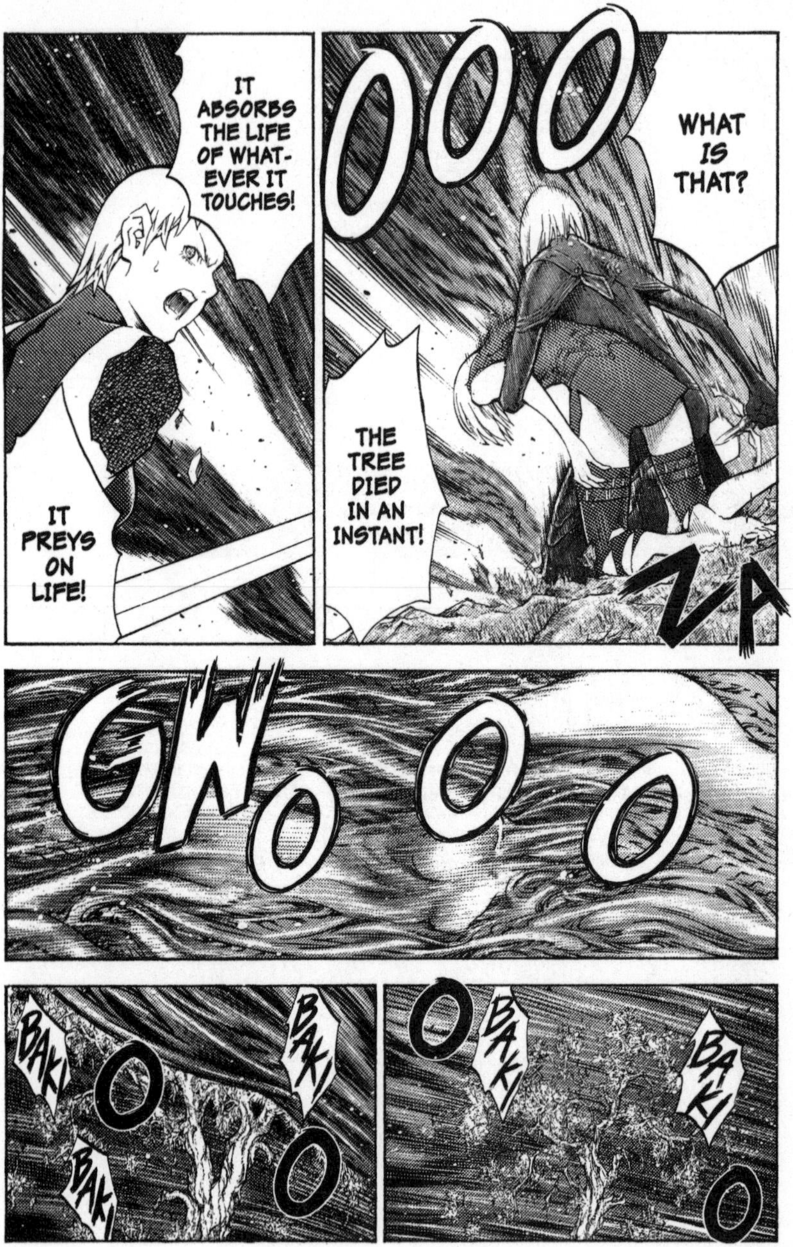
OOO
WHAT IS THAT?
THE TREE DIED IN AN INSTANT!
ZA
IT ABSORBS THE LIFE OF WHAT-EVER IT TOUCHES!
IT PREYS ON LIFE!
GWOOOO
BAKI
BAKI
O
O
BAKI
O
BAKI
O
BAKI

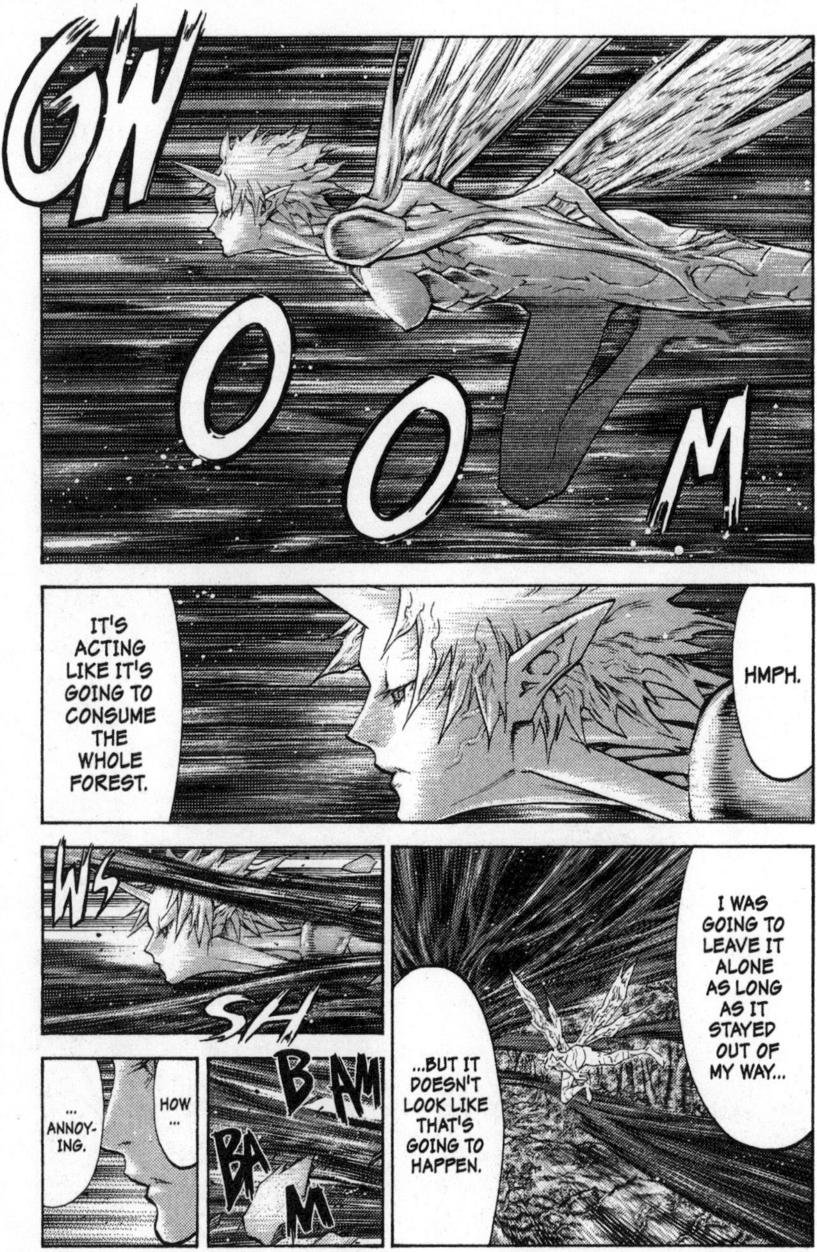
GWOOOM
HMPH.
IT'S ACTING LIKE IT'S GOING TO CONSUME THE WHOLE FOREST.
I WAS GOING TO LEAVE IT ALONE AS LONG AS IT STAYED OUT OF MY WAY...
...BUT IT DOESN'T LOOK LIKE THAT'S GOING TO HAPPEN.
WSSH
BAM
BAM
HOW ...
... ANNOY-ING.

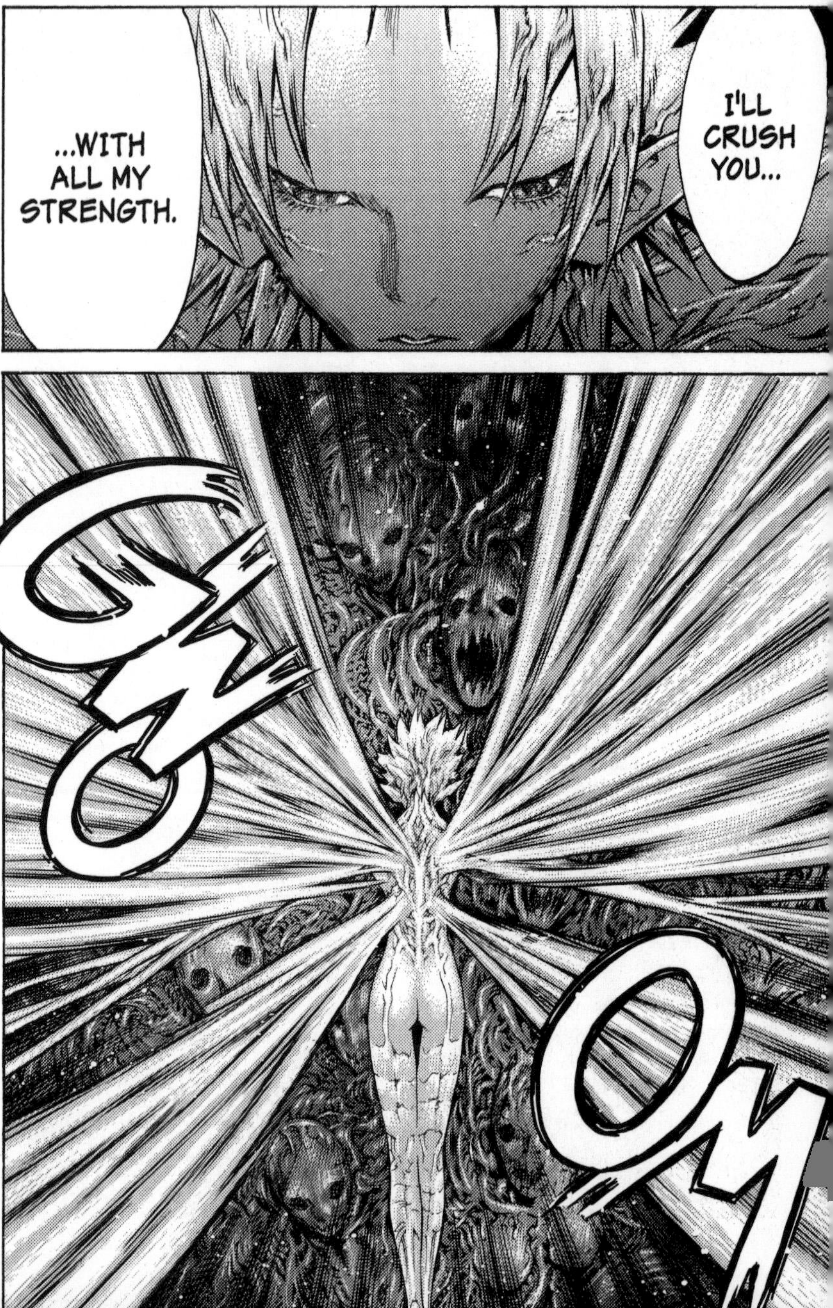
I'LL CRUSH YOU...
...WITH ALL MY STRENGTH.
GO
OM

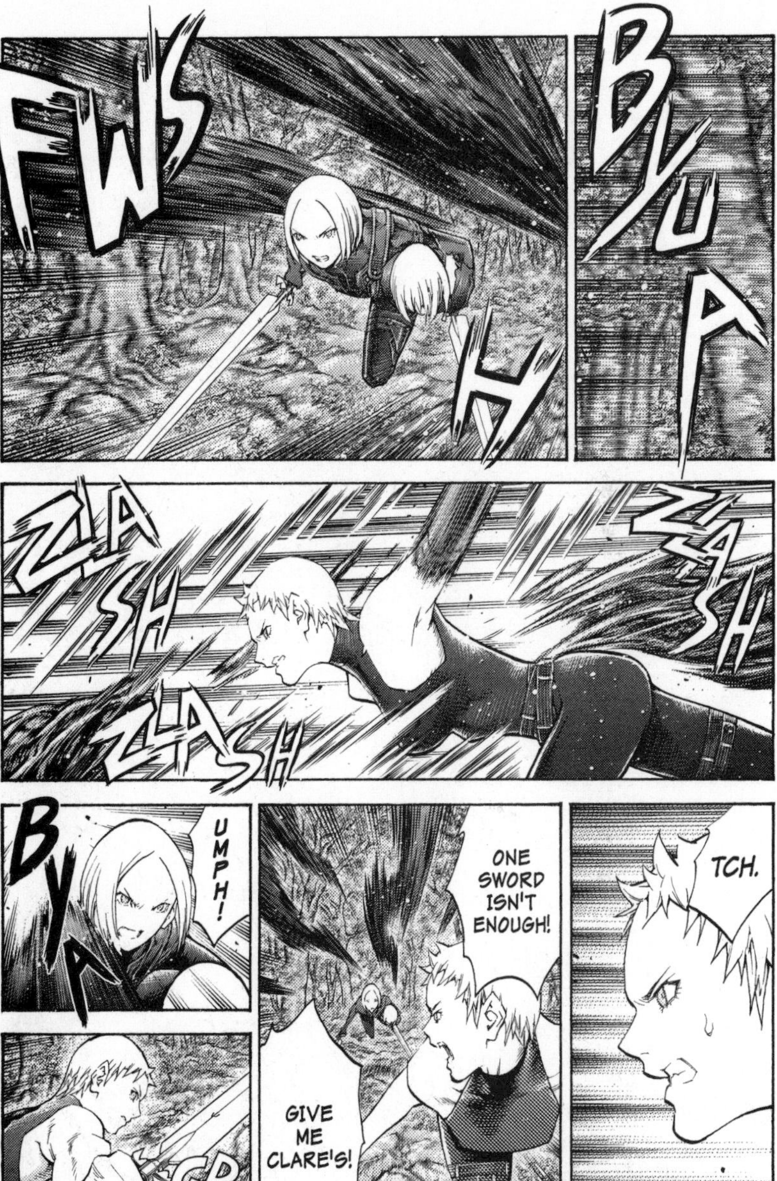
BYUA
FWSH
ZASH
ZASH
ZASH
TCH.
ONE SWORD ISN'T ENOUGH!
GIVE ME CLARE'S!
UMPH!
BYA
GRIP

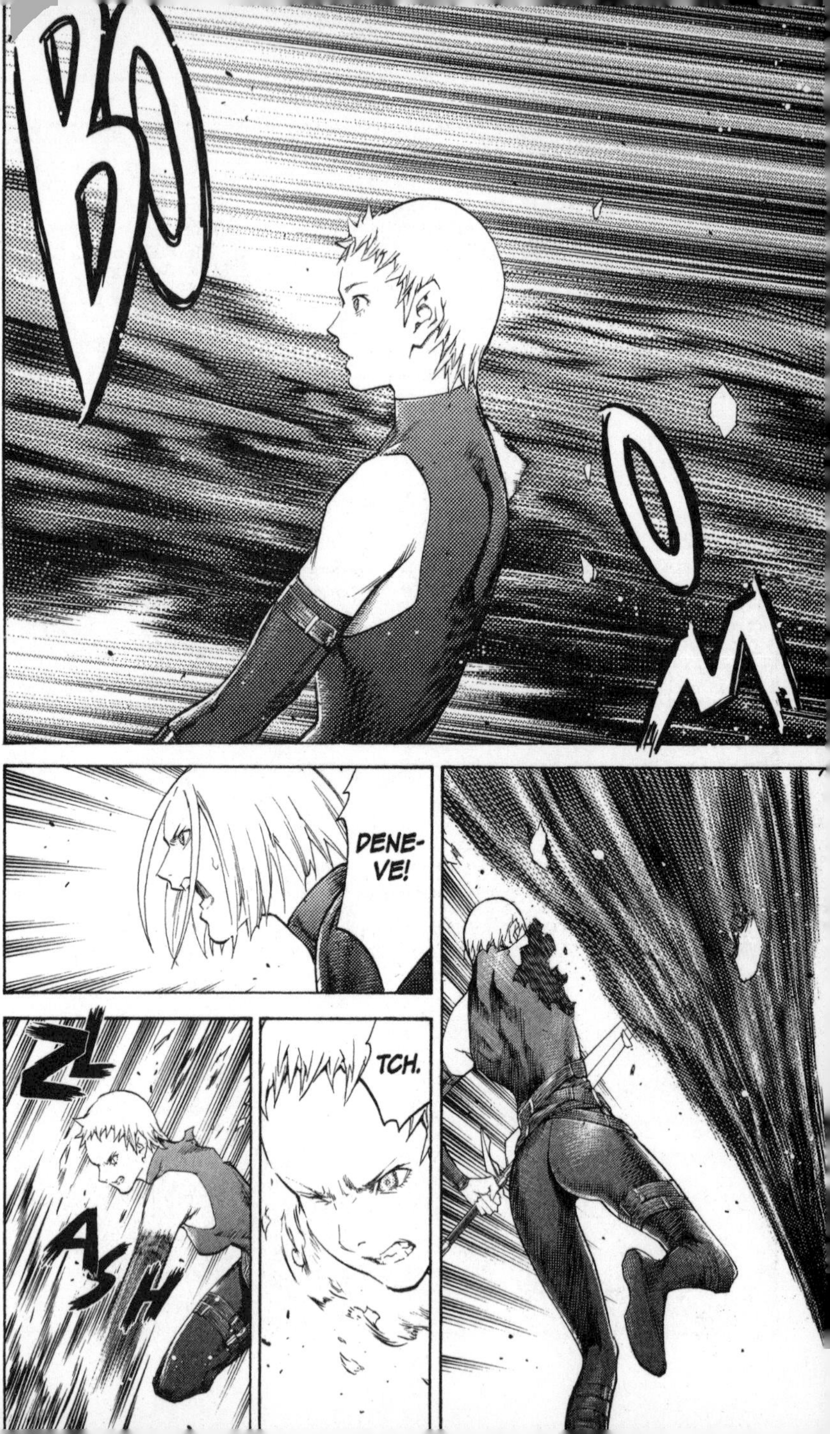
BOOM
DENEVE!
TCH.
ZASH

READ THIS WAY

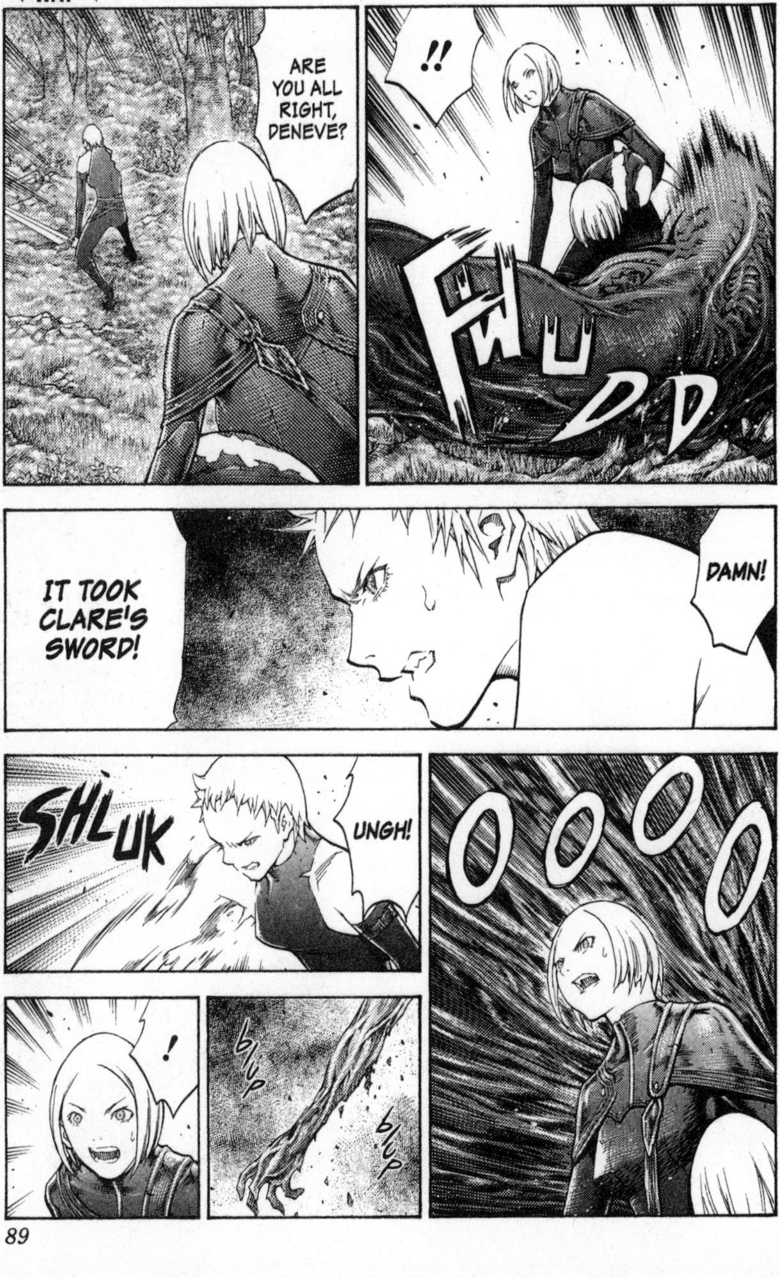
!!
FWUDD
ARE YOU ALL RIGHT, DENEVE?
DAMN!
IT TOOK CLARE'S SWORD!
OOOOO
SHLUK
UNGH!
blup
blup
!

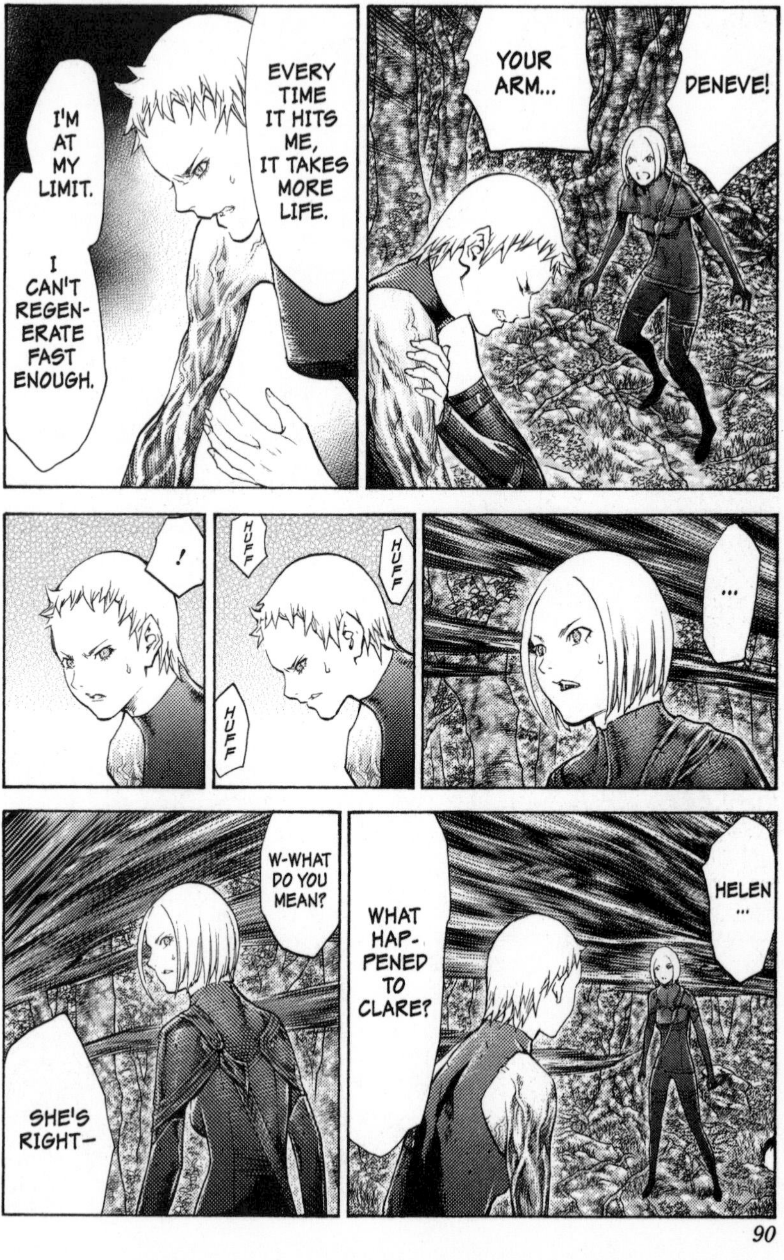
DENEVE!
YOUR ARM...
EVERY TIME IT HITS ME, IT TAKES MORE LIFE.
I'M AT MY LIMIT.
I CAN'T REGEN-ERATE FAST ENOUGH.
...
HUFF
HUFF
HUFF
!
HELEN ...
WHAT HAP-PENED TO CLARE?
W-WHAT DO YOU MEAN?
SHE'S RIGHT—

READ THIS WAY

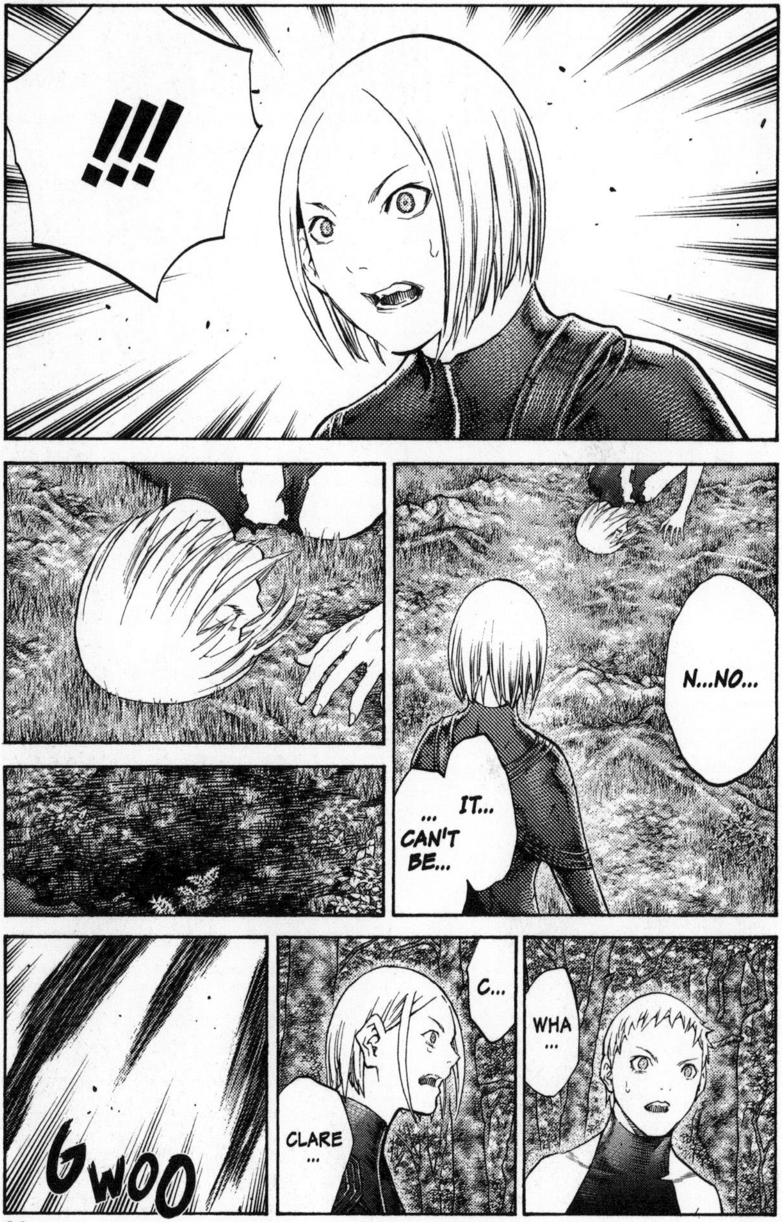
!!!
N...NO...
IT... ... CAN'T BE...
WHA ...
C...
CLARE ...
GWOO

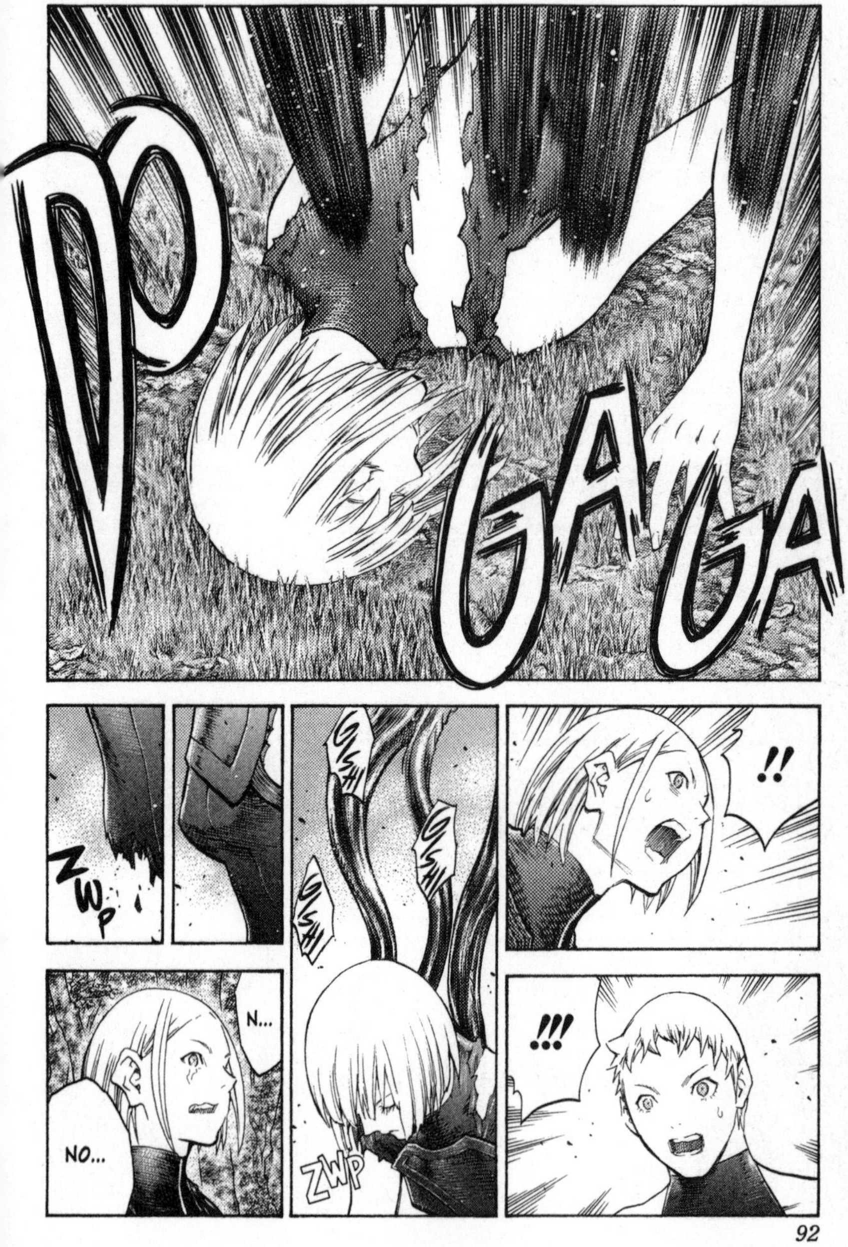
DO
GAGA
!!
GUSH!
GUSH!
GUSH!
ZWP
ZWP
!!!
N...
NO...

READ THIS WAY

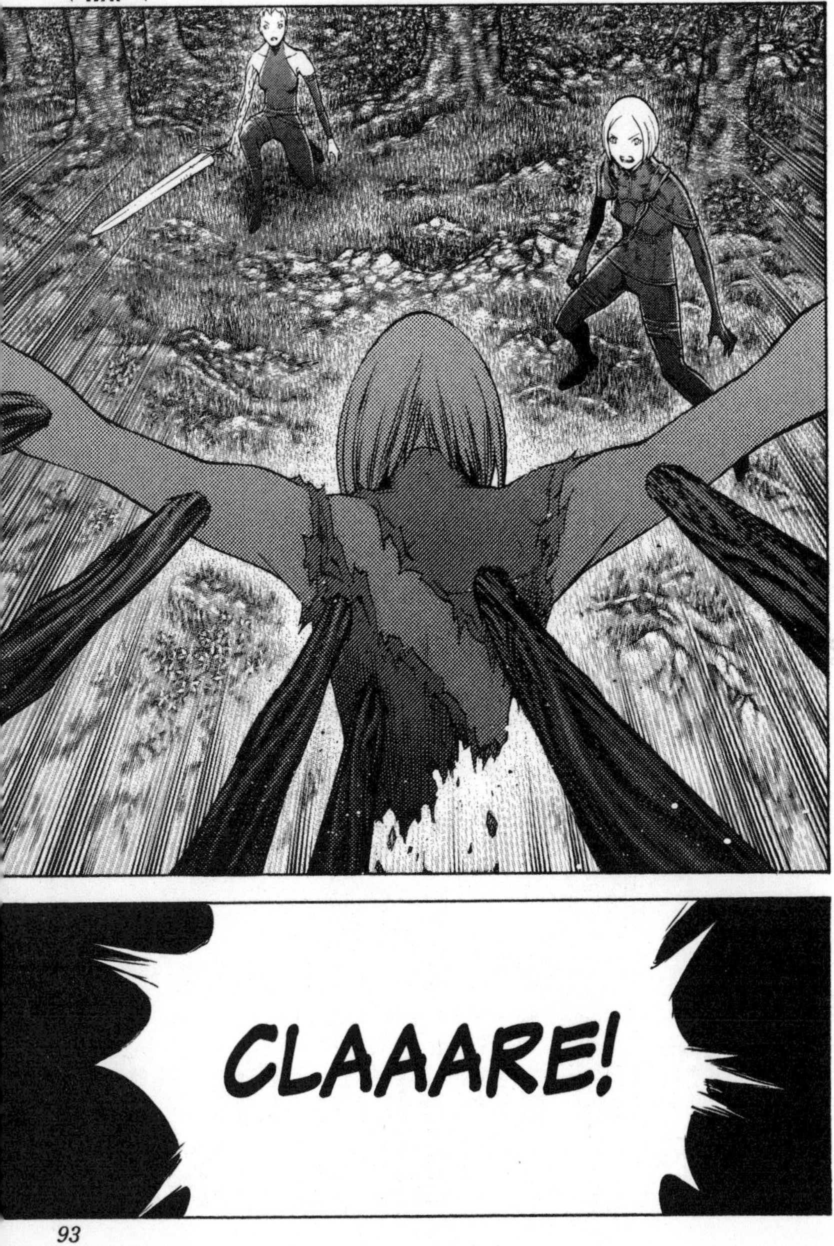
CLAAARE!

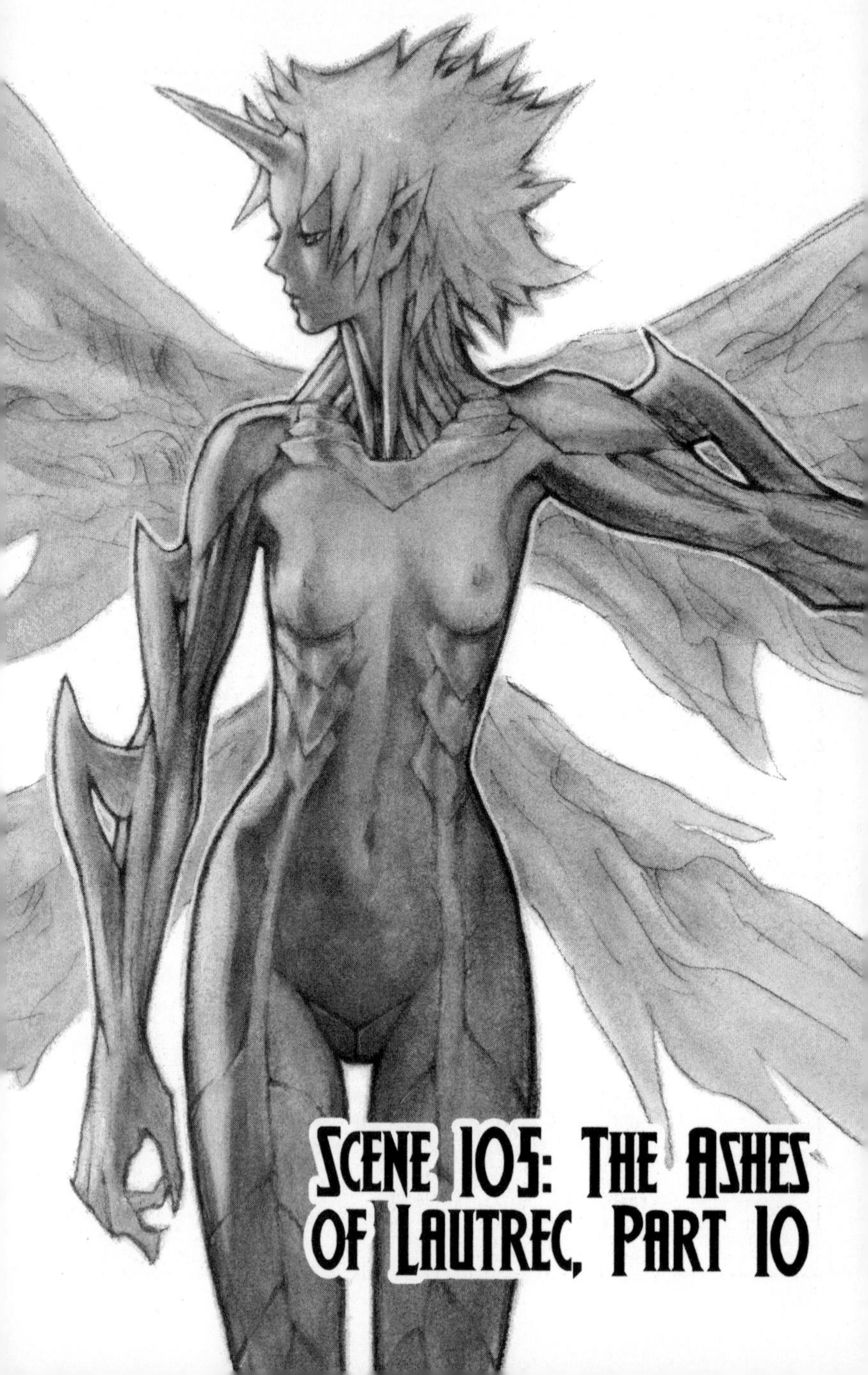

Scene 105: The Ashes of Lautrec, Part 10

READ THIS WAY

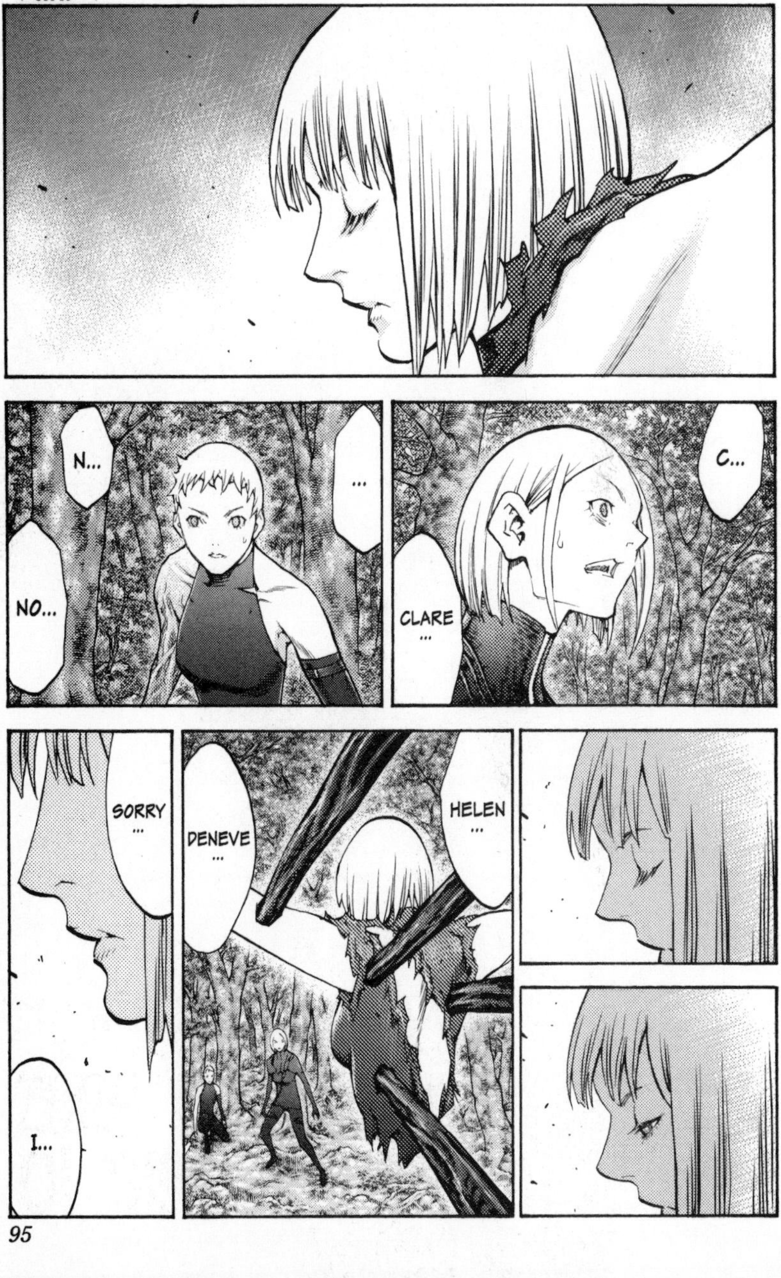
C...
CLARE ...
...
N...
NO...
HELEN ...
DENEVE ...
SORRY ...
I...

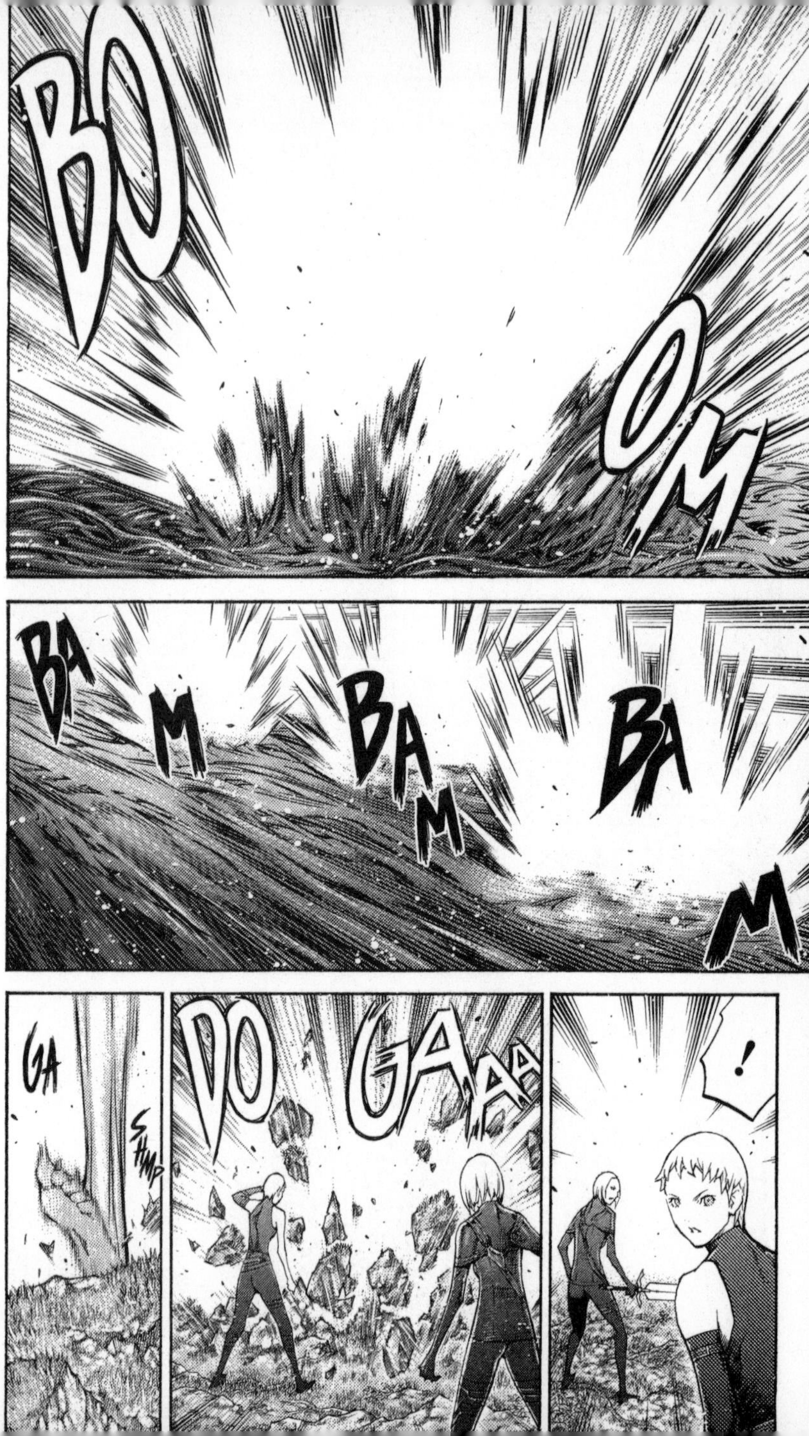
BOOM
BAM
BAM
BAM
!
DOGAAA
GA
SHMP

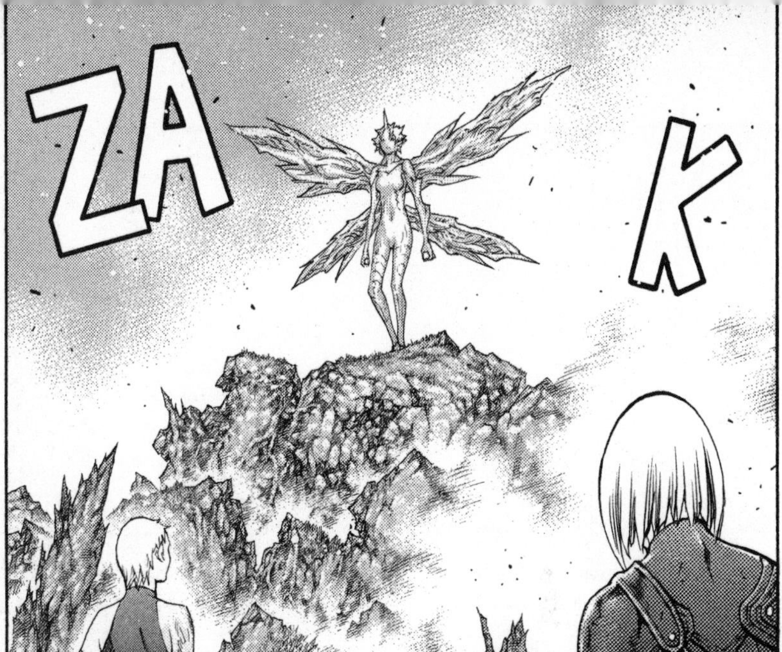
ZA
K
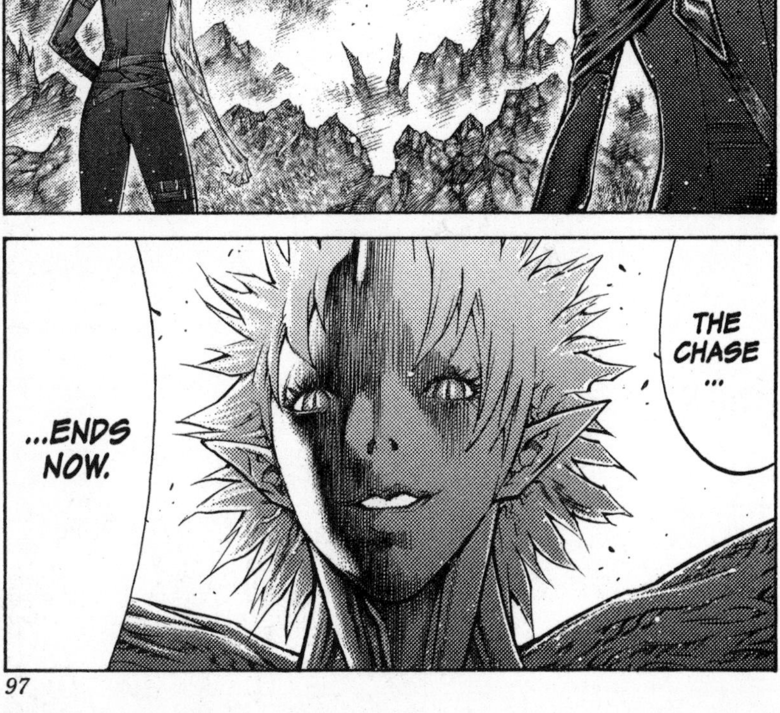
THE CHASE ...
...ENDS NOW.

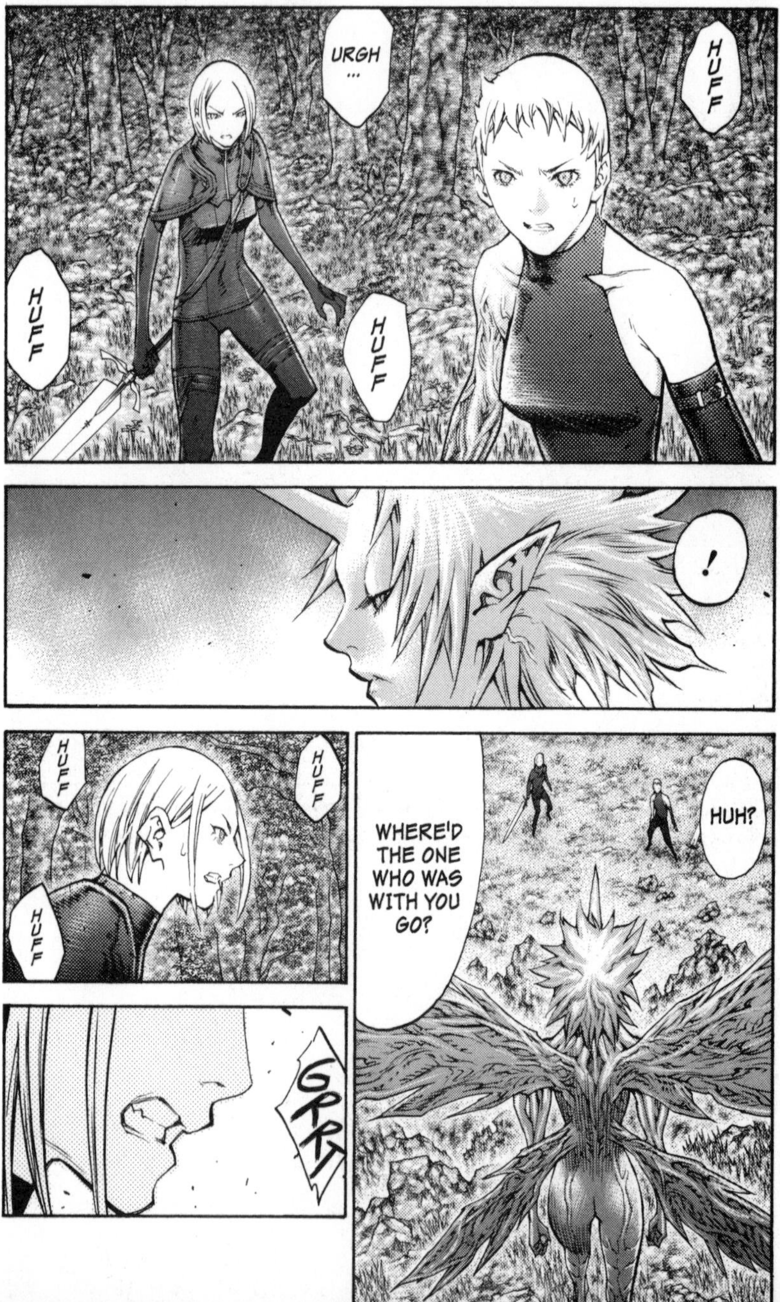
HUFF
URGH ...
HUFF
HUFF
!
HUH?
WHERE'D THE ONE WHO WAS WITH YOU GO?
HUFF
HUFF
HUFF
GRRT

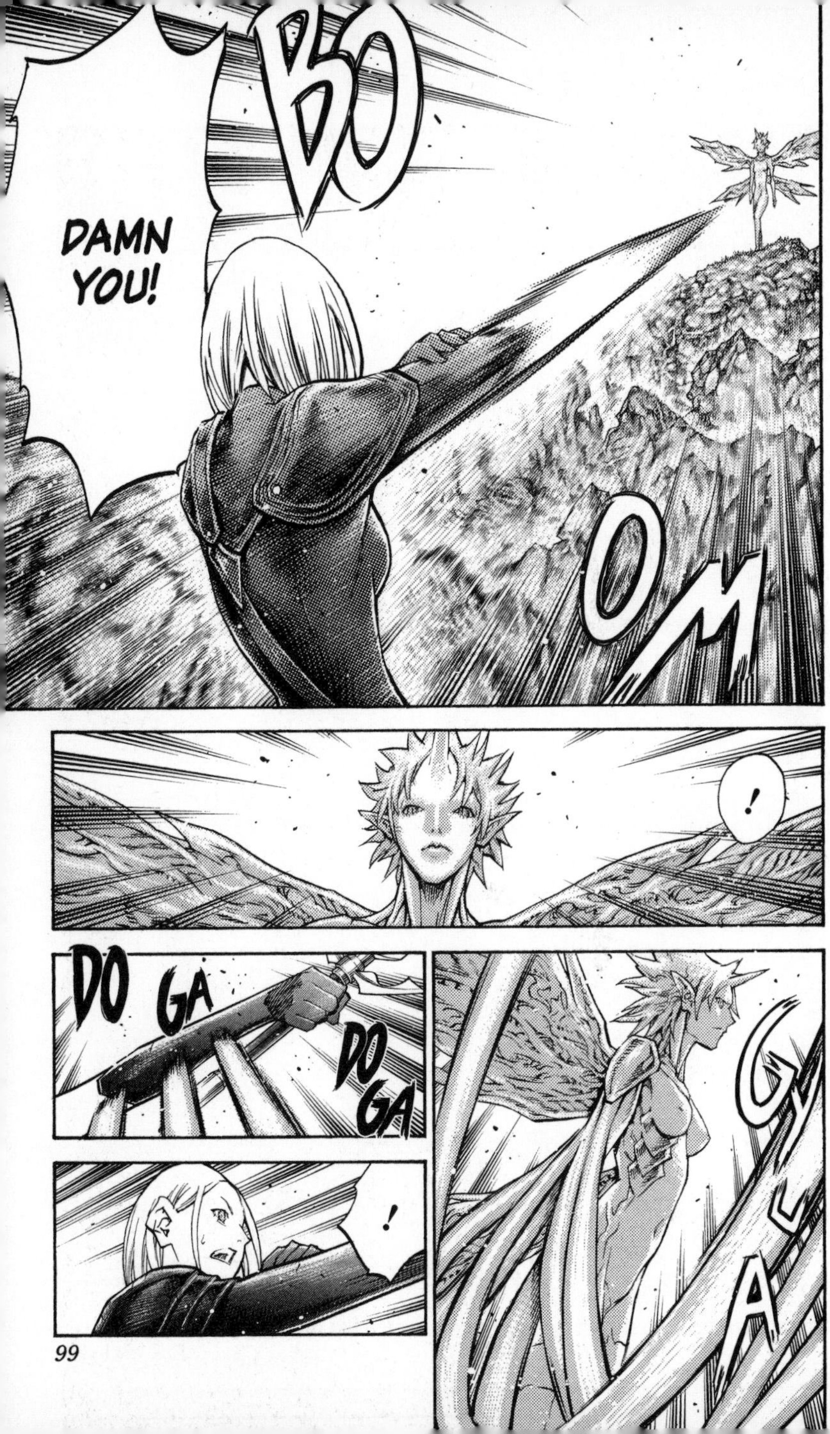

BO
DAMN YOU!
OM
!
GUA
DO GA
DO GA
!

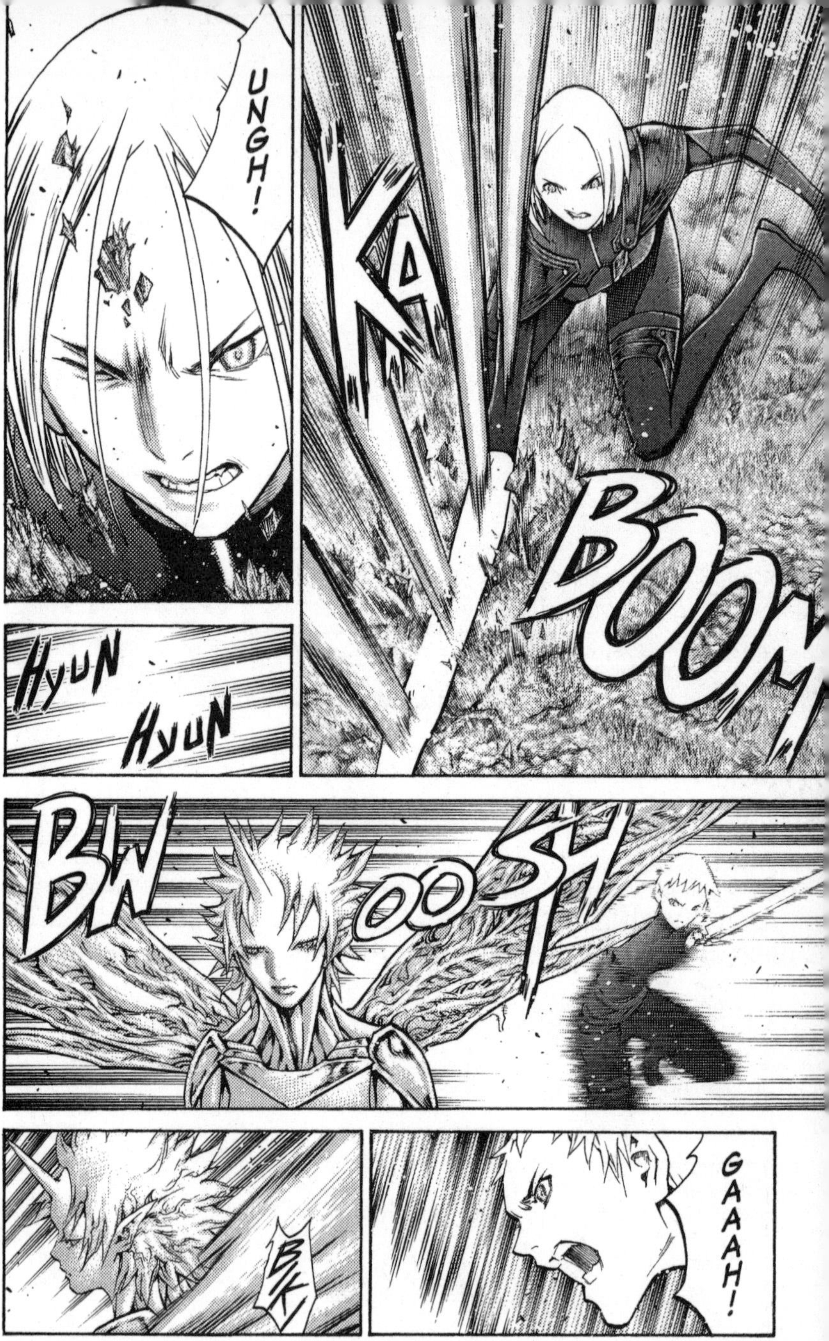
KA
BOOM
UNGH!
HYUN
HYUN
BWOOSH
GAAAH!
BK

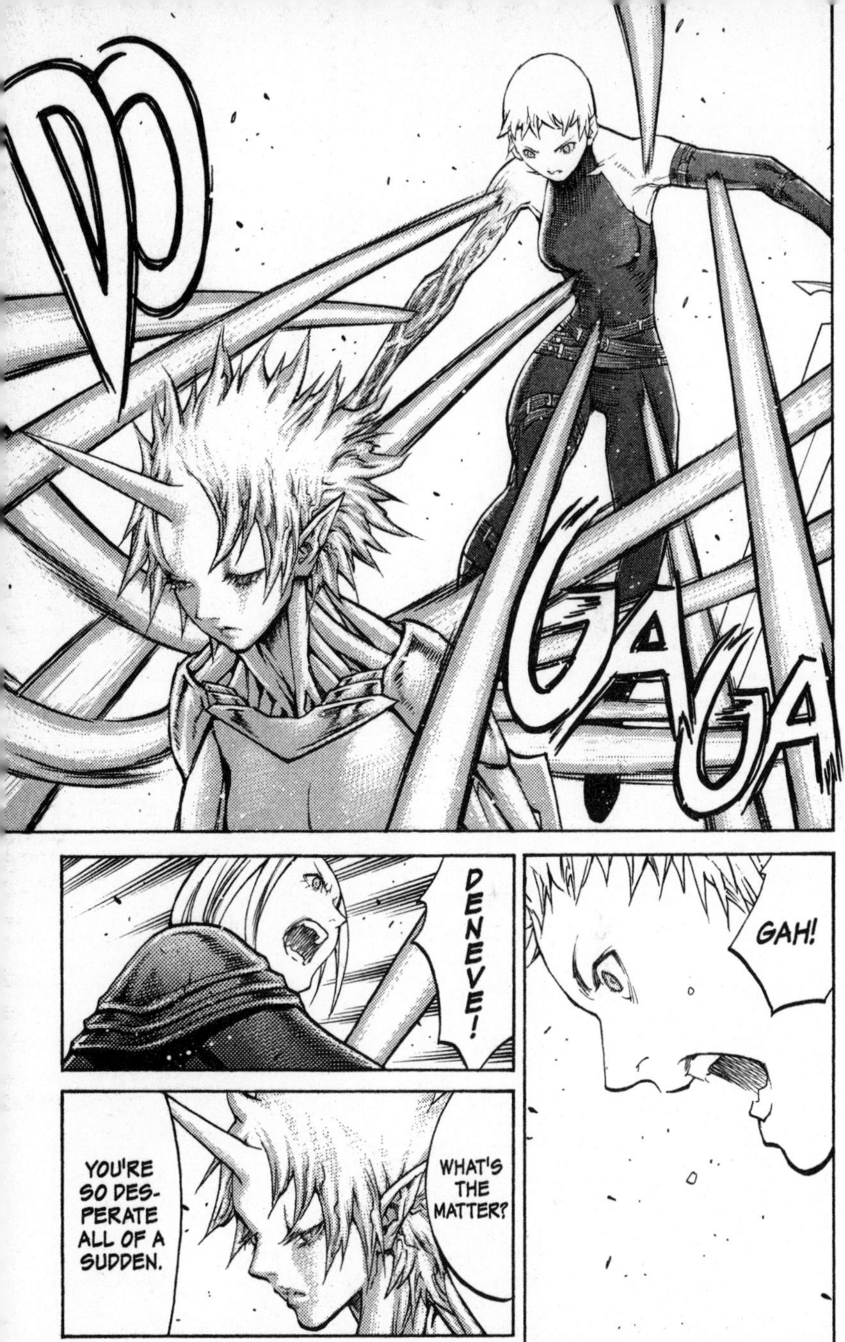
DO
GAGA
GAH!
DENEVE!
WHAT'S THE MATTER?
YOU'RE SO DESPERATE ALL OF A SUDDEN.

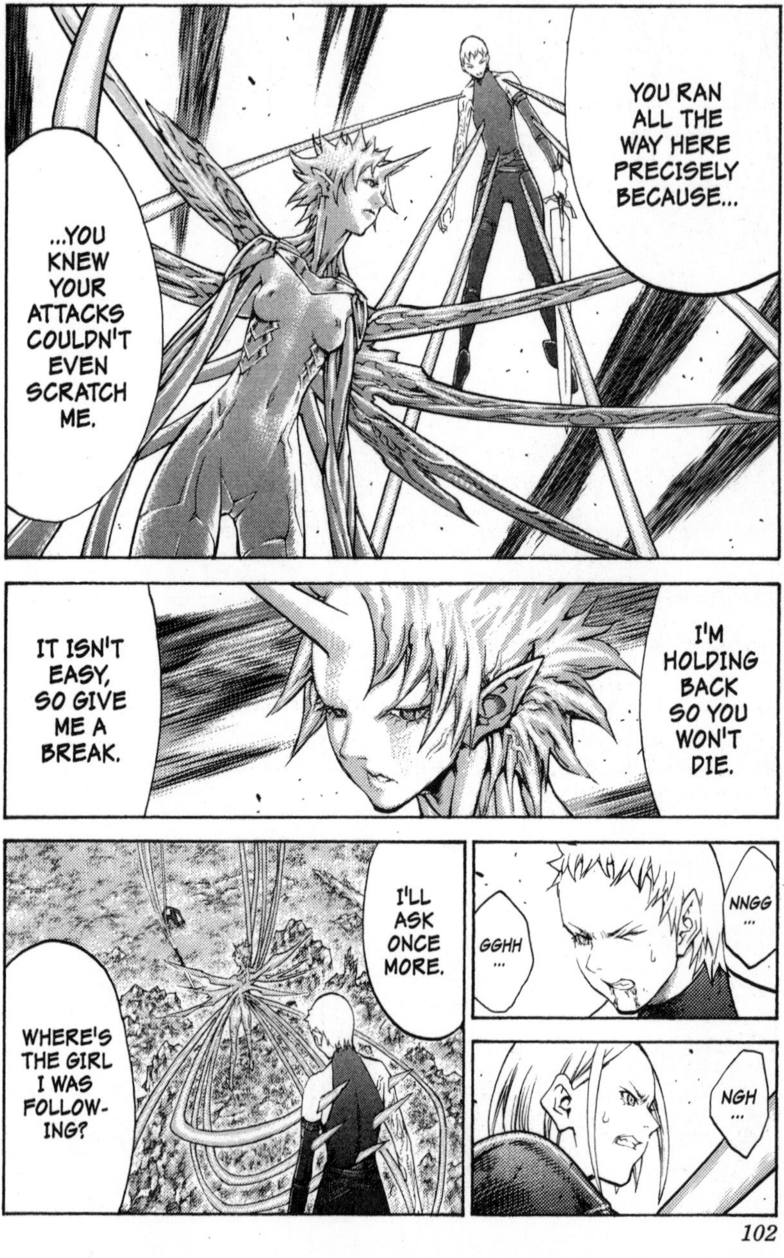
YOU RAN ALL THE WAY HERE PRECISELY BECAUSE...
...YOU KNEW YOUR ATTACKS COULDN'T EVEN SCRATCH ME.
I'M HOLDING BACK SO YOU WON'T DIE.
IT ISN'T EASY, SO GIVE ME A BREAK.
NNGG...
GGHH...
NGH...
I'LL ASK ONCE MORE.
WHERE'S THE GIRL I WAS FOLLOWING?

READ THIS WAY

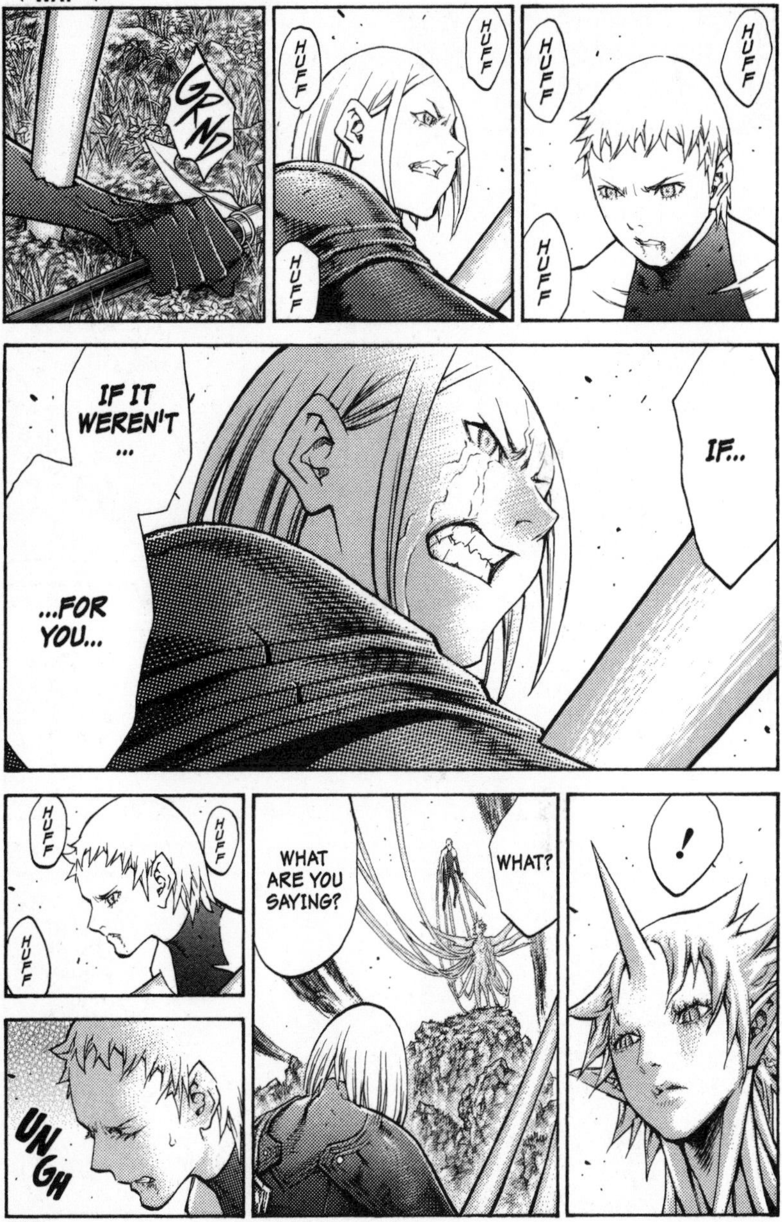
HUFF
HUFF
HUFF
HUFF
HUFF
HUFF
HUFF
GRNN
IF...
IF IT WEREN'T ...
...FOR YOU...
!
WHAT?
WHAT ARE YOU SAYING?
HUFF
HUFF
HUFF
UNGH

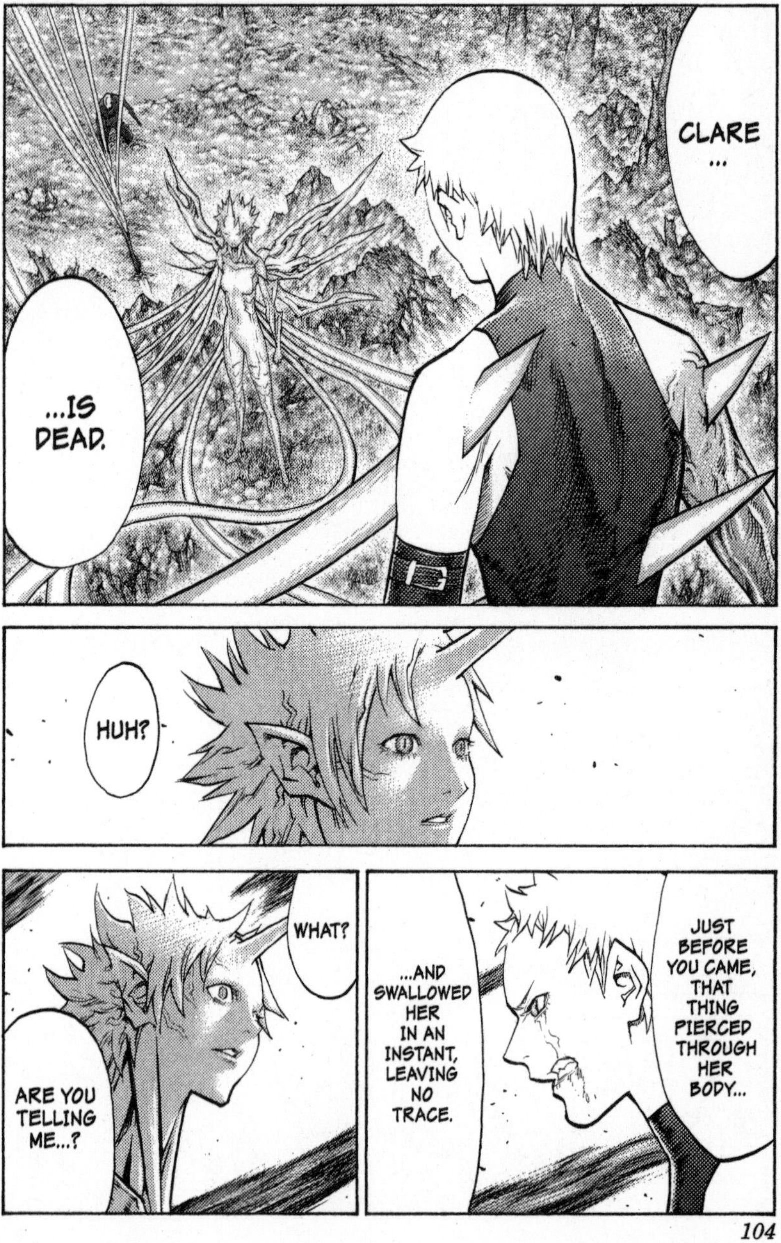
CLARE ...
...IS DEAD.
HUH?
JUST BEFORE YOU CAME, THAT THING PIERCED THROUGH HER BODY...
...AND SWALLOWED HER IN AN INSTANT, LEAVING NO TRACE.
WHAT?
ARE YOU TELLING ME...?

READ THIS WAY

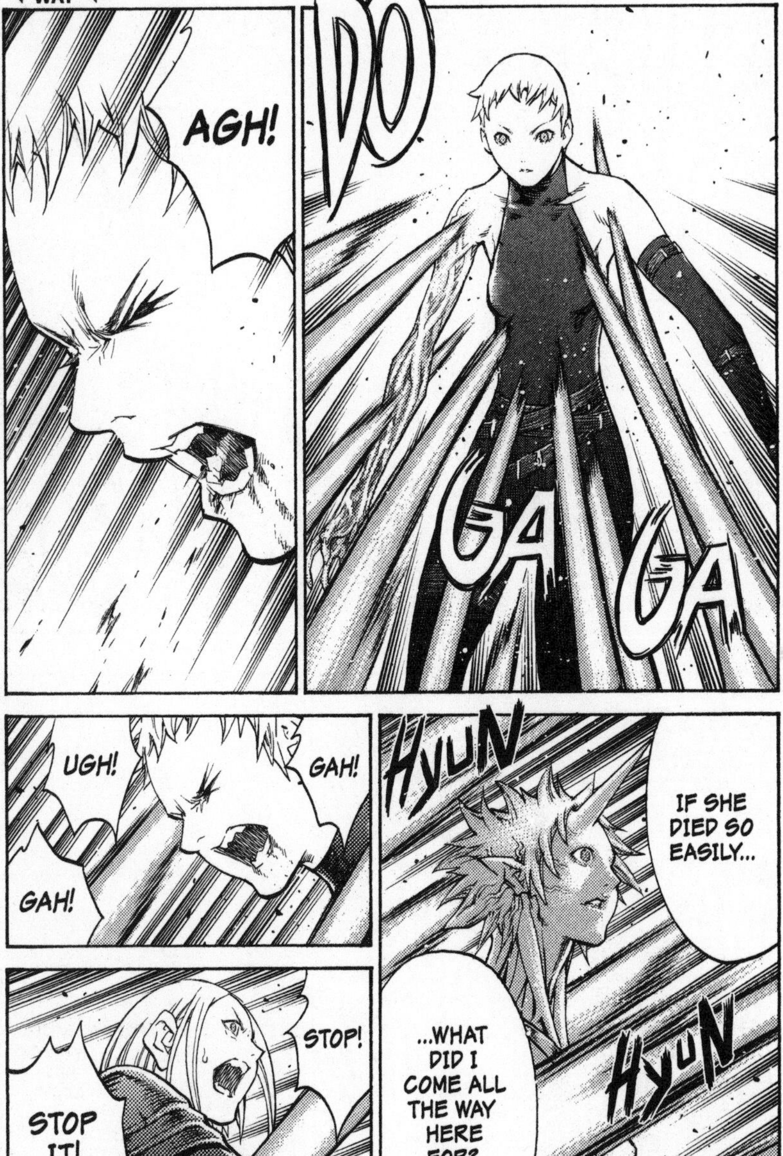
DO
GA GA
AGH!
IF SHE DIED SO EASILY...
HYUN
...WHAT DID I COME ALL THE WAY HERE FOR?
HYUN
GAH!
UGH!
GAH!
STOP!
STOP IT!

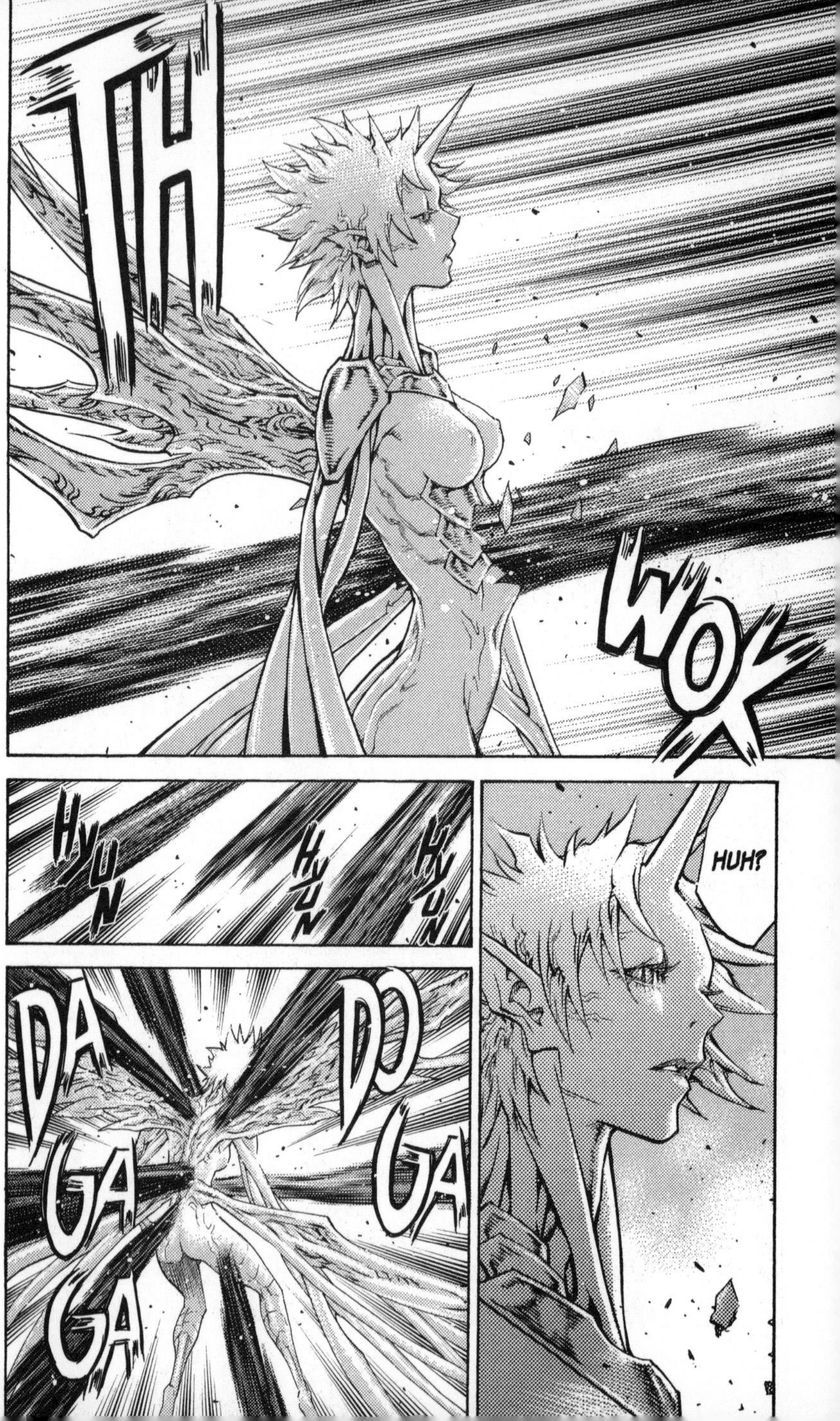
TH
WOX
HUH?
HYUN
HYUN
HYUN
DO GA
DA GA GA

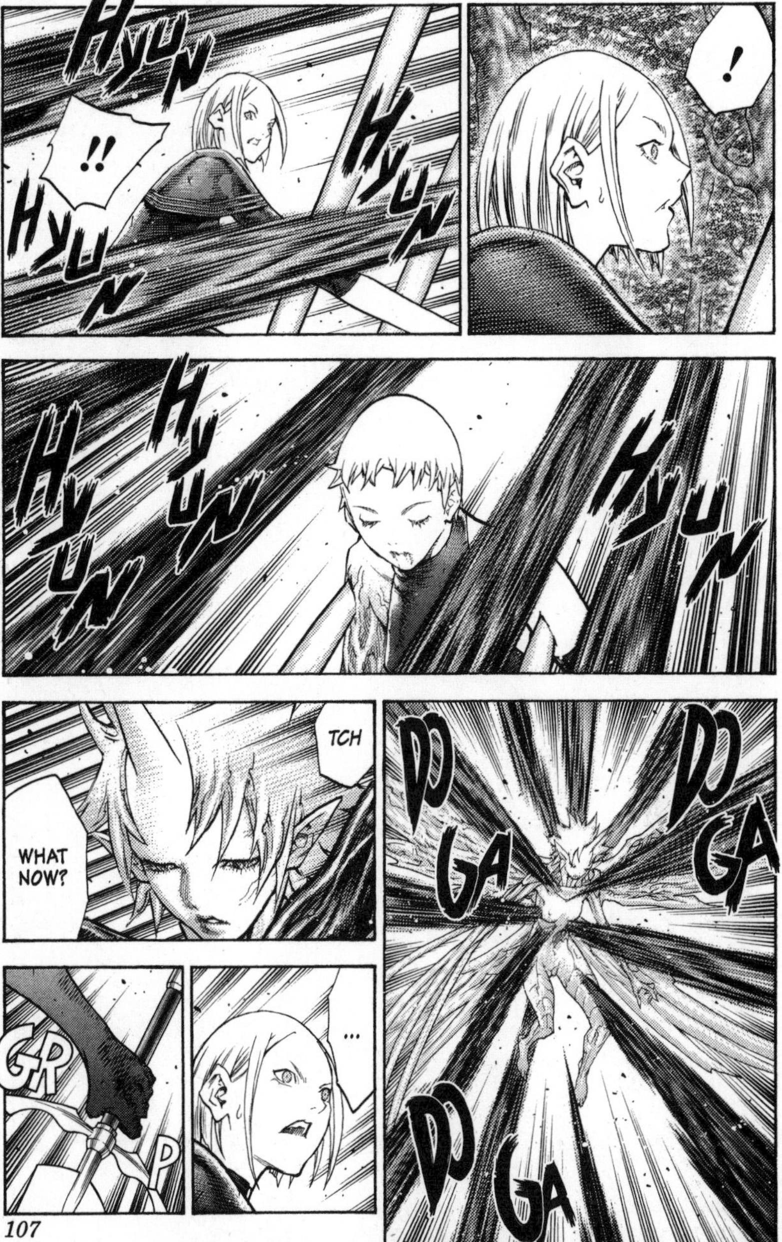
!
HYUN
HYUN
!!
HYUN
HYUN
HYUN
HYUN
DOGA
DOGA
DOGA
TCH
WHAT NOW?
...
GRP

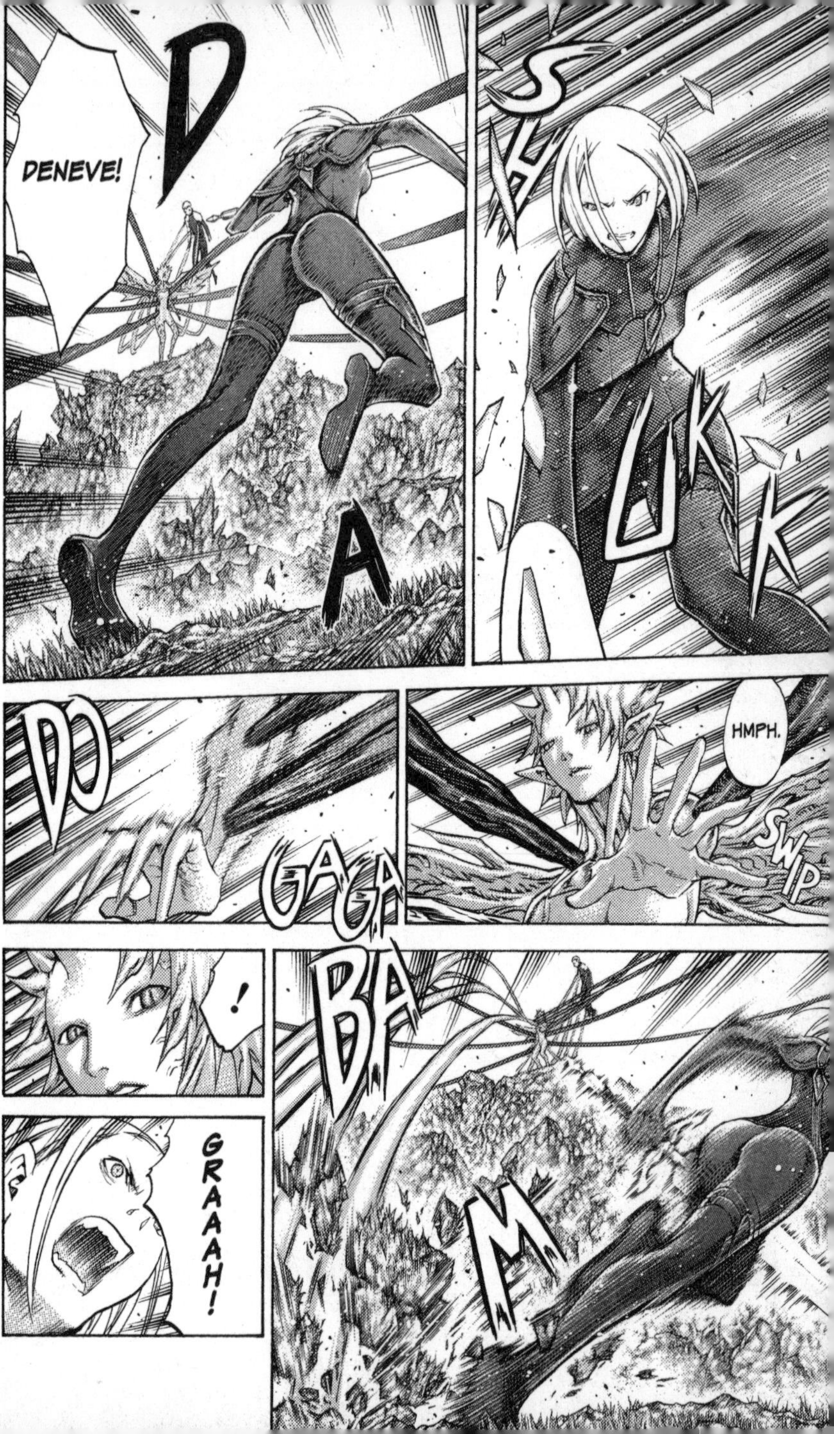
SHUKK
DENEVE!
DA
HMPH.
SWIP
DO
GAGA
BA
M
!
GRAAAH!

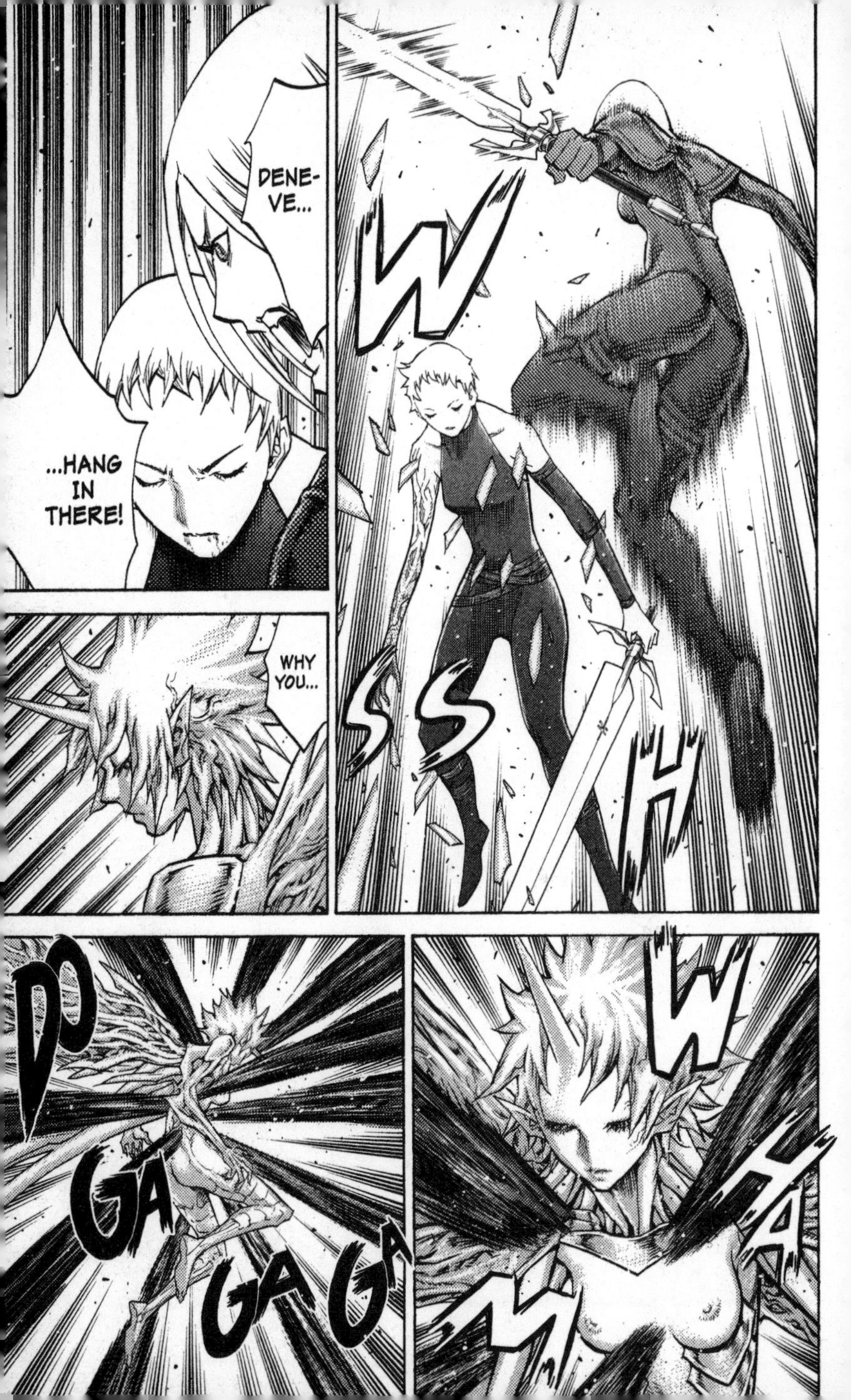
WSSH
DENE-VE...
...HANG IN THERE!
WHY YOU...
WHAM
DOGAGAGA

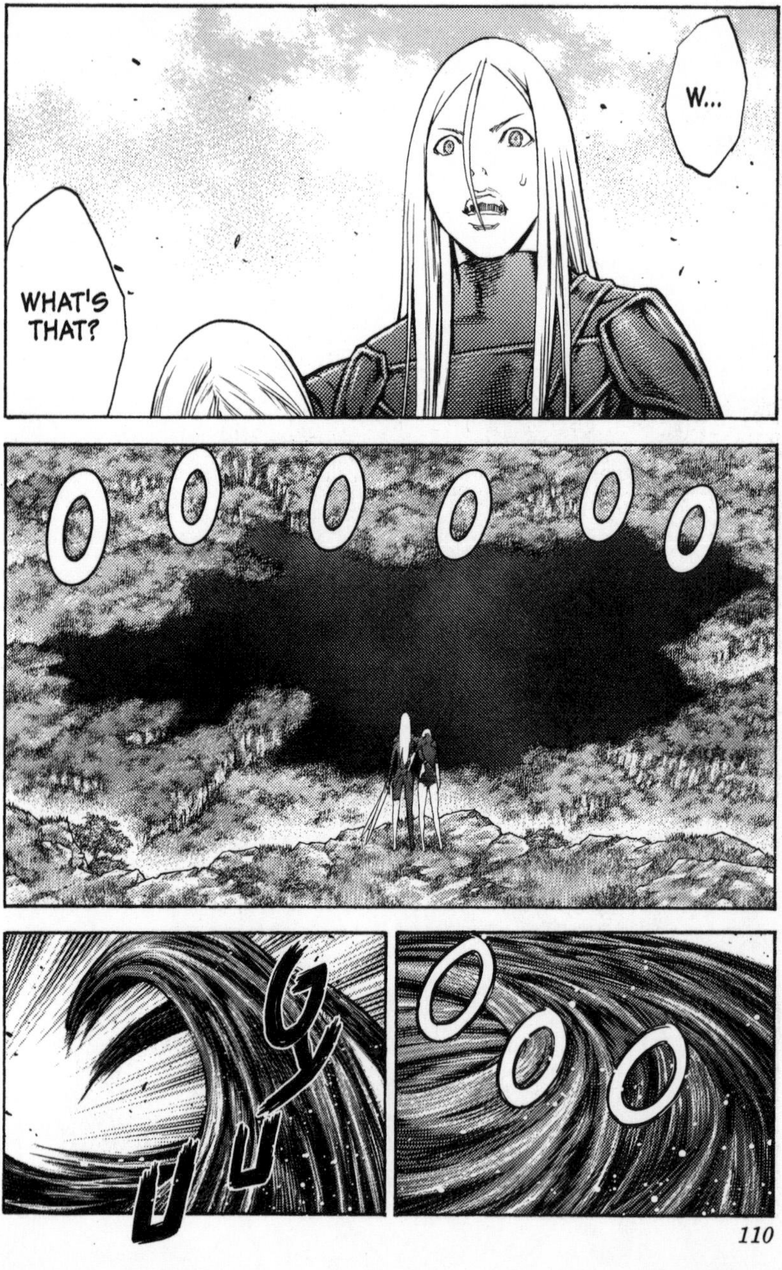
W...
WHAT'S THAT?
OOOOOOO
OOOO

READ THIS WAY

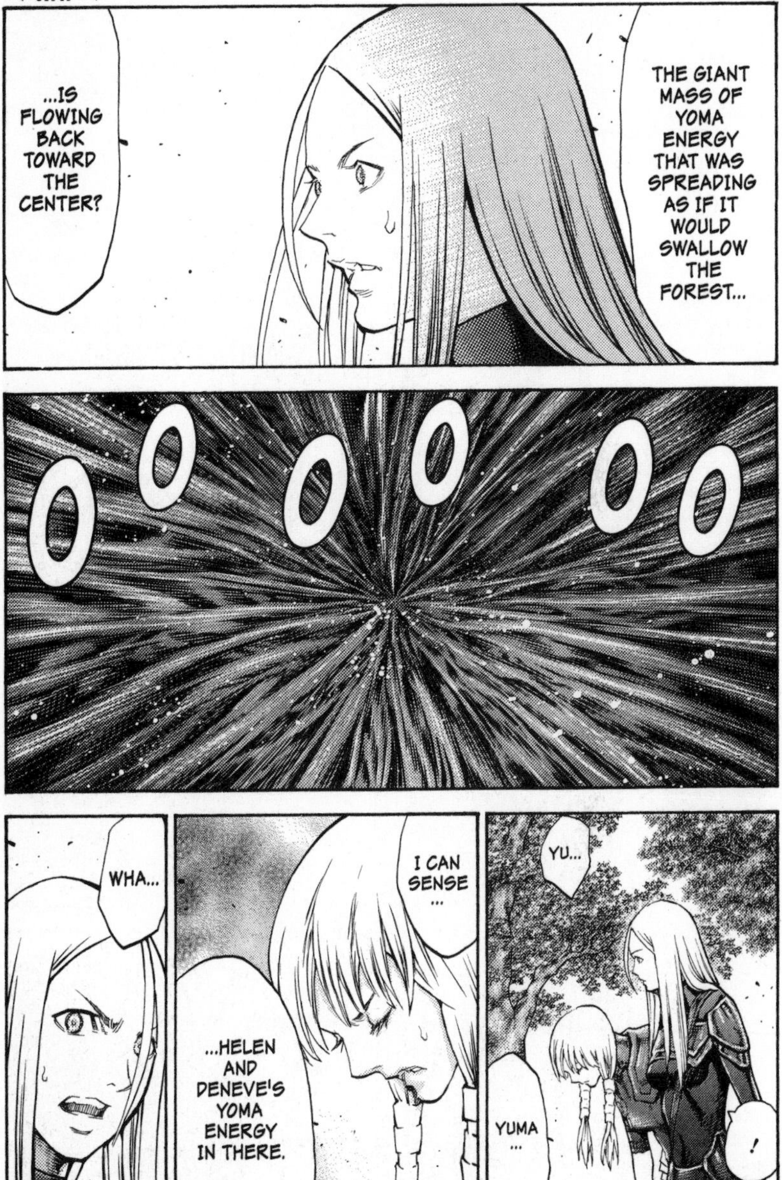
THE GIANT MASS OF YOMA ENERGY THAT WAS SPREADING AS IF IT WOULD SWALLOW THE FOREST...
...IS FLOWING BACK TOWARD THE CENTER?
OOOOOO
YU...
YUMA...
!
I CAN SENSE...
...HELEN AND DENEVE'S YOMA ENERGY IN THERE.
WHA...

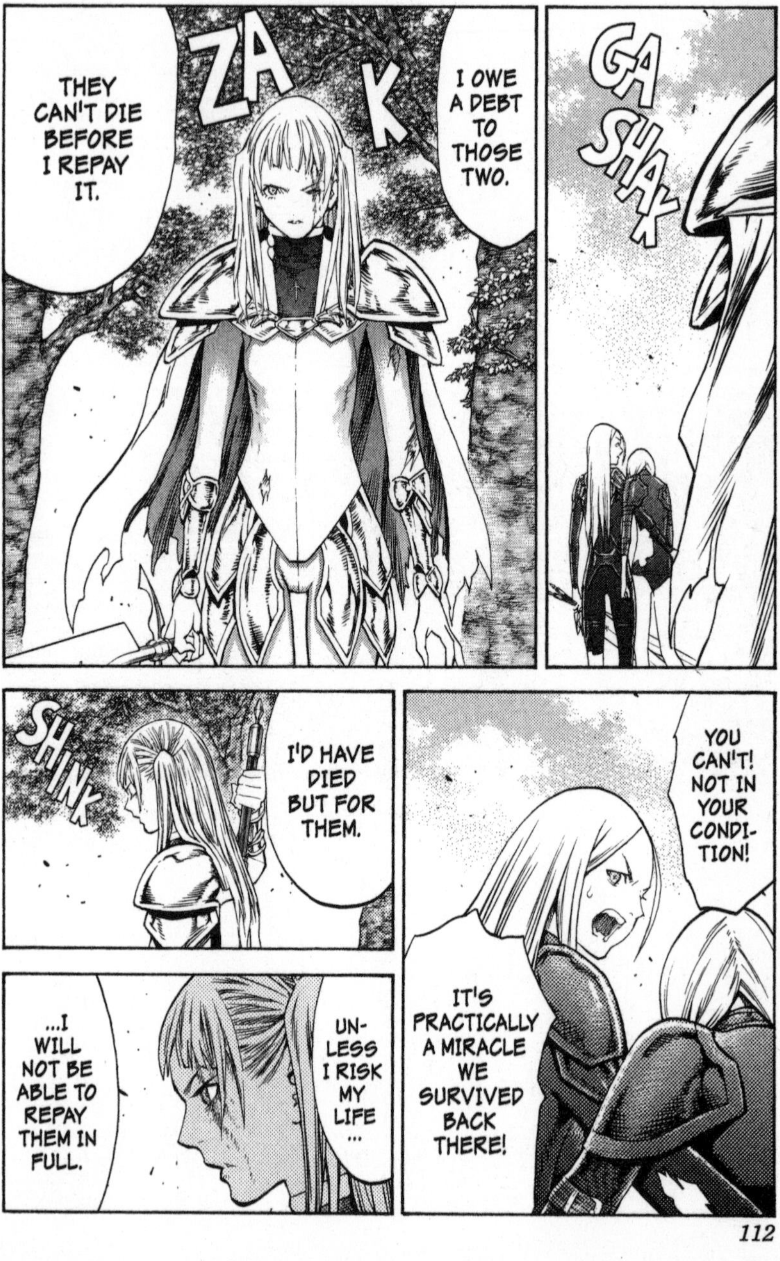
GA SHAK
I OWE A DEBT TO THOSE TWO.
ZA K
THEY CAN'T DIE BEFORE I REPAY IT.
YOU CAN'T! NOT IN YOUR CONDITION!
IT'S PRACTICALLY A MIRACLE WE SURVIVED BACK THERE!
SHINK
I'D HAVE DIED BUT FOR THEM.
UNLESS I RISK MY LIFE...
...I WILL NOT BE ABLE TO REPAY THEM IN FULL.

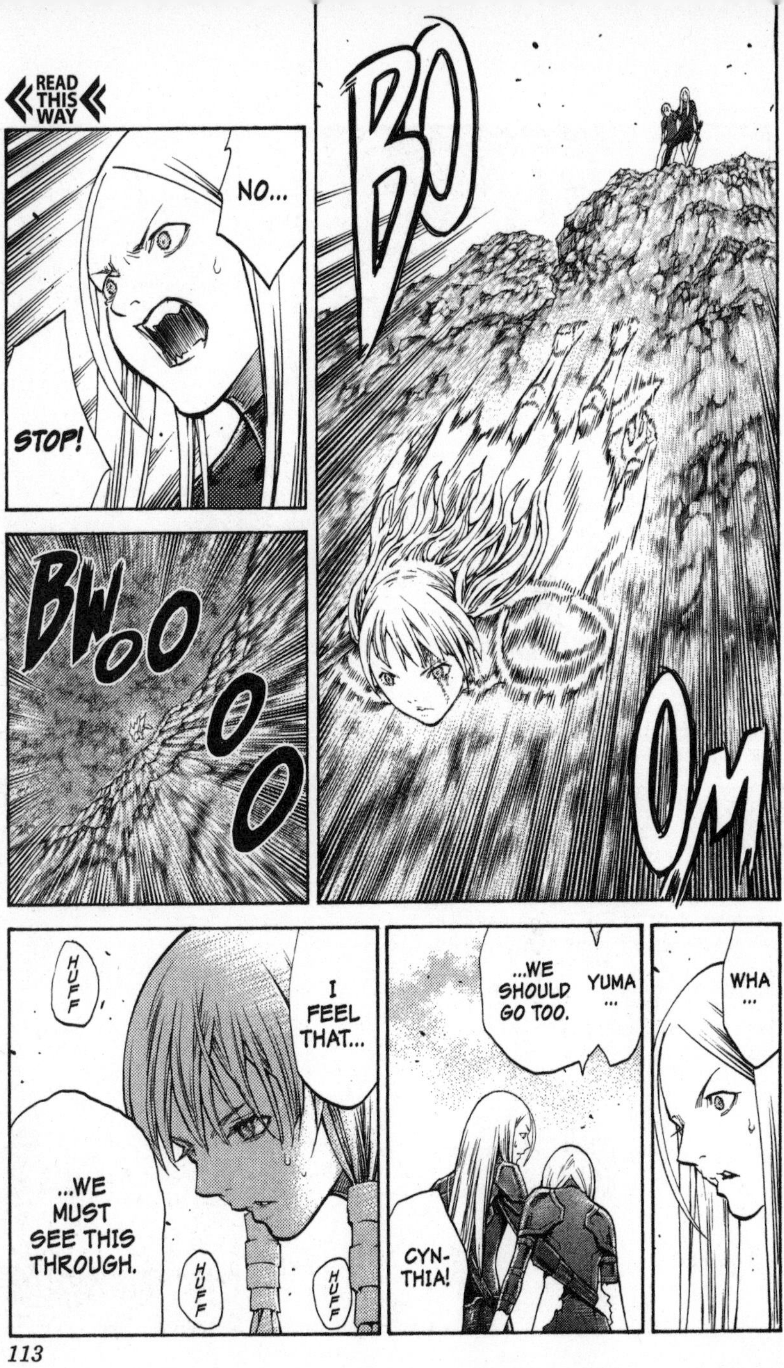
READ THIS WAY
BOOM
NO...
STOP!
BWOOOOO
WHA ...
YUMA ...
...WE SHOULD GO TOO.
CYN-THIA!
I FEEL THAT...
...WE MUST SEE THIS THROUGH.
HUFF
HUFF
HUFF

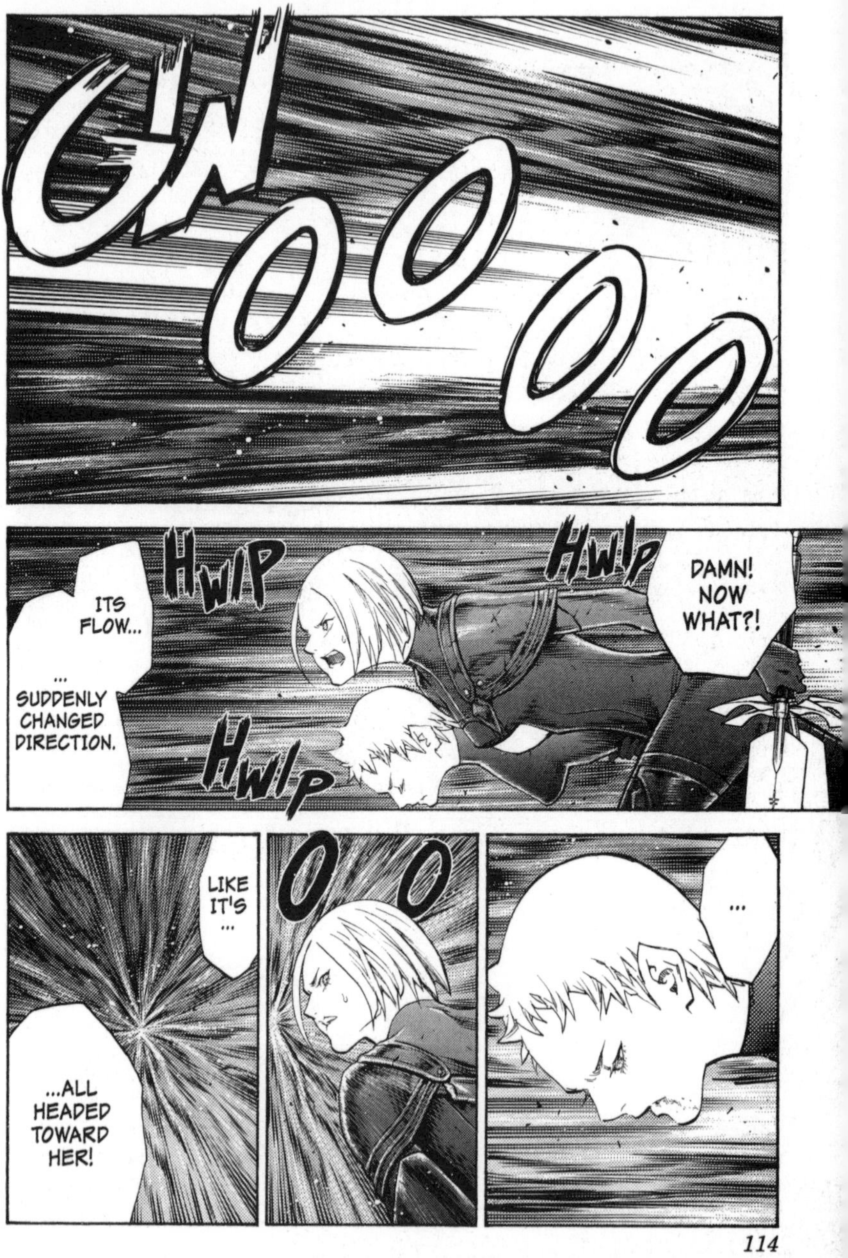
GWOOOOOO
HWIP
DAMN! NOW WHAT?!
HWIP
ITS FLOW...
HWIP
... SUDDENLY CHANGED DIRECTION.
...
OO
LIKE IT'S ...
...ALL HEADED TOWARD HER!

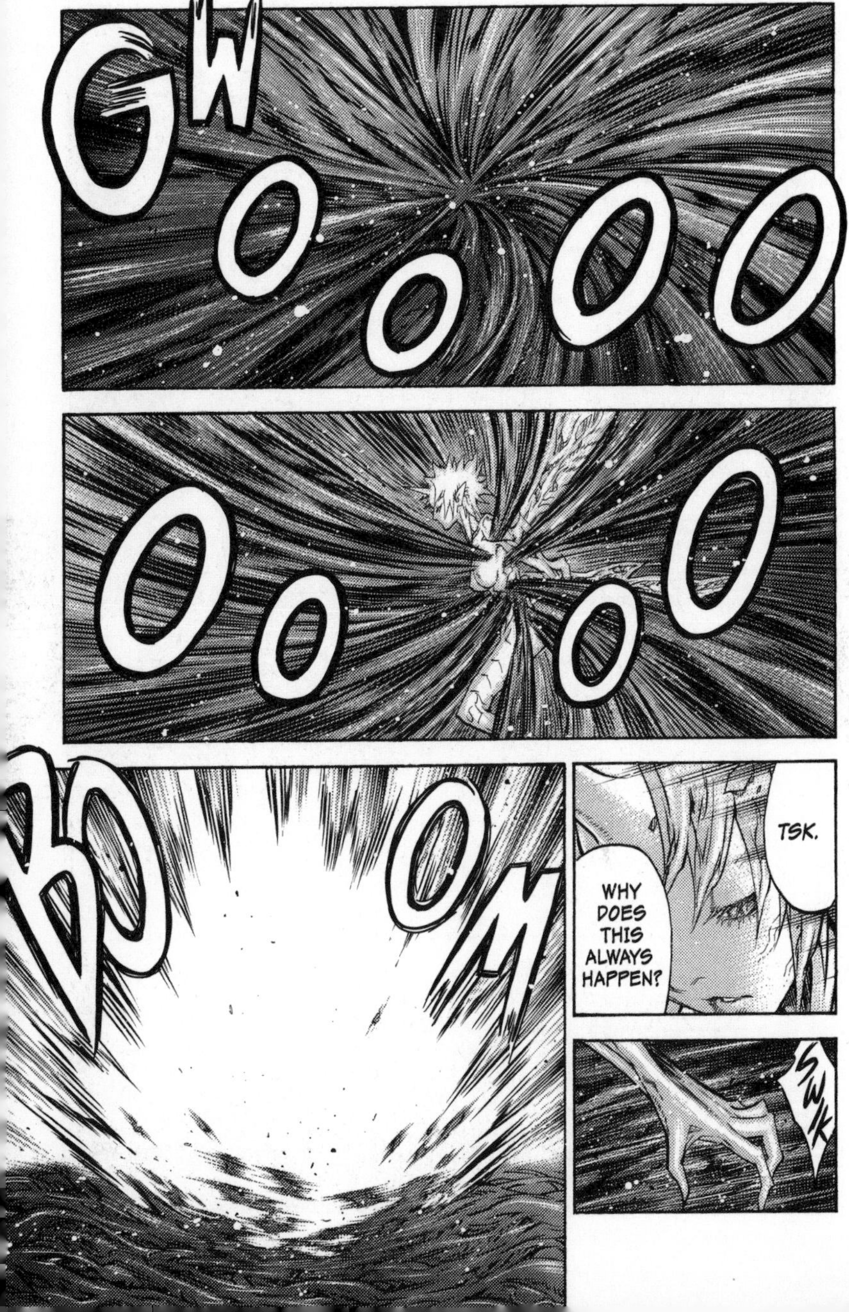
GWOOOO
OOOO
TSK.
WHY DOES THIS ALWAYS HAPPEN?
SWIK
BOOM

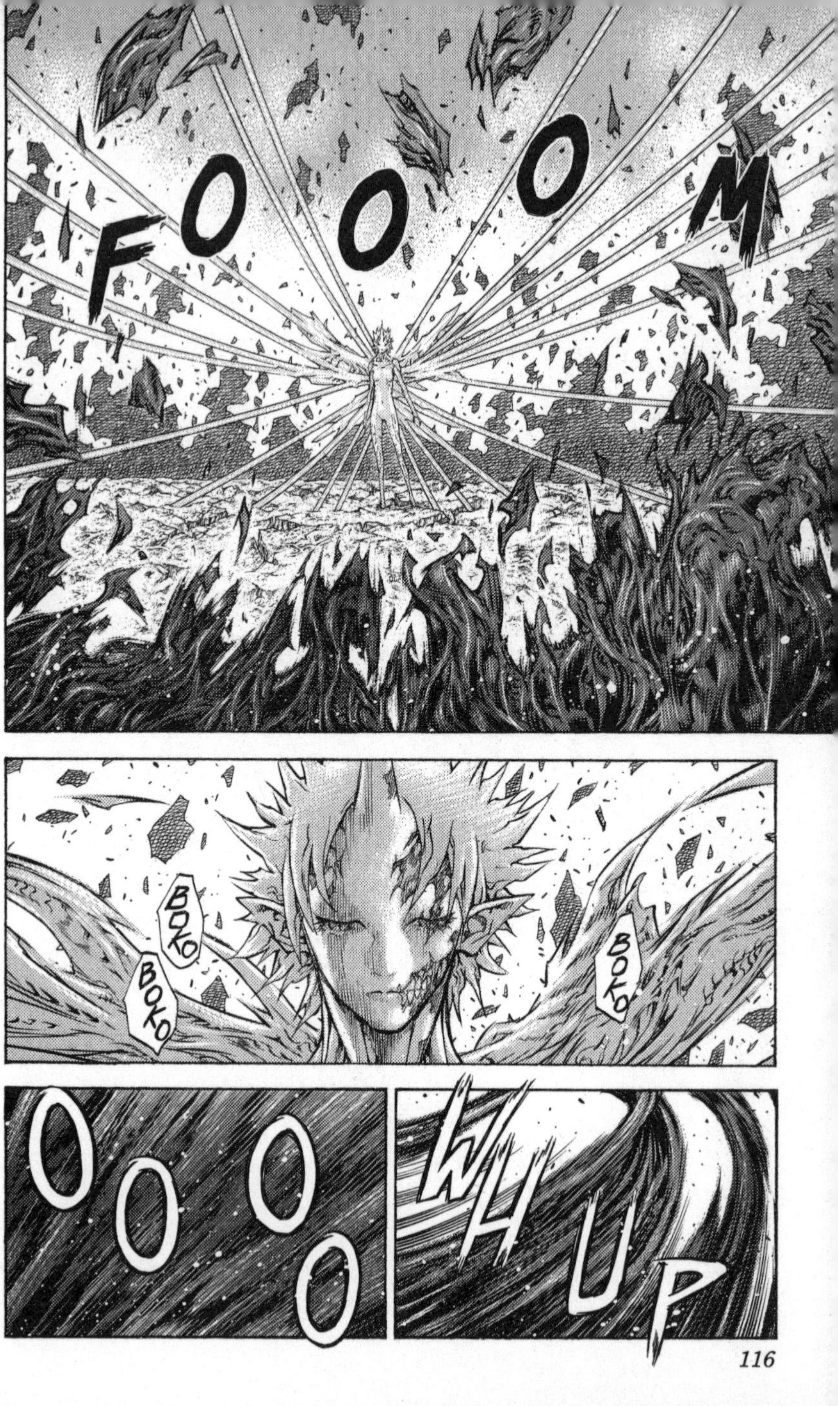
FOOOM
BOKO
BOKO
BOKO
WHUP
OOOO

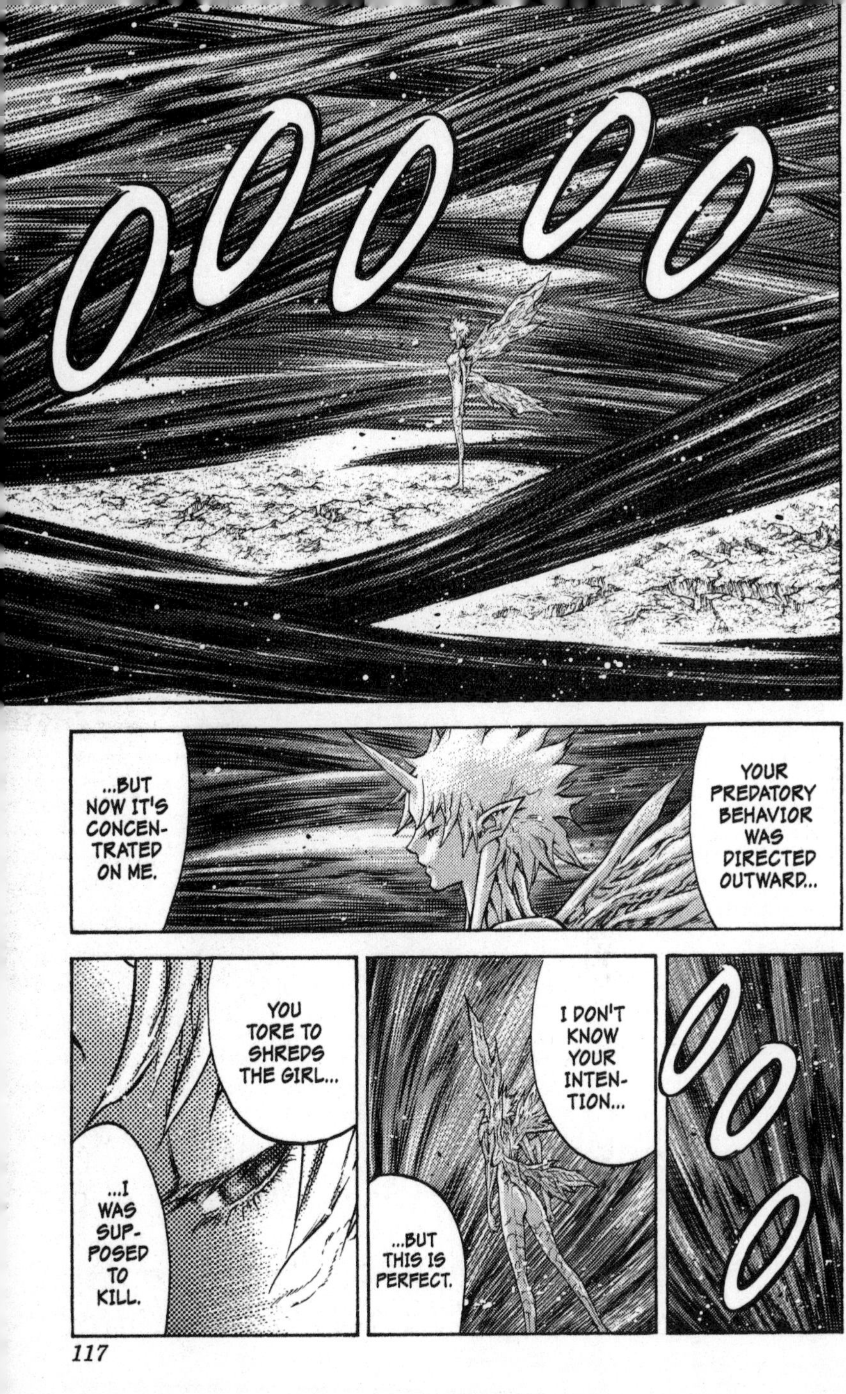
OOOOO
YOUR PREDATORY BEHAVIOR WAS DIRECTED OUTWARD...
...BUT NOW IT'S CONCEN-TRATED ON ME.
OOO
I DON'T KNOW YOUR INTEN-TION...
...BUT THIS IS PERFECT.
YOU TORE TO SHREDS THE GIRL...
...I WAS SUP-POSED TO KILL.

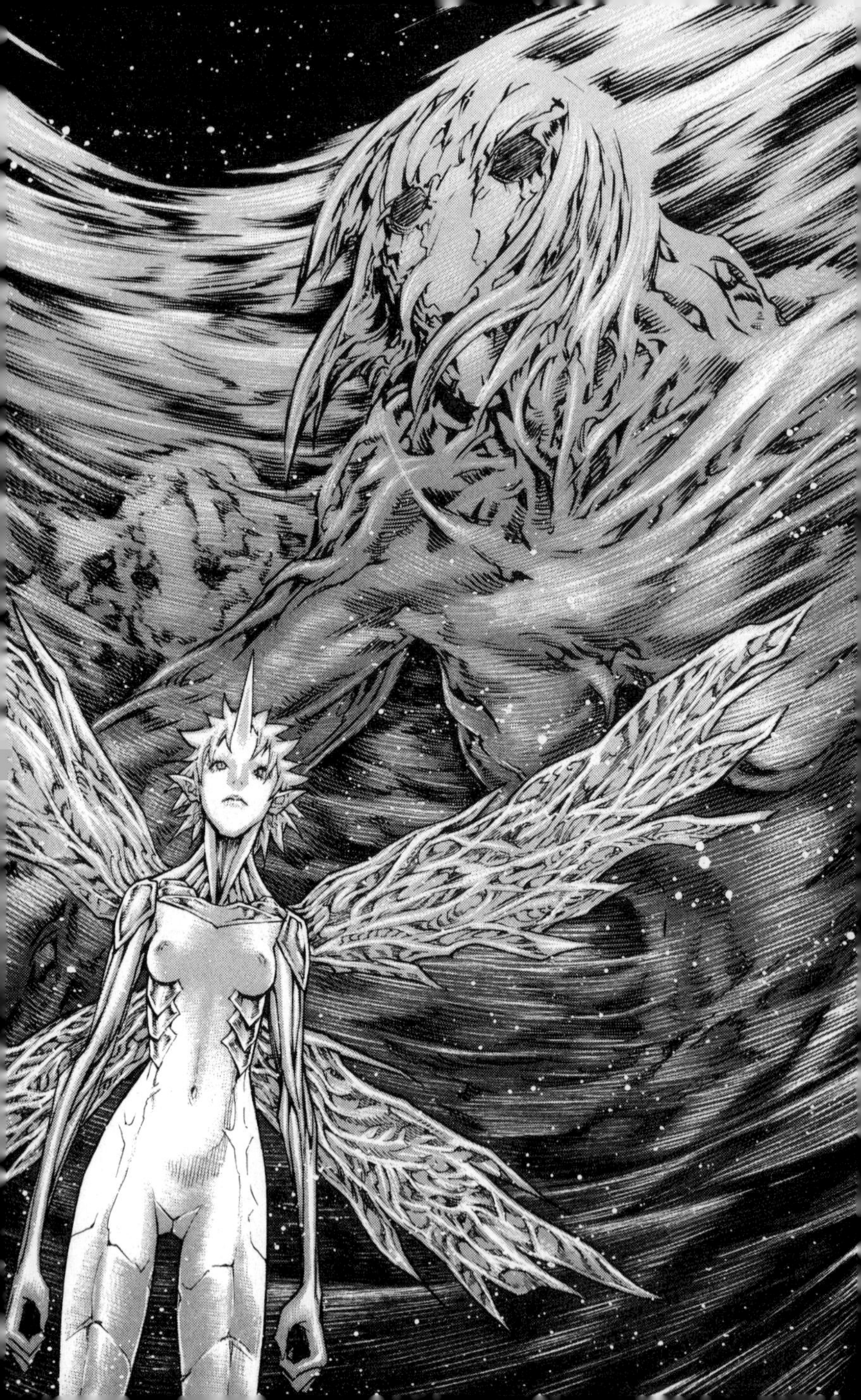

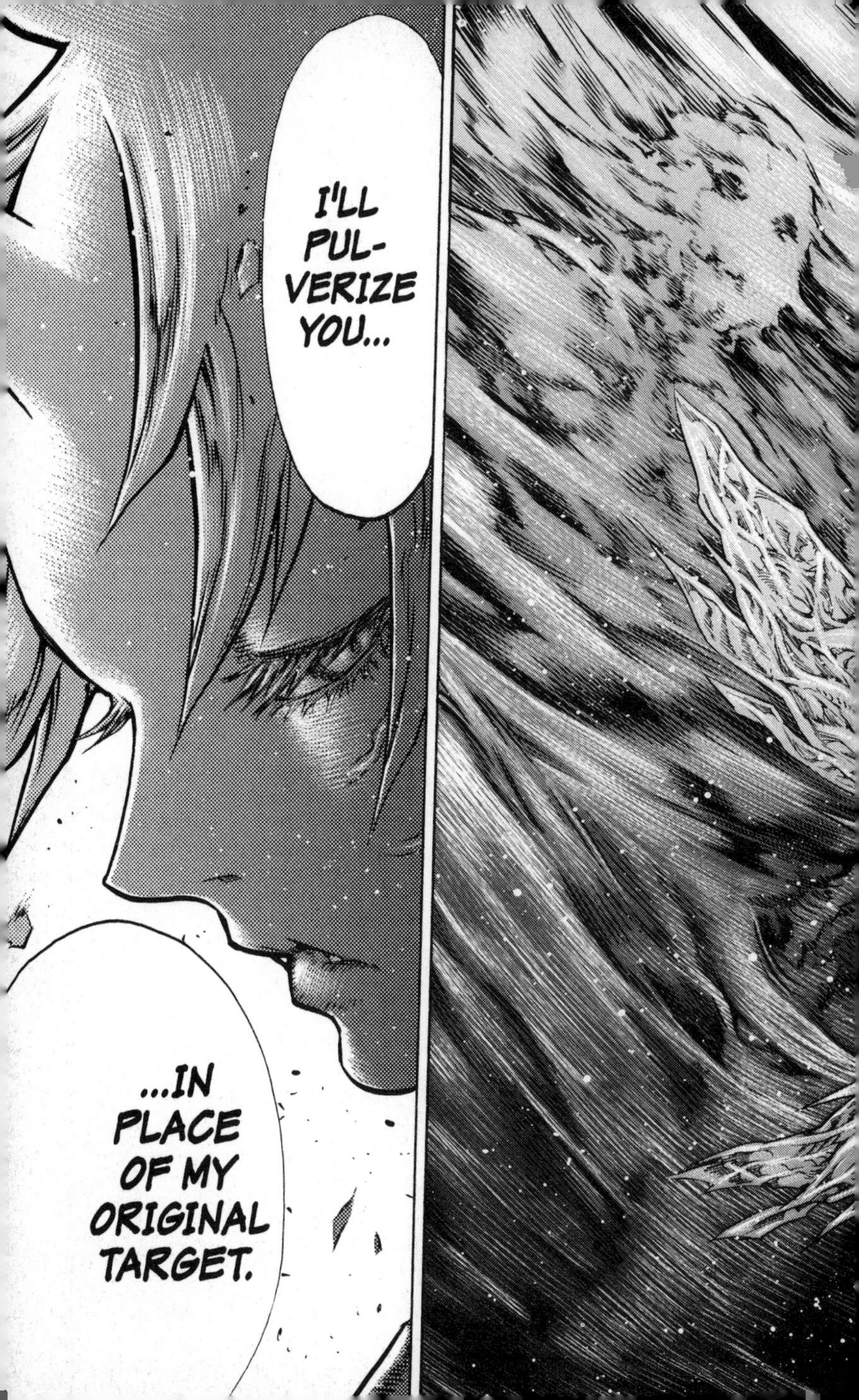
I'LL PUL-VERIZE YOU...
...IN PLACE OF MY ORIGINAL TARGET.

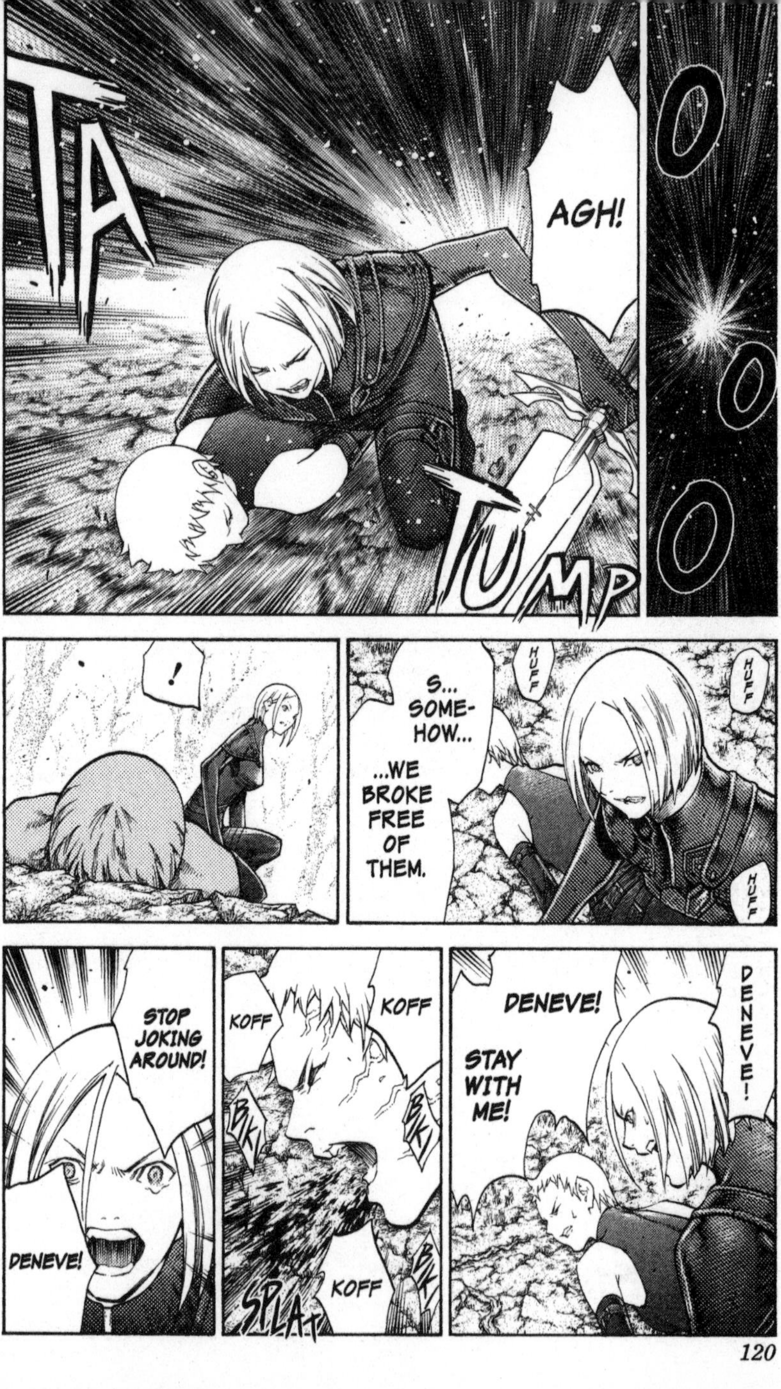
OOO
AGH!
TA
TUMP
HUFF
S... SOME-HOW...
...WE BROKE FREE OF THEM.
HUFF
HUFF
!
DENEVE!
DENEVE!
STAY WITH ME!
KOFF
KOFF
BIKI
BIKI
BIKI
KOFF
SPLAT
STOP JOKING AROUND!
DENEVE!

« READ THIS WAY «

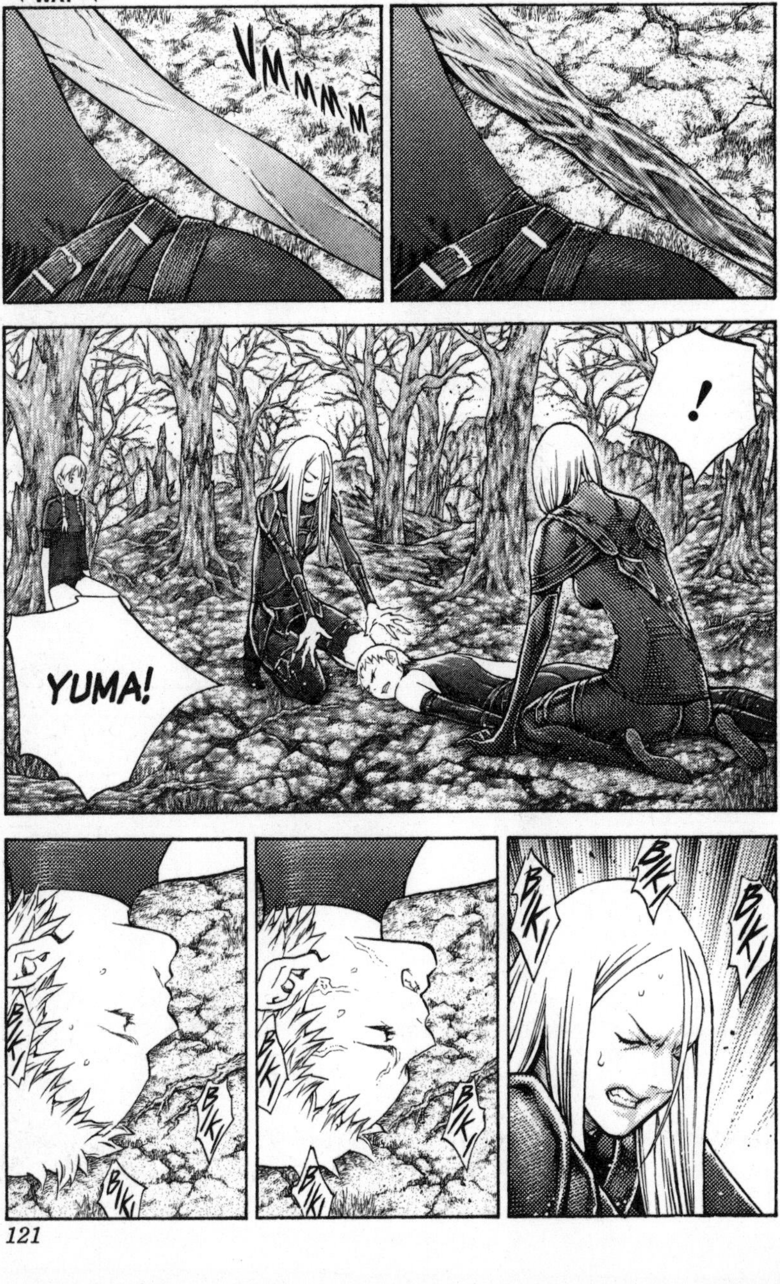
VMMMM
!
YUMA!
BIKI
BIKI
BIKI
BIKI
BIKI
BIKI
BIKI
BIKI

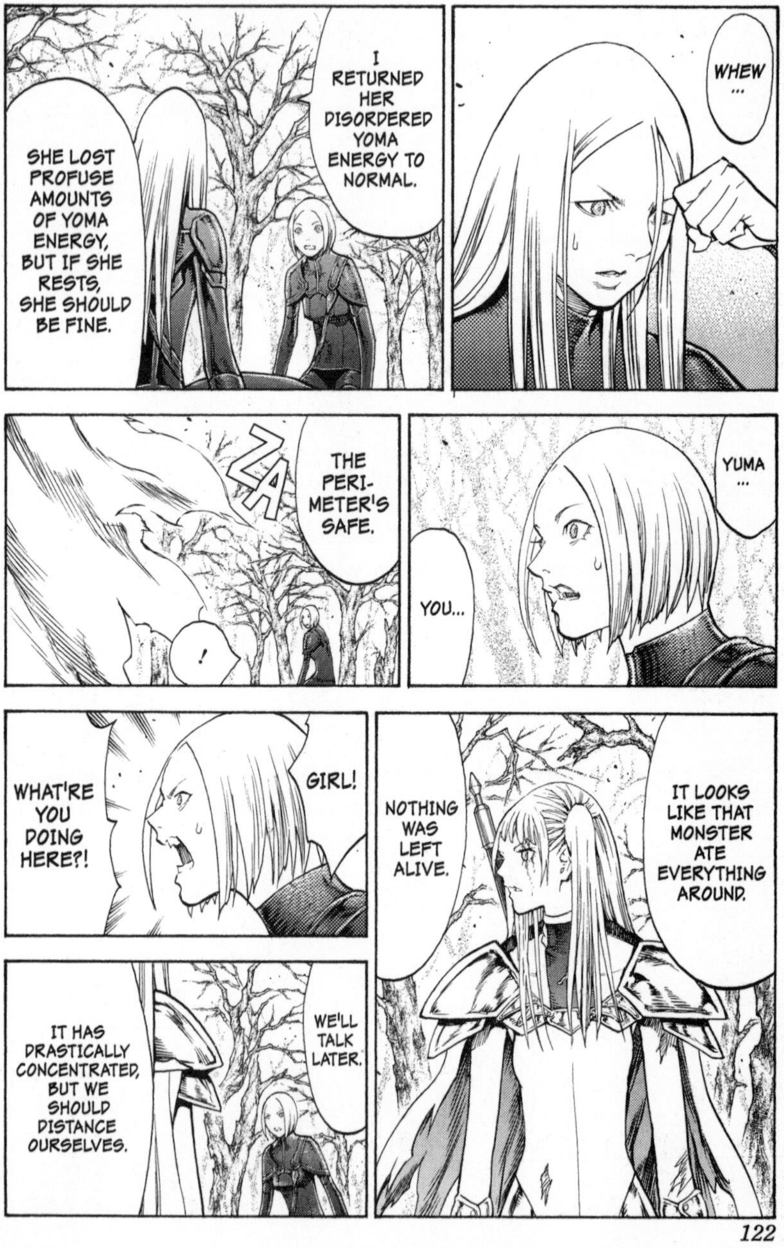
WHEW...
I RETURNED HER DISORDERED YOMA ENERGY TO NORMAL.
SHE LOST PROFUSE AMOUNTS OF YOMA ENERGY, BUT IF SHE RESTS, SHE SHOULD BE FINE.
YUMA...
YOU...
THE PERI-METER'S SAFE.
ZA
!
IT LOOKS LIKE THAT MONSTER ATE EVERYTHING AROUND.
NOTHING WAS LEFT ALIVE.
GIRL!
WHAT'RE YOU DOING HERE?!
WE'LL TALK LATER.
IT HAS DRASTICALLY CONCENTRATED, BUT WE SHOULD DISTANCE OURSELVES.

READ THIS WAY

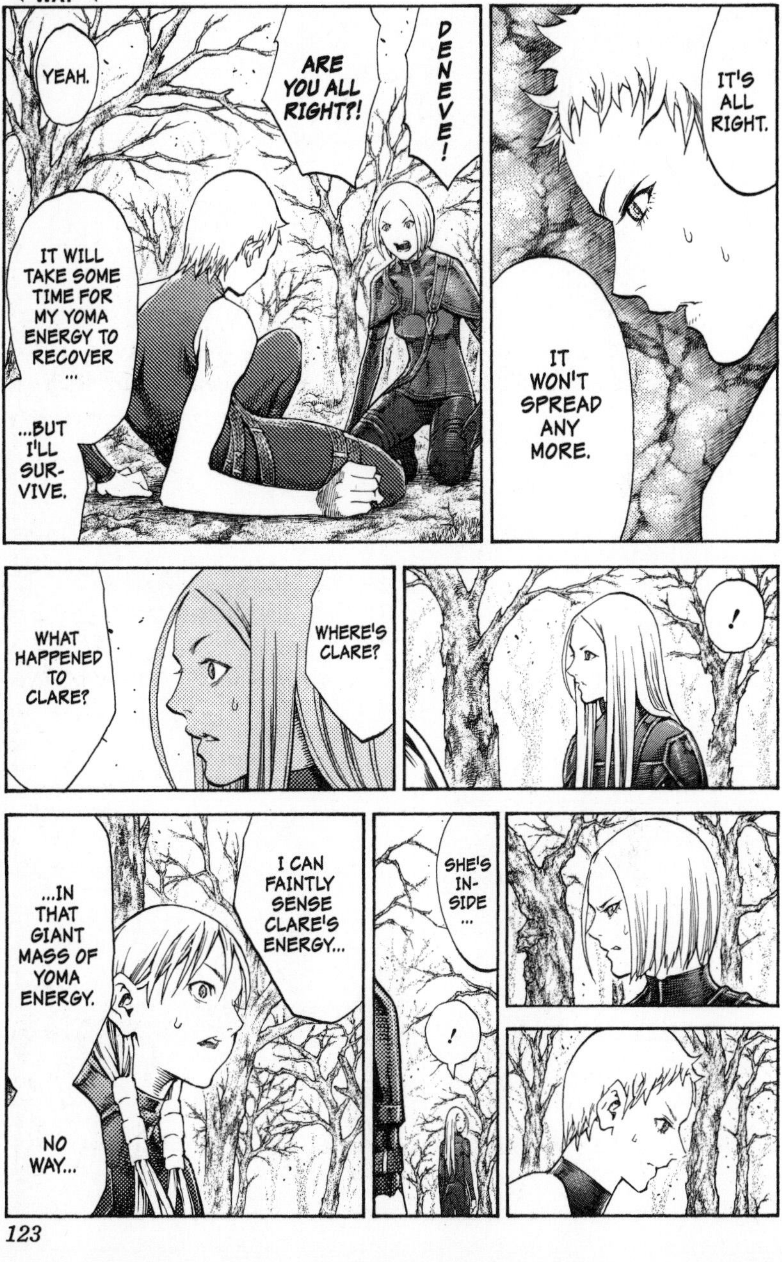

IT'S ALL RIGHT.
IT WON'T SPREAD ANY MORE.
DENEVE!
ARE YOU ALL RIGHT?!
YEAH.
IT WILL TAKE SOME TIME FOR MY YOMA ENERGY TO RECOVER ...
...BUT I'LL SUR-VIVE.
!
WHERE'S CLARE?
WHAT HAPPENED TO CLARE?
SHE'S IN-SIDE ...
!
I CAN FAINTLY SENSE CLARE'S ENERGY...
...IN THAT GIANT MASS OF YOMA ENERGY.
NO WAY...

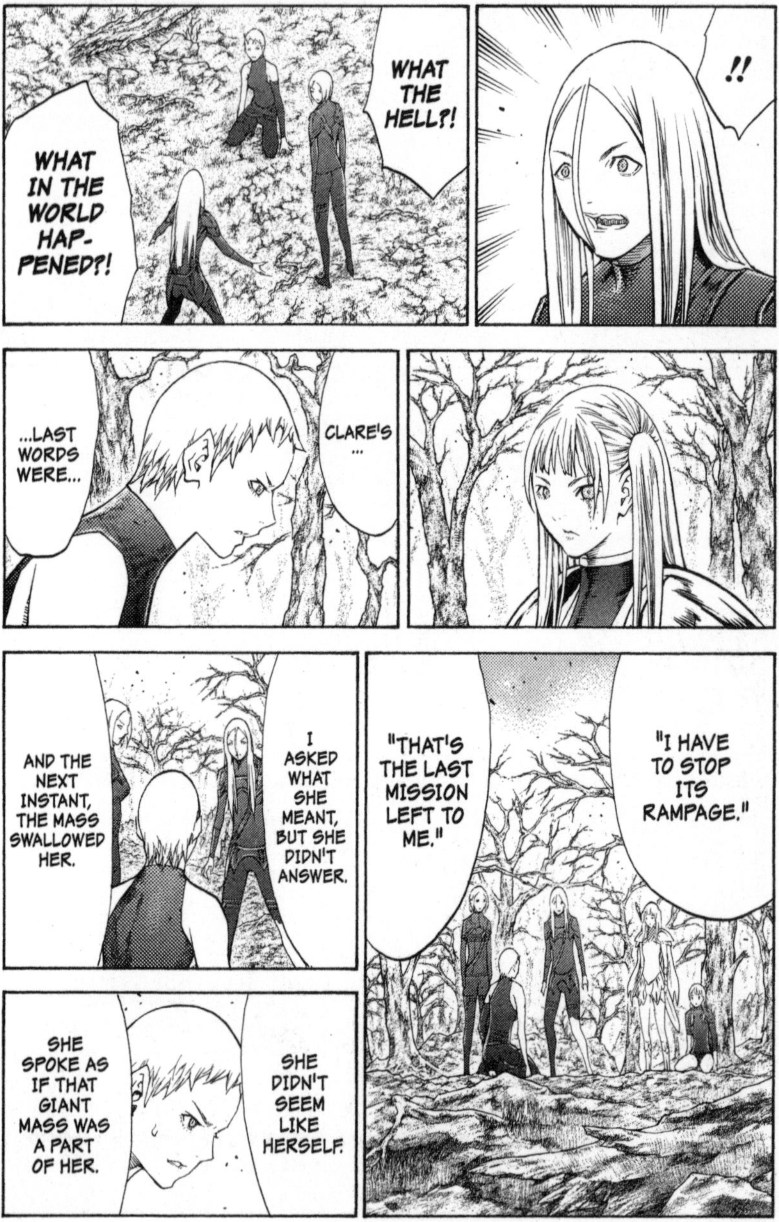
!!
WHAT THE HELL?!
WHAT IN THE WORLD HAP-PENED?!
CLARE'S ...
...LAST WORDS WERE...
"I HAVE TO STOP ITS RAMPAGE."
"THAT'S THE LAST MISSION LEFT TO ME."
I ASKED WHAT SHE MEANT, BUT SHE DIDN'T ANSWER.
AND THE NEXT INSTANT, THE MASS SWALLOWED HER.
SHE DIDN'T SEEM LIKE HERSELF.
SHE SPOKE AS IF THAT GIANT MASS WAS A PART OF HER.

READ THIS WAY

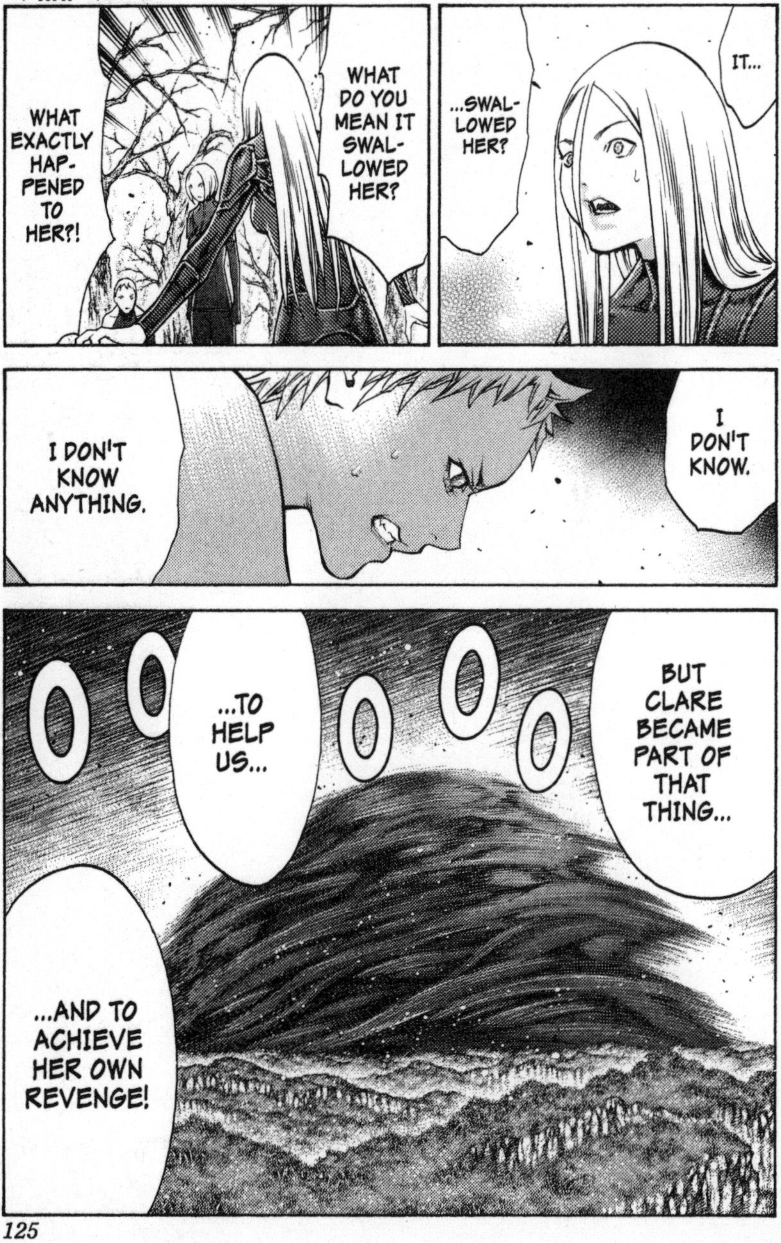
IT...
...SWALLOWED HER?
WHAT DO YOU MEAN IT SWALLOWED HER?
WHAT EXACTLY HAPPENED TO HER?!
I DON'T KNOW.
I DON'T KNOW ANYTHING.
BUT CLARE BECAME PART OF THAT THING...
...TO HELP US...
...AND TO ACHIEVE HER OWN REVENGE!

クレイモア

Claymore

Scene 106: Phantoms in the Heart, Part 1

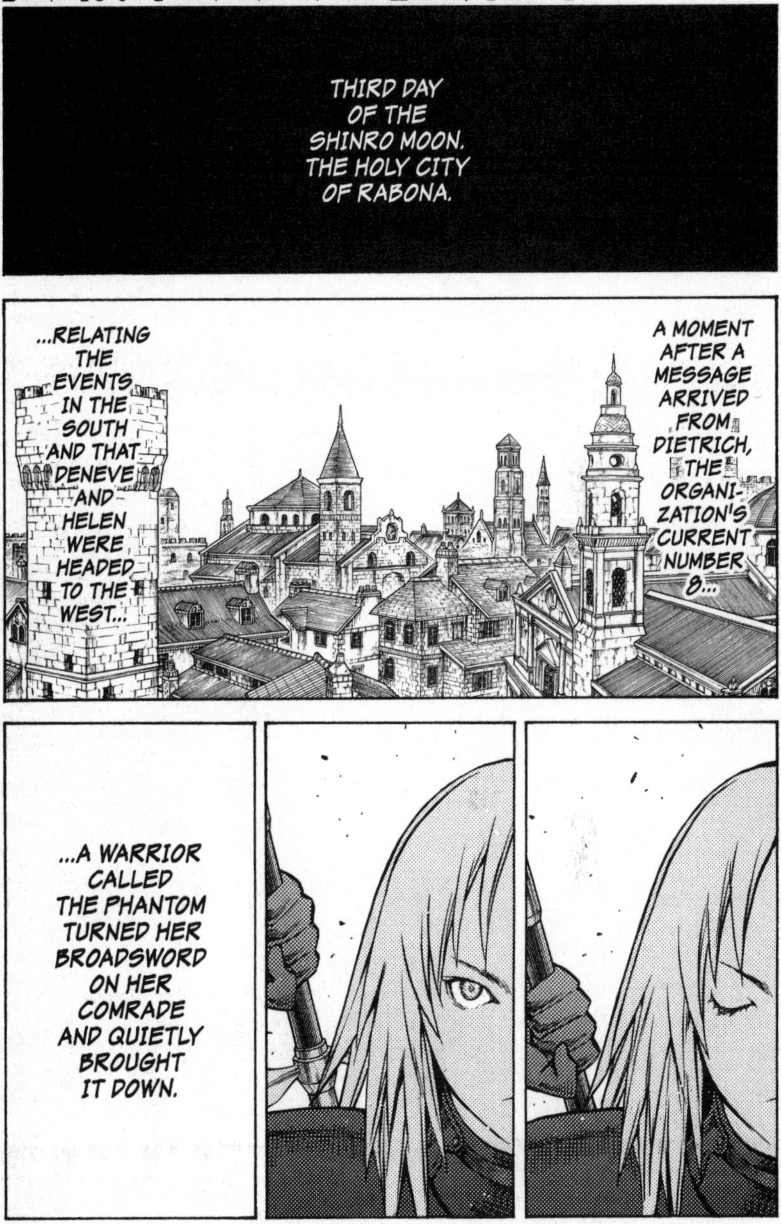
THIRD DAY OF THE SHINRO MOON. THE HOLY CITY OF RABONA.
A MOMENT AFTER A MESSAGE ARRIVED FROM DIETRICH, THE ORGANI-ZATION'S CURRENT NUMBER 8...
...RELATING THE EVENTS IN THE SOUTH AND THAT DENEVE AND HELEN WERE HEADED TO THE WEST...
...A WARRIOR CALLED THE PHANTOM TURNED HER BROADSWORD ON HER COMRADE AND QUIETLY BROUGHT IT DOWN.

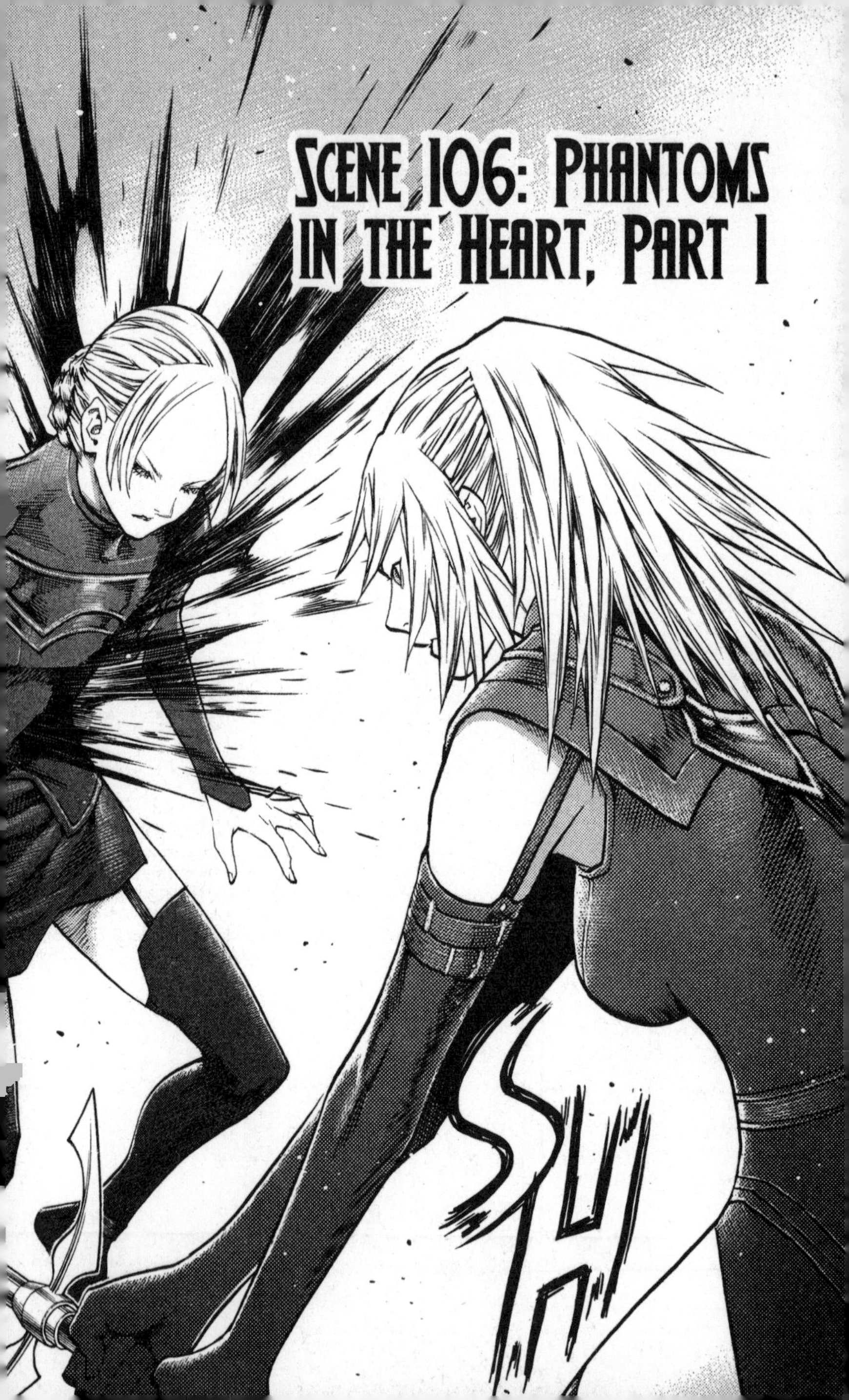
Scene 106: Phantoms in the Heart, Part 1
SHH

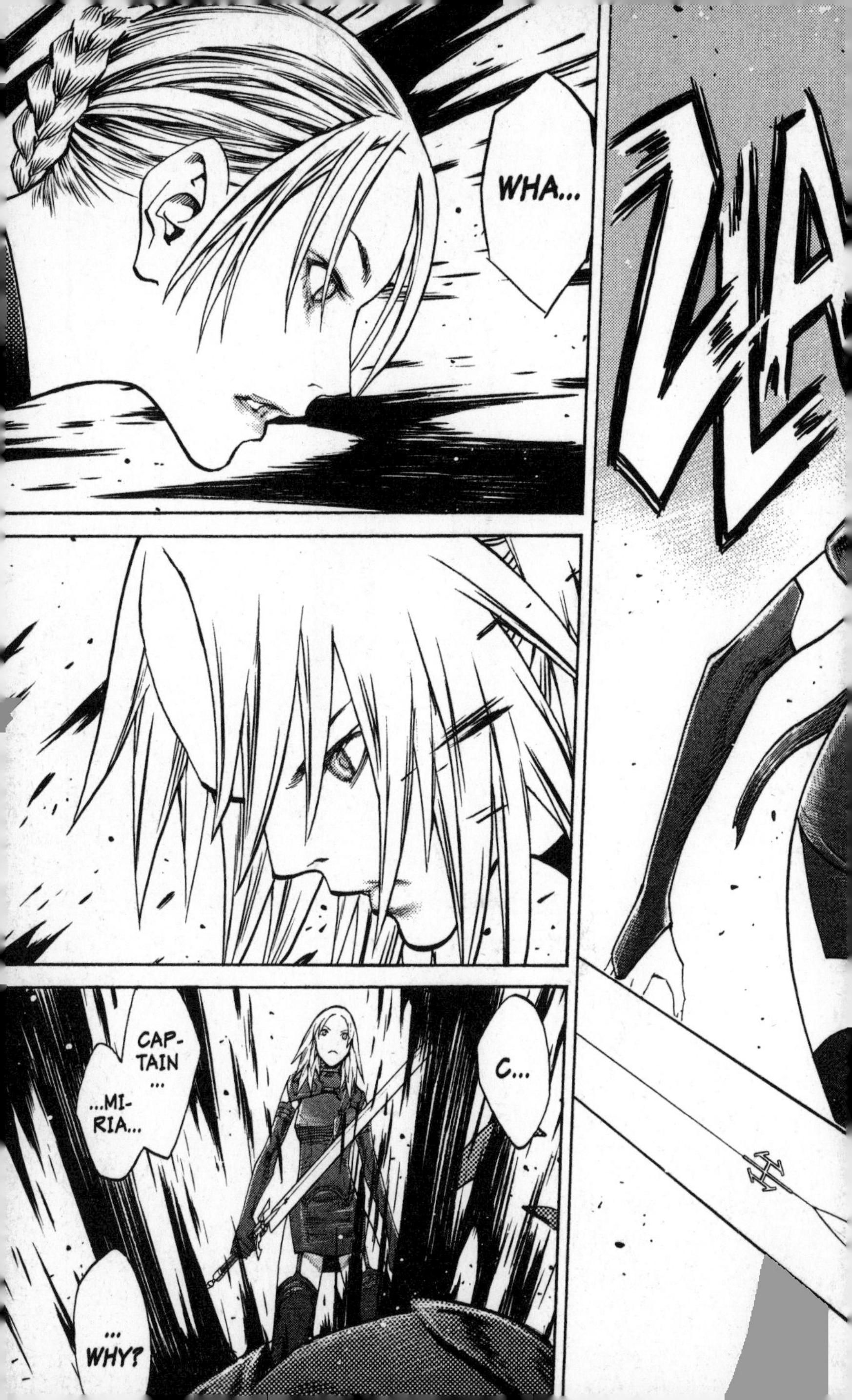
WHA...
C...
CAP-TAIN ...
...MI-RIA...
... WHY?

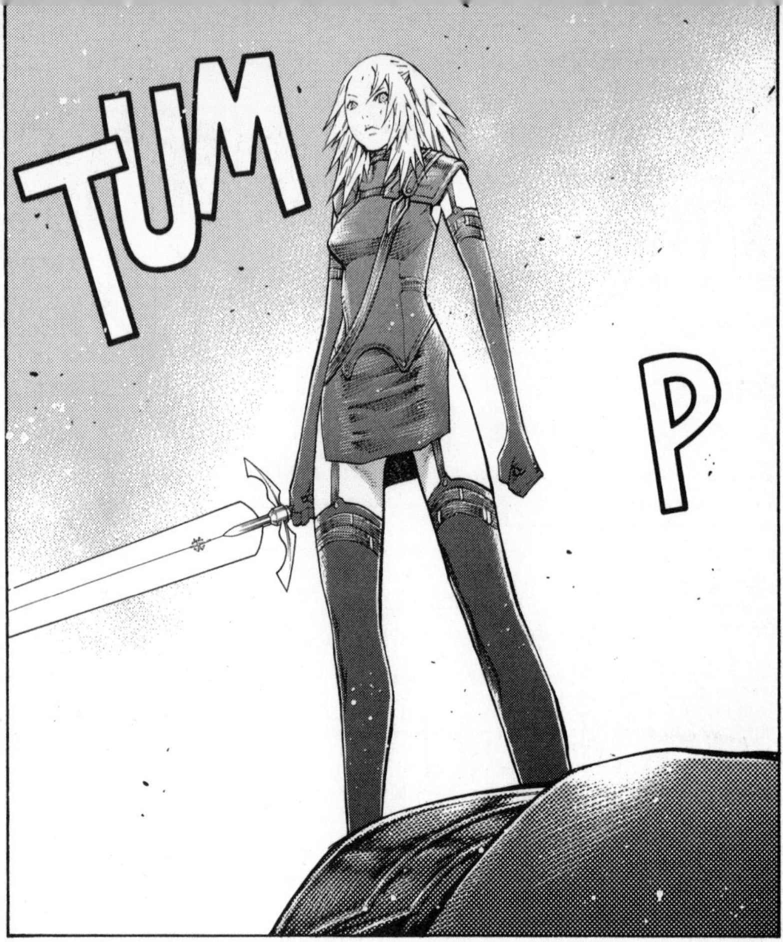
TUM
P

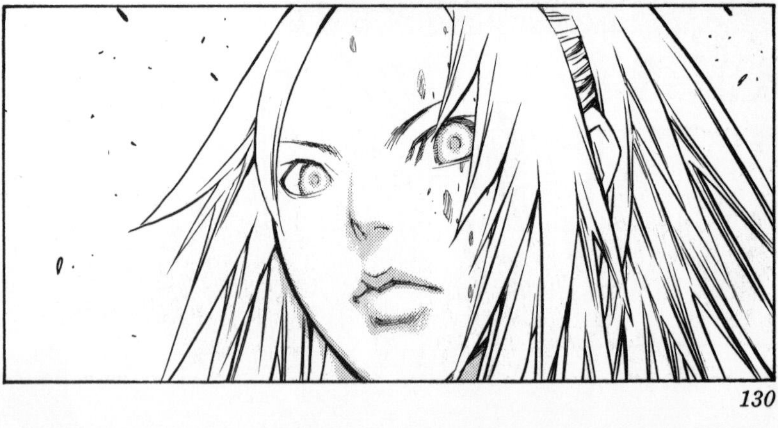

READ THIS WAY

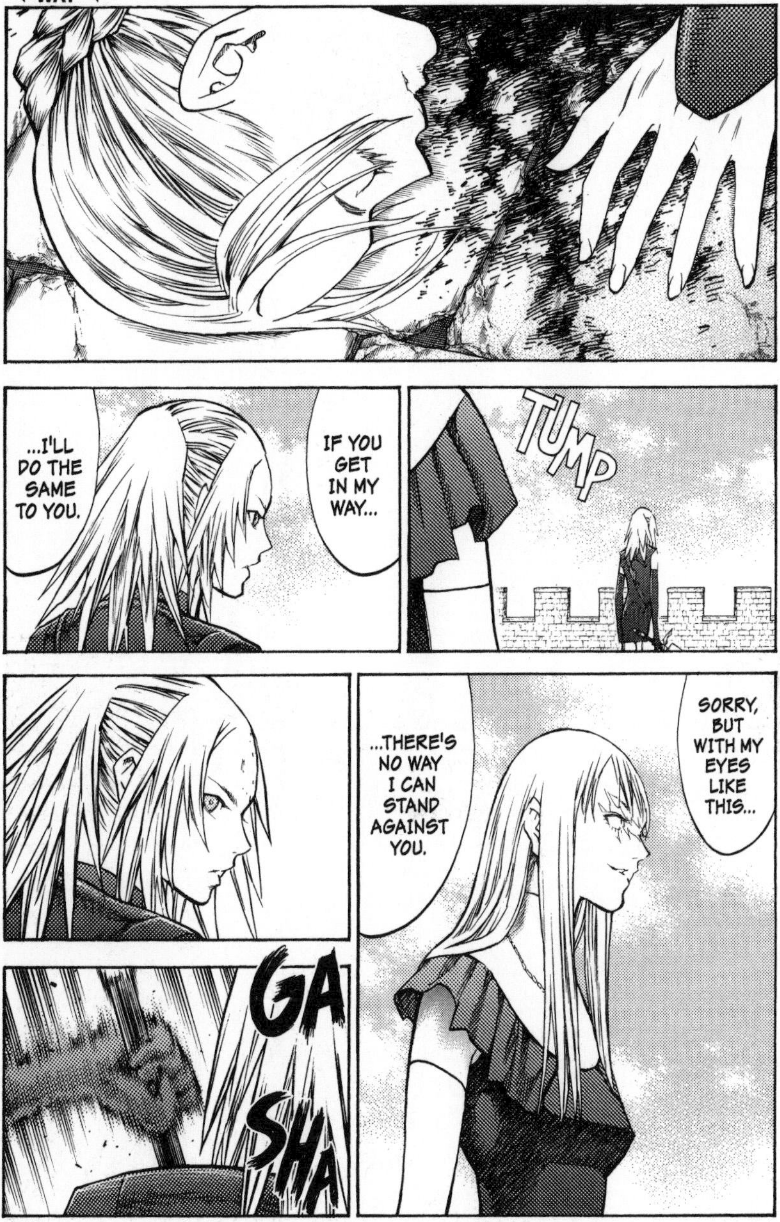
TUMP
IF YOU GET IN MY WAY...
...I'LL DO THE SAME TO YOU.
SORRY, BUT WITH MY EYES LIKE THIS...
...THERE'S NO WAY I CAN STAND AGAINST YOU.
GASHA

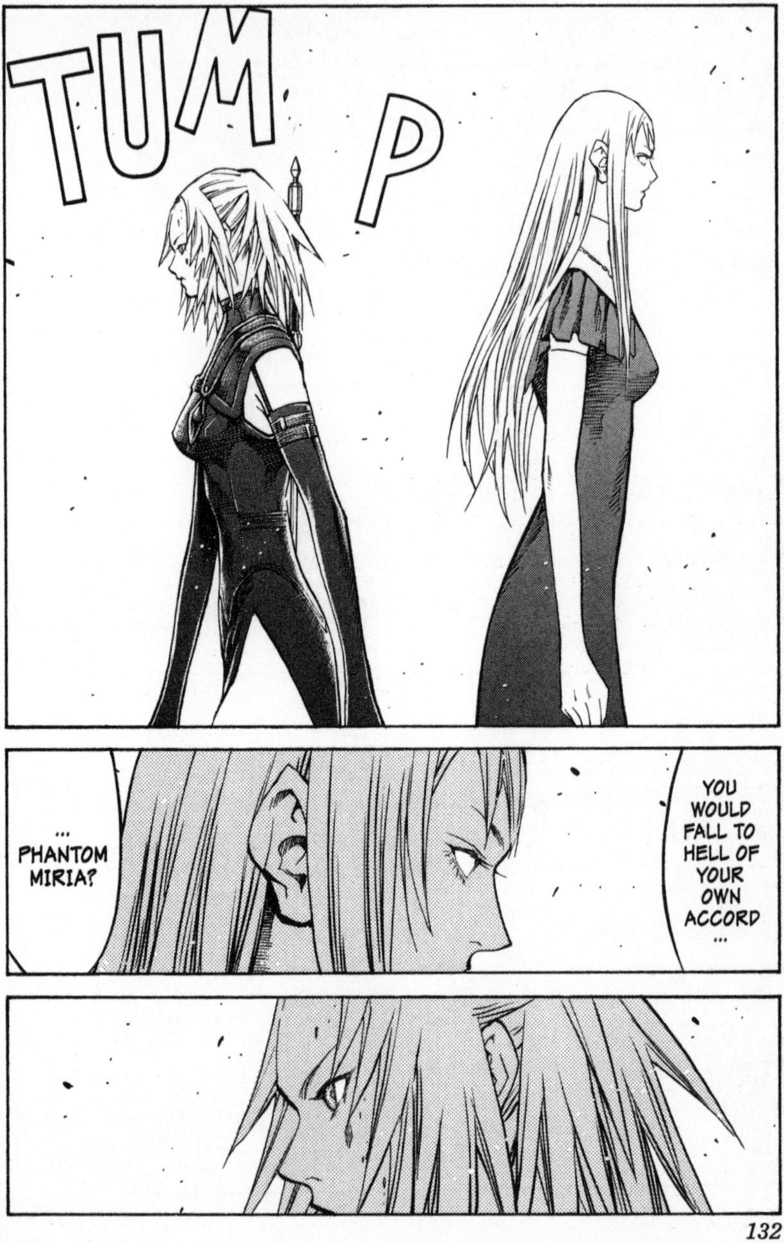
TUMP
YOU WOULD FALL TO HELL OF YOUR OWN ACCORD ...
... PHANTOM MIRIA?

READ THIS WAY

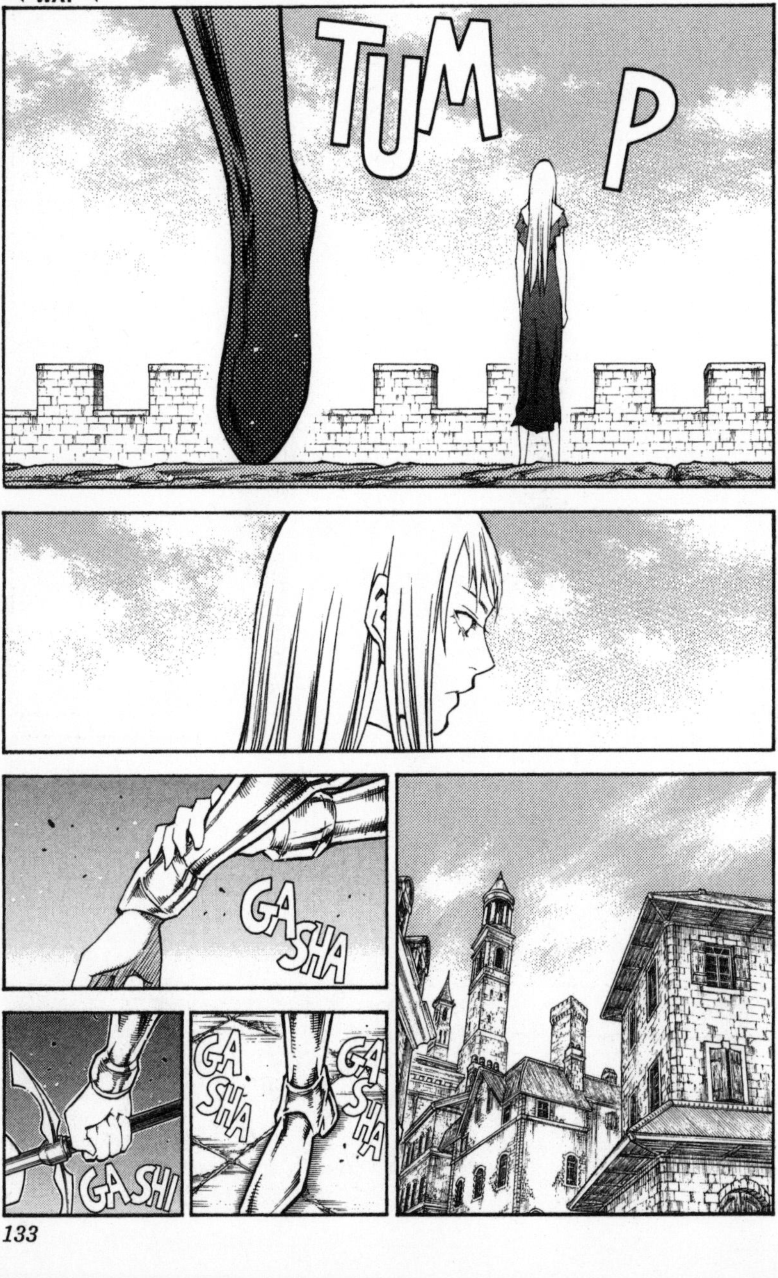
TUMP
GASHA
GASHA
GASHA
GASHI

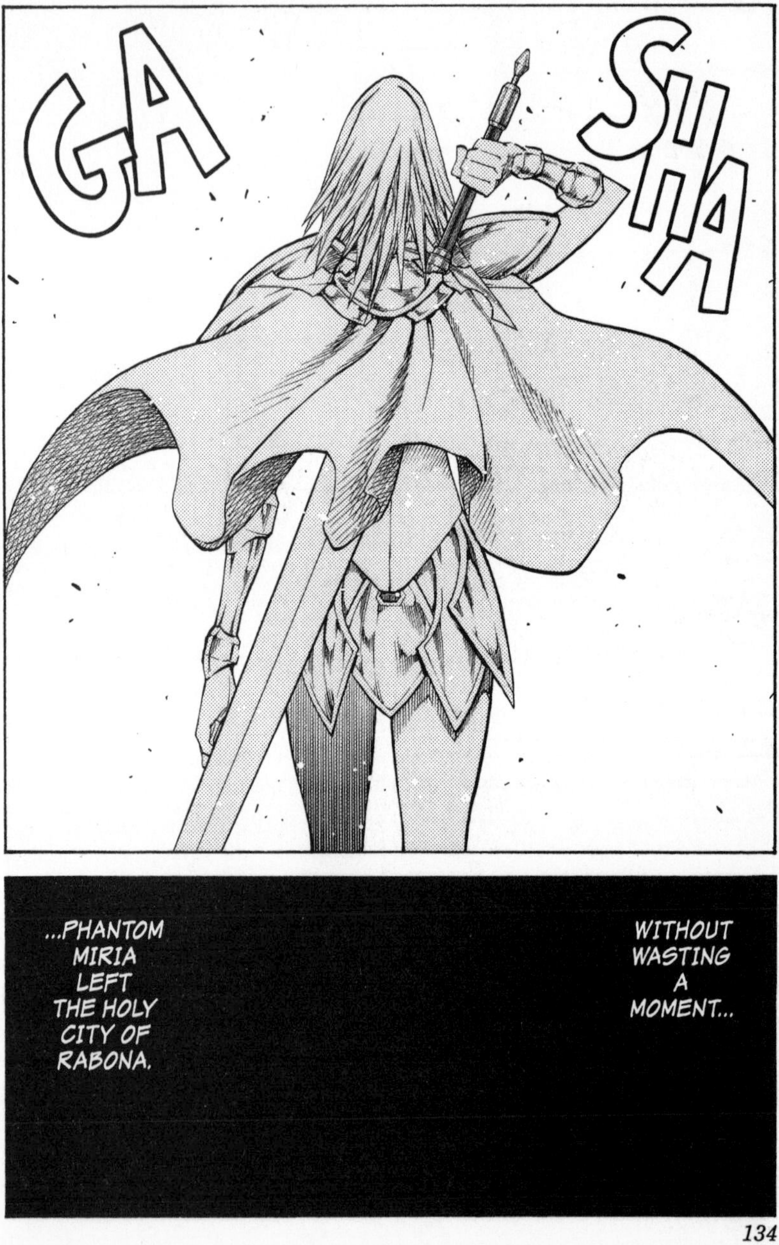
GA SHA
WITHOUT WASTING A MOMENT...
...PHANTOM MIRIA LEFT THE HOLY CITY OF RABONA.

READ THIS WAY

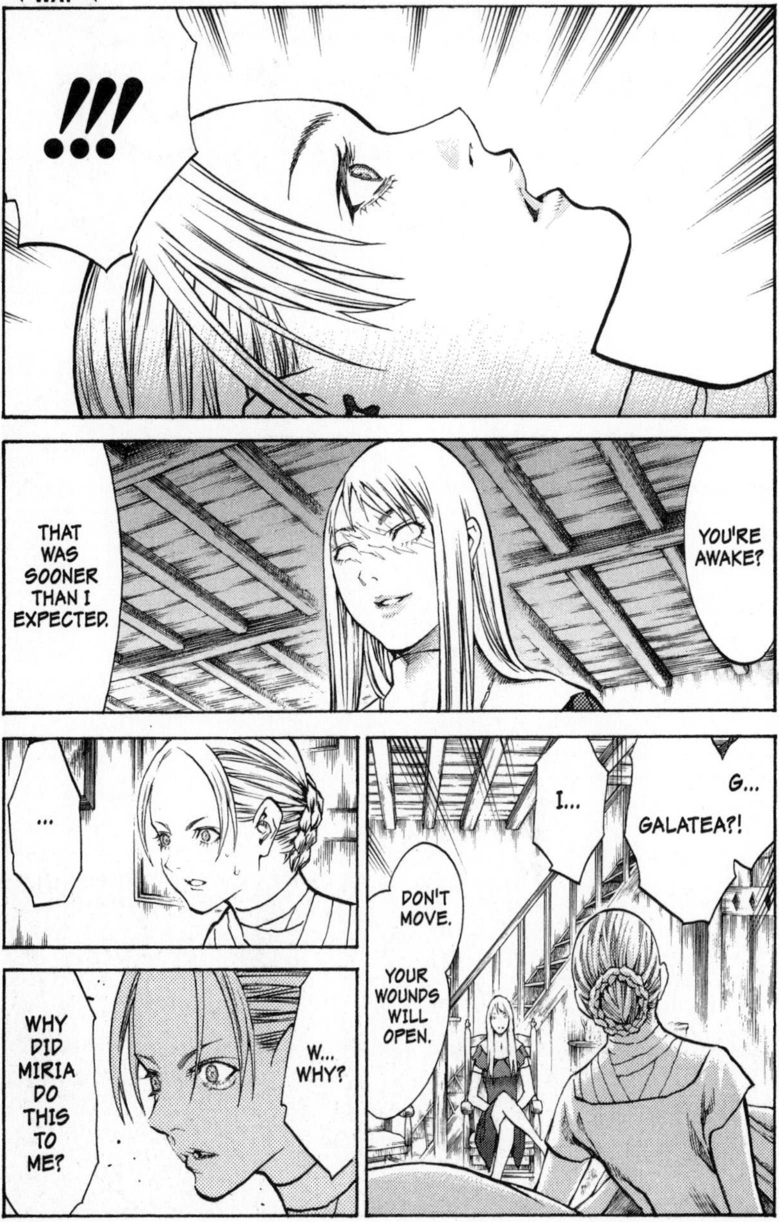
!!!
YOU'RE AWAKE?
THAT WAS SOONER THAN I EXPECTED.
G... GALATEA?!
I...
DON'T MOVE.
YOUR WOUNDS WILL OPEN.
...
W... WHY?
WHY DID MIRIA DO THIS TO ME?

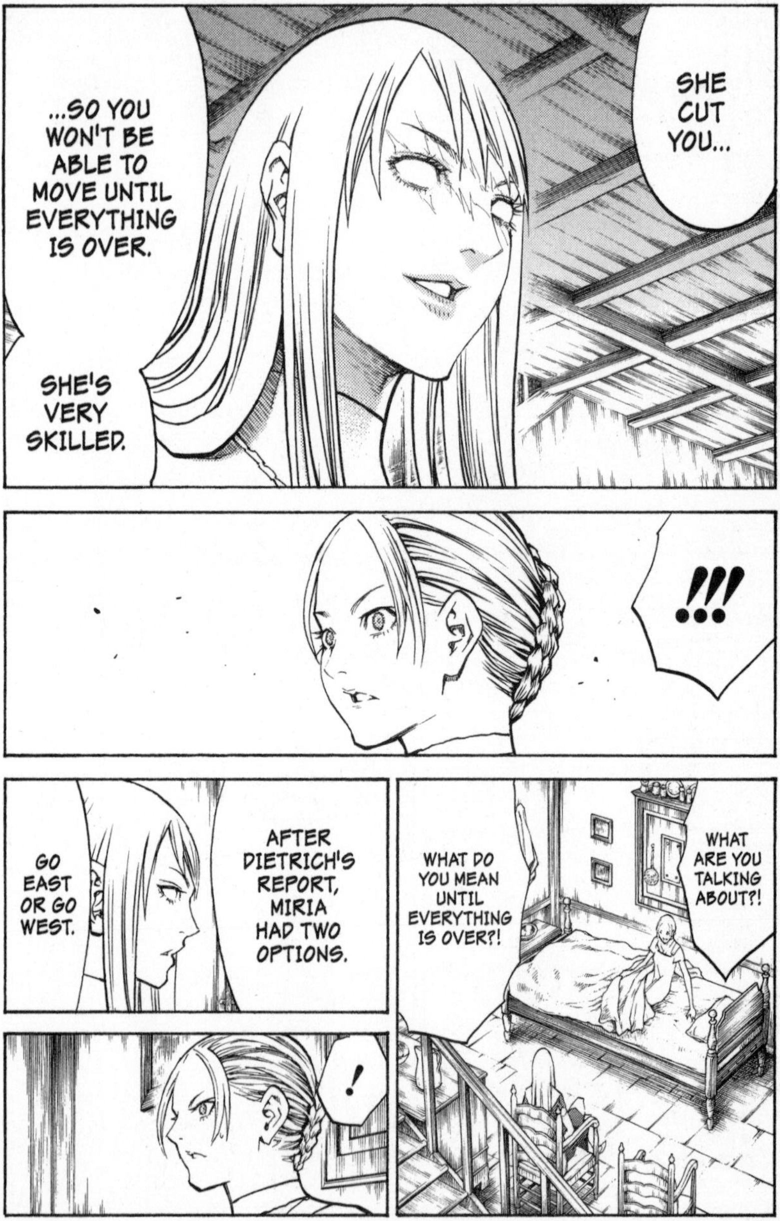
SHE CUT YOU...
...SO YOU WON'T BE ABLE TO MOVE UNTIL EVERYTHING IS OVER.
SHE'S VERY SKILLED.
!!!
WHAT ARE YOU TALKING ABOUT?!
WHAT DO YOU MEAN UNTIL EVERYTHING IS OVER?!
AFTER DIETRICH'S REPORT, MIRIA HAD TWO OPTIONS.
GO EAST OR GO WEST.
!

READ THIS WAY

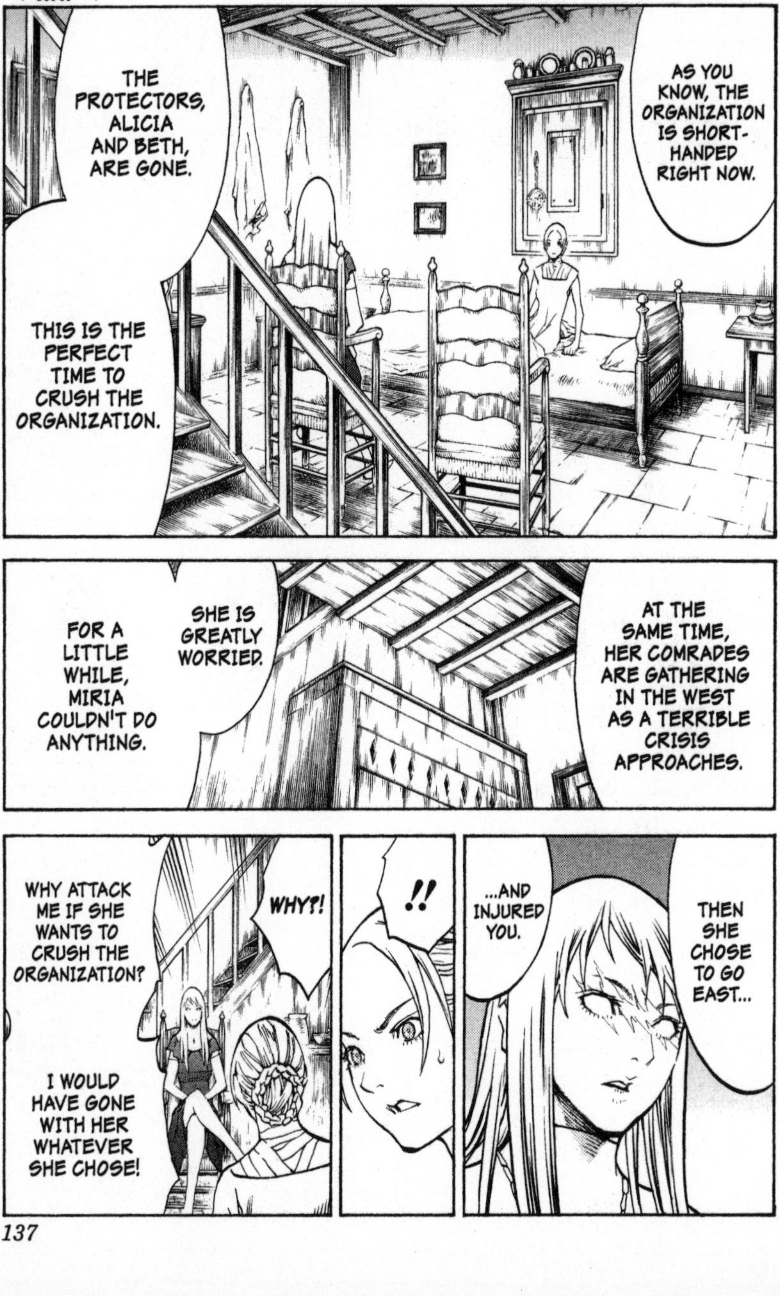
AS YOU KNOW, THE ORGANIZATION IS SHORT-HANDED RIGHT NOW.
THE PROTECTORS, ALICIA AND BETH, ARE GONE.
THIS IS THE PERFECT TIME TO CRUSH THE ORGANIZATION.
AT THE SAME TIME, HER COMRADES ARE GATHERING IN THE WEST AS A TERRIBLE CRISIS APPROACHES.
SHE IS GREATLY WORRIED.
FOR A LITTLE WHILE, MIRIA COULDN'T DO ANYTHING.
THEN SHE CHOSE TO GO EAST...
...AND INJURED YOU.
!!
WHY?!
WHY ATTACK ME IF SHE WANTS TO CRUSH THE ORGANIZATION?
I WOULD HAVE GONE WITH HER WHATEVER SHE CHOSE!

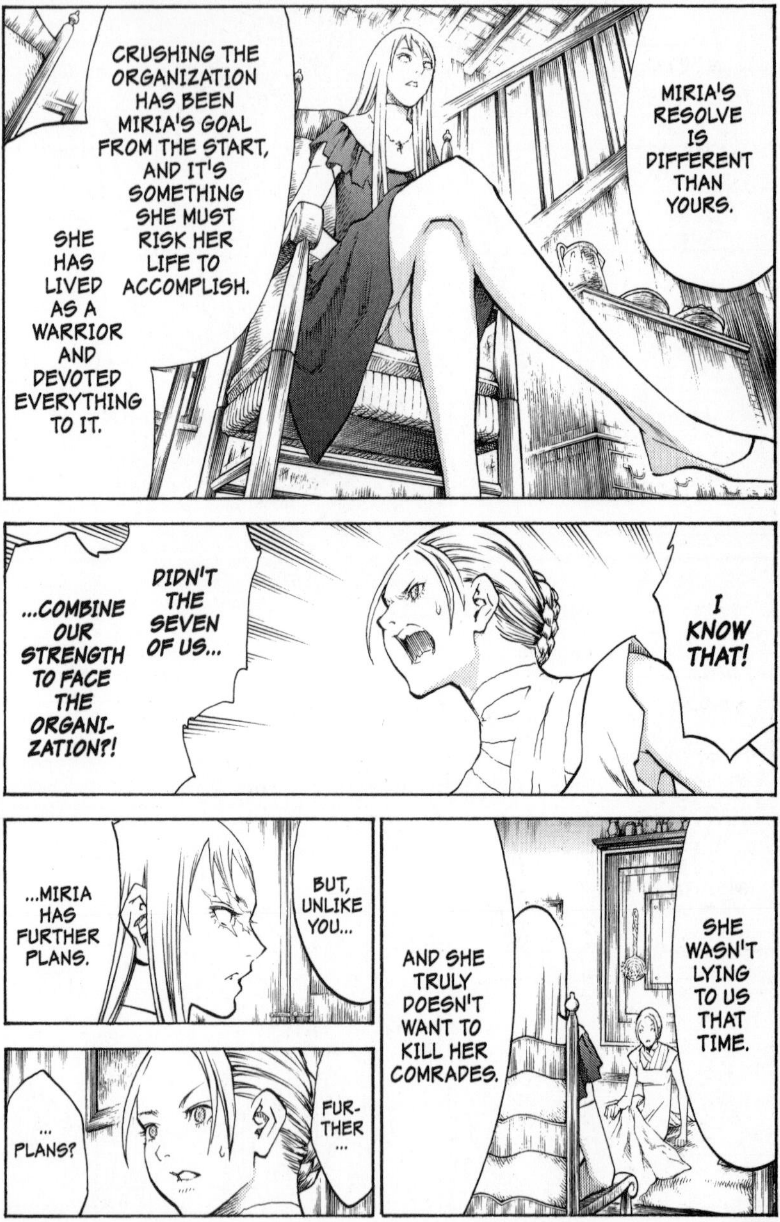
MIRIA'S RESOLVE IS DIFFERENT THAN YOURS.
CRUSHING THE ORGANIZATION HAS BEEN MIRIA'S GOAL FROM THE START, AND IT'S SOMETHING SHE MUST RISK HER LIFE TO ACCOMPLISH.
SHE HAS LIVED AS A WARRIOR AND DEVOTED EVERYTHING TO IT.
I KNOW THAT!
DIDN'T THE SEVEN OF US...
...COMBINE OUR STRENGTH TO FACE THE ORGANIZATION?!
SHE WASN'T LYING TO US THAT TIME.
AND SHE TRULY DOESN'T WANT TO KILL HER COMRADES.
BUT, UNLIKE YOU...
...MIRIA HAS FURTHER PLANS.
FURTHER...
...PLANS?

READ THIS WAY

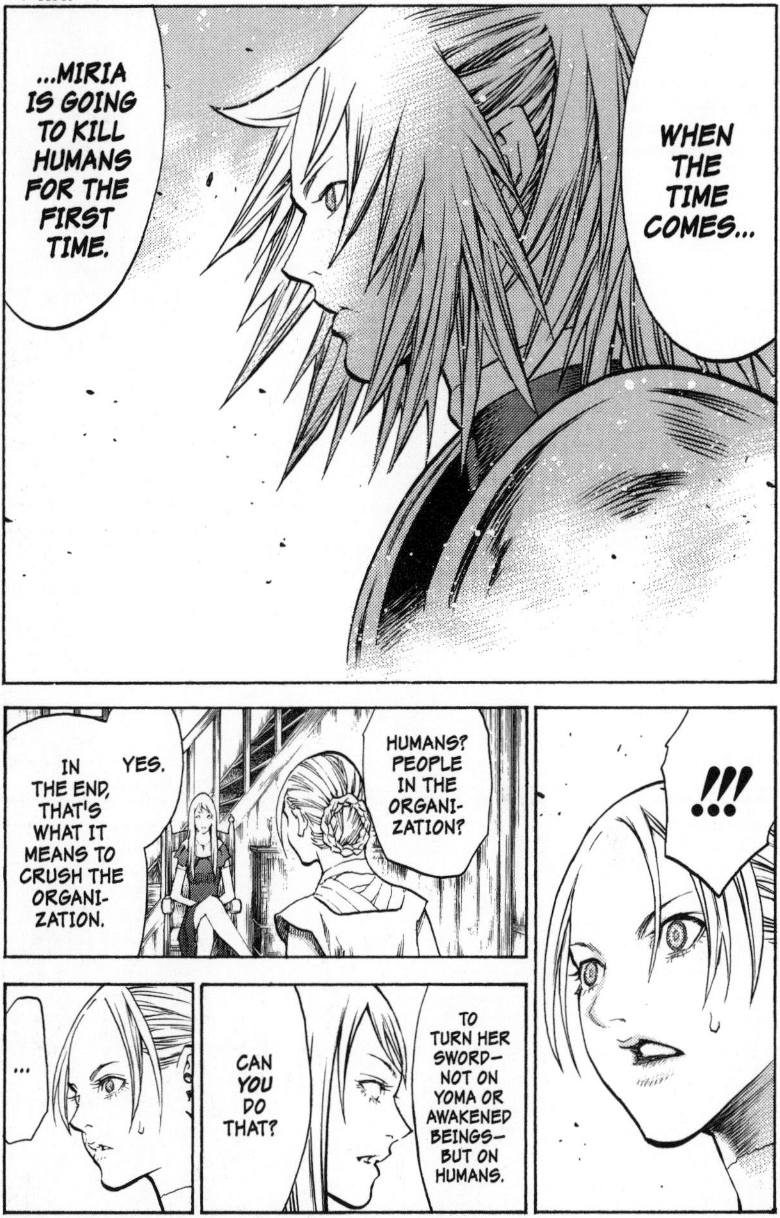

WHEN THE TIME COMES...
...MIRIA IS GOING TO KILL HUMANS FOR THE FIRST TIME.
!!!
HUMANS? PEOPLE IN THE ORGANIZATION?
YES.
IN THE END, THAT'S WHAT IT MEANS TO CRUSH THE ORGANIZATION.
TO TURN HER SWORD—NOT ON YOMA OR AWAKENED BEINGS—BUT ON HUMANS.
CAN YOU DO THAT?
...

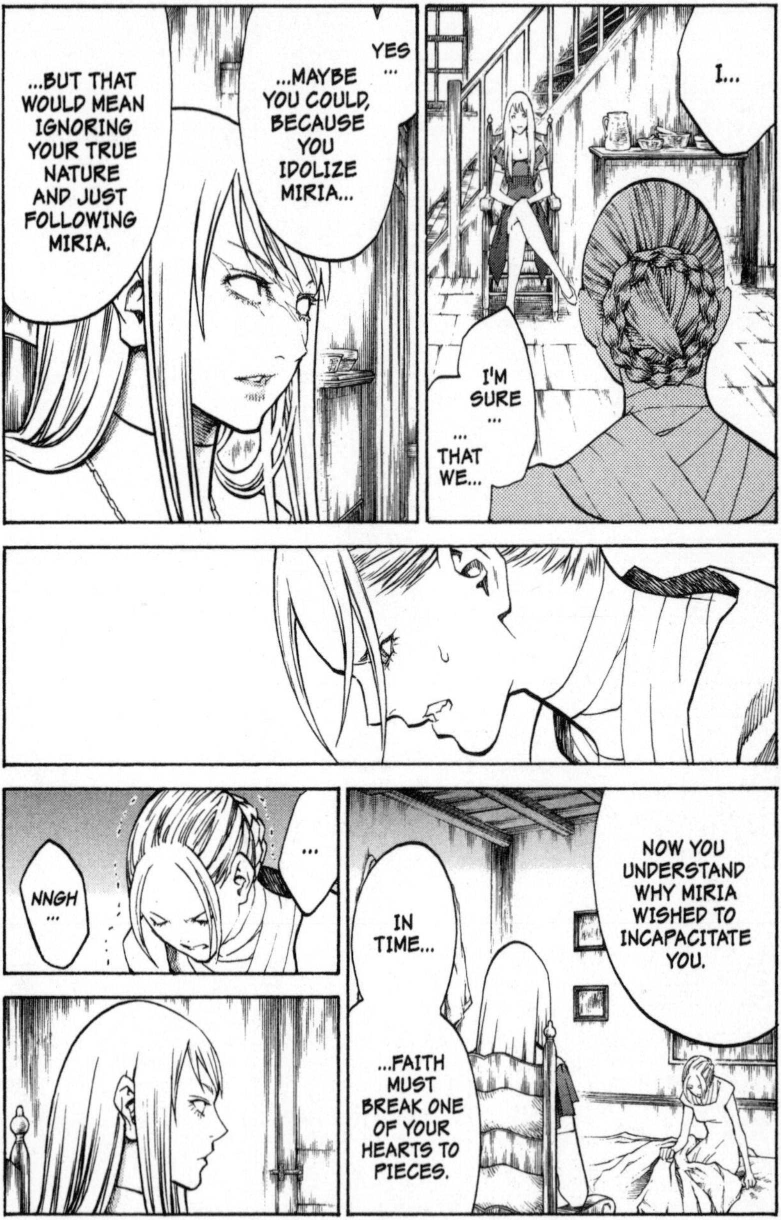
I...
I'M SURE...
...THAT WE...
YES...
...MAYBE YOU COULD, BECAUSE YOU IDOLIZE MIRIA...
...BUT THAT WOULD MEAN IGNORING YOUR TRUE NATURE AND JUST FOLLOWING MIRIA.
NOW YOU UNDERSTAND WHY MIRIA WISHED TO INCAPACITATE YOU.
IN TIME...
...FAITH MUST BREAK ONE OF YOUR HEARTS TO PIECES.
...
NNGH...

READ THIS WAY

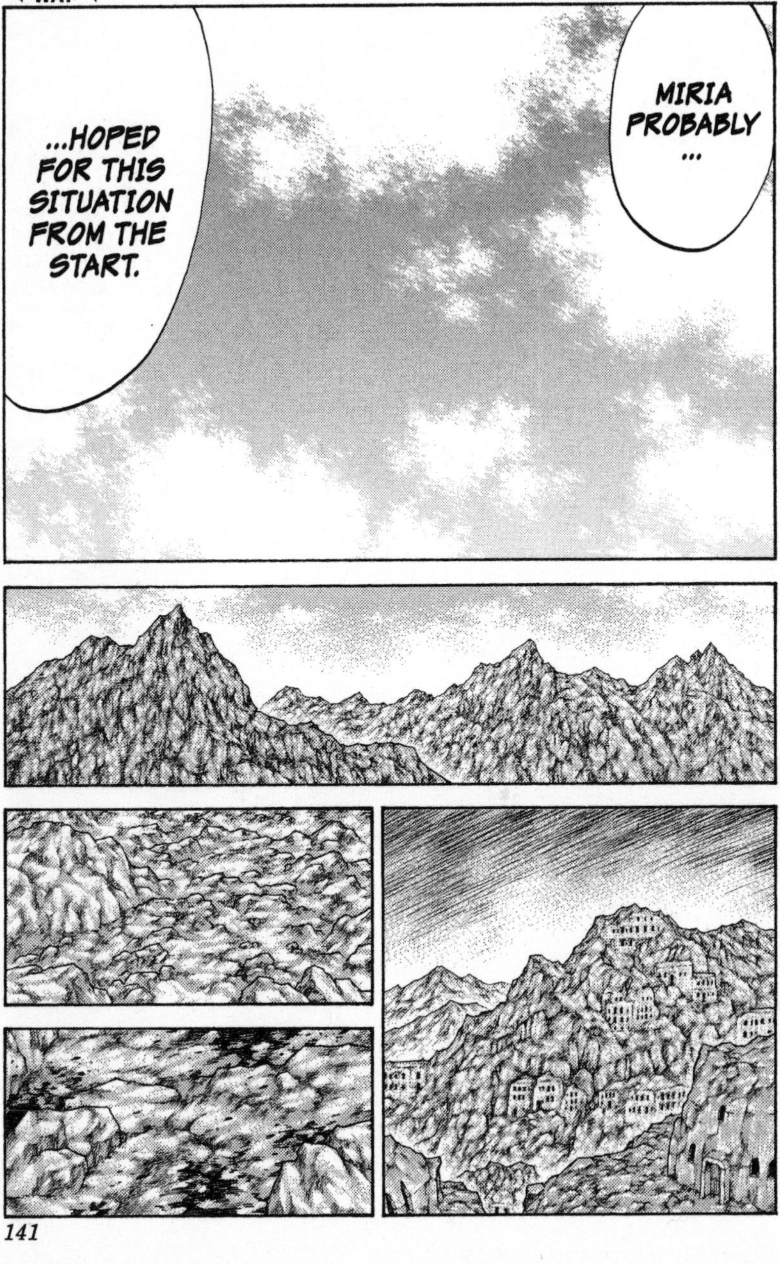
MIRIA PROBABLY ...
...HOPED FOR THIS SITUATION FROM THE START.

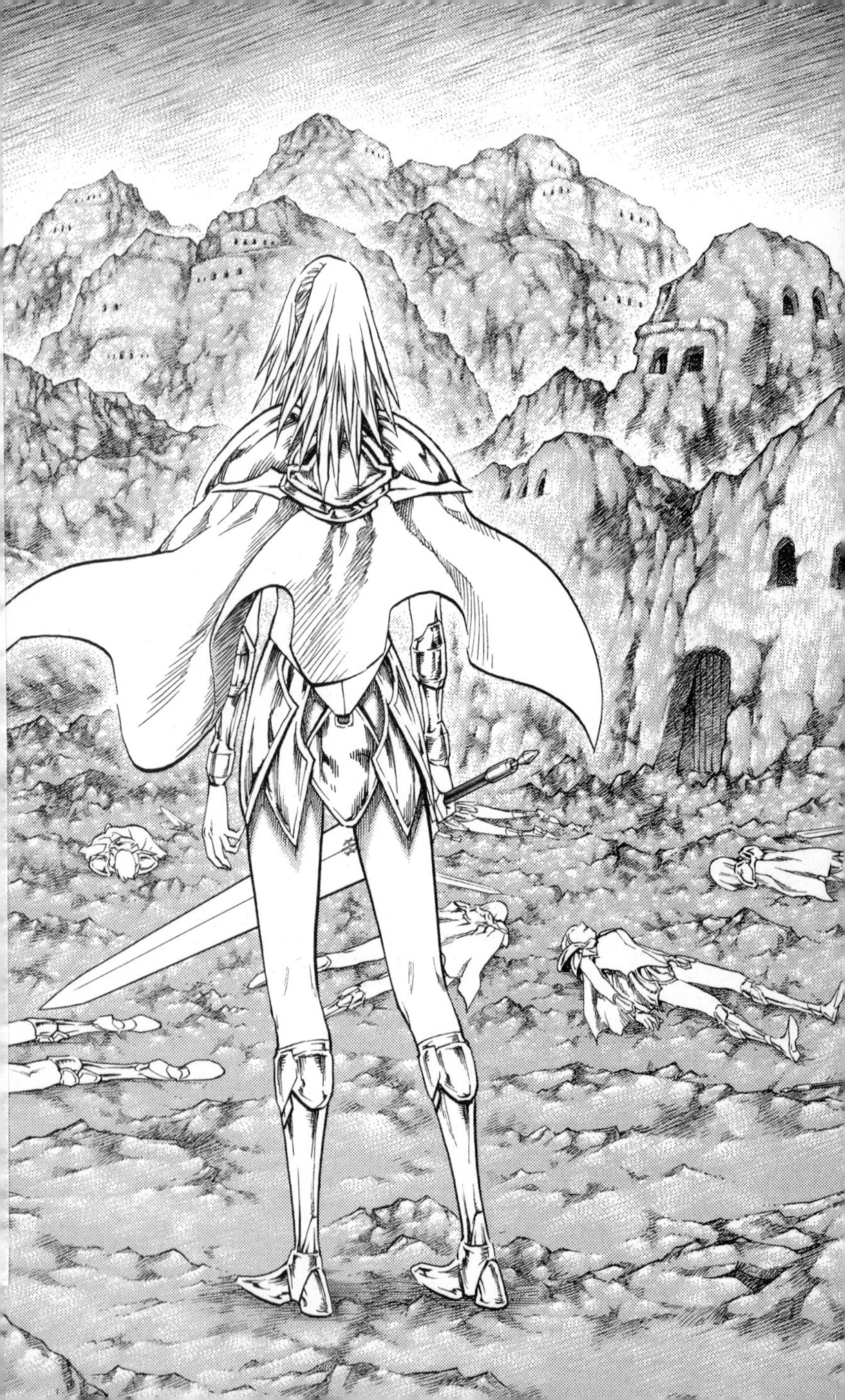

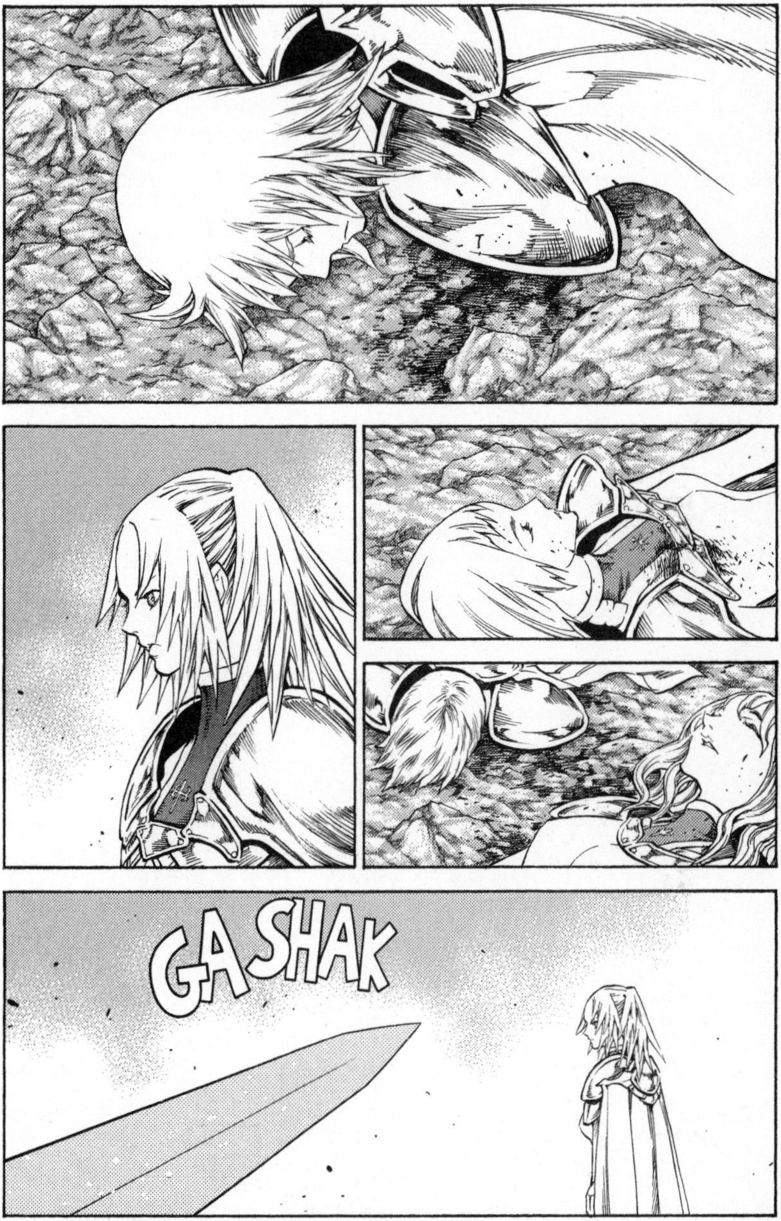
GASHAK

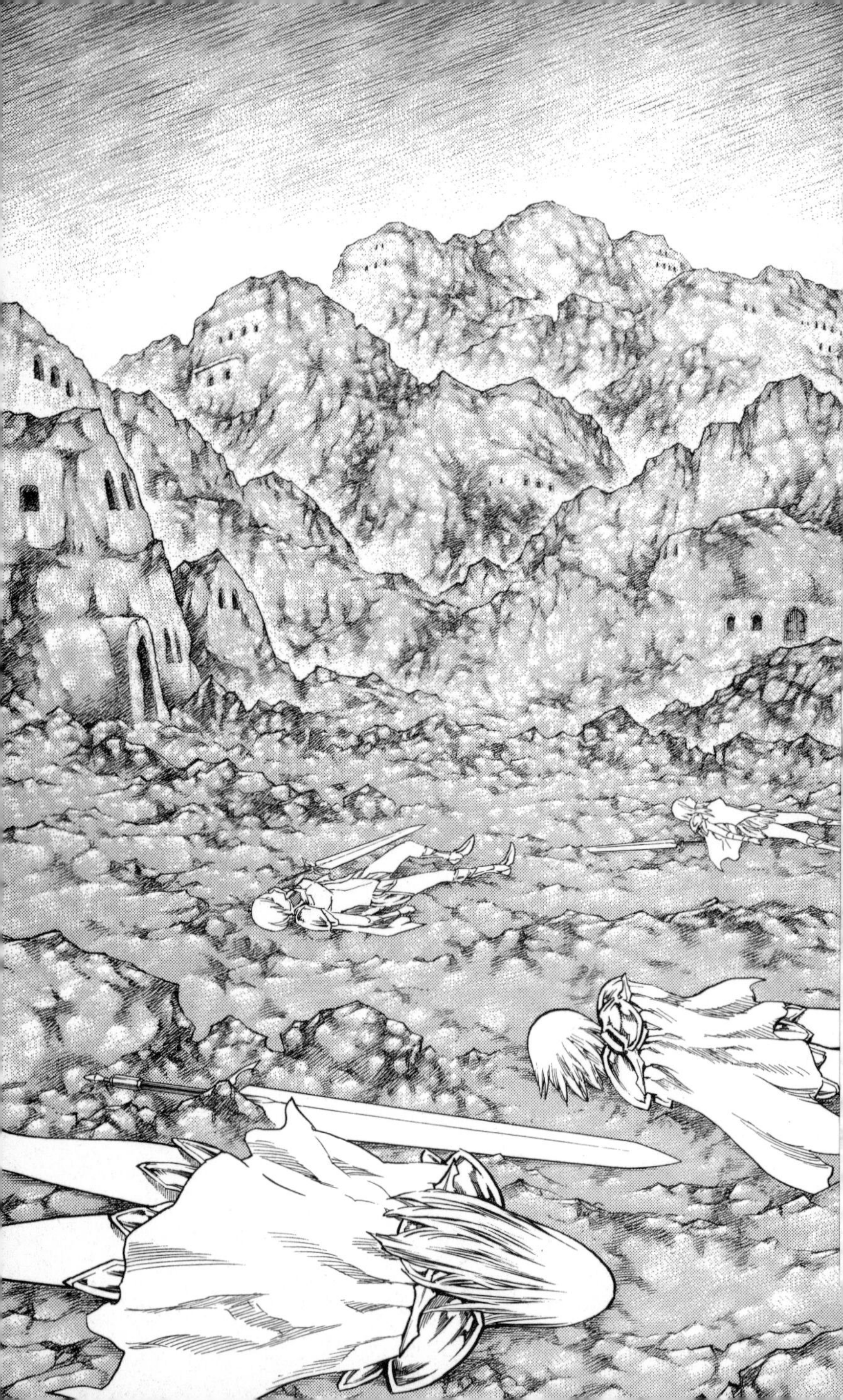

READ THIS WAY

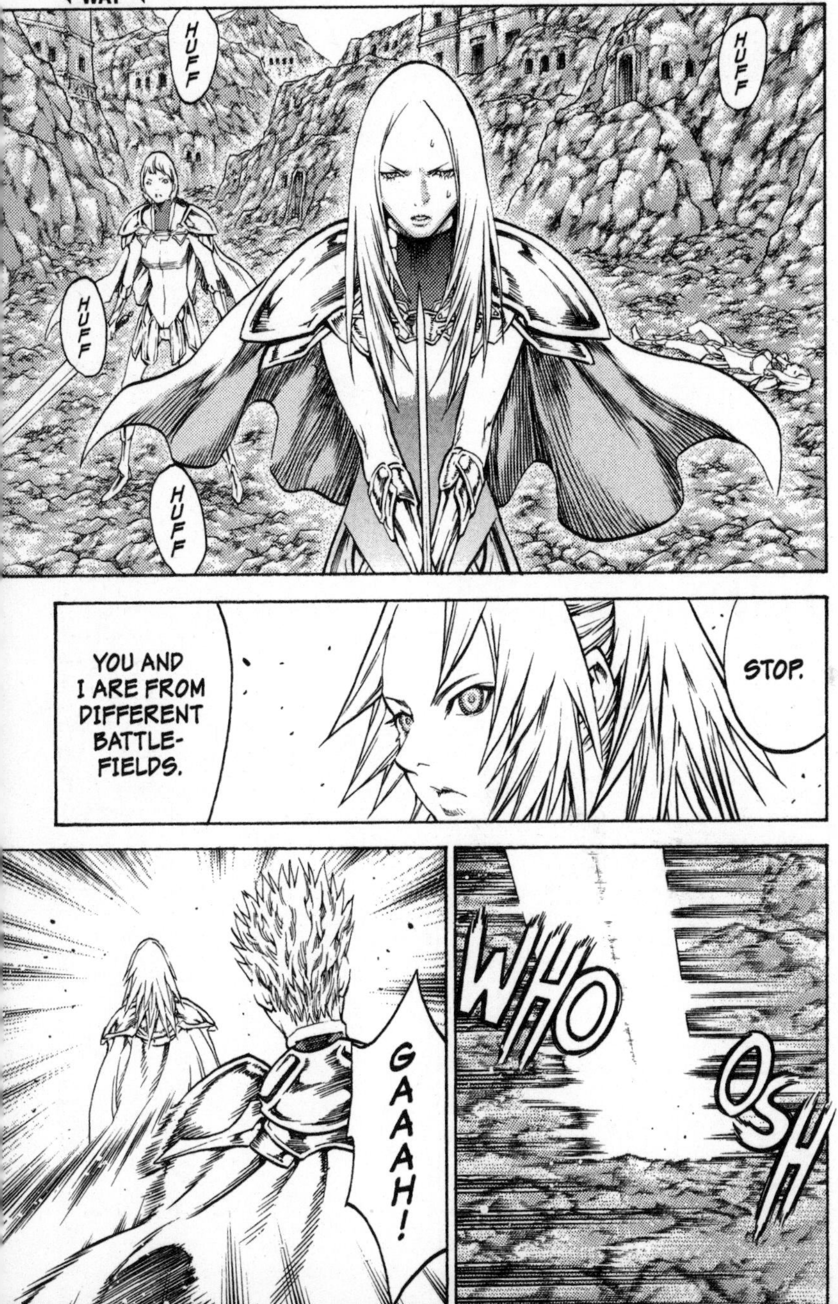
HUFF
HUFF
HUFF
HUFF
STOP.
YOU AND I ARE FROM DIFFERENT BATTLE-FIELDS.
WHOOSH
GAAAH!

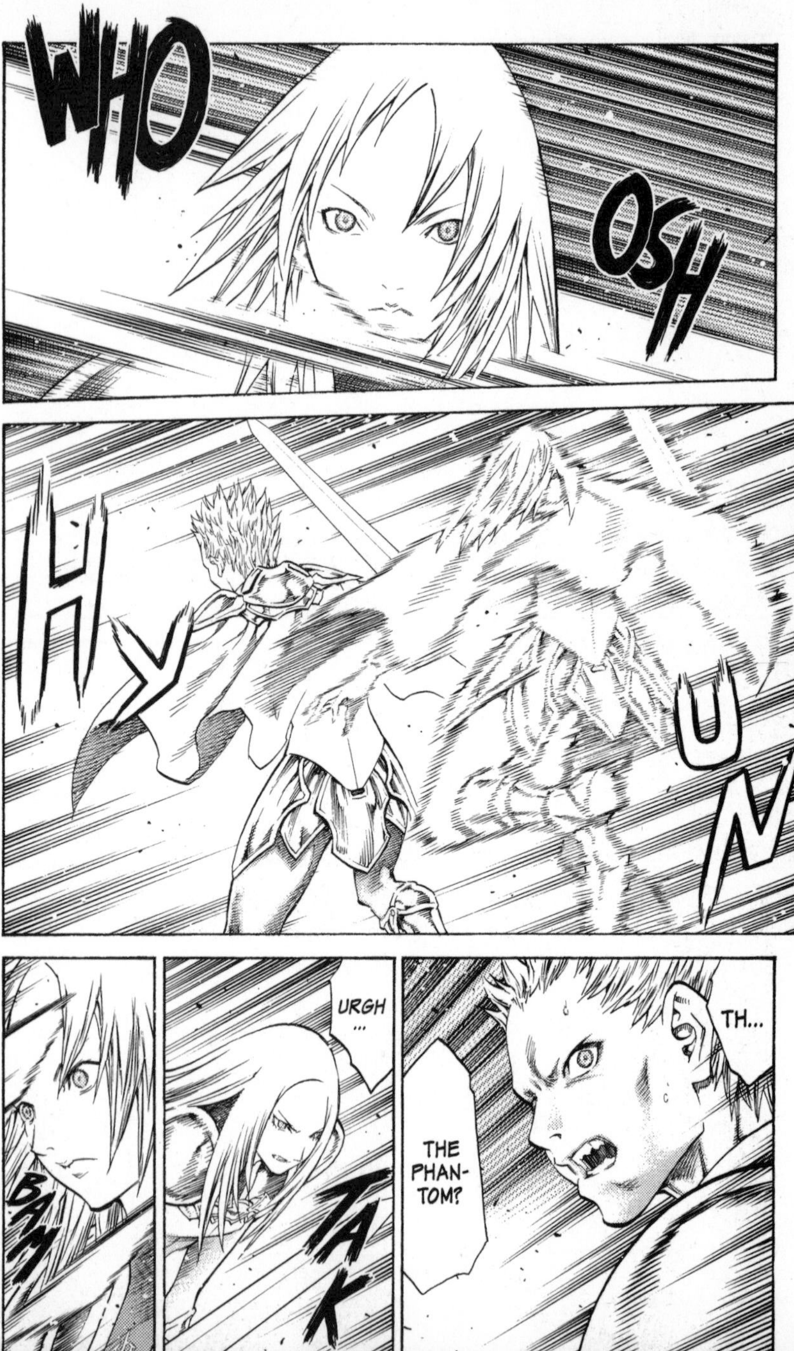
WHO
OSH
HY
UN
TH...
THE PHAN-TOM?
URGH ...
TAK
BAM

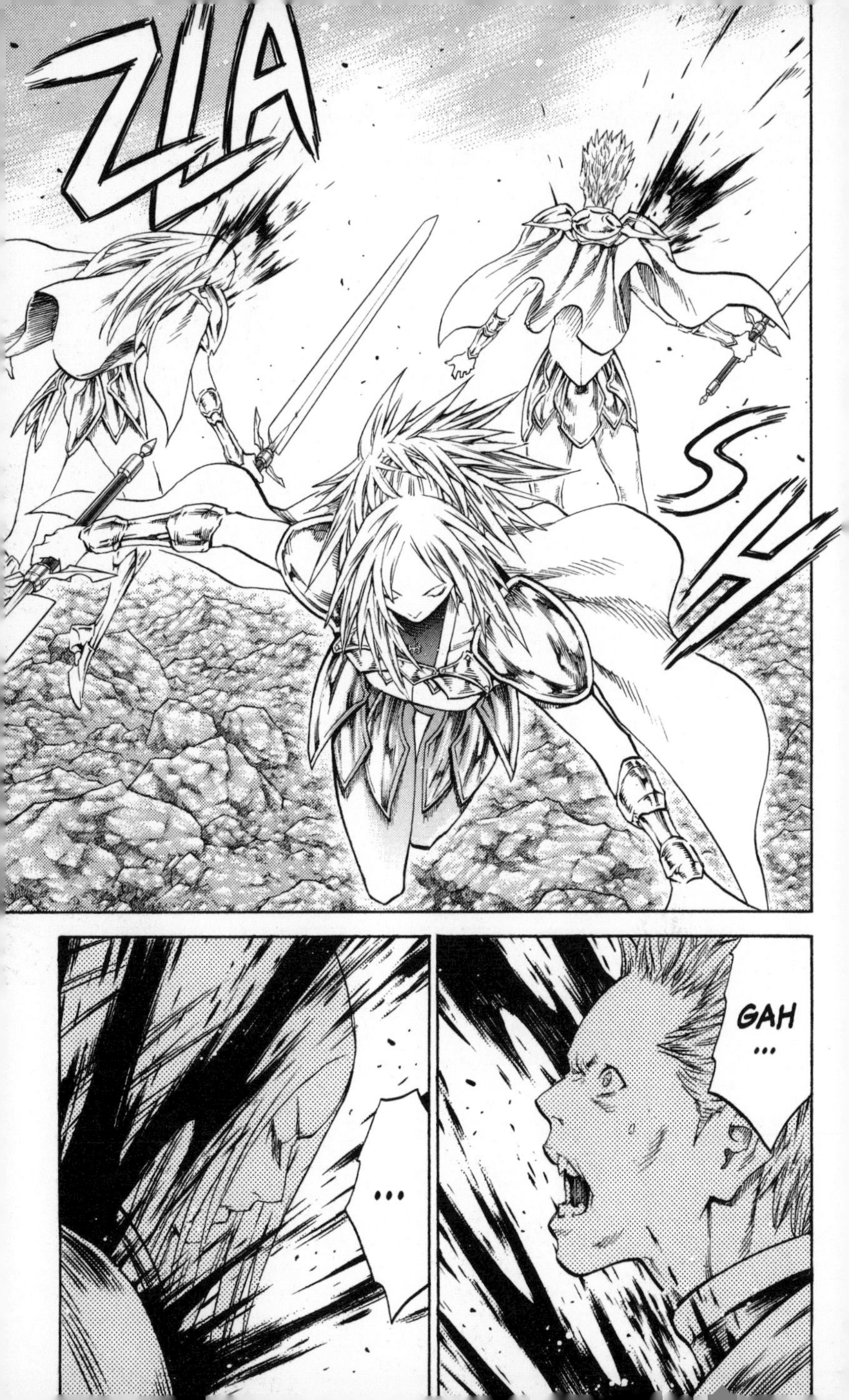
ZZA
SH
GAH ...
...

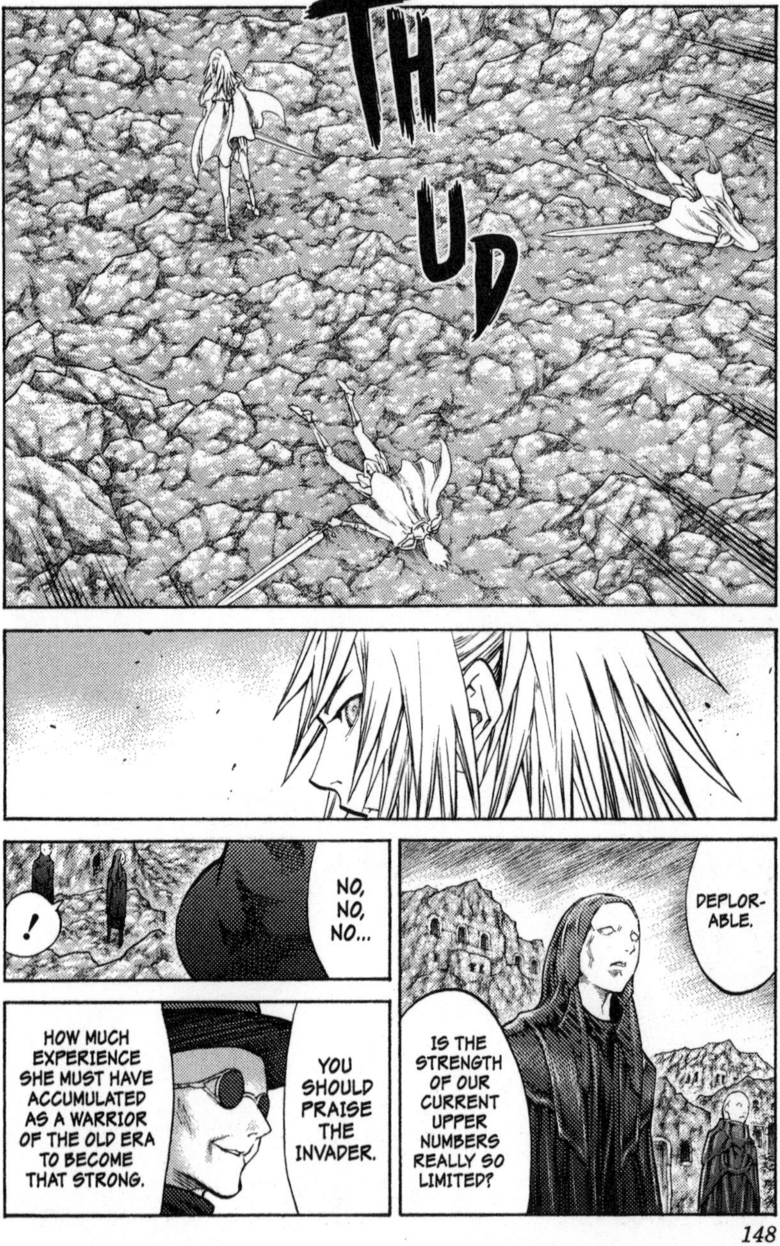
THUD
DEPLOR-ABLE.
IS THE STRENGTH OF OUR CURRENT UPPER NUMBERS REALLY SO LIMITED?
!
NO, NO, NO...
YOU SHOULD PRAISE THE INVADER.
HOW MUCH EXPERIENCE SHE MUST HAVE ACCUMULATED AS A WARRIOR OF THE OLD ERA TO BECOME THAT STRONG.

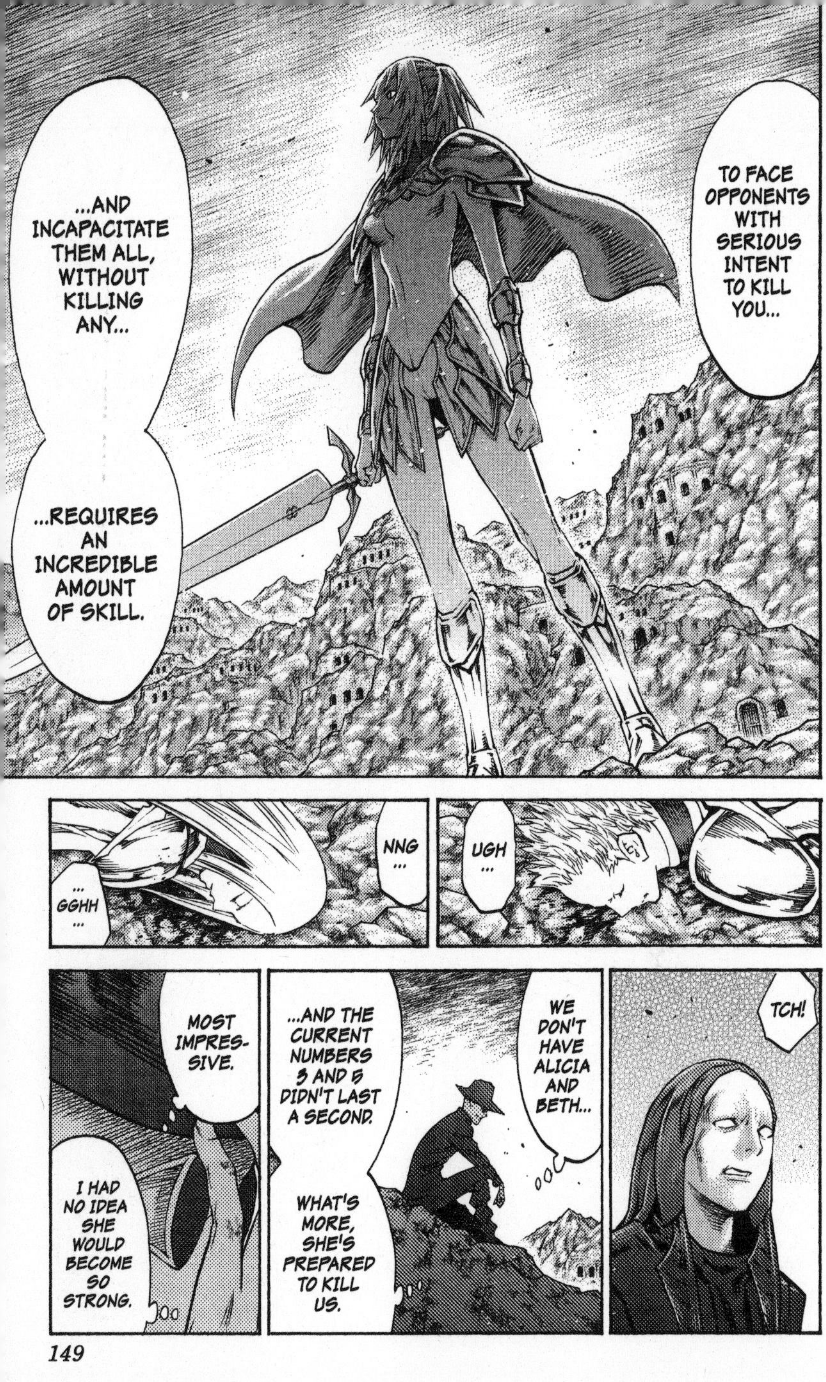
TO FACE OPPONENTS WITH SERIOUS INTENT TO KILL YOU...
...AND INCAPACITATE THEM ALL, WITHOUT KILLING ANY...
...REQUIRES AN INCREDIBLE AMOUNT OF SKILL.
UGH...
NNG...
...GGHH...
TCH!
WE DON'T HAVE ALICIA AND BETH...
...AND THE CURRENT NUMBERS 3 AND 5 DIDN'T LAST A SECOND.
WHAT'S MORE, SHE'S PREPARED TO KILL US.
MOST IMPRES-SIVE.
I HAD NO IDEA SHE WOULD BECOME SO STRONG.

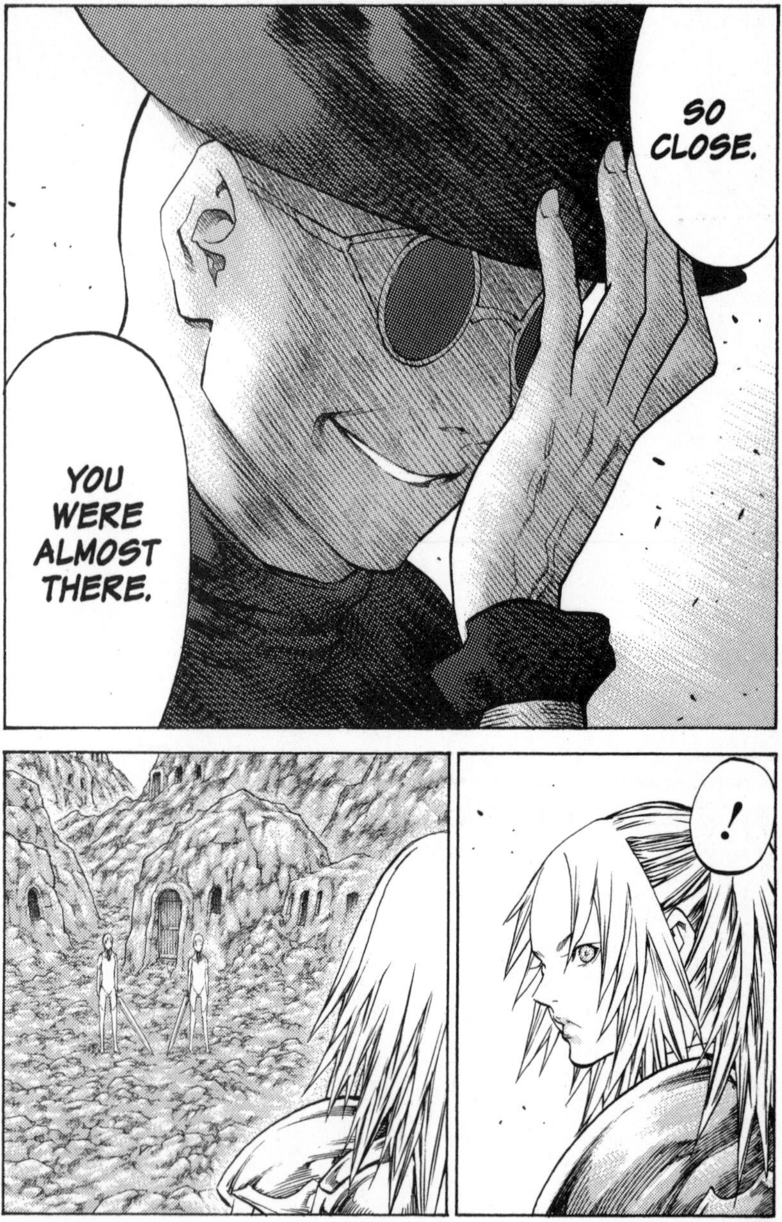
SO CLOSE.
YOU WERE ALMOST THERE.
!

READ THIS WAY

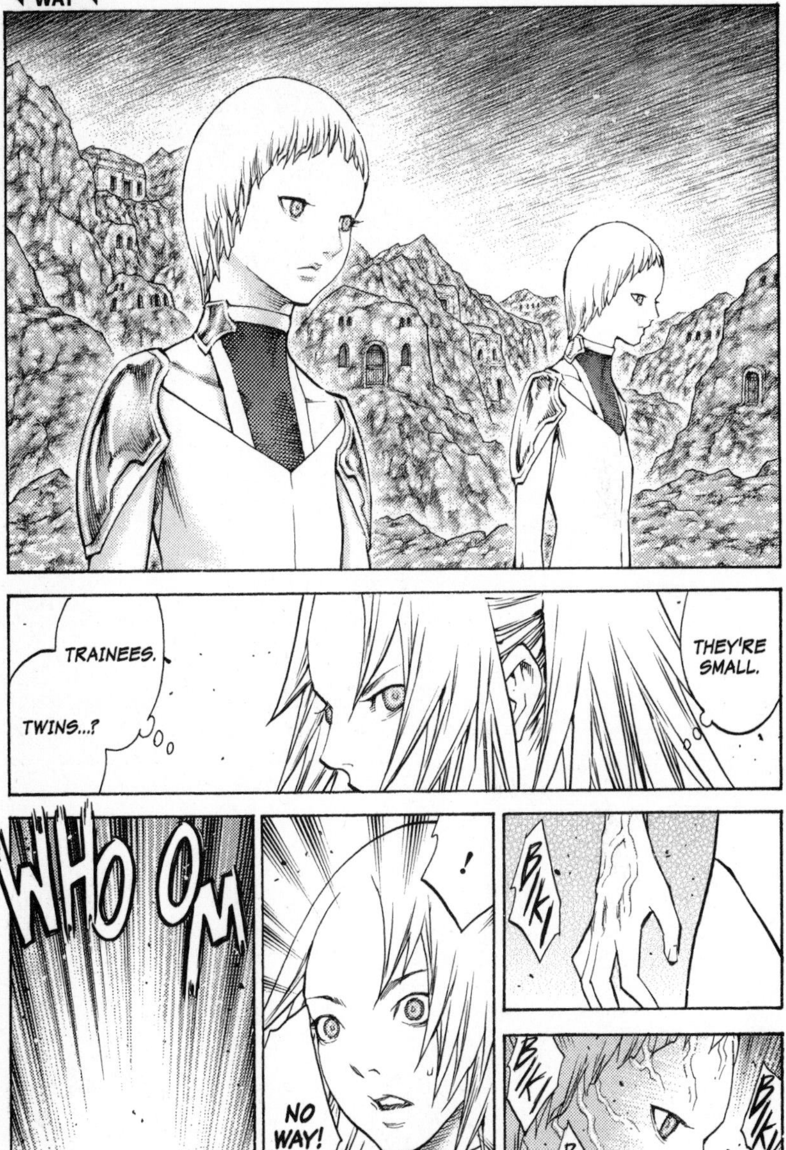
THEY'RE SMALL.
TRAINEES.
TWINS...?
BIKI
BIKI
BIKI
BIKI
!
NO WAY!
WHOOM

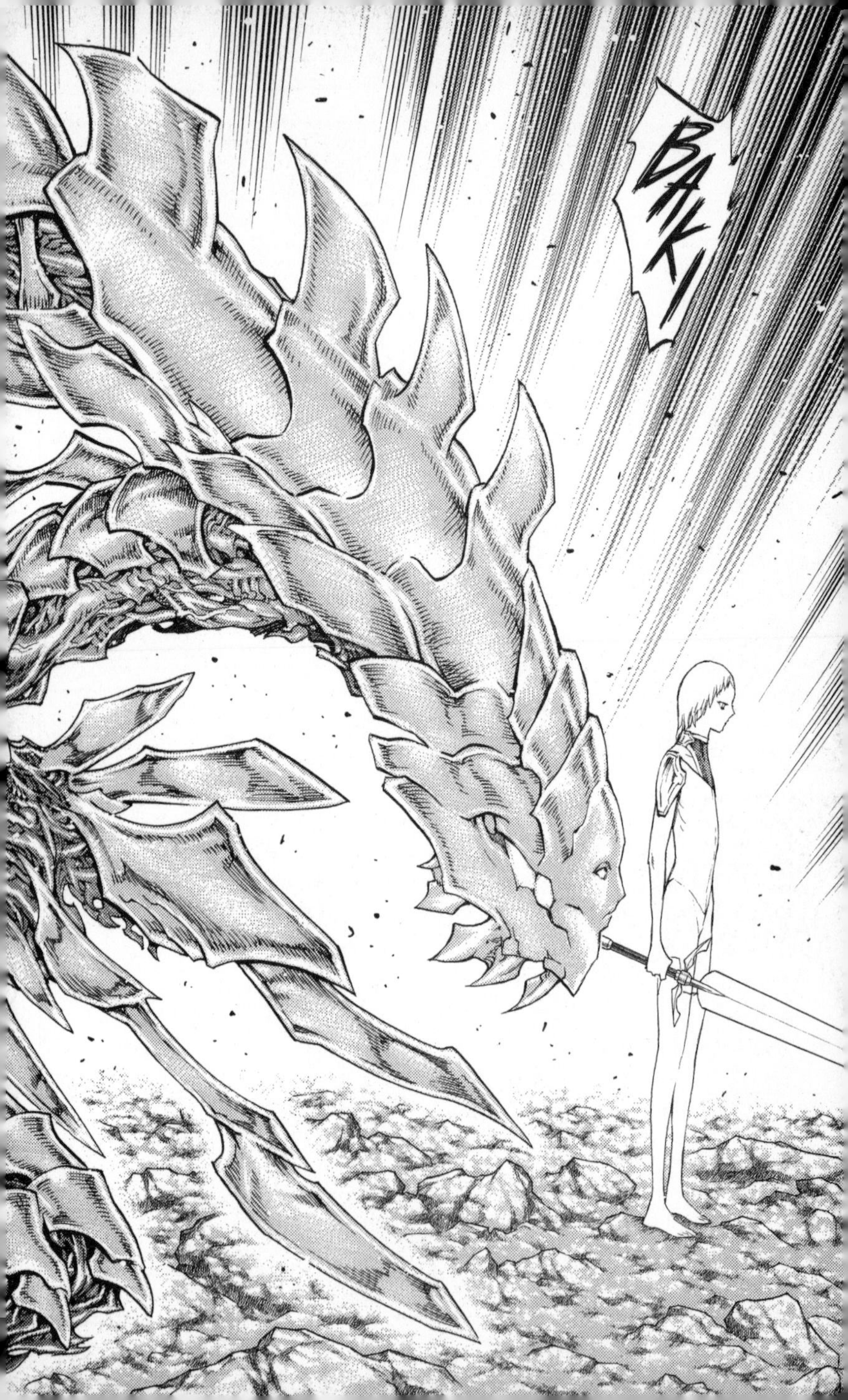
BAKI

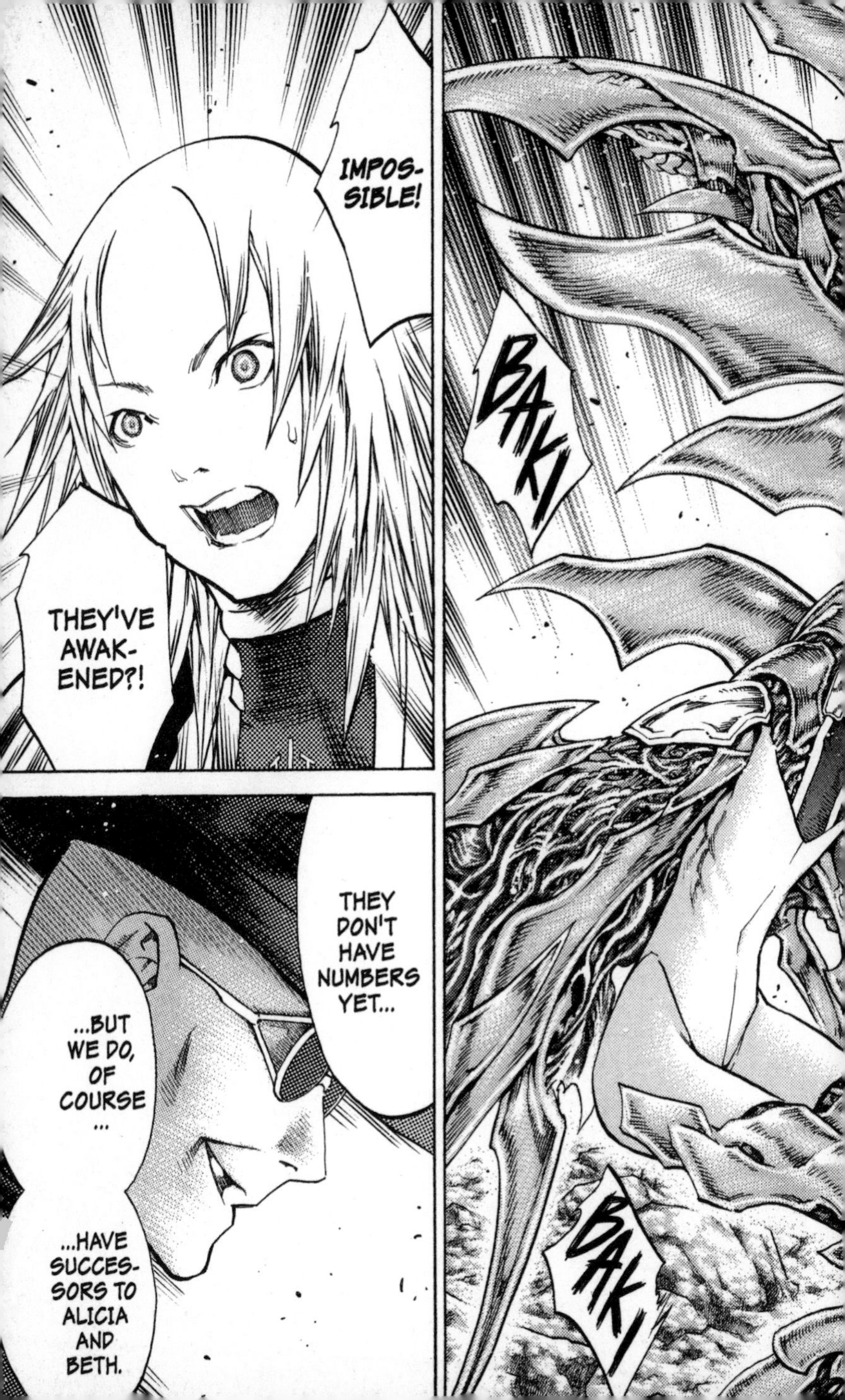
BAKI
BAKI
IMPOSSIBLE!
THEY'VE AWAKENED?!
THEY DON'T HAVE NUMBERS YET...
...BUT WE DO, OF COURSE...
...HAVE SUCCESSORS TO ALICIA AND BETH.

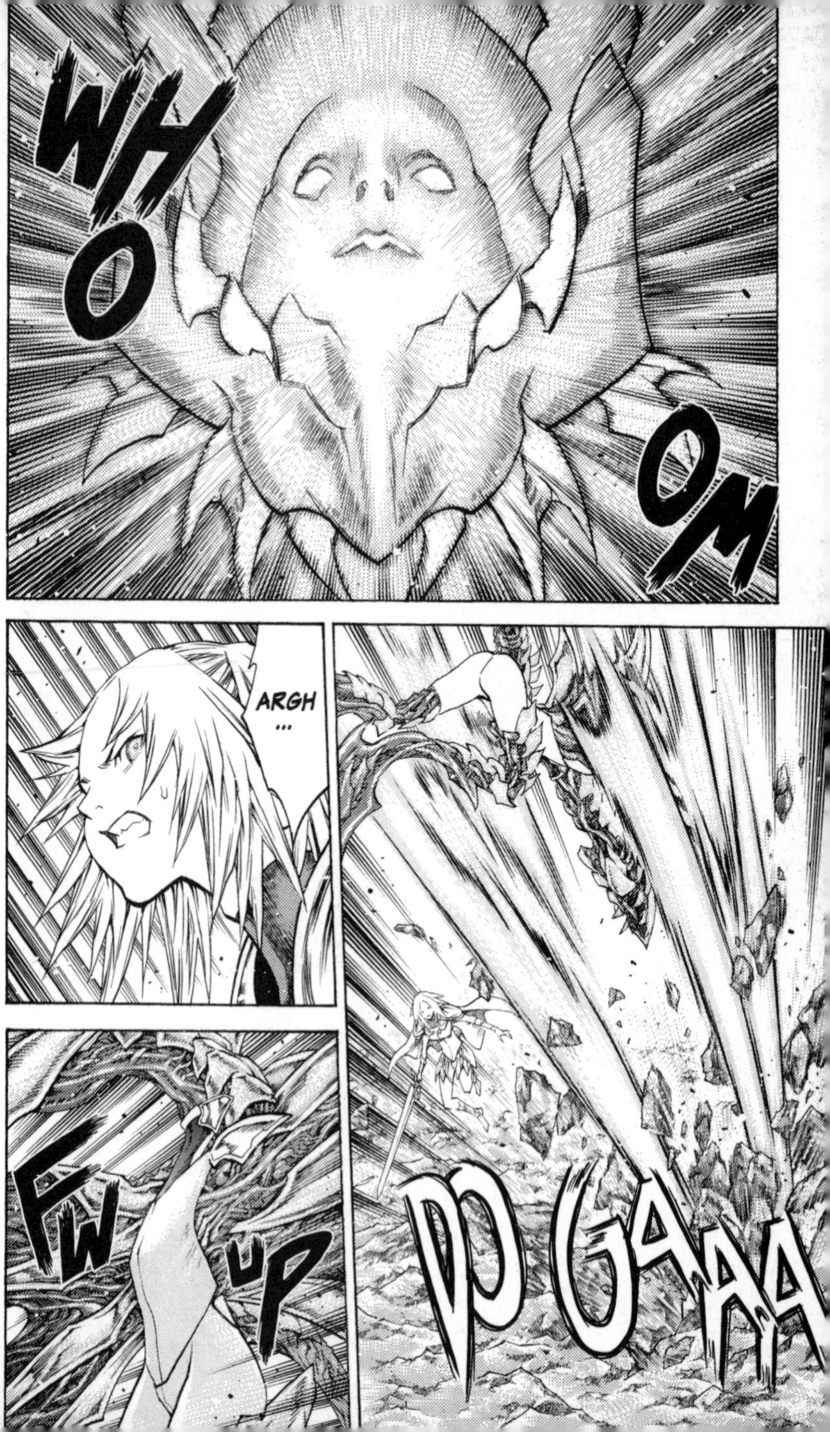
WHOOM
DOGAAA
ARGH ...
FWUP

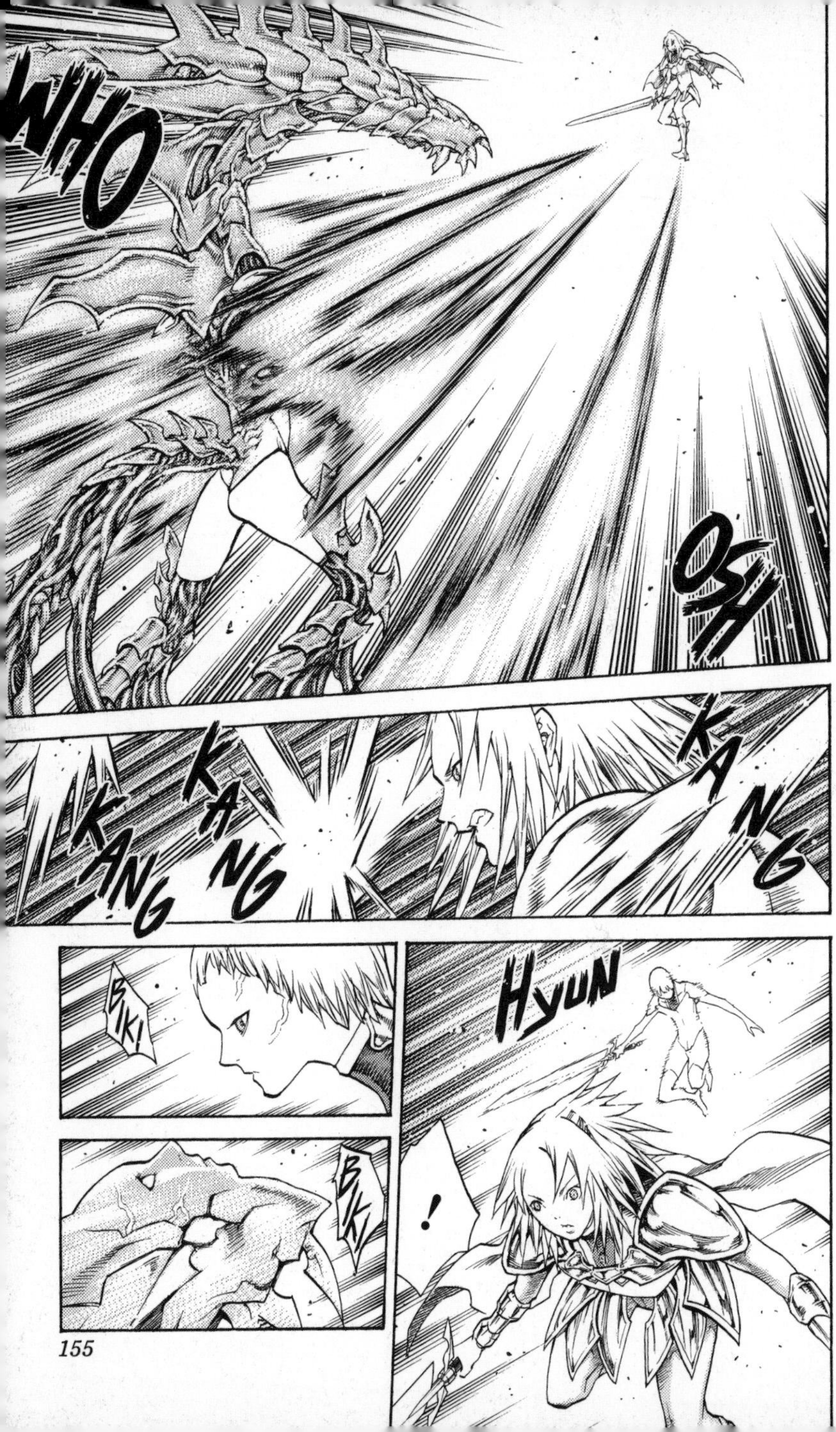
WHO
OSH
KANG
KANG
KANG
HYUN
!
BIKI!
BIKI!

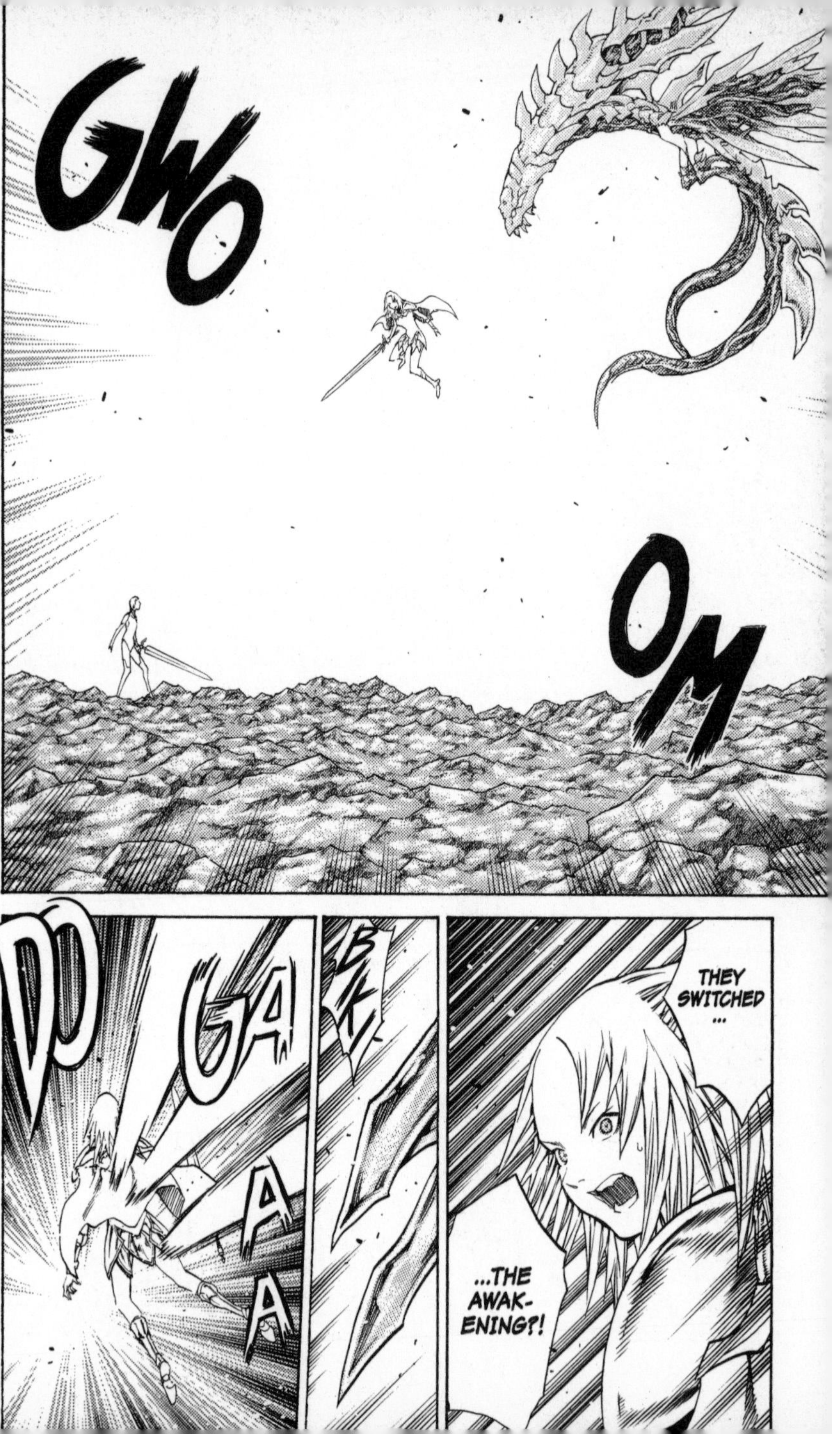
GWO
OM
THEY SWITCHED ...
...THE AWAKENING?!
BKI
DO
GA
A
A

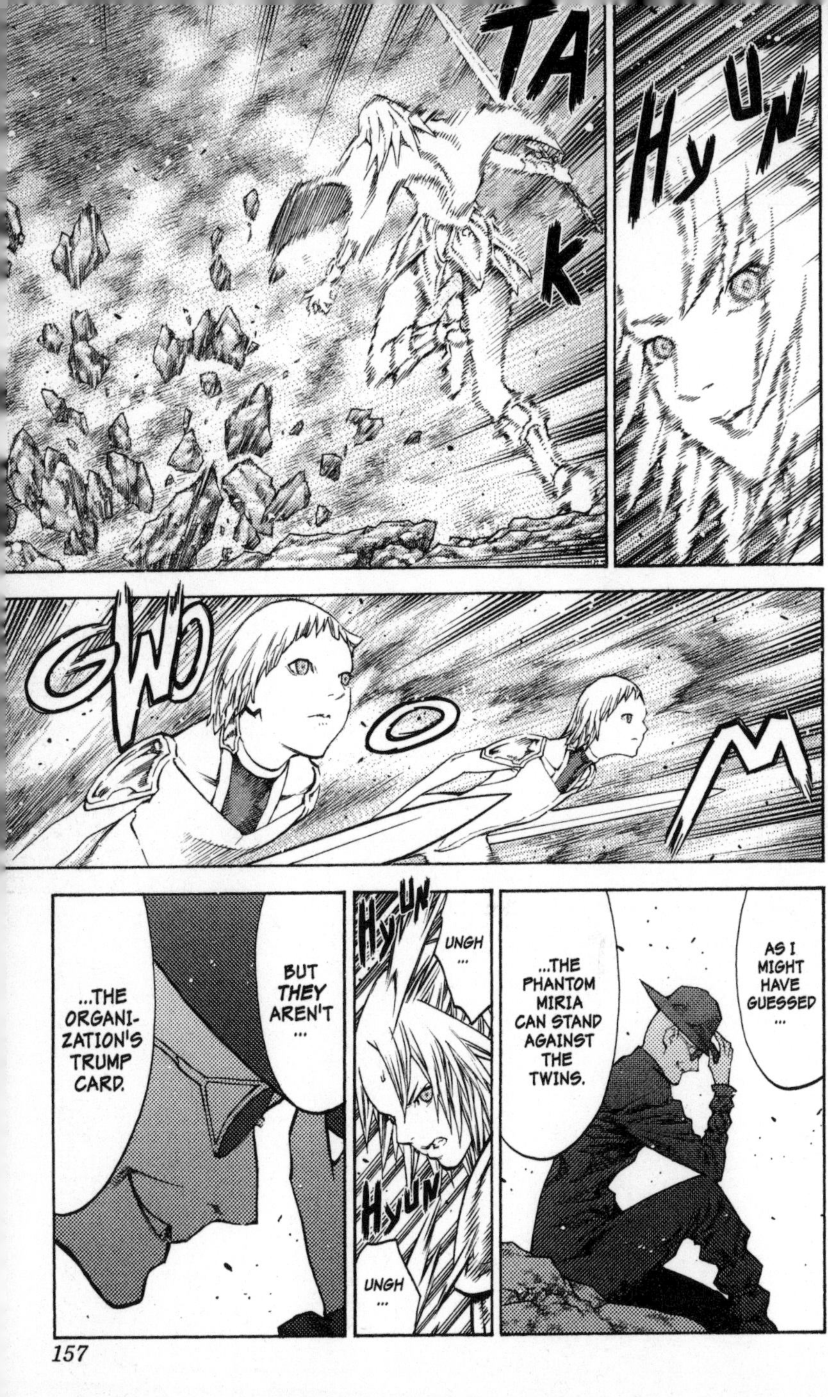
HyUN
TAK
GWOOM
AS I MIGHT HAVE GUESSED...
...THE PHANTOM MIRIA CAN STAND AGAINST THE TWINS.
HyUN
UNGH...
HyUN
UNGH...
BUT THEY AREN'T...
...THE ORGANIZATION'S TRUMP CARD.

クレイモア
Claymore

Scene 107: Phantoms in the Heart, Part 2

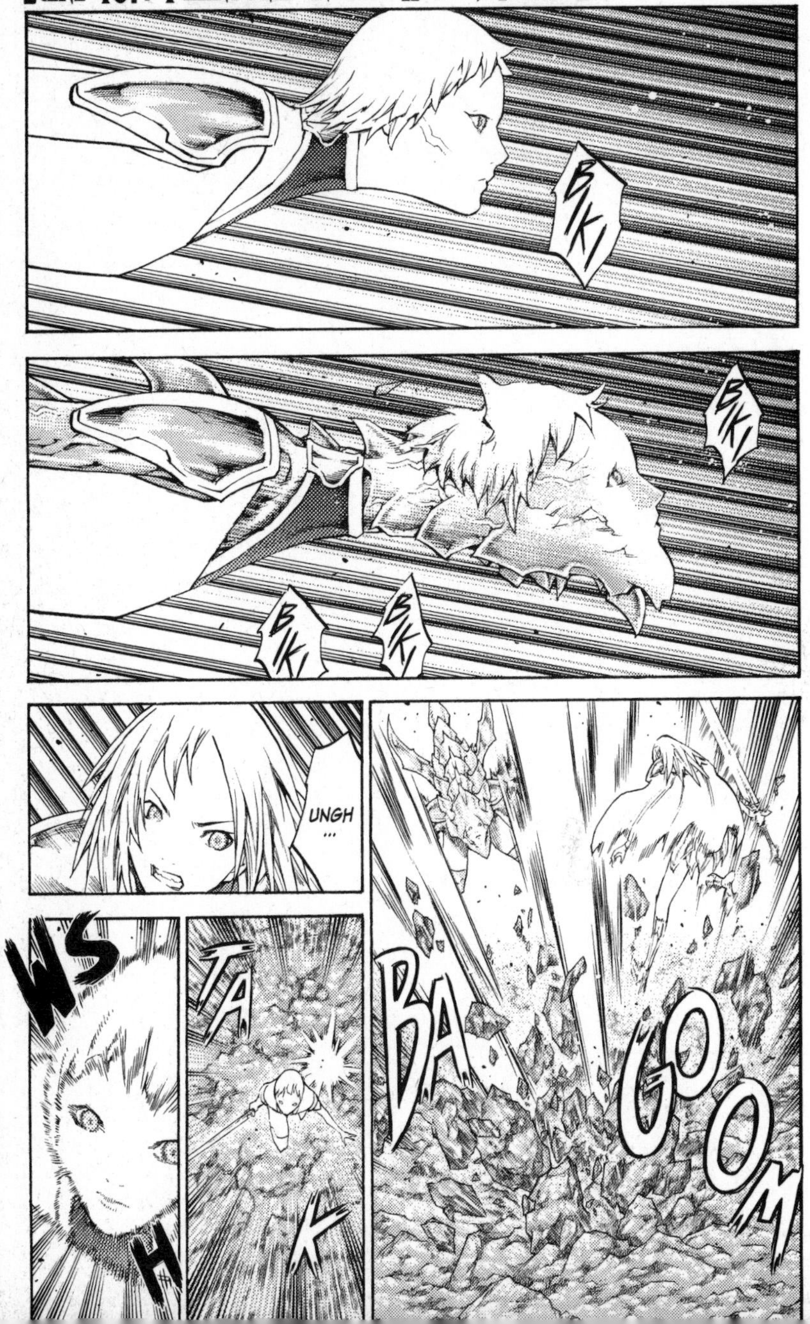
BIKI
BIKI
BIKI
BIKI
BAGOOOM
UNGH ...
TAK
WSH

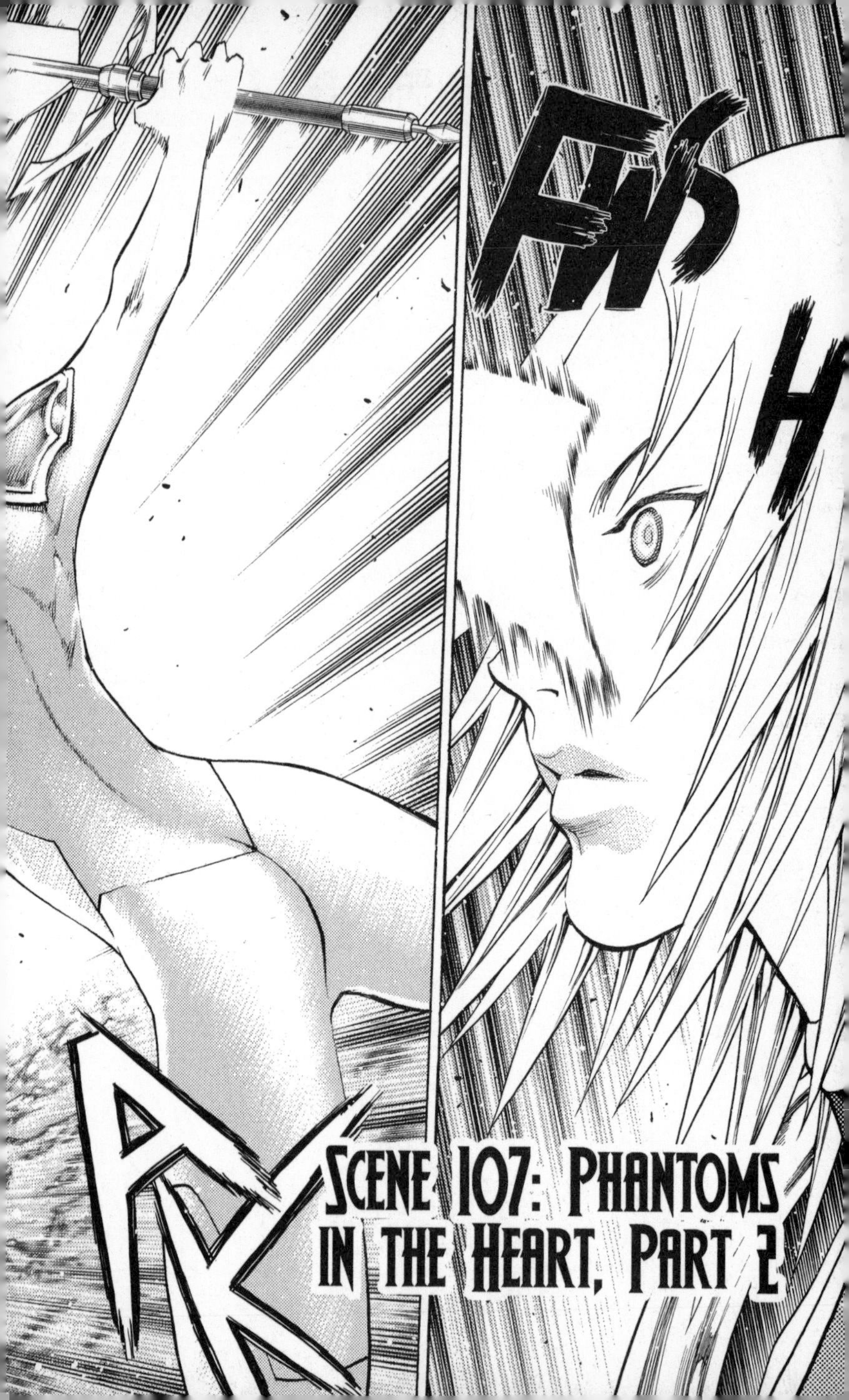
FWS
H
Scene 107: Phantoms in the Heart, Part 2
AK

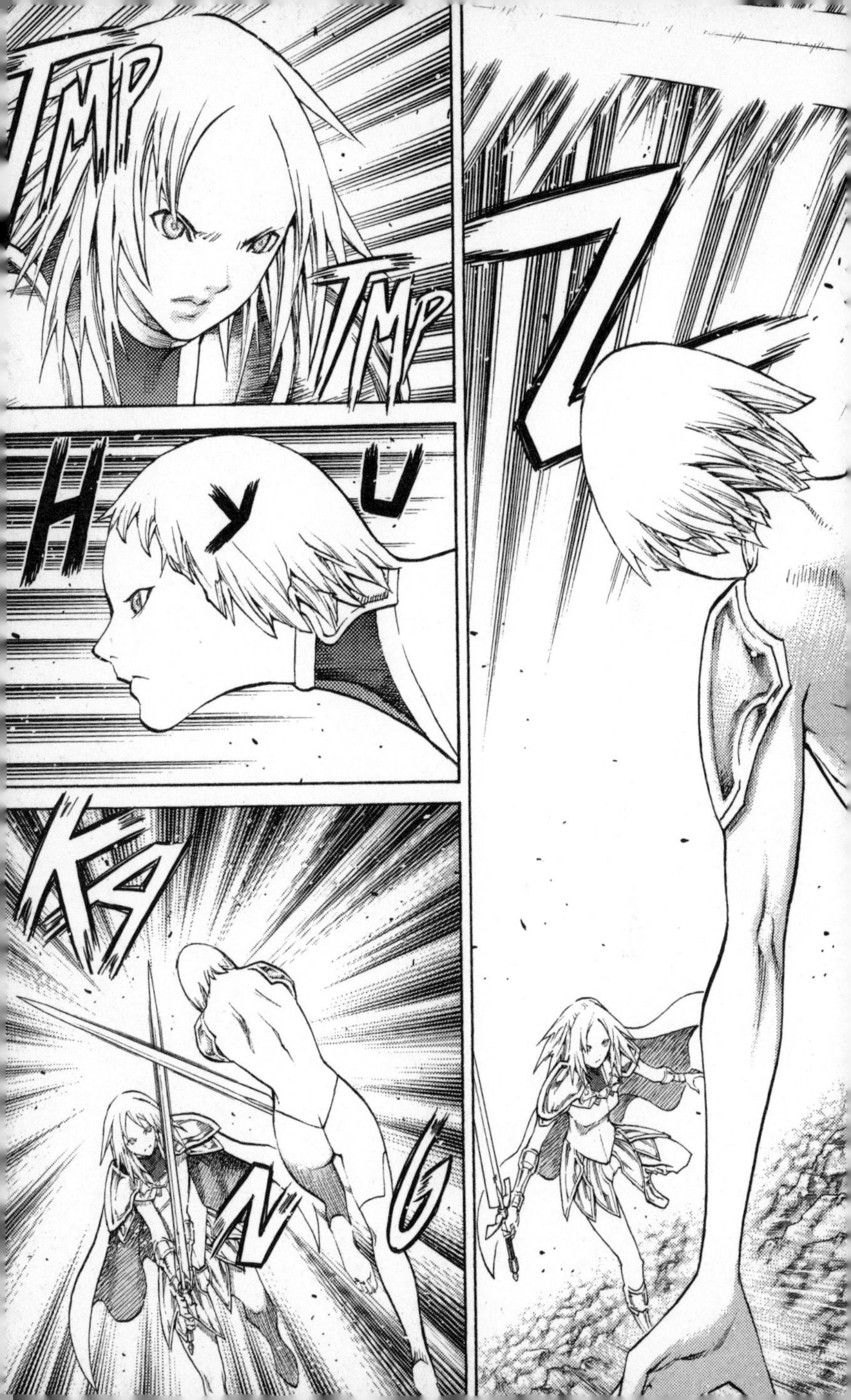
Z
TMP
TMP
HYU
KA
NG

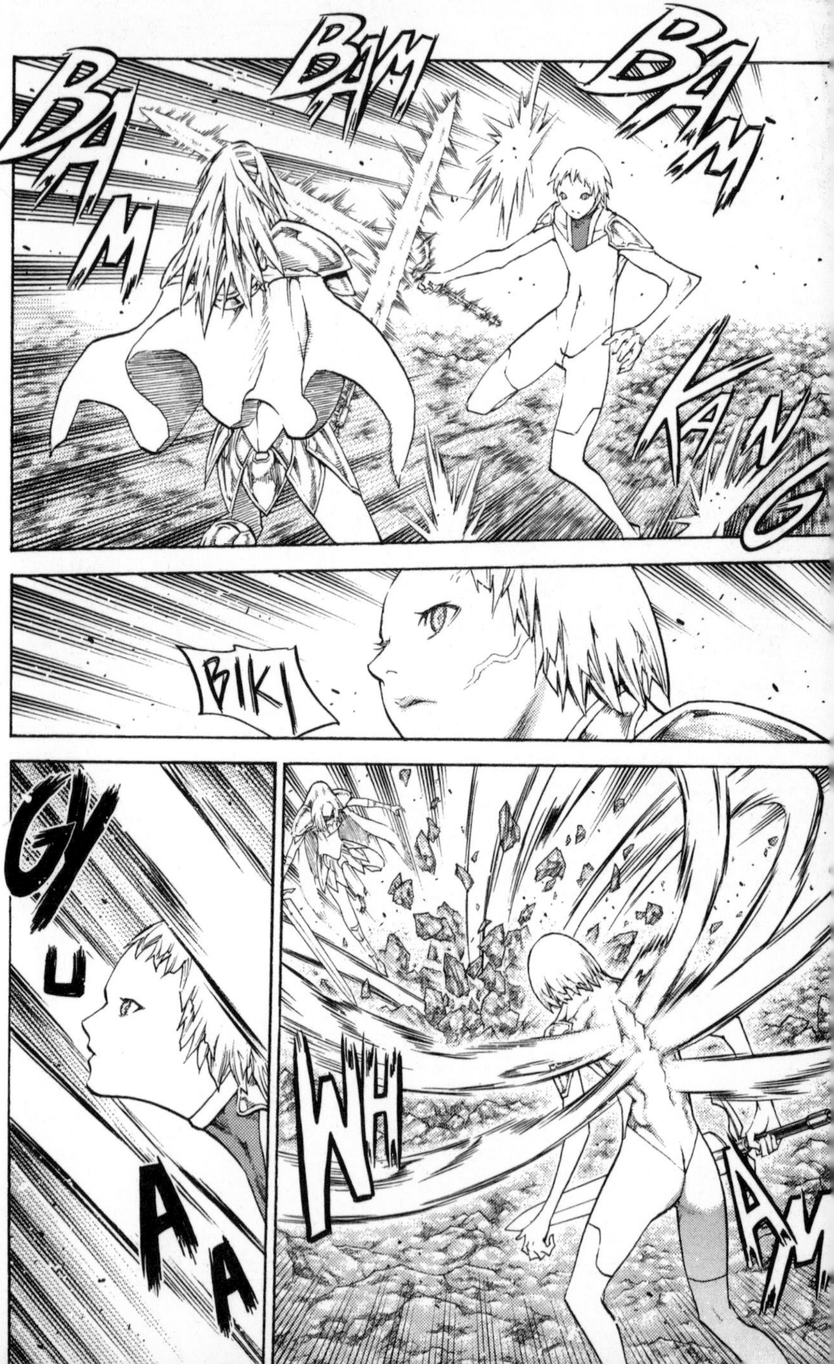
BAM
BAM
BAM
KANG
BIKI
WHAM
GYUAAA

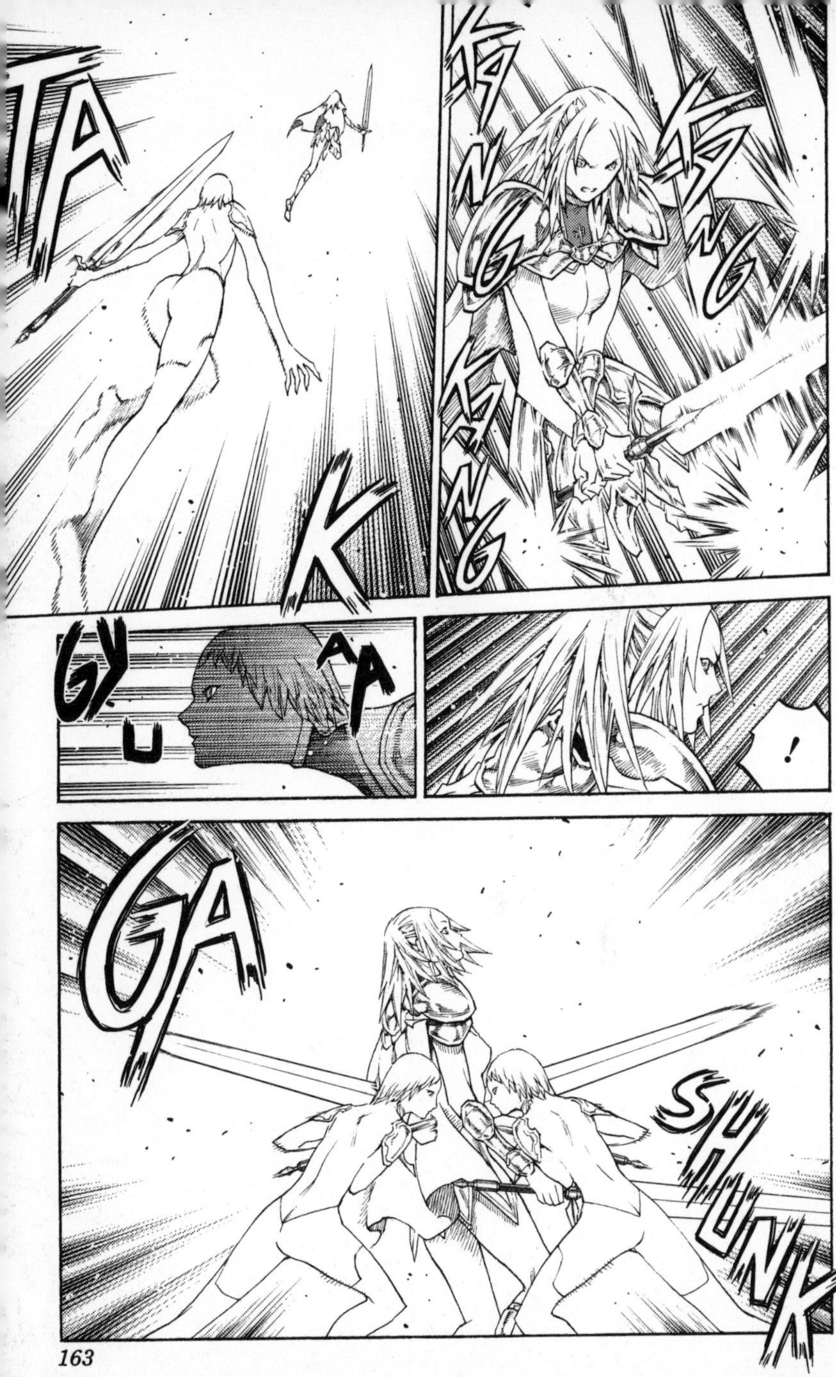
KANG
KANG
KANG
TA
K
!
GYU
AA
GA
SHUNK

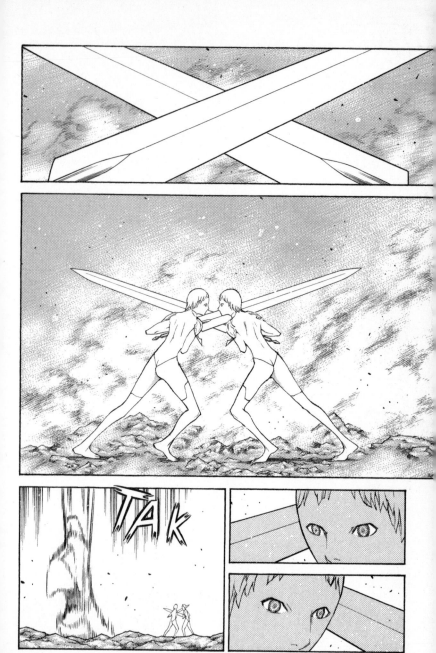

TAK

READ THIS WAY

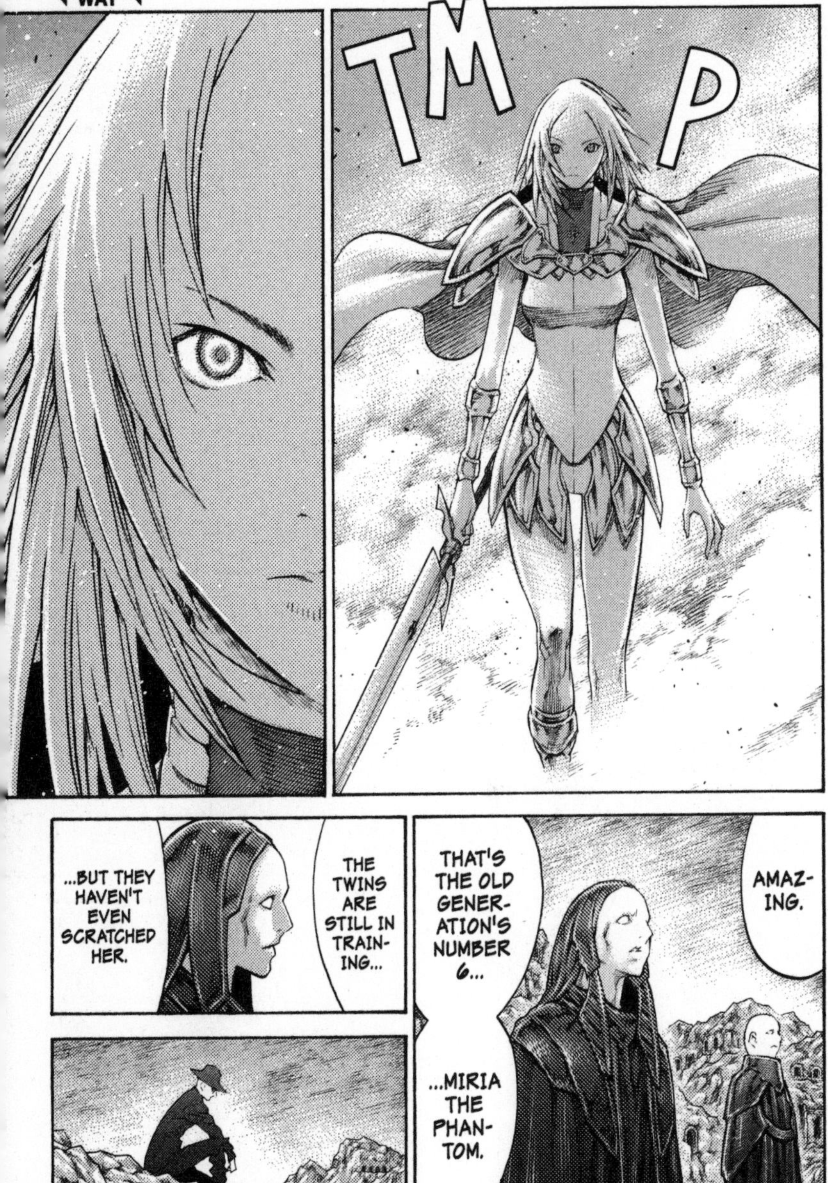
TMP
AMAZING.
THAT'S THE OLD GENERATION'S NUMBER 6...
...MIRIA THE PHANTOM.
THE TWINS ARE STILL IN TRAINING...
...BUT THEY HAVEN'T EVEN SCRATCHED HER.

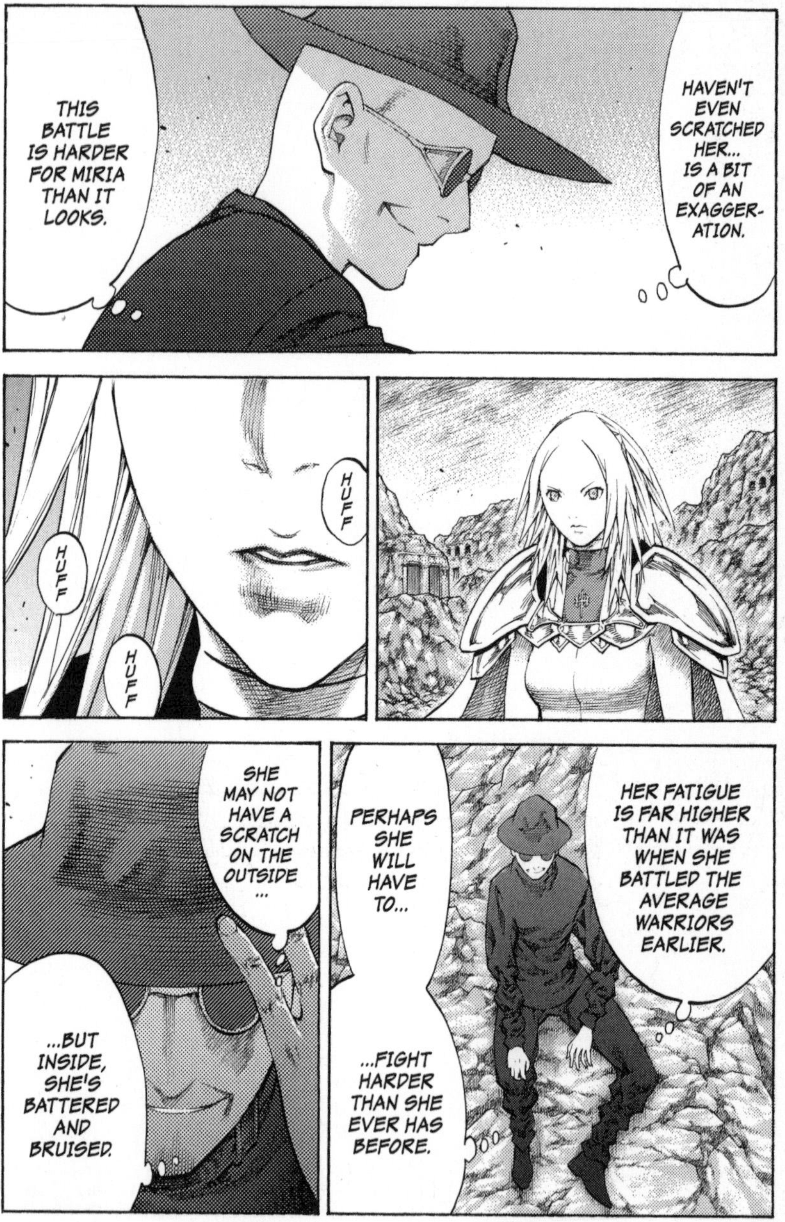
HAVEN'T EVEN SCRATCHED HER... IS A BIT OF AN EXAGGER-ATION.
THIS BATTLE IS HARDER FOR MIRIA THAN IT LOOKS.
HUFF
HUFF
HUFF
HER FATIGUE IS FAR HIGHER THAN IT WAS WHEN SHE BATTLED THE AVERAGE WARRIORS EARLIER.
PERHAPS SHE WILL HAVE TO...
...FIGHT HARDER THAN SHE EVER HAS BEFORE.
SHE MAY NOT HAVE A SCRATCH ON THE OUTSIDE ...
...BUT INSIDE, SHE'S BATTERED AND BRUISED.

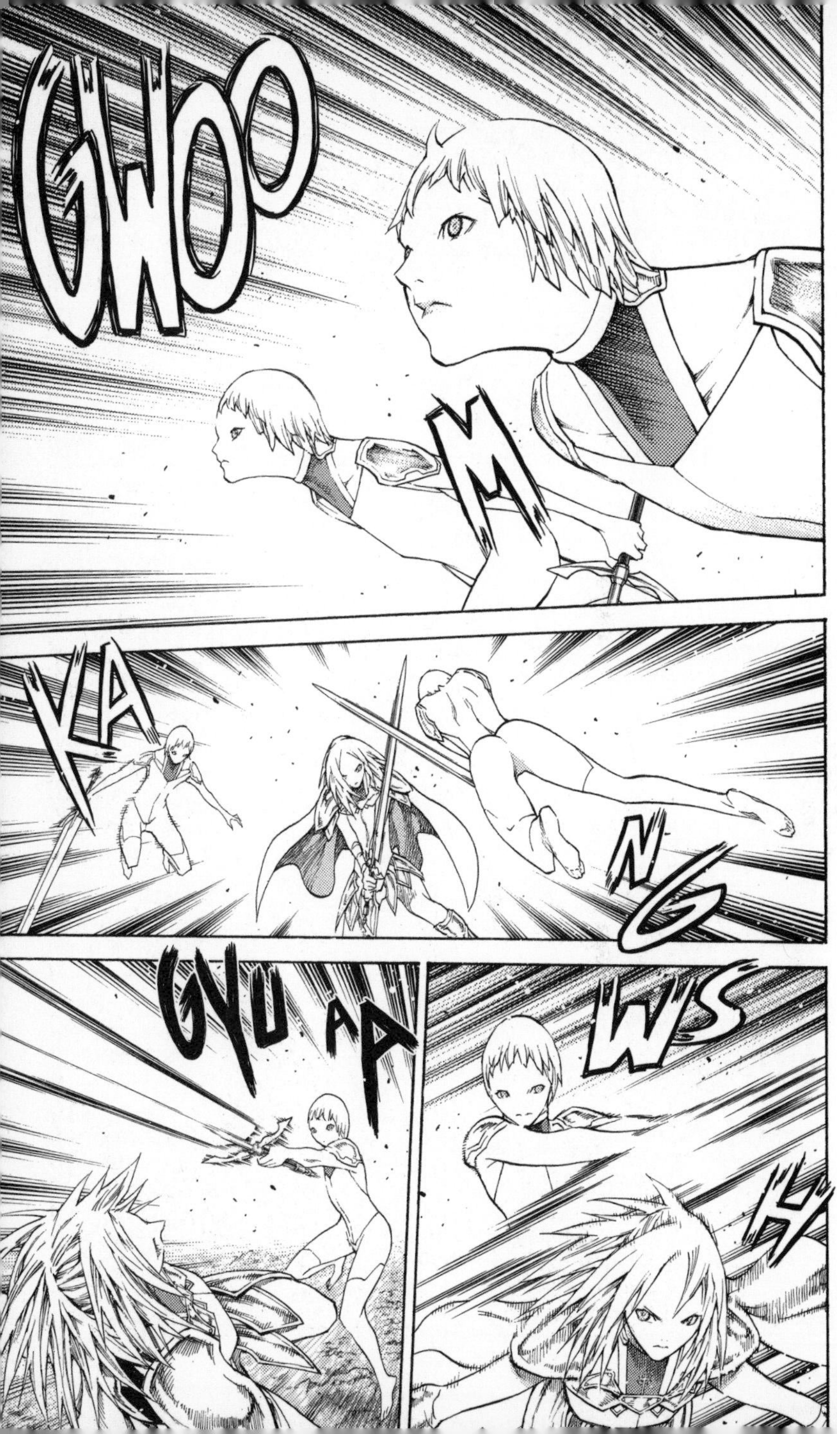
GWOO
M
KA
NG
WS
KY
GYU
AP

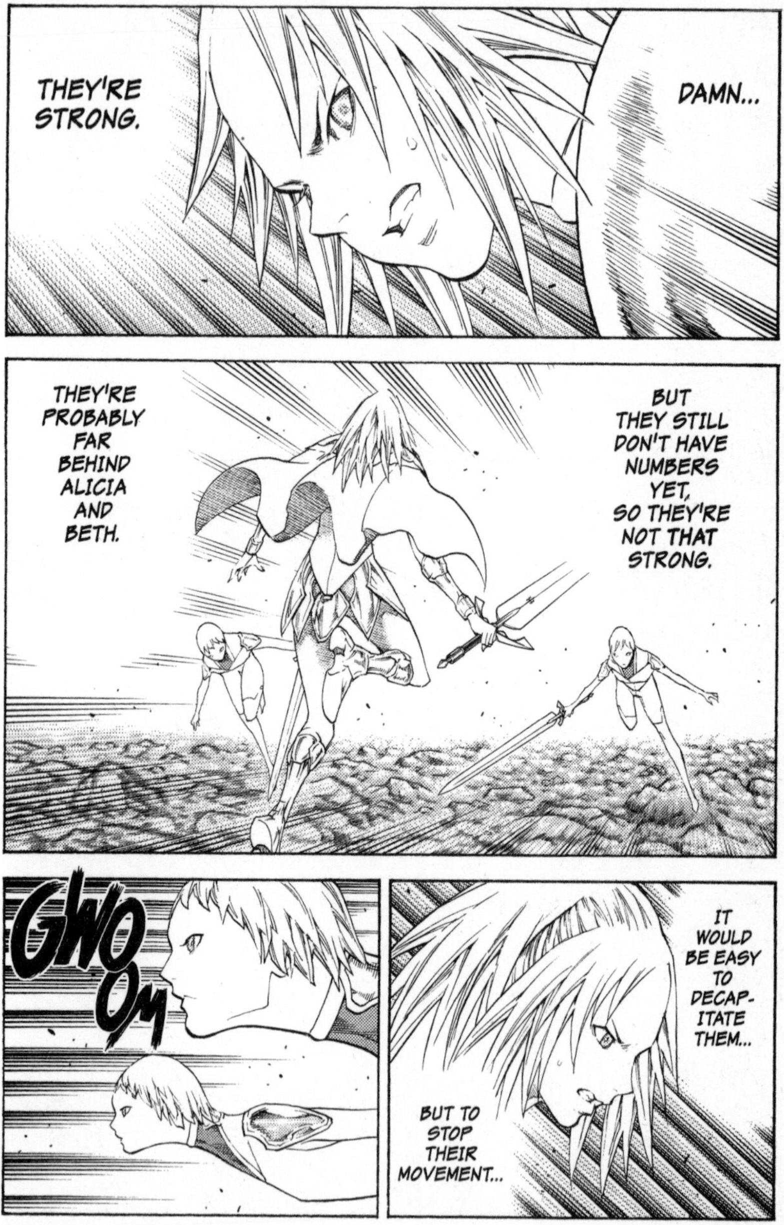
DAMN...
THEY'RE STRONG.
BUT THEY STILL DON'T HAVE NUMBERS YET, SO THEY'RE NOT THAT STRONG.
THEY'RE PROBABLY FAR BEHIND ALICIA AND BETH.
IT WOULD BE EASY TO DECAP-ITATE THEM...
BUT TO STOP THEIR MOVEMENT...
GWOOM

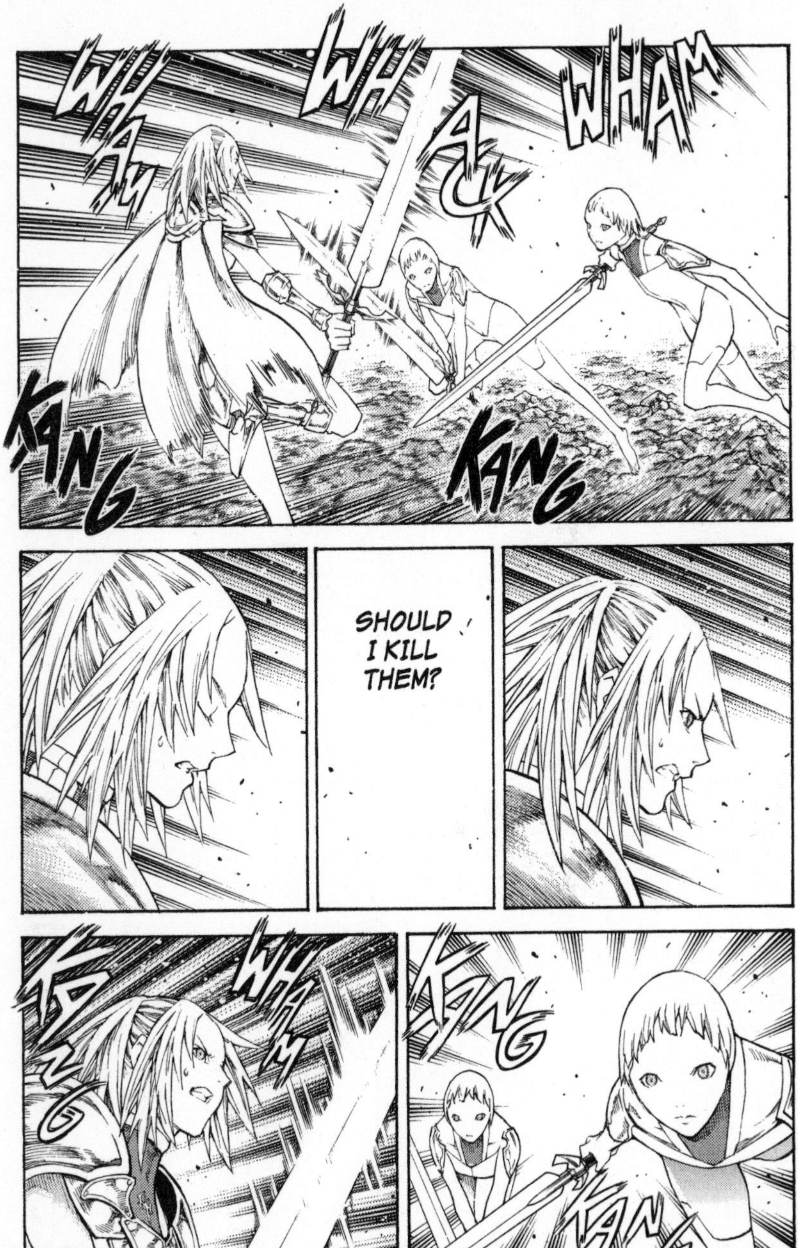
WHAM
WHACK
WHAM
KANG
KANG
SHOULD I KILL THEM?
KANG
KANG
WHAM
KANG

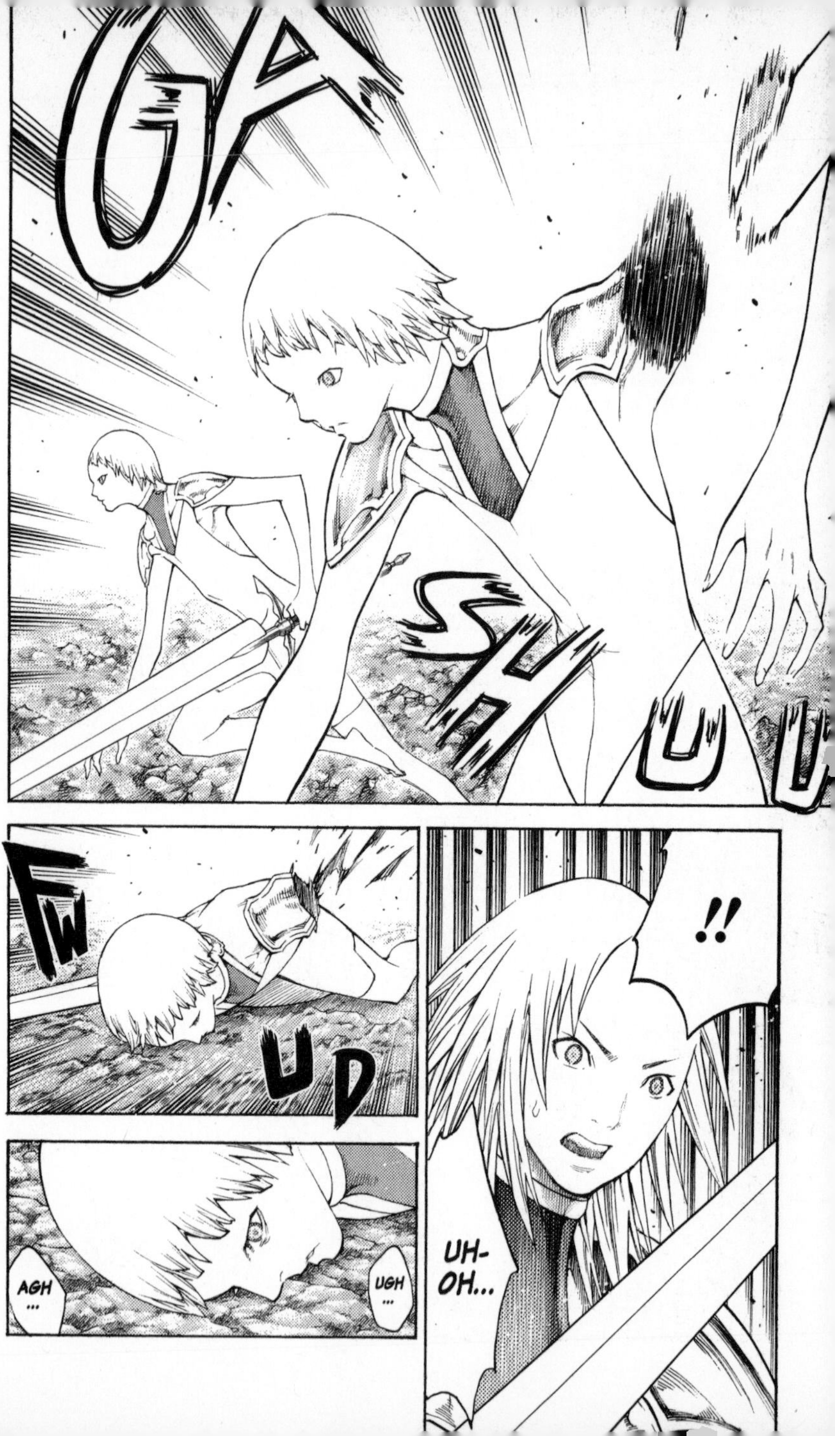
GA
SHUU
!!
UH-OH...
FWUD
UGH...
AGH...

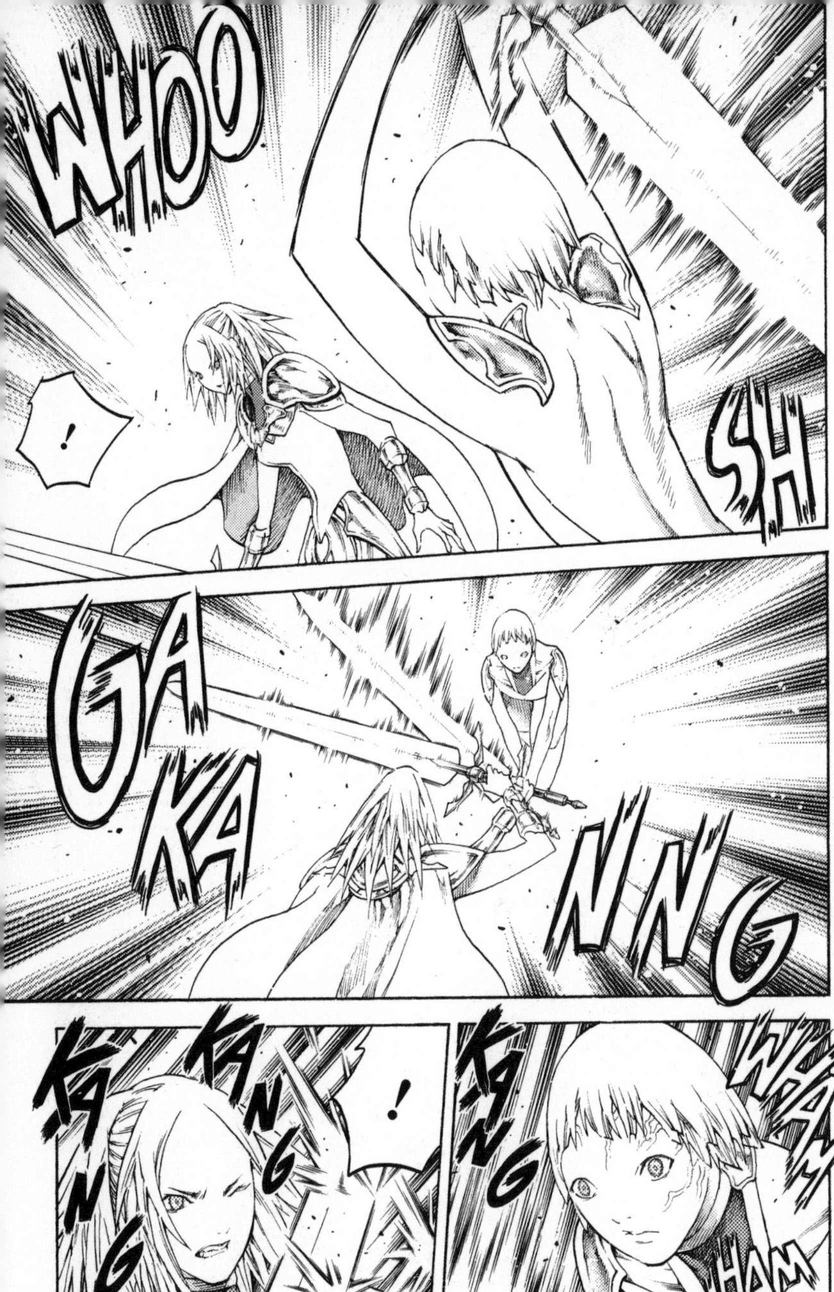
WHOO
SH
!
GAKA
NNG
KANG
WHAM
WHAM
KANG
KANG
!

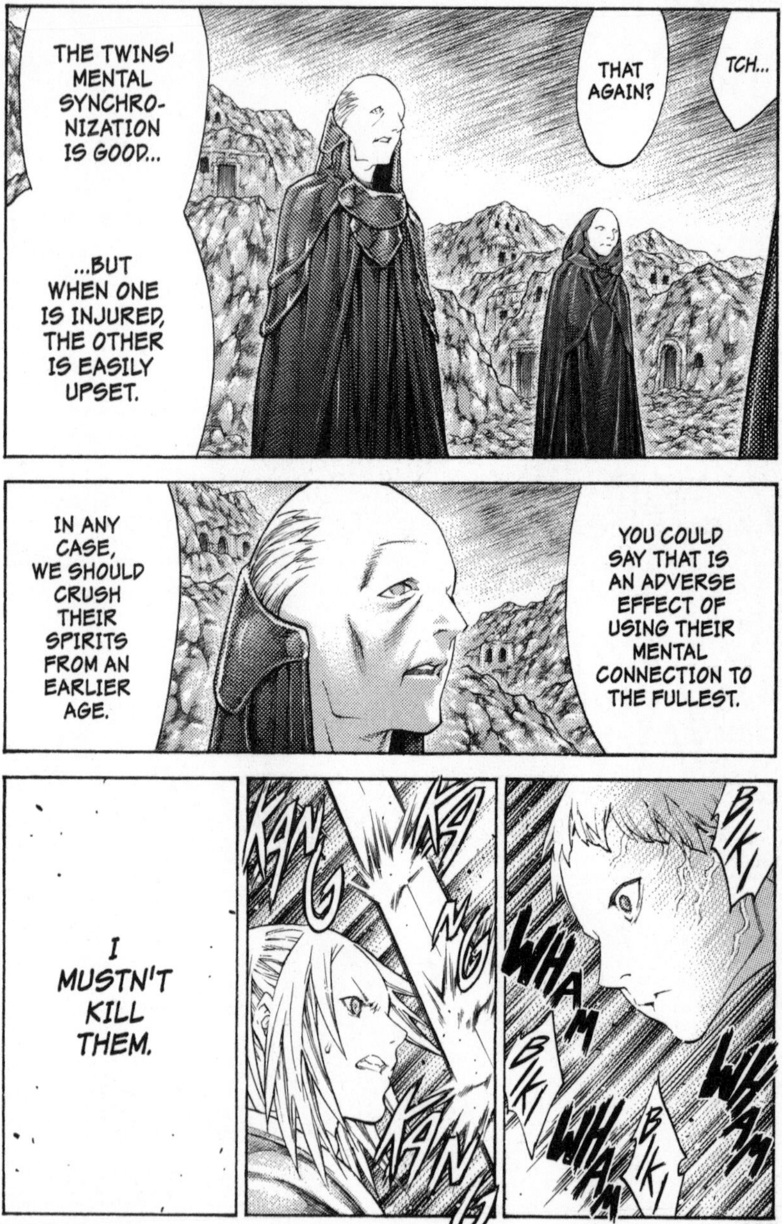
TCH...
THAT AGAIN?
THE TWINS' MENTAL SYNCHRONIZATION IS GOOD...
...BUT WHEN ONE IS INJURED, THE OTHER IS EASILY UPSET.
YOU COULD SAY THAT IS AN ADVERSE EFFECT OF USING THEIR MENTAL CONNECTION TO THE FULLEST.
IN ANY CASE, WE SHOULD CRUSH THEIR SPIRITS FROM AN EARLIER AGE.
BIKI
WHAM
WHAM
BIKI
WHAM
BIKI
KANG
KANG
KANG
I MUSTN'T KILL THEM.

READ THIS WAY

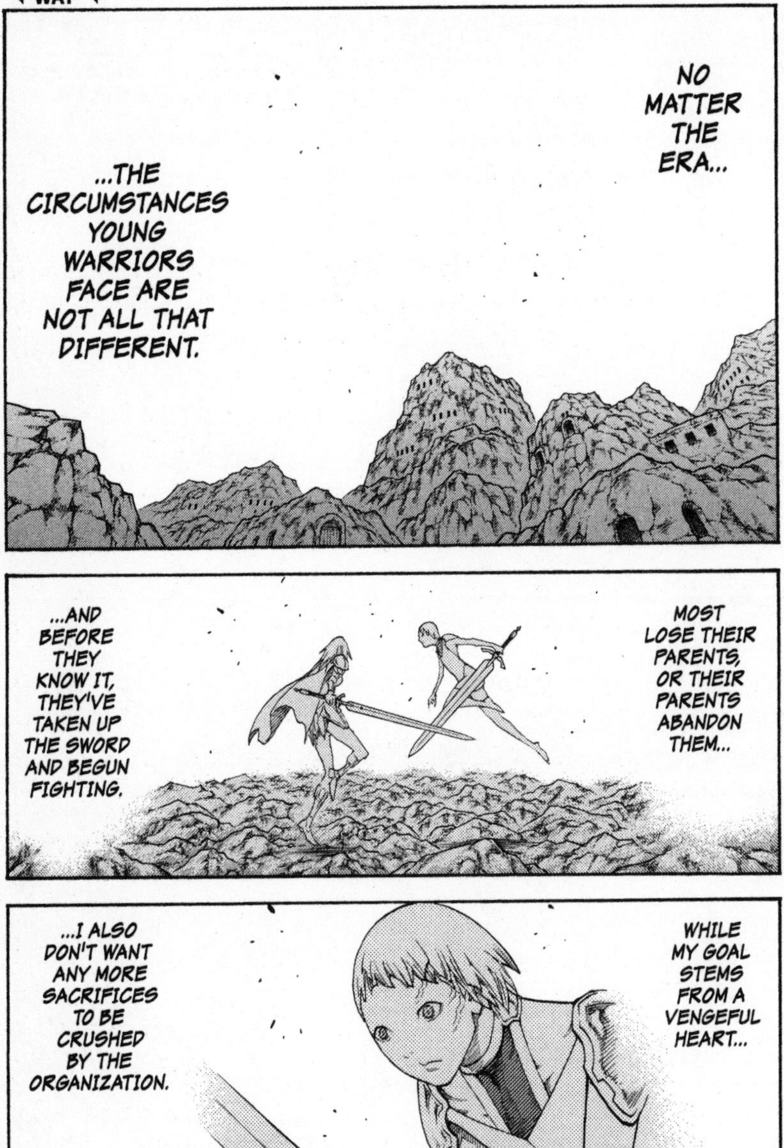
NO MATTER THE ERA...
...THE CIRCUMSTANCES YOUNG WARRIORS FACE ARE NOT ALL THAT DIFFERENT.
MOST LOSE THEIR PARENTS, OR THEIR PARENTS ABANDON THEM...
...AND BEFORE THEY KNOW IT, THEY'VE TAKEN UP THE SWORD AND BEGUN FIGHTING.
WHILE MY GOAL STEMS FROM A VENGEFUL HEART...
...I ALSO DON'T WANT ANY MORE SACRIFICES TO BE CRUSHED BY THE ORGANIZATION.

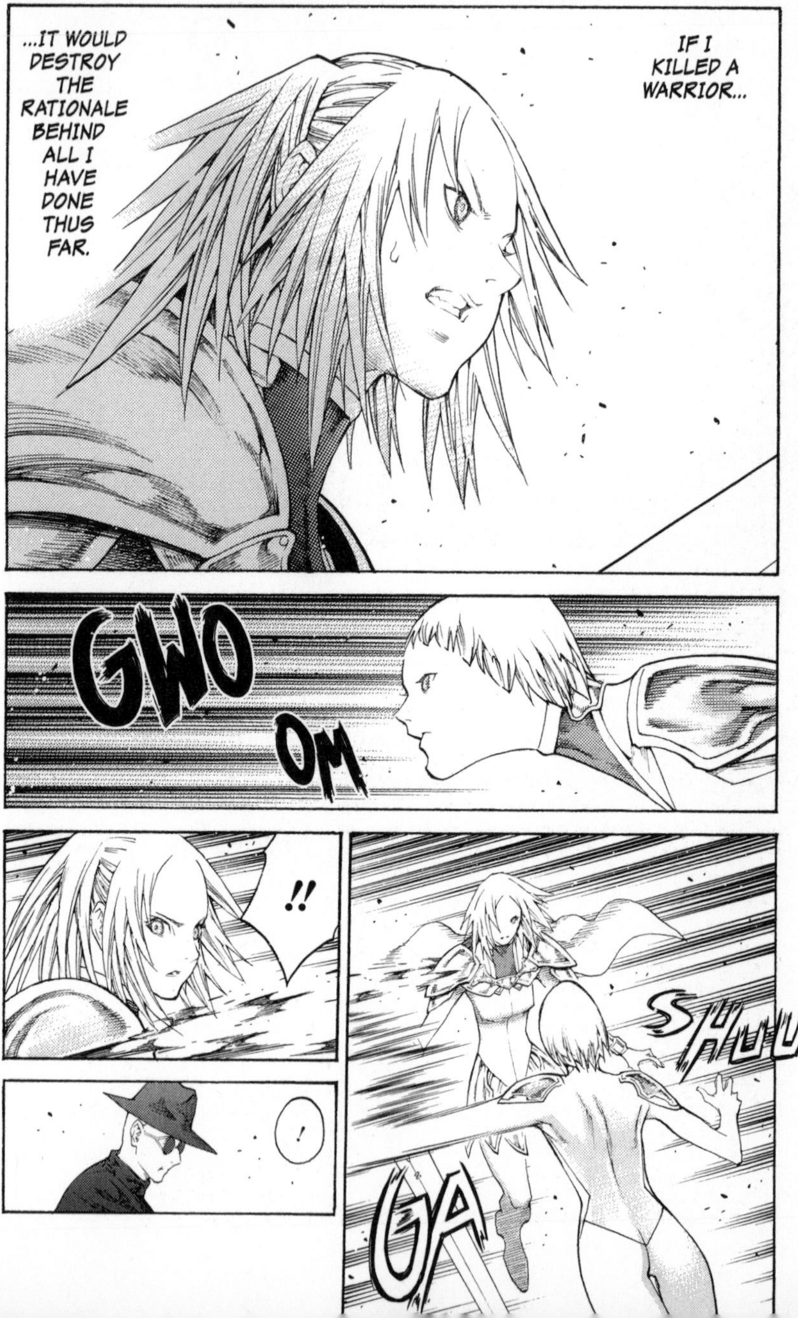
IF I KILLED A WARRIOR...
...IT WOULD DESTROY THE RATIONALE BEHIND ALL I HAVE DONE THUS FAR.
GWO
OM
SHUU
GA
!!
!

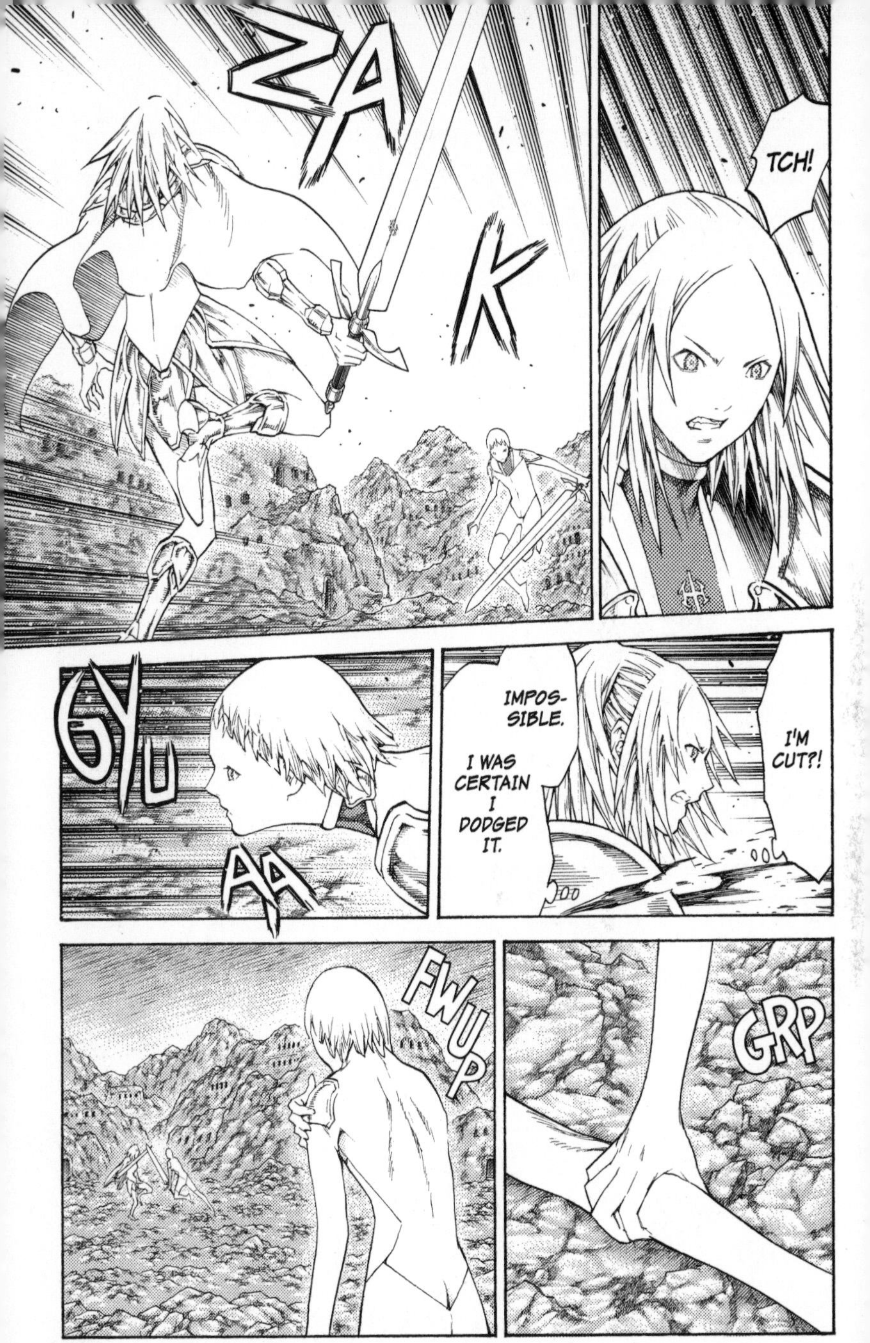
TCH!
ZAK
I'M CUT?!
IMPOS-SIBLE.
I WAS CERTAIN I DODGED IT.
GYUAA
GRP
FWUP

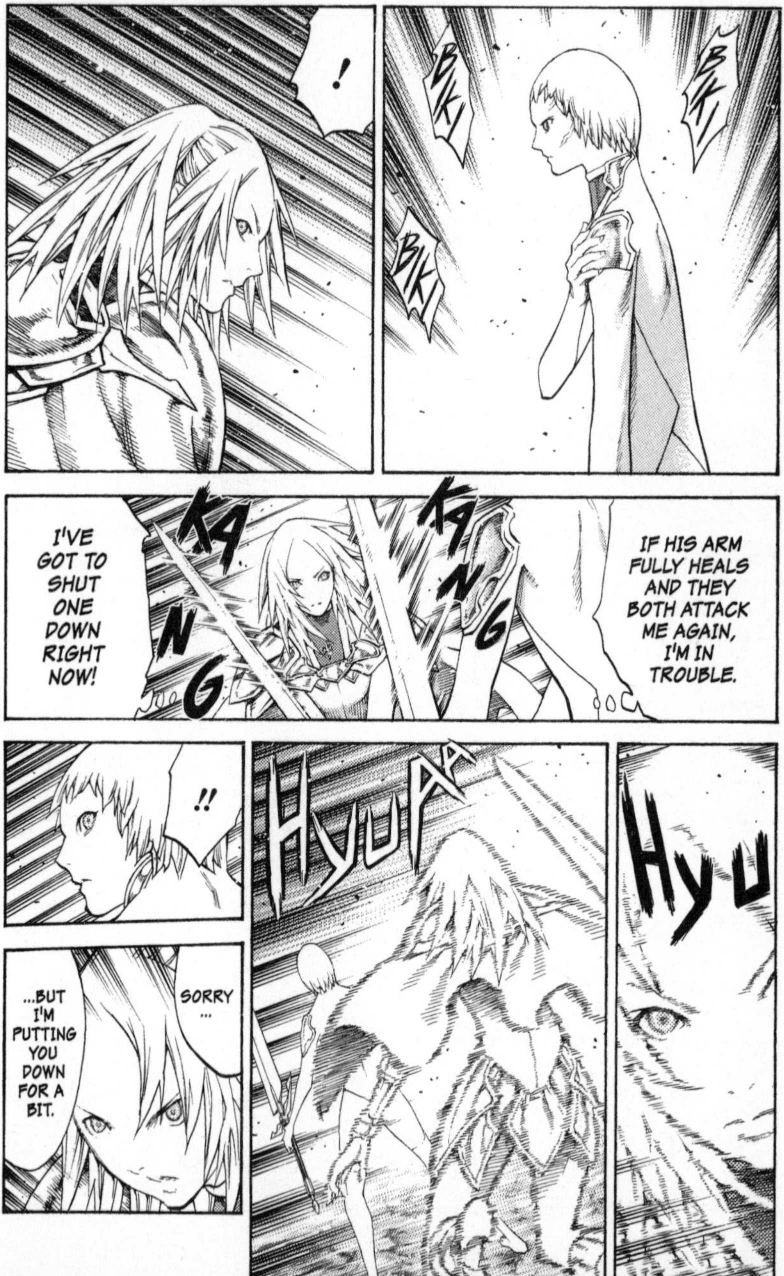
BIKI
BIKI
BIKI
!
IF HIS ARM FULLY HEALS AND THEY BOTH ATTACK ME AGAIN, I'M IN TROUBLE.
KANG
KANG
I'VE GOT TO SHUT ONE DOWN RIGHT NOW!
HYU
HYUA
!!
SORRY...
...BUT I'M PUTTING YOU DOWN FOR A BIT.

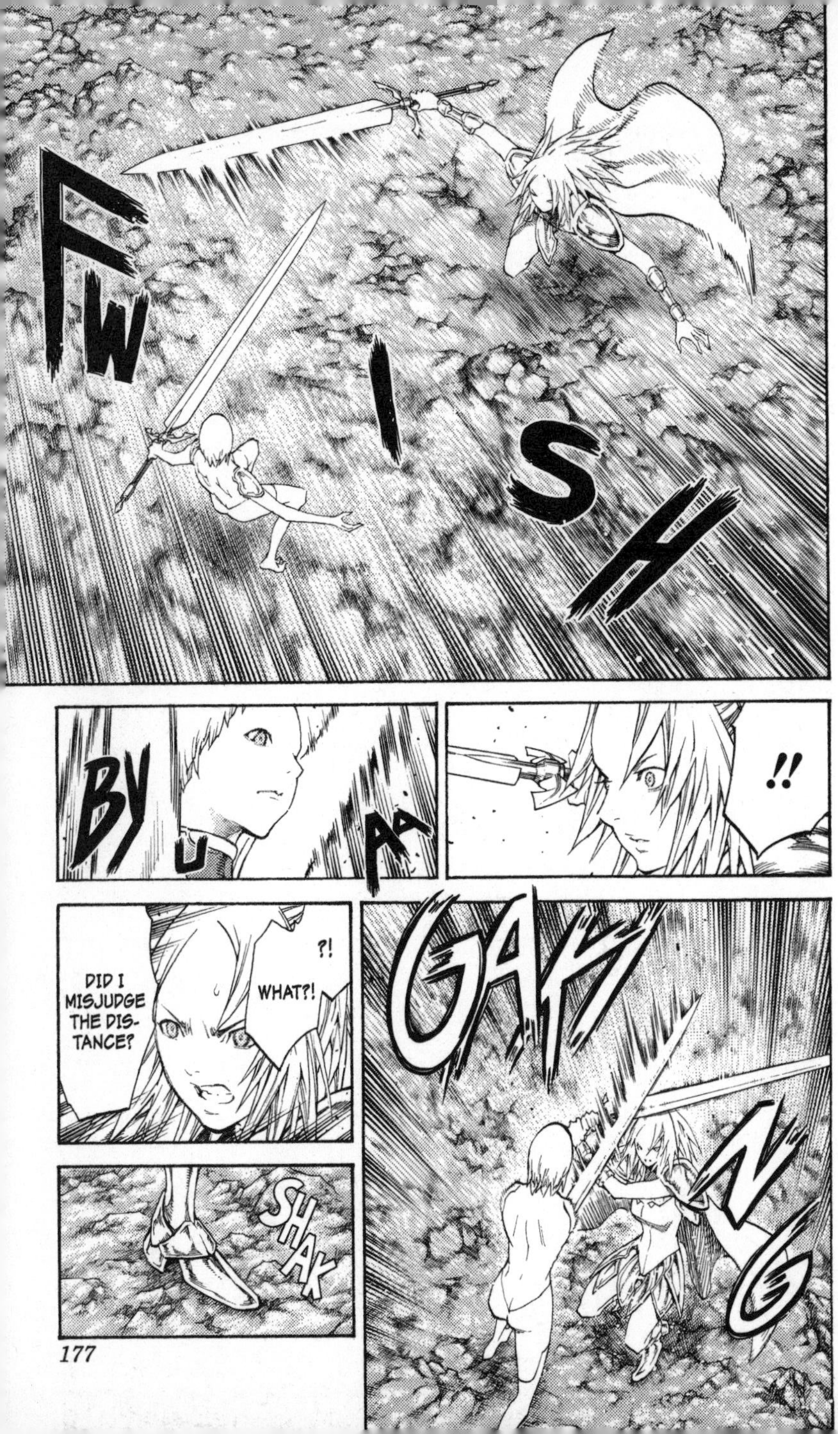
FWISH
!!
BYUAA
GAK
NG
?!
WHAT?!
DID I MISJUDGE THE DIS-TANCE?
SHAK

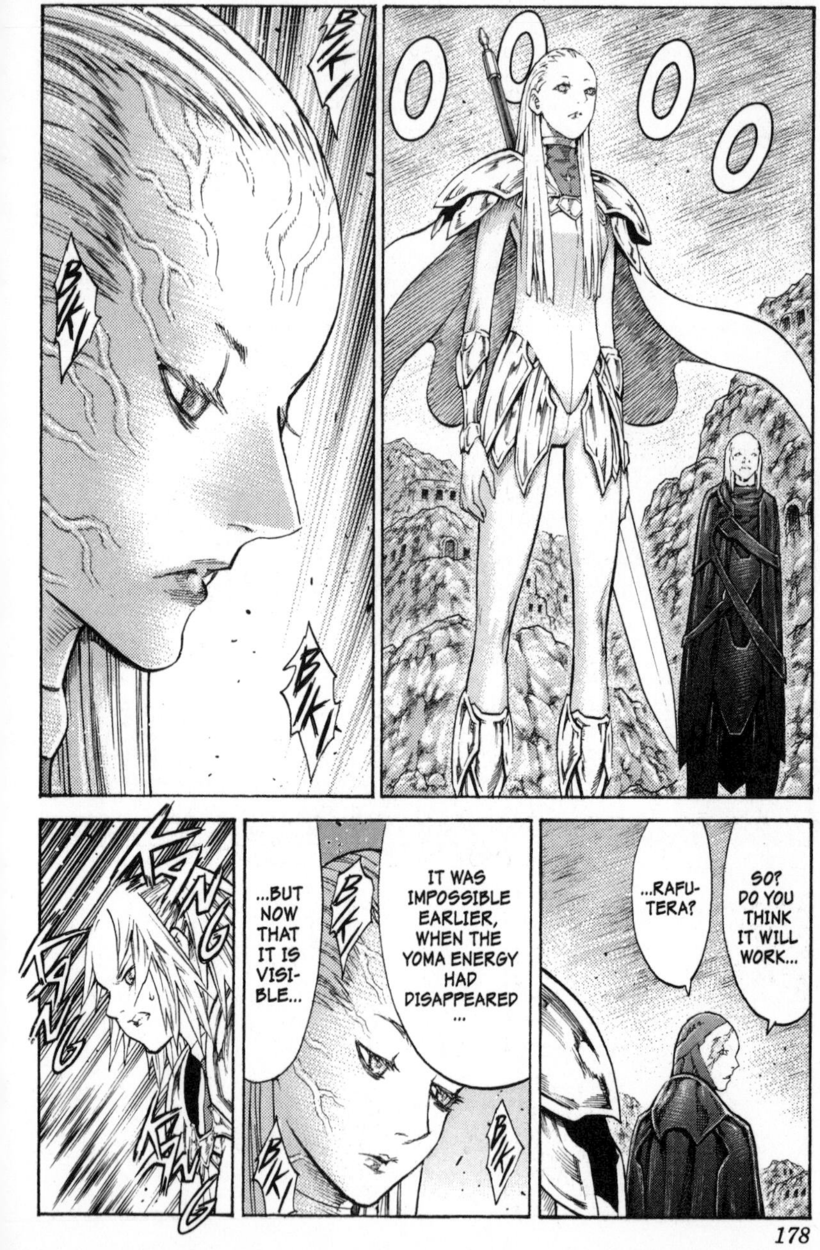
OOOO
BIKI
BIKI
BIKI
SO? DO YOU THINK IT WILL WORK...
...RAFUTERA?
IT WAS IMPOSSIBLE EARLIER, WHEN THE YOMA ENERGY HAD DISAPPEARED...
...BUT NOW THAT IT IS VISIBLE...
BIKI
BIKI
BIKI
KANG
KANG
KANG

READ THIS WAY

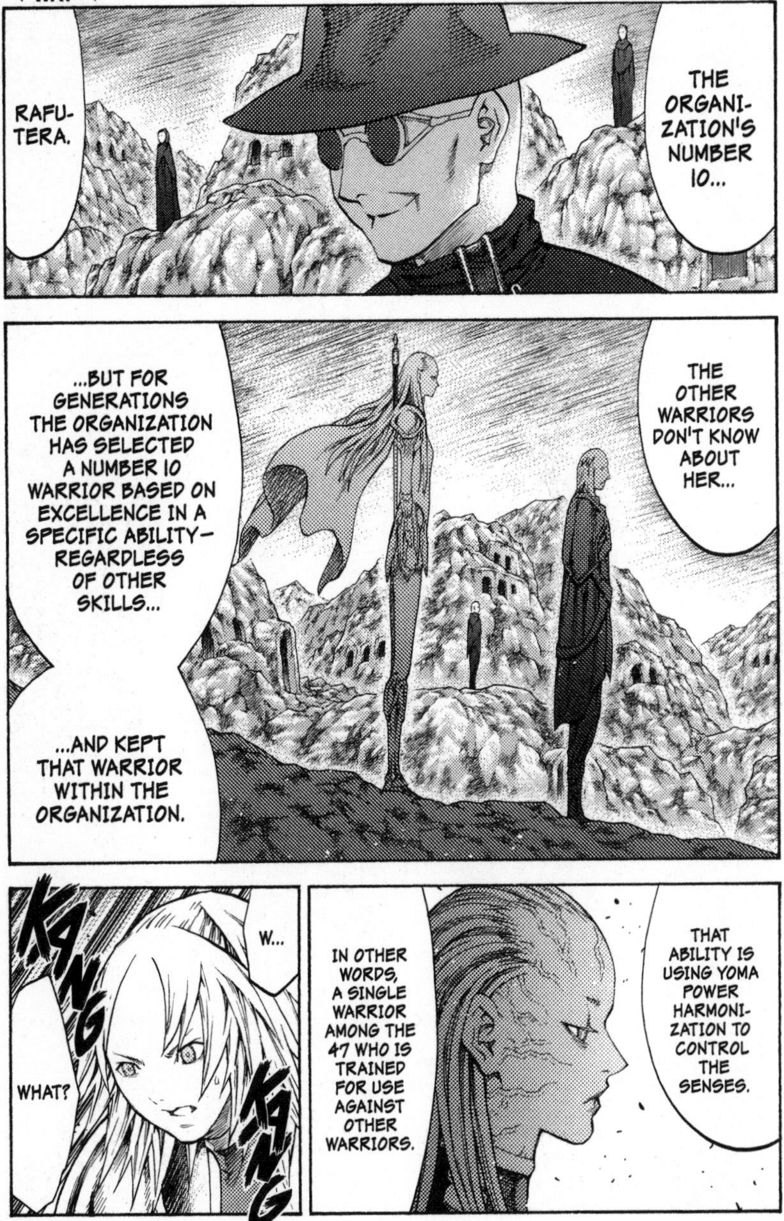
THE ORGANIZATION'S NUMBER 10...
RAFUTERA.
THE OTHER WARRIORS DON'T KNOW ABOUT HER...
...BUT FOR GENERATIONS THE ORGANIZATION HAS SELECTED A NUMBER 10 WARRIOR BASED ON EXCELLENCE IN A SPECIFIC ABILITY—REGARDLESS OF OTHER SKILLS...
...AND KEPT THAT WARRIOR WITHIN THE ORGANIZATION.
THAT ABILITY IS USING YOMA POWER HARMONIZATION TO CONTROL THE SENSES.
IN OTHER WORDS, A SINGLE WARRIOR AMONG THE 47 WHO IS TRAINED FOR USE AGAINST OTHER WARRIORS.
W...
KANG
WHAT?
KANG

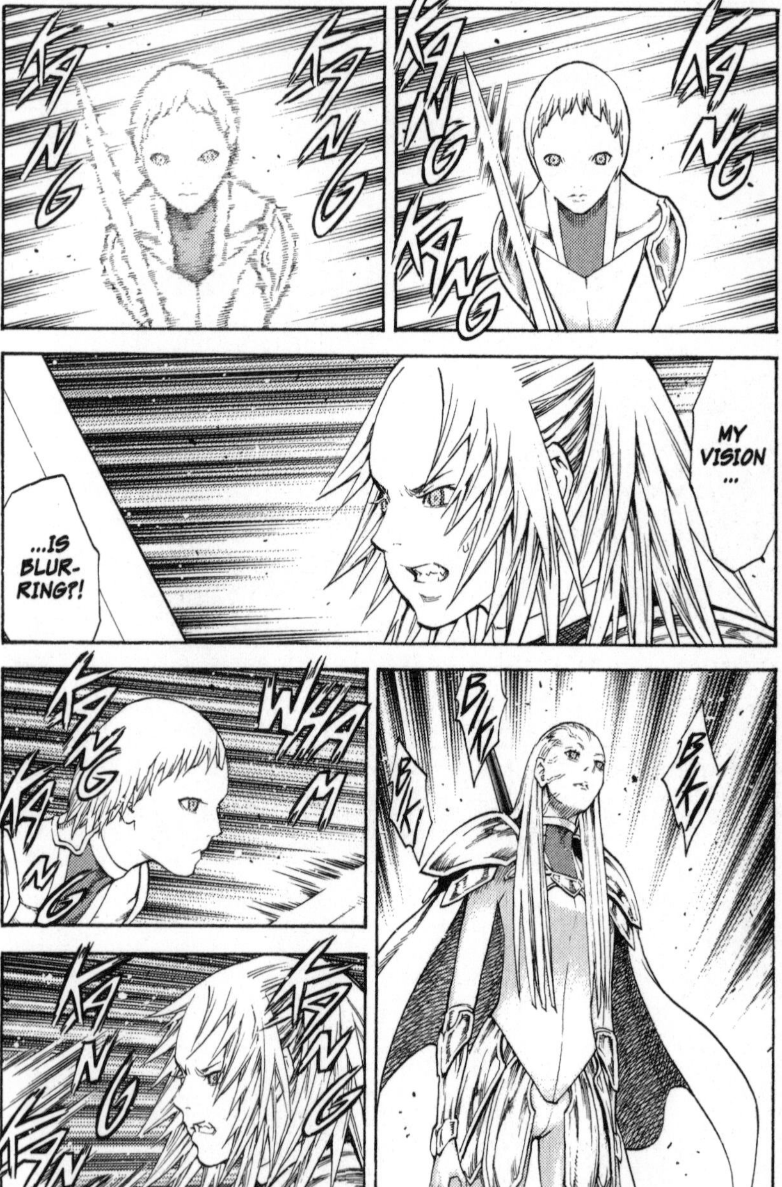

KANG
KANG
KANG
KANG
KANG
KANG
MY VISION...
...IS BLUR-RING?!
BIKI
BIKI
BIKI
WHAMM
KANG
KAKANG
KANG
KANG
KANG

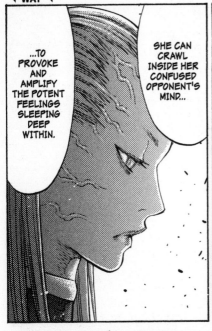

READ THIS WAY

NUMBER 10'S CONTROL OF THE SENSES ALLOWS HER TO OBSCURE HER OPPONENT'S VISION AND UP-SET HER SENSE OF DISTANCE SOMEWHAT...
...BUT SHE WILL NOW USE HER *TRUE* POWER.
SHE CAN CRAWL INSIDE HER CONFUSED OPPONENT'S MIND...
...TO PROVOKE AND AMPLIFY THE POTENT FEELINGS SLEEPING DEEP WITHIN.
!
KANG
KANG
KANG
KANG
KANG
KANG
WHY?
WHY ARE *YOU* HERE?

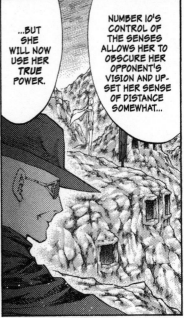

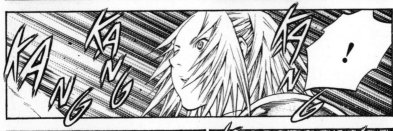

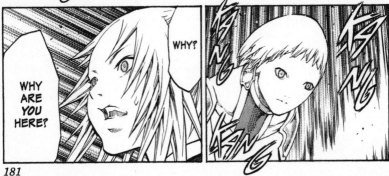

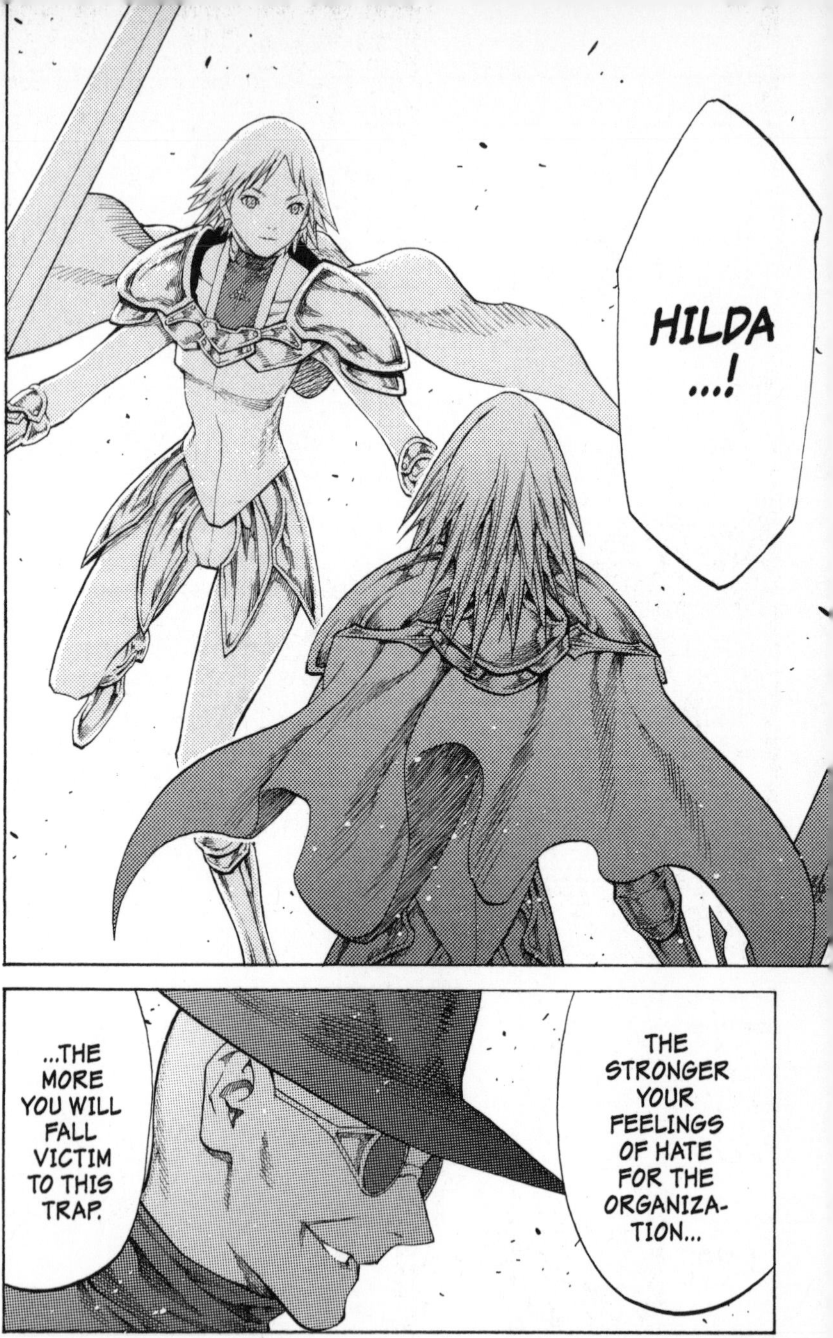
HILDA ...!
THE STRONGER YOUR FEELINGS OF HATE FOR THE ORGANIZATION...
...THE MORE YOU WILL FALL VICTIM TO THIS TRAP.

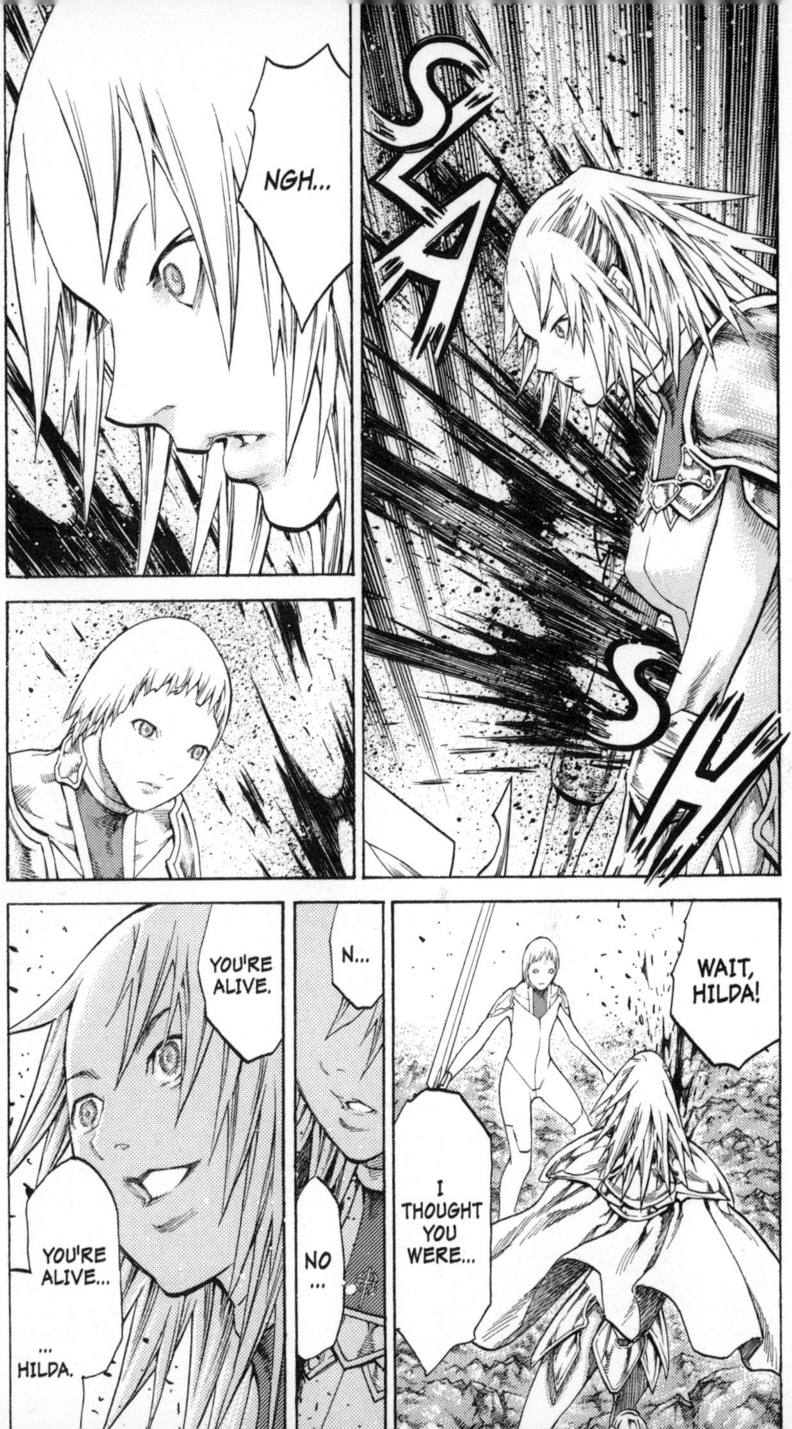
SLASH
NGH...
WAIT, HILDA!
I THOUGHT YOU WERE...
N...
NO ...
YOU'RE ALIVE.
YOU'RE ALIVE...
... HILDA.

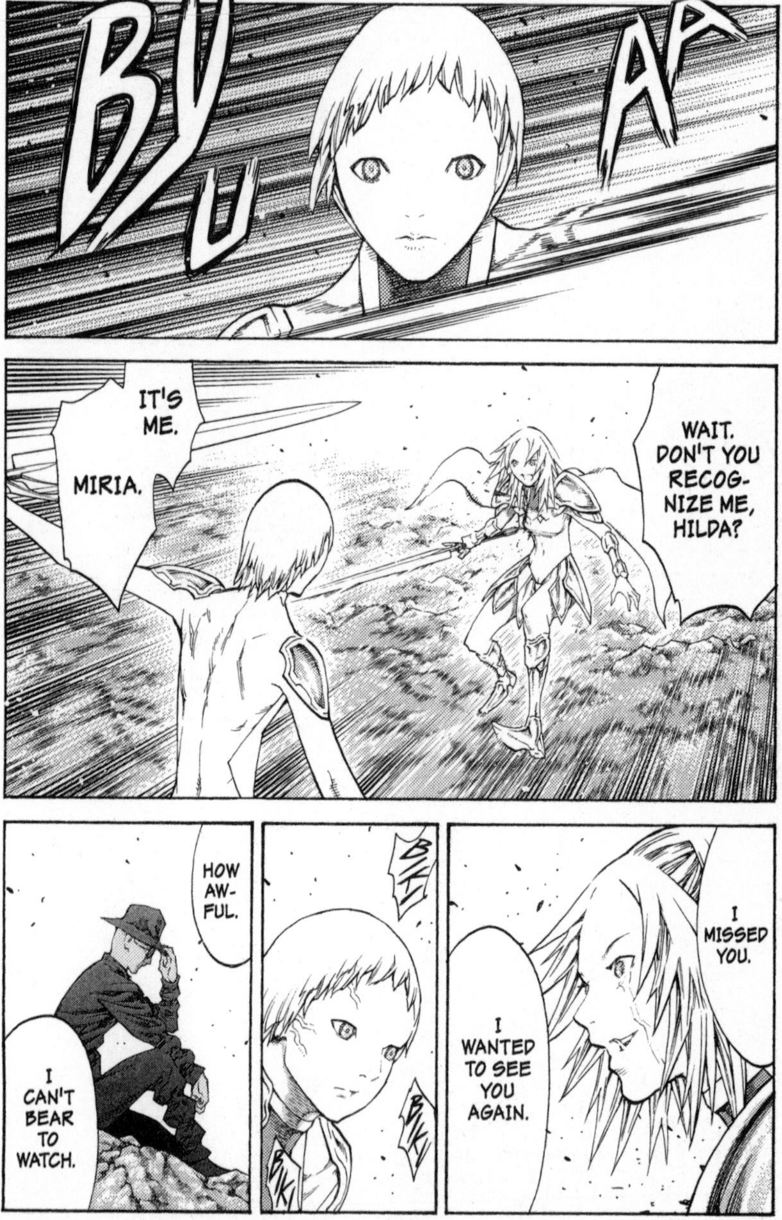
BYUUAA
WAIT. DON'T YOU RECOGNIZE ME, HILDA?
IT'S ME.
MIRIA.
I MISSED YOU.
I WANTED TO SEE YOU AGAIN.
BIKI
BIKI
BIKI
HOW AWFUL.
I CAN'T BEAR TO WATCH.

READ THIS WAY

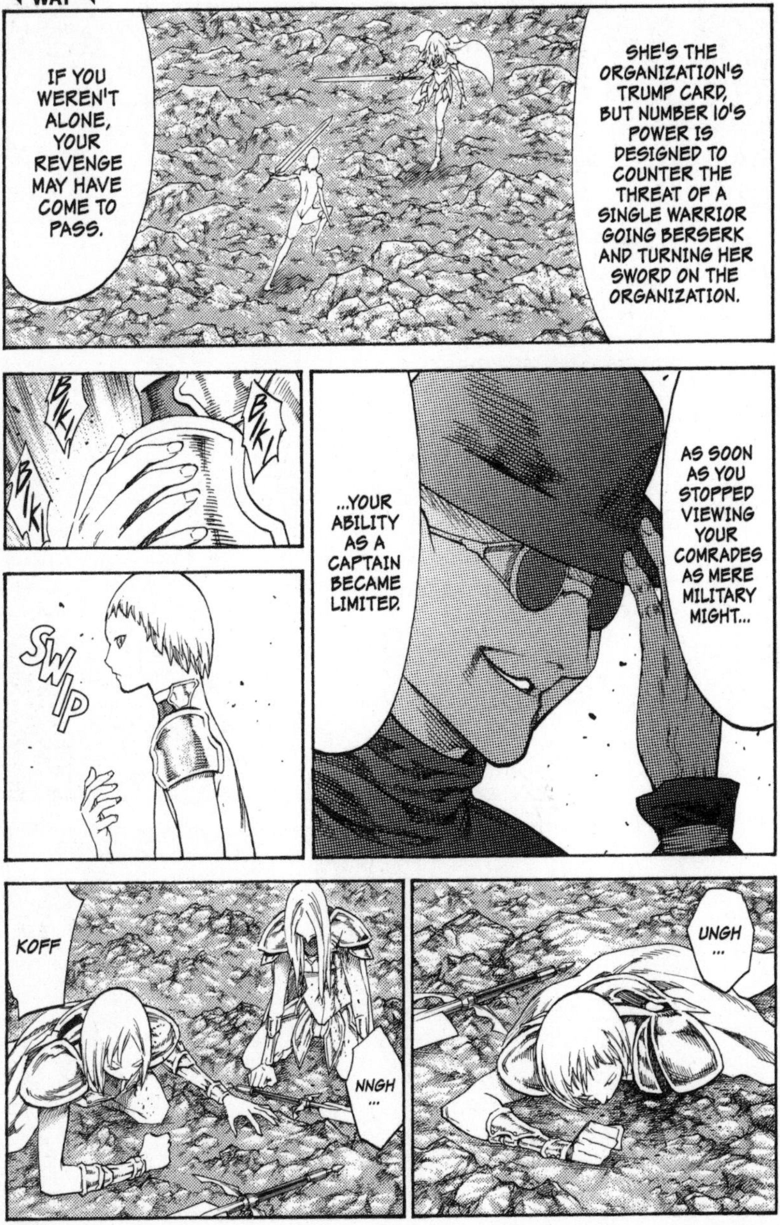

SHE'S THE ORGANIZATION'S TRUMP CARD, BUT NUMBER 10'S POWER IS DESIGNED TO COUNTER THE THREAT OF A SINGLE WARRIOR GOING BERSERK AND TURNING HER SWORD ON THE ORGANIZATION.
IF YOU WEREN'T ALONE, YOUR REVENGE MAY HAVE COME TO PASS.
AS SOON AS YOU STOPPED VIEWING YOUR COMRADES AS MERE MILITARY MIGHT...
...YOUR ABILITY AS A CAPTAIN BECAME LIMITED.
BIKI
BIKI
BIKI
SWIP
UNGH...
KOFF
NNGH...

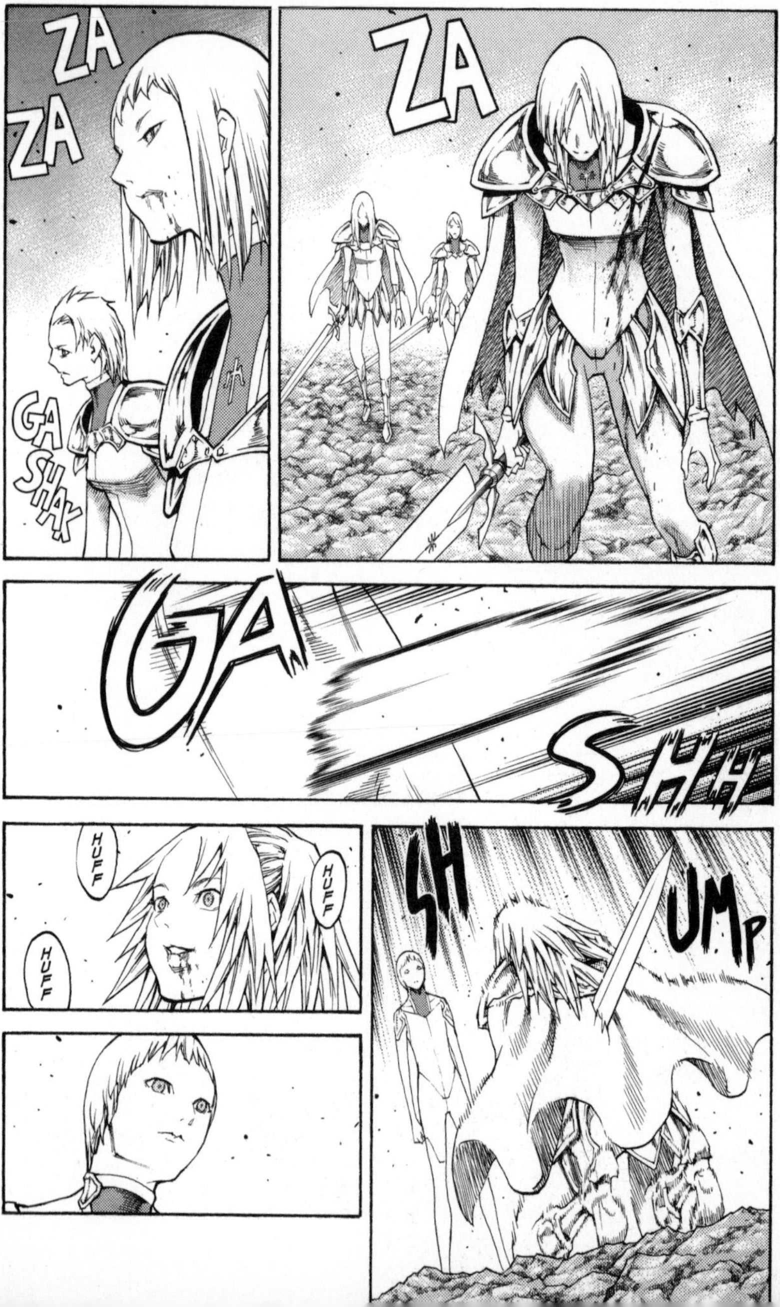
ZA
ZA
ZA
GA SHAK
GA
SHH
SH
UMP
HUFF
HUFF
HUFF

READ THIS WAY

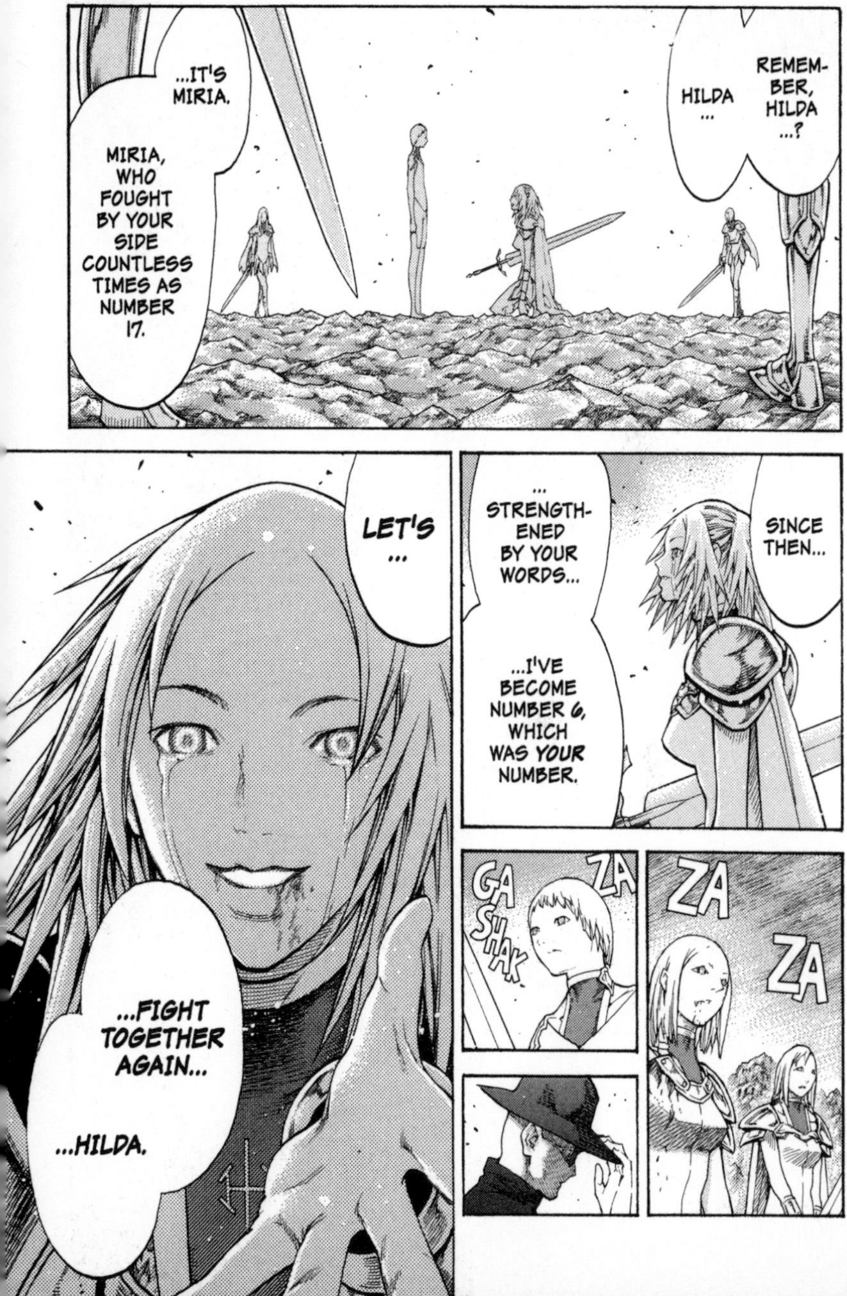
REMEMBER, HILDA...?
HILDA...
...IT'S MIRIA.
MIRIA, WHO FOUGHT BY YOUR SIDE COUNTLESS TIMES AS NUMBER 17.
SINCE THEN...
...STRENGTHENED BY YOUR WORDS...
...I'VE BECOME NUMBER 6, WHICH WAS YOUR NUMBER.
ZA
ZA
ZA
GA SHAK
LET'S...
...FIGHT TOGETHER AGAIN...
...HILDA.

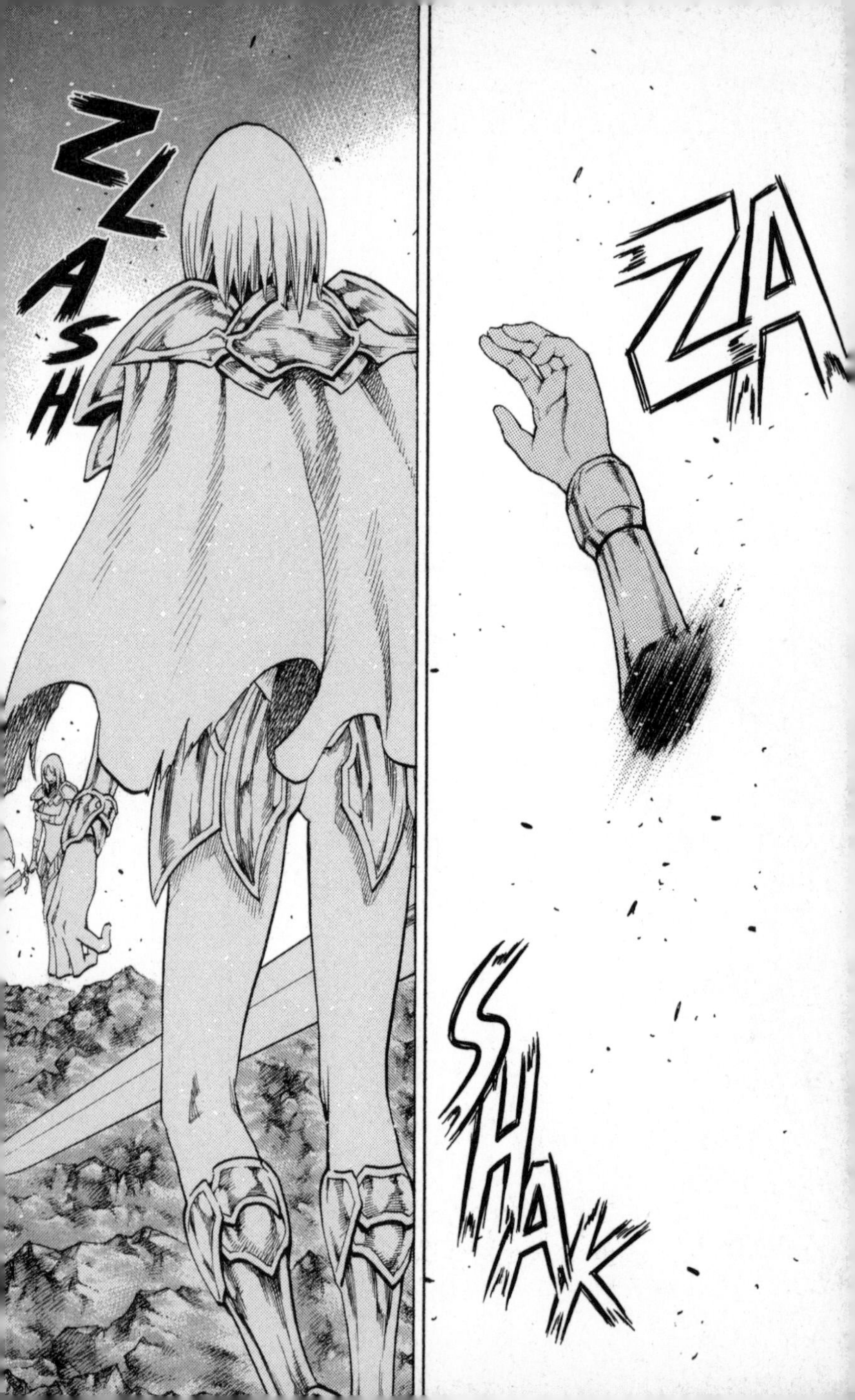
ZA
SHAK
ZLASH

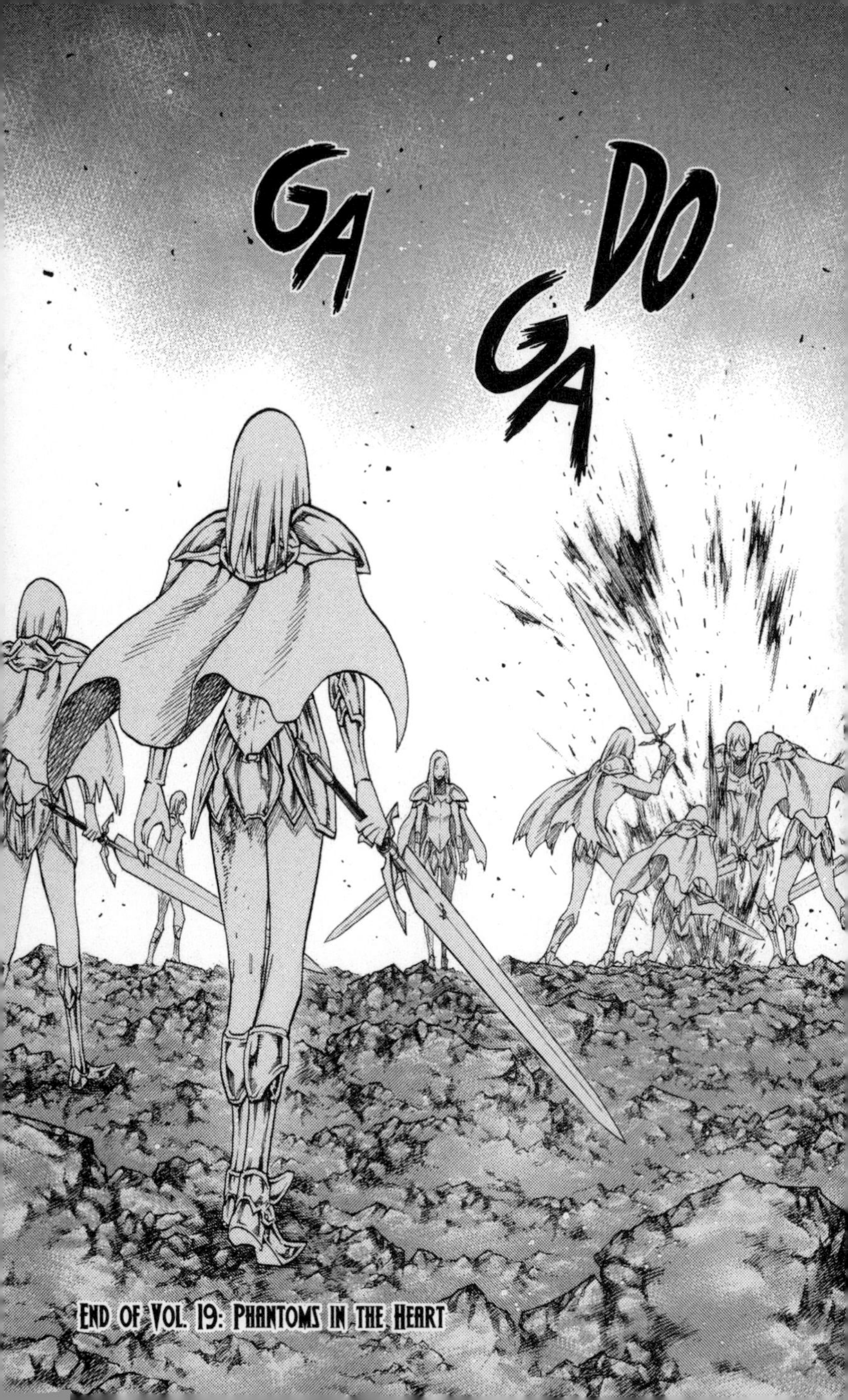
DO
GA
GA
End of Vol. 19: Phantoms in the Heart

クレイモア

Claymore

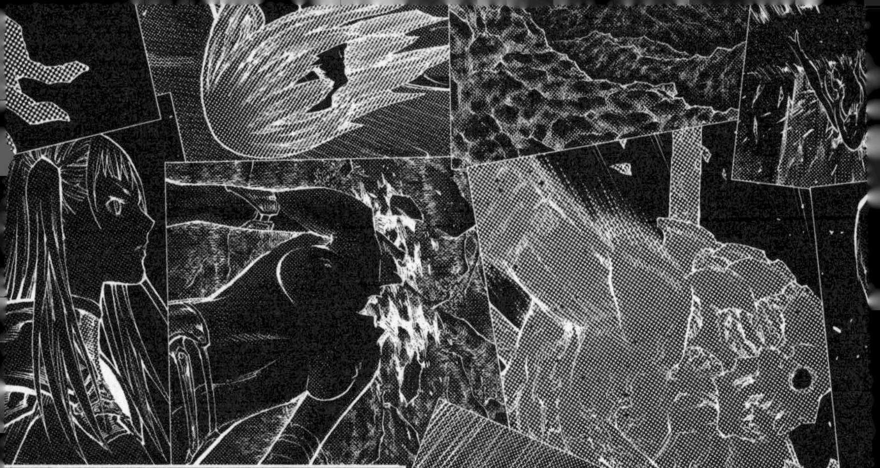

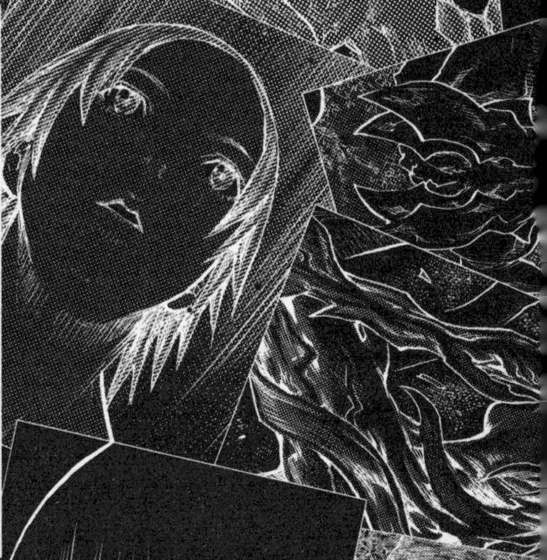

Seven years have passed since the Battle of the North. In the West, the sisters Alicia and Beth begin fighting Riful. Meanwhile, Rafaela and Luciela have transformed into a horrible destroyer. In the midst of this upsetting state of affairs, Priscilla awakens and appears before Clare!

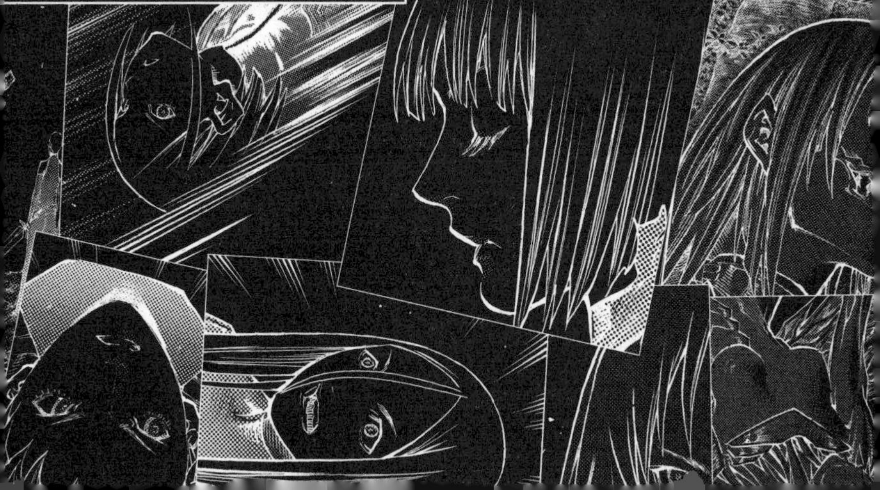

SHONEN JUMP ADVANCED Manga Edition

Claymore

クレイモア

Vol. 19
Phantoms in the Heart

Story and Art by **Norihiro Yagi**